Contents

JEWISH APOSTASY IN THE MODERN WORLD

JEWISH APOSTASY

IN THE

MODERN WORLD

Edited and with an Introduction by

TODD M. ENDELMAN

HM

HOLMES & MEIER

New York / London

Holmes & Meier Publishers, Inc.
30 Irving Place
New York, NY 10003

Great Britain:
1–3 Winton Close
Letchworth, Hertfordshire SG61 1BA
England

Book design by Dale Cotton

This book has been printed on acid-free paper.

Library of Congress Cataloging-in-Publication Data

Jewish apostasy in the modern world.

 Bibliography: p.
 Includes index.
 1. Converts from Judaism.   2. Jews—Cultural
assimilation.   I. Endelman, Todd M.
BV2620.J48   1987   261.2′6   86-31889
ISBN 0-8419-1029-4 (alk. paper)

Manufactured in the United States of America

Preface

THE origins of this volume can be traced to a seminar on Jewish apostasy and Christian missionary activity that we taught together in the Bernard Revel Graduate School of Yeshiva University in the spring term 1979. As frequently happens, each of us came to the topic in a different way. Professor Endelman had written previously about the efforts of Jews to enter the mainstream of English society in the eighteenth and early nineteenth centuries and at the time was already pursuing his interest in radical forms of social assimilation in western European Jewish history, while Professor Gurock was concerned primarily with examining American Jewish responses to Christianizing efforts in immigrant neighborhoods. A generous grant from the Memorial Foundation for Jewish Culture and encouragement and support from the Bernard Revel Graduate School allowed us to prepare curricular materials and an extensive bibliography for the course and to bring a number of guest lecturers to Yeshiva University to speak on topics related to the theme of the seminar.

Our teaching experience that semester galvanized our own interest in the dual phenomena of apostasy and missionizing and encouraged us to continue our work in the area. We soon became aware, however, that despite the importance of the topic in terms of both the history of Jewish-Christian relations and the history of Jewish assimilation it had not attracted much serious academic attention. In order to promote interest in the subject, we decided to convene a number of scholarly meetings at which persons who were beginning to work in the area could present their research to colleagues for comment and criticism. With funding from the Memorial Foundation for Jewish Culture, a public conference on the theme "Apostates and Missionaries: A Historical Perspective" was held at Yeshiva University in December 1983. The essays in this volume by Jonathan Sarna and Michael Stanislawski, as well as our own essays, were first presented as papers at the Yeshiva University conference. The remaining essays were initially presented at a series of three seminars Professor Endelman convened in 1984 at Indiana University, where he was then teaching. These seminars were part of an ongoing program in Jewish-Christian relations sponsored by the Jewish Studies Program at Indiana University with the financial support of the religious affairs division of the Lilly Endowment of Indianapolis.

We believe that the essays in this volume offer a fresh perspective on problems that have long troubled Jews and Christians alike. Although historians and religious thinkers have addressed the questions of apostasy and missionizing before, they have usually done so in a polemical spirit, their work generating as a consequence as much heat as light. This is perhaps the first work to consider Christian missionaries, Jewish apostates, and related topics dispassionately, without a hidden agenda, as important matters in their own right in the social and religious history of the modern period. The essays included here explore major themes in European social history, intergroup relations in America, Jewish assimilation, and the intellectual and psychological dynamics of conversion. In his introduction Professor Endelman highlights these themes and provides a broad overview of Jewish apostasy that allows each essay to be seen in historical context. To clarify the character of apostasy in the *modern* period, an essay on varieties of Jewish conversion in the *medieval* world by Jeremy Cohen has been included and appears as the first essay in the volume. The chapters that follow are arranged on a rough geographical basis, beginning with Germany, the starting point for most discussions of modern Jewish history, and ending with the United States. The last essay—William Toll's on intermarriage in the American West—may seem at first to be out of place in a collection devoted to converts and missionaries. However, as Toll makes clear, in recent decades conversion *from* Judaism has ceased to be significant, while intermarriage and conversion *to* Judaism have risen dramatically—largely due to shifts in the position of Jews in American society. Thus Toll's essay seemed an appropriate one with which to close this collection.

It would have been impossible to convene the various gatherings out of which this volume grew and to prepare this collection for publication without the support of a number of key individuals and institutions, and we would like to acknowledge our indebtedness to them. For their assistance and encouragement we are particularly grateful to Professor Leo Landman, Dean of the Bernard Revel Graduate School of Yeshiva University; Professor Alvin Rosenfeld, Director of the Jewish Studies Program at Indiana University; the Memorial Foundation for Jewish Culture; and Dr. Robert Wood Lynn, Senior Vice President of the Lilly Endowment of Indianapolis.

Jeffrey S. Gurock
Todd M. Endelman

JEWISH APOSTASY IN THE MODERN WORLD

Introduction

TODD M. ENDELMAN

In the aftermath of emancipation Christian efforts to convert Jews consistently bedeviled Jewish-Christian relations. For Jews, missionary activity expressed an ancient hostility that seemingly threatened the existence of the Jewish people and, at the very minimum, questioned the legitimacy of Jewish survival in the modern world. Christians, on the other hand, saw the evangelization of the Jews in a very different light. For them, missionary work was an expression of love and concern rather than intolerance and bigotry. Whereas Jews evinced little interest in Christian doctrine and none whatsoever in turning Christians into Jews—desiring, above all, to be left alone—Christians were unable to take such a detached view. Christian origins—and, in particular, the ambivalence of Christianity toward Judaism that was a consequence of these origins—created an obsessive attitude toward Judaism that was altogether disproportionate to the numbers or influence of Jews in Christendom.

Initially a sect within first-century Palestinian Judaism, Christianity grew to maturity bearing the impress of its genesis within another faith. Christians, like Jews, regarded Hebrew Scripture as the word of God and, like them, employed exegetical techniques to flesh out its meaning. By comparison with their pagan neighbors, both Jews and Christians worshiped God in similar ways, gathering together in public assemblies to offer prayers and hear Scripture expounded. In addition, Christians regarded the history of the Jewish people before the appearance of Jesus as the earliest part of their own

1

history, for they saw themselves not as newcomers or usurpers but as inheritors of an unbroken covenant with the God of Israel. Where the two faiths differed, of course, was over messianic claims regarding Jesus. For Christians, Jesus was the anointed redeemer whose coming Scripture foretold. For Jews, he was not a messianic figure. For them, the world was no better after Jesus' death—the yoke of Rome was more burdensome than ever—so they continued to pray for the coming of their own savior who would release them from foreign oppression and restore their glory. Yet, however much Judaism and Christianity differed about the identity of the messiah, they were in accord, even on this issue, that their salvation was linked to his coming, whoever he might be.

The intimate character of the initial relationship between Judaism and Christianity, which has frequently been characterized in familial terms as that between a father and his son or between an elder and a younger brother, did not bring harmony and fellowship in its wake. Indeed, as so often happens within families, the very closeness of the relationship produced extraordinarily intense feelings of rivalry and jealousy—in this case, on the part of the younger sibling. The source of the discord was that both religions claimed the same patrimony; both saw themselves as the favored children of their divine father. However, since Christians claimed to have displaced Jews as the chosen people, yet appeared on the stage of history only after much of Israelite history had already unfolded, the task of setting forth their claims was particularly pressing. Unfortunately for the Jewish people, the younger religion chose to defend its claims at the expense of the elder's understanding of its relationship to God. By attacking the authenticity of Judaism's interpretation of Scripture, its reading of history, its traditions and practices, Christianity hoped to establish the validity of its own theology and exegesis. Christian self-definition, in other words, came to rest on the disparagement of Judaism, and thus from the earliest centuries Christian doctrine incorporated an attack on fundamental Jewish beliefs.

However, although hostile, Christian attitudes were not unrelievedly so. The fact that Jews and Christians shared in common Hebrew Scripture—as well as the fact that the gospel was first preached to the Jewish people—encouraged the hope that one day Jews would acknowledge their error and convert to Christianity. When the time was ripe, all Israel would be saved. Thus, though Christians might in good conscience humiliate and oppress Jews, they

were not to destroy them. Accordingly, at the outset of the Second Crusade in 1146, Bernard of Clairvaux warned the knights of England against slaughtering Jews: "The Jews are for us the living words of Scripture, for they remind us always of what our Lord suffered. They are dispersed all over the world so that by expiating their crime they may be everywhere the living witnesses of our redemption." They were to be preserved in a degraded state, as a symbol of the triumph of Christianity, until that time that their hearts were turned, their obstinacy overcome, their unbelief uprooted. "If the Jews are utterly wiped out," the abbot of Clairvaux asked, "what will become of our hope for their promised salvation, their eventual conversion?"[1]

On the other hand, the belief that Jewish degradation testified to the triumph of Christianity did not discourage attempts to turn Jews into Christians before the time was ripe. Spreading the good news was a critical element in Christianity from its infancy; the perception that unconverted Jews were witnesses to Christian truth was not an obstacle to efforts to remove the veil from their eyes. Indeed, in one sense, there was greater satisfaction in converting Jews than pagans. The persistent refusal of Jews to admit their error, after all, was a constant affront to Christianity, since the gospel had been preached to them before other peoples and their own Scripture, so it was argued, contained the evidence for Jesus' messiahship. In this light, Jewish acknowledgment of Jesus could be seen as a weightier testimony to Christian truth than that of heathens. Thus, the conversion of Jews was considered particularly desirable, and over the centuries an inordinate amount of attention was devoted to this objective.

The missionary impulse, however, was not equally strong at all times. In the first centuries of Christianity, preachers of the new faith actively sought converts within the Jewish communities of the Hellenistic world and frequently met with considerable success, particularly among recent heathen converts to Judaism and their descendants. The vigor of patristic polemics against Judaism testifies to these efforts (as well as to the need of the church to claim the inheritance of Israel as its own). In the early Middle Ages, on the other hand, there was little anti-Jewish polemical literature, and, when a resurgence of polemic occurred in the late eleventh and twelfth centuries, these works disavowed any significant interest in proselytizing Jews. Peter of Blois (d. 1200), for example, believed that the Jews could not be converted before the time set by God. Here and there a convert might be made, but the people as a whole would persist in their stubborn-

ness. Yet in the thirteenth century, when the church's attitude toward the Jews in general hardened, it began to pursue their proselytization in a fairly systematic fashion. Public disputations were staged in Paris in 1240 and in Barcelona in 1263 in order to discredit Judaism and pressure Jews into abandoning their faith. In Spain the Dominicans established schools to teach missionaries Hebrew so they would be able to convince Jews of the truth of Christianity on the basis of their own sacred texts. Armed with Hebrew learning, the friars went into synagogues to preach conversionist sermons that Jews were compelled to attend. At the theoretical level, polemical literature enthusiastically embraced the desirability of missionary activity, an outlook that was not questioned until the nineteenth century.

Although the church did not actively pursue the evangelization of the Jews at all times, conversionist activity of a more informal character seems to have been fairly constant throughout the medieval period. The lower clergy, who were more likely have close contact with Jews than abbots and bishops, were always alert to opportunities for bringing Jews to an acknowledgment of their errors. Religious discussions between the lower clergy and Jews were not uncommon, and from time to time Jews were won over to the majority faith as a result. The story of Hermann of Cologne in the early twelfth century, which Jeremy Cohen analyzes in his contribution to this volume, is an instructive example of how frequent and intensive contact between ordinary Jews and Christians could lead to apostasy.

The effects of Christian missionizing, whether formal or informal, in the medieval and early modern periods are difficult to gauge, at least within the Ashkenazi Jewish world. The evidence is too meager to allow even rough calculations about the number of Jews who voluntarily accepted baptism. Jacob Katz, who surveyed the evidence in rabbinic literature for northern and central Europe, concluded that what was most striking about the incidence of voluntary apostasy was its isolated character.[2] On the other hand, Jeremy Cohen believes that the phenomenon was probably less isolated than Katz and others have maintained. Yet he also concludes that the sources are too scanty to permit any quantification. What is certain is that converts in northern and central Europe before the modern period were never sufficiently numerous to form a distinctive social unit within the majority society as they did in Spain from the late fourteenth century on. Of course, there were instances of mass conversion when whole groups were forced to choose between baptism and death, the most famous cases occurring in the Rhineland during the First Crusade. Such conversions were not, naturally, genuine, and frequently the secular authorities permitted these persons to return to their former faith, usually in the face of ecclesiastical opposition.

The motives of those who became Christians at this time were, not surprisingly, mixed. Some conversions, although probably not the majority, were clearly pragmatic in character. There were always some Jews who found the insecurity and inferiority of Jewish status too difficult to bear and for whom conversion was an opportunity to improve their personal situation. Similarly, there were persons on the periphery of Jewish society—the poor, for example, and those who ran afoul of community standards—who found the material inducements offered to converts too tempting to resist. However, in an age when religious values suffused the totality of life, most conversions were undoubtedly sincere, the outcome of spiritual and intellectual convictions rather than unprincipled opportunism. This is not to say, of course, that religious considerations alone were at work in the majority of cases; pragmatic considerations may also have played a role, but not always at a conscious level. In medieval society, as Jacob Katz has observed, in which religion provided the framework for so much of human activity, "it is very likely that a Jew who was captivated by the values of Christian society experienced this process subjectively in the form of religious conversion."[3]

Those who were drawn to the Christian faith from conviction came from all segments of Jewish society and not just from the periphery as is sometimes imagined. The three medieval converts at the center of Jeremy Cohen's essay all came from intellectually or socially prominent backgrounds: Peter Alfonsi was one of the leaders of the Jewish community of the eleventh-century Andalusian city of Huesca prior to his apostasy; Hermann of Cologne's father was a substantial moneylender with business dealings in a number of German cities; Pablo Christiani, whose origins are less well known, studied rabbinic literature with two prominent Provençal rabbis. The conversion experiences of these three apostates, however, were all quite distinct. Alfonsi's faith in Judaism was undermined by rationalism; his decision to be baptized was calculated and deliberate, "the capstone of extended intellectual inquiry," in Cohen's words, that led him to believe that Christianity had superseded Judaism. Hermann's conversion was a more emotional experience: Christianity offered him spiritual relief from the inner turbulence and restlessness of adolescence. Pablo Christiani's conversion, which is not as well documented as the other two, probably had its roots in the communal strife surrounding the Maimonidean controversy in Montpellier in the early 1230s. Whatever his motives, he emerged from his conversion a bitter enemy of his former coreligionists, a vicious polemicist in the Dominican offensive against Judaism in the thirteenth century. Like so many other converts, he was unable to merge quietly into the majority community but felt compelled to testify publicly to the truth of his new faith and to force the rest of Jewry to acknowledge the correctness of his own step by taking the same step themselves.

In only one Jewish community in the premodern period did apostasy cease to be an occasional phenomenon and take on epidemic proportions. In the last century of medieval Spanish Jewry, between the pogroms of 1391 and the expulsion of 1492, tens of thousands of Jews voluntarily converted in the face of militant church missionizing and popular threats to the security of their lives and property. The disputation of Tortosa in 1413–14, in particular, in which the chief Christian spokesman (Geronimo de Santa Fe) was a former Jew (Yehoshua Ha-Lorki), left in its wake as many as twenty-five thousand converts. Whole communities were caught up in the flight, and in some places synagogues were turned into churches. This unprecedented mass apostasy was only in part the outcome of pressure from without. Equally critical were cultural trends within Spanish Jewry that weakened its ability to withstand angry mobs and crusading friars. The Jews of the Iberian peninsula, unlike their counterparts in northern and central Europe, were not cut off from intellectual currents in the larger society in which they lived. Their immersion in non-Jewish learning, as well as their economic well-being, frequently eroded their faith in the religion of their fathers and left them mentally unprepared to face the persecution that plagued them from 1391 on. In addition, some felt that history itself, as it was being played out on Spanish soil, was testifying to the truth of the Christian faith. With their own eyes they witnessed the military triumph of Christianity over Islam—the last Muslim forces in Spain were defeated in 1492—at the same time that they themselves experienced a radical decline in their own status and power. In these circumstances, it is not difficult to understand how thousands came to accept the Christian claim that the "old" Israel had been cast aside.

The success of Christian missionizing in Spain and elsewhere in the premodern world derived in part from the insecurity of Jewish life in societies that were religiously intolerant. Theological claims about Jewish wickedness and rejection carried conviction because secular authorities were willing to translate church doctrine into public policy and persecute Jews in their territories. (The church itself had no powers of coercion at its disposal and was dependent on the state to enforce measures against Jews.) When the West became more tolerant toward religious diversity in general in the seventeenth and eighteenth centuries—and toward Jews in particular—the churches could no longer rely on the state to supply the atmosphere of intimidation that had underwritten previous missionary efforts. Moreover, Protestantism, in whose sphere the thriving new Jewish communities of northern Europe were to be found, saw conversion, whether of Jews or Gentiles, as the result of an intensive process of self-exploration. It never envisioned the use of state coercion to effect a mass conversion of the Jews. Accordingly, the missionary movements that developed within the Protestant denominations from the seventeenth century on (and which are still active, if not flourishing, today) developed new techniques for attracting Jews to Christianity. They sought to win Jewish souls with sympathy and goodwill, through gentle persuasion and with assurances of brotherly love rather than fiery polemic. Indeed, they attributed the failure of Roman Catholic missionizing over the centuries to the church's persecutory policy.

The first Protestant missions devoted exclusively to winning Jewish souls were founded in Germany—in Hamburg in 1667 by Esdras Edzard, a disciple of Johannes Buxtorf, and in Halle in 1728 by Johann Heinrich Callenberg. The idea of *Judenmission*, however, never aroused widespread enthusiasm among German Protestants, by comparison with elsewhere, and the growth of missionary groups there was slow and fitful. The convert Paulus Cassel, a preacher and missionary in Berlin, told two visiting missionaries from London in 1886 that German pastors had no interest in missions to the Jews and that the majority of Christians, like the Jews, were "heathens," with "no sense of religion."[4] British and American Protestants were more enthusiastic, not only because religion played a more prominent role in public and private life in those countries (as Cassel's comments suggest), but also because currents within Anglo-American Protestantism—such as millennialism, bibliolatry, and evangelicalism—encouraged the missionary impulse. In the nineteenth and early twentieth centuries, conversionist organizations of every hue flourished in both countries, the oldest of which, the London Society for

Promoting Christianity among the Jews (founded in 1809 and still operating today), not only conducted missionary work within Anglo-Jewry but also supported an extensive network of missionary stations abroad—in central and eastern Europe, North Africa, and the Middle East (including the Holy Land itself). It was the chief backer, for example, of Joseph Rabinovich's New Israel movement in Odessa in the early 1880s, a Jewish-Christian sect whose curious history Steven Zipperstein describes in his contribution to this volume.

In the heyday of Anglo-American missionary activity, the prime targets of the conversionist societies were the Jewish poor, who, by virtue of their poverty, were more receptive to missionaries bearing spiritual and material gifts than middle-class Jews. (Missionaries had few opportunities to even speak with the latter, who, in their comfortable homes in pleasant residential neighborhoods, were beyond the reach of street corner preachers and storefront conversionists.) The hundreds of thousands of eastern European immigrants who crowded into the great manufacturing cities of the West from the 1870s on were considered especially ripe for evangelization and became the focus of an intensive missionary effort. In the East End of London, more than a dozen missionary organizations operated at the turn of the century, offering a wide range of free social services to the newcomers—medical care, reading rooms, vocational training, youth clubs, country holidays, even food, clothing, and, in some instances, help with the rent. On New York's Lower East Side, as Jeffrey Gurock explains in his essay below, Protestant groups attempted to disarm wary Jewish parents by sponsoring summer programs for Jewish children (vacation Bible schools and fresh-air excursions, for example) in which the conversionist aims of the programs were consciously muted. The Federation of Churches and Christian Organizations of New York City, which in 1905 operated eight vacation Bible schools enrolling two thousand Jewish children, explained that while "their inspiration is Christian" their "management is human and their mission is not a proselytizing one."

Conversionist welfare programs in immigrant neighborhoods in England and America served thousands of Jews, almost all of whom would have resisted any contact with missionaries were it not for their poverty and, in some instances, their distance from family and friends in the old country. Most who took advantage of these services remained deaf to the message that accompanied them. Nevertheless, the fact that large numbers of Jews were exposed to Christian proselytization troubled communal leaders, even if the results were rather meager in the end. As Jonathan Sarna and Jeffrey Gurock show in their respective essays, American Jewish leaders responded to this challenge with vigor but not with unanimity. Some believed that exposés of missionary "rascality" were sufficient to arouse Jews from their indifference and alert them to the conversionist threat; others felt that since missionary activity took advantage of weaknesses in Jewish communal life, strengthening these areas would be the only effective means of countering the challenge. In fact, in both America and England, missionary work in immigrant neighborhoods forced native leaders to provide a greater range of welfare services for recent arrivals than they would otherwise have done. Conversionist activity also stimulated the development of Jewish education by forcing communal leaders to provide Jewish alternatives to Christian-sponsored charity schools for the poor and by highlighting the need for English-language instructional materials for Jews who were ignorant of their own faith. Indeed, Sarna concludes that missionary activity in America was a blessing, not a curse, for the development of communal institutions.

In the modern period, however, the role of missions in turning Jews into Christians has been rather unimportant, despite the energy and money invested in the enterprise. Most Jews who became Christians in the years between the French Revolution and World War II chose baptism on their own initiative, without clerical encouragement, since, unlike apostates in the medieval and early modern periods, they did not convert from conviction but instead for largely pragmatic reasons. Some sought to bolster their social status by escaping the stigma attached to Jewishness. Others wished to advance their careers outside the range of traditional Jewish occupations and found their Jewishness an obstacle. Still others, like Heinrich Heine, believed that baptism was the ticket of admission to European civilization. For the most part, these persons were indifferent to religious practices and beliefs of any kind. Some were raised in homes already devoid of Jewish customs and symbols; others were exposed, while at school and university, to intellectual currents critical of religious faith. Whatever the case, they moved from a nominal Judaism to a nominal Christianity. The novelist and philosopher Fritz Mauthner remarked in 1912 that while it was not impossible for an educated Jewish adult to become a Christian out of conviction he had never personally encountered such a case. In his experience, expediency brought the overwhelming majority of adult converts to profess their belief in Christianity.[5]

Although conversion in the modern period never became a mass movement, as in Spain after 1391, it was a characteristic form of radical assimilation in most western Jewish societies in the nineteenth and early twentieth centuries. Several hundred thousand Jews abandoned Judaism during this period. (It is impossible to be any more precise.)[6] The rate of conversion, however, was by no means equally strong at all times, in all countries, and among all strata of Jewish society. Instead, distinctive patterns of apostasy emerged in different settings, bearing the impress of larger social and political conditions.

The first substantial wave of conversions in the modern period occurred in Germany in the late eighteenth and early nineteenth centuries, especially among the offspring of banking and merchant families in cities like Berlin, Frankfurt, and Hamburg. These converts were drawn from the first generation of central European Jews to receive a western education and to be exposed to cultural trends in the majority society. They often grew up without firm roots in the world of Jewish tradition and found social and intellectual life in gentile society broader, more stimulating, and better mannered. It was, to use a term from Deborah Hertz's essay, "seductive." At the same time, these converts came to despise their own heritage—as parochial, desiccated, and anachronistic—for in the process of their acculturation to German values and perceptions they had internalized German prejudices about Judaism. They also discovered that despite their own "enlightenment" and distance from ghetto ways they remained Jews in the eyes of German society unless they took the final step in the assimilatory process and formally converted.

Apostasy remained a noticeable feature of Jewish life in Germany throughout the modern period and did not decline, as some historians have maintained, after the Prussian edict of emancipation in 1812 and similar acts in other German states. As Hertz demonstrates in her study of Berlin converts, there was a definite rise in the incidence of conversion during the first half of the nineteenth century. Converts became sufficiently numerous that even the orthodox rabbinate was eventually compelled to take note of their presence in the formation of halachic (legal) decisions, as we learn in David Ellenson's essay. The reason for the continual increase in apostasy is that, while emancipation removed some of the more onerous restrictions on Jewish activity, it could not compel Germans to welcome Jews as fellow citizens and intimate friends. Jews in Germany continued to experience widespread occupational and social discrimination throughout the nineteenth century, and consequently they continued to leave Judaism. In fact, the bestowal of emancipation raised their expectations about the possibilities for integration into German life, and when these expectations failed to be realized, their disappointment was that much greater, and thus the impetus to abandon a religious identity that had ceased to be meaningful was even stronger. In the last decades of the nineteenth century, when antisemitism gained widespread respectability and the public campaign against Jews intensified, the increase in the number of conversions became especially dramatic, as I show in my comparative study of apostasy in Victorian England and Imperial Germany.

In the capital cities of the Habsburg Empire—Vienna, Budapest, and Prague—with their largely westernized Jewish populations, similar motives for abandoning Judaism operated, although not with the same force everywhere. (In those regions of the empire where traditional Jewish life still flourished, as in Galicia or Subcarpathian Ruthenia, for example, apostasy was an infrequent occurrence.) In late imperial Vienna, the rate of defection was perhaps the highest of any city in Europe. In an average year at the turn of the century, there was one conversion for every 270 Jews in Vienna, while in Berlin there was one for every 600 Jews and in Budapest one for every 1,050 Jews.[7] In Vienna, however, more than occupational and social discrimination contributed to the high rate of conversion, for there a Jew who wanted to marry a Catholic had first to convert in order to do so. In Budapest, although baptism was necessary to obtain certain government posts and gain entry into elite social circles, state and society were sufficiently liberal to forestall the emergence of conversion as a common response to antisemitism. However, after the collapse of the Habsburg Empire, the number of conversions shot up dramatically, as William McCagg explains in his survey of conversion in modern Hungarian history. The antisemitic White Terror that followed the four-and-a-half-month communist regime of Béla Kun (a Jew) in 1919 shattered Hungarian Jewry's sense of security. Riots and acts of violence sent thousands of Jews streaming into the arms of the church seeking conversion as quickly as possible. Between 1919 and 1921, when the political situation stabilized, almost ten thousand Jews were baptized.

In the liberal states of the West—Britain, America, Holland, and

France—pragmatic conversions, while not absent, were far less common, although it is impossible to know how much so. (Because religious affiliation was voluntary and not an aspect of civil status in these states, there are no records of movement from one group to another.) Legal equality and social integration came more easily than in central Europe. In the second half of the nineteenth century, it became possible for Jews to move into elite social circles, prestigious occupations, and the mainstream of national politics without casting aside their Judaism. Public denigration of Jews and Judaism was restrained by comparison with the situation elsewhere; only in France did the Jewish Question play a prominent role in politics, and even here it was not sufficiently strong to exclude Jews from public life. In general, Jews and Christians mixed more freely in these liberal societies. Social intimacy was not unusual, especially in the case of second- and third-generation acculturated Jews. With the weakening of old taboos and allegiances, intermarriage became increasingly common, particularly from the late nineteenth century on, as William Toll's study of intermarriage in the American West clearly reveals. Jews who married outside their religion in these countries were not required to convert and usually did not do so. However, in most cases they allowed their children to be raised as Christians, since some social stigma always adhered to Jewishness, regardless of how tolerant these societies were in other respects. Thus, the demographic outcome was the same as if they had converted in the first place.

In both liberal and illiberal societies, those who converted were not representative (in a sociological and demographic sense) of the Jewish community as a whole, but came in disproportionate numbers from groups that were most exposed to exclusion and defamation. Young men in occupations outside those in which Jews had been traditionally concentrated (or students planning to enter these fields), in the face of obstacles to their social and professional advancement, were more likely to convert than those who, following in their fathers' footsteps, entered business or finance. Francis Ephraim Cohen, the son of a stockbroker in late Georgian London, became an Anglican and changed his name to Palgrave (his wife's maiden name) because he harbored literary and scholarly ambitions at a time when most middle-class Anglo-Jewish men were unlearned merchants and brokers. (His second son, the subject of Benjamin Braude's essay, reversed the process by embracing his ancestral identity and reveling in those very roots his father had sought to bury.) Daniel Chwolson, who grew up in great poverty in Vilna, converted in 1855 to become professor of Semitics at the University of St. Petersburg. When later asked whether he changed his religion from conviction, he supposedly replied, "Yes, I was convinced it is better to be a professor in St. Petersburg than a *melamed* [a teacher in a Jewish elementary school] in Eyshishok." Jews who intended to make careers in the public sector—in the civil service, the judiciary, the army, the university, etc.—were especially likely to convert, since discrimination in these areas, from which Jews had been completely banned before emancipation, was pervasive. In a sample of 370 male converts in Vienna in the period 1870–1910, civil servants, professionals, and students represented slightly more than half of the total number of apostates, while in Berlin in the period 1873–1906 university students alone constituted 36 percent of converts of known occupation.[8] In tsarist Russia, young men converted to gain the right to live outside the Pale of Settlement or to enter university. (Those with qualms about submitting to regular baptism could frequently obtain—for a fee—the necessary baptismal certificate from an obliging Protestant clergyman or missionary.) In western and central Europe, merchants, small traders, and business employees, who were far more representative of the mass of Jewish householders than university graduates, also converted—to promote their social fortunes or to intermarry (the two motives were frequently linked) or simply to escape the stigma of Jewishness. However, their contribution to the total number of converts was quite small relative to their numerical weight in Jewry as a whole.

Young women as well became Christians for pragmatic reasons. In central Europe, women who married into Christian upper-middle-class and aristocratic circles almost always converted prior to marriage. Further down the social hierarchy, as more women in the lower middle class entered the marketplace toward the end of the nineteenth century—as teachers, clerical workers, shop assistants, seamstresses, etc.—and came into contact with occupational discrimination or fell in love with non-Jewish fellow workers, their share of the total number of conversions rose. For example, in Berlin in the period 1873–82, women accounted for only 7 percent of those converting; by 1912, they constituted 40 percent, most of whom were from the lower middle class.[9] Even in the Russian Empire there were female converts in this category. Michael Stanislawski relates the story of Sima Keller, a twenty-seven-year-old single woman who graduated from the Odessa gymnasium for women in 1900 with a teaching certificate and then had herself baptized in the Orthodox church in order to obtain a position. In general, though, women at all ranks within Jewish society were less likely than men to cut their ties with Judaism. Until the midtwentieth century, most remained at home, outside the marketplace and public life, enclosed in the private sphere of friends and family, cut off from the temptations that led ambitious young men to change their religious affiliation.

While pragmatic considerations motivated most conversions in the modern period, there were instances, though not many in relative terms, of Jews changing their faith for genuine religious reasons. These converts came from diverse backgrounds and seem to have had equally diverse religious needs and experiences. In tsarist Russia, as Stanislawski demonstrates in his essay below, there were Jews who received a traditional Jewish upbringing and lived within the norms of rabbinic Judaism for years, then rejected them (for reasons that are not always clear) and found their way to the Orthodox church. Yosef Dreyzin, for example, a graduate of the government sponsored rabbinical seminary at Zhitomir, converted in 1891—at age forty-eight—having already served as rabbi of several towns in the Pale of Settlement in the previous decade. Joseph Rabinovich, the subject of Zipperstein's essay, came from a hasidic family (followers of the Belzer rebbe), was won over to the *haskalah* as a young man, then embraced the proto-Zionism of the Hibbat Zion movement, and finally found his way, around 1883, to a form of Judeo-Christianity that he propagated in South Russia until his death in 1899. On the other hand, there were Jews who embraced Christianity from genuine conviction who grew up in a largely secular atmosphere and received no significant religious training. This was the case with Boris Pasternak in Russia, Simone Weil in France, Eugen Rosenstock-Huessy in Germany, and Hugh Montefiore in England, to cite only a few well-known examples. In short, there was no uniform path from Judaism to Christianity for those who changed their religion for spiritual reasons.

As in earlier periods, a disproportionate number of these sincere converts felt compelled to testify publicly to the truth of their new faith—by writing glowingly about their conversion experiences or by dedicating their lives to converting other Jews. In fact, the most prominent missionaries to the Jews in the nineteenth and twentieth centuries in Europe and America were former Jews. The London Society for Promoting Christianity among the Jews, as well as other British missionary groups, employed dozens of converts at home and abroad, like Joseph Rabinovich in Odessa, to spread the gospel among their former coreligionists; indeed, it is hard to imagine the various British societies being able to carry on their extensive work overseas without the use of agents who were former Jews. (Several hundred Jews also became Church of England clergymen and pursued conventional, nonmissionary clerical careers.) In France the only church organization devoted exclusively to evangelizing Jews, the congregation Notre Dame de Sion, was established in 1843 by Theodore and Alphonse Ratisbonne, sons of a Strasbourg banker who was president of the Jewish consistory of Alsace.

In addition to those Jews who converted for pragmatic reasons and those who did so for spiritual ones, there were also apostates whose motives were not wholly opportunistic yet at the same time not religious in the usual sense of the term. These persons left Judaism partly for negative reasons—that is, they wanted to escape anti-semitism—but they also were moved by cultural loyalties and allegiances of a positive sort. In their eyes, Christianity was an integral part of the larger culture in which they lived; to cement their relationship to this culture, they felt they needed to become Christians, regardless of their personal religious beliefs. For the Nobel laureate chemist Fritz Haber, for example, who became a Christian before he had decided to pursue an academic career, conversion was not a religious decision but a public demonstration of his identification with *Deutschtum*. He and his Jewish friends considered themselves to be thoroughly German. Science and philosophy, they felt, had eroded their ties to Judaism. Why should they remain within the Jewish community? Maximilian Harden claimed that he had adopted Christianity because it had seemed to him "the way of life corresponding to the higher culture."[10] When westernized Hungarian Jews, initially enthusiasts for the German-language Danubian *haskalah*, passionately embraced Magyar nationalism in the midnineteenth century, some felt, as McCagg points out, that becoming a pure Magyar also required conversion to the Magyar faith.

The modern period produced one further category of apostasy—Jews who believed that the theological differences between Judaism and Christianity were rapidly disappearing and that, since the two religions would merge into one enlightened faith in the near future, it was no longer desirable for Jews to maintain a separate group identity. Rather, they believed, they should ally themselves with the progressive forces within Christianity. Perhaps the first Jew to advocate this position was David Friedländer, a wealthy Berlin silk manufacturer, disciple of Moses Mendelssohn, and prominent communal leader. In an anonymous pamphlet published in 1799, Friedländer proposed that the Berlin community convert en masse to a rationalized form of Christianity. The circumstances that gave birth to the proposal and the reception it received are described by Hertz in her essay on "seductive conversion" in Berlin. A century later in America, where both Reform Judaism and liberal Protestantism had discarded much of their respective traditions, it was not uncommon for Reform rabbis to envision a day when the two faiths would draw together. Most, however, probably believed that the universal faith that would emerge would be Judaism. Solomon Sonneschein of St. Louis, a rabbi in the radical Reform camp, was the exception: he actually attempted to become a Unitarian preacher. (Like Friedländer, his terms were rejected.) His near defection, as Benny Kraut explains below, was a product of the radicalization of the Reform movement in the United States and, simultaneously, the social and intellectual rapprochement between Unitarians and Reform Jews in the last third of the nineteenth century.

Whatever the motives that led Jews to abandon Judaism, they frequently found that the formal act of conversion was insufficient to convince gentile society that they had ceased to be Jews. The best-known apostates of the modern period—Rahel Varnhagen, Heinrich Heine, Karl Marx, Benjamin Disraeli, Bernard Berenson, Gustav Mahler—were all regarded by their contemporaries as Jews, even when, like Marx and Disraeli, they had been baptized as children. Popular opinion in most countries accepted the notion of the immutability of Jewishness. In strongly antisemitic societies, Jewish character was considered inflexible and thus impervious to baptism, and converts in these countries usually faced obstacles to their advancement. Even in the more liberal states of the West, converts' origins were not easily forgotten, although they did not prevent acceptance by gentile society as frequently as they did in central and eastern Europe. On the other hand, in most cases the children or grandchildren of converts were able to enjoy the fruits of their parents' or grandparents' apostasy, particularly if this multi-generational process of integration was well advanced before antisemitism became virulent at the end of the last century.

Most Jews who became Christians were eager to leave their Jewishness behind them and worked assiduously to promote their own and their children's absorption into the larger society. In a few instances, however, converts and their descendants found it psychologically impossible to bury their origins. Their sense of Jewishness would not quietly fade away, relinquishing its hold on them, allowing them to transform themselves effortlessly into gentile citizens. Old attachments and former concerns resurfaced to disturb their peace of mind. On occasion, the children of converts, much to their parents' horror and confusion, reclaimed attachments that their parents had sought to bury. In some cases, such as those of Benjamin Disraeli and Heinrich Heine, the return to Jewishness was motivated or reinforced by pressure from without—the gentile world constantly reminded both of them of their origins. Disraeli, who encountered considerable hostility on account of his background when he launched his political career in the 1830s, boldly embraced his Jewishness a decade later, compensating for his parvenu origins by creating a myth of racial chosenness. Having returned to and then refashioned his Jewish identity, he felt able to stand up to the caste pride of the well-born landowners of ancient lineage by whom he wished to be accepted. There were also former Jews and their children who reclaimed their Jewish heritage on their own initiative. The Victorian diplomat and literary traveler, William Gifford Palgrave, whose turbulent career Braude examines, left the Church of England, to which his father had converted, to become a Catholic—and a Jesuit, to boot—but within a few years, without renouncing his allegiance to Rome, began calling himself Cohen (his father's name originally) and observing some Jewish rituals. Hostility to Jews apparently played no role in the genesis of his judaizing. The Palgraves, as Braude stresses, were remarkably successful in integrating into the mainstream of British life; few families could match their success in capturing positions of eminence in Victorian society.

Since the end of World War II, both missionizing and apostasy have changed their character. The densely populated immigrant neighborhoods to which missionaries devoted most of their attention have disappeared, as has the poverty that formed the backdrop to their activity. In light of these changes, the focus of missionary activity has shifted in recent decades to other equally vulnerable groups within the Jewish community, college students and the aged, in particular. In general, however, the missionary impulse is not as strong as it once was. In the aftermath of the Holocaust, most mainline churches have rethought the traditional Christian position on the damnation of the

Jews and the possibility of salvation outside Christianity. The outcome of this theological reappraisal has been the renunciation of efforts to make Jews into Christians. Today only right-wing fundamentalist Protestant groups work actively at evangelizing Jews. Their labors, while frequently eliciting expressions of near hysteria within the Jewish community, have, in fact, not been very fruitful. Similarly, conversions for social and occupational reasons have also become increasingly infrequent in recent decades. Although antisemitism has not disappeared by any means, it has ceased to be a major obstacle to economic and social mobility in most western societies. When Jews cease to be Jews in the contemporary world, it is not because they have become Christians but because they have become indifferent.

NOTES

1. Quoted in Robert Chazan, ed., *Church, State, and Jew in the Middle Ages* (New York: Behrman House, 1980), p. 103.

2. Jacob Katz, *Exclusiveness and Tolerance: Studies in Jewish-Gentile Relations in Medieval and Modern Times* (New York: Schocken Books, 1962), pp. 67–68.

3. Katz, *Exclusiveness and Tolerance*, p. 76.

4. W. Ord-Mackenzie and Thomas Chaplin, *Report of Visit to Continental Missions, August & September 1886* (London: Alexander and Shepherd, n.d.), pp. 10, 13.

5. Fritz Mauthner, in *Judentaufen*, ed. Arthur Landsberger (Munich: Georg Muller Verlag, 1912), p. 76.

6. The German conversionist J. F. A. de le Roi estimated that 224,000 European and American Jews were baptized in the nineteenth century. *Judentaufen im 19. Jahrhundert: Ein statistischer Versuch*, Schriften des Institutum Judaicum in Berlin no. 27 (Leipzig: J. C. Hinrichs Buchhandlung, 1899). [A summary of his findings has been reprinted in Paul R. Mendes-Flohr and Jehuda Reinharz, eds., *The Jew in the Modern World: A Documentary History* (New York: Oxford University Press, 1980), p. 539.] Some of de le Roi's country-by-country estimates are more trustworthy than others. In the case of those countries where neither the churches nor the government recorded Jewish baptisms, his calculations do not inspire great confidence. For example, in the case of Great Britain, he used the following dubious method: in Germany, the ratio of Jews converted under missionary auspices to Jews baptized in regular churches was 1:8 or 1:9; thus, in Great Britain, where missionary groups recorded the number of Jews they converted, it is possible to calculate the number of Jews baptized in parish churches by using the same ratio, more or less, that prevailed in Germany. (In fact, so as not to overestimate the total number of converts, he used a ratio of 1:6 [p. 22]). De le

Roi's implicit assumption was that circumstances affecting conversion in England were roughly the same as in Germany, an assumption that is clearly ill-founded, as I show in my essay below. However, de le Roi's estimates are the only ones we have, and while not always reliable on a country by country basis, taken together they do give a sense of the extent of Jewish apostasy in the modern period.

7. Jacob Lestschinsky, "Ha-shemad be-aratsot shonot" [Apostasy in Different Lands], *Ha-olam* 5, no. 10 (1911): 6.

8. Marsha L. Rozenblit, *The Jews of Vienna, 1867–1914: Assimilation and Identity* (Albany: State University of New York Press, 1983), p. 137; Arthur Ruppin, *The Jews of Today*, trans. Margery Bentwich (London: G. Bell and Sons, 1913), p. 194.

9. Lestschinsky, "Ha-shemad be-aratsot shonot," *Ha-olam* 5, no. 11 (1911): 6; Marion A. Kaplan, "Tradition and Transition—The Acculturation, Assimilation, and Integration of Jews in Imperial Germany—A Gender Analysis," *Leo Baeck Institute Year Book* 27 (1982): 18.

10. Harry F. Young, *Maximilian Harden: Censor Germaniae* (The Hague: Martinus Nijhoff, 1959), p. 12.

1

The Mentality of the Medieval Jewish Apostate: Peter Alfonsi, Hermann of Cologne, and Pablo Christiani

JEREMY COHEN

THE vast array of influences on the medieval Jew who contemplated conversion to Christianity highlights the distinctive complexity of Jewish life in western Europe during the Middle Ages.[1] The medieval church, which constantly looked forward to the establishment of a universal Christian commonwealth on earth, placed a special value on the conversion of the Jews. Belonging to a religious minority which had persistently survived the Christianization of Rome, the disintegration of the Empire, and the various sociopolitical upheavals of the Dark Ages, the Jew by his mere existence as a non-Christian thwarted the universalistic aspirations of the *ecclesia*. The fact of his Jewishness posed an additional challenge to Christians; for they deemed him a faithless deicide whose biblical legacy—the status of God's chosen people Israel—God had long ago transferred to them. From the earliest days of ecclesiastical history, the teachings of *Adversus Judaeos*, through which Christians asserted their own beliefs by negating those of the Jews, had played a key role in literary, homiletical, and iconographic expressions of Christian theology; and they continued to do so throughout the entire medieval period. The letter of canon law, to be sure, insisted that the Jews be wooed to the church not by physical compulsion but with softer forms of persuasion (*blandimentis*),[2] including an enforced level of marked social and legal inferiority. Yet the message of *Adversus Judaeos* theology, to which all members of medieval society were exposed, remained unmitigated: "When Christ-killers gather," St. John Chrysostom had taught, "the cross is ridiculed, God

20

blasphemed, the father unacknowledged, the son insulted, the grace of the Spirit rejected. . . . If the Jewish rites are holy and venerable, our way of life must be false. But if our way is true, as indeed it is, theirs is fraudulent."³ Such anger readily fueled the quasi-nationalistic intentions of Christian monarchs who, in an effort to unify their subjects along religious lines, offered their Jews a choice between conversion and expulsion, in both the opening and closing centuries of the medieval period. Friendship with Jews could easily motivate Christian notables to sacrifice the welfare of their comrades' bodies for that of their souls. In times of social unrest and cultural ferment—e.g., during the early Crusades—legal proscription could do little to quell the threat of popular anti-Jewish violence and forced baptism. And beginning in the twelfth and thirteenth centuries, the church as an institution promoted concerted missionary efforts among the Jews, dispatching preachers (often at the head of angry mobs) into the synagogues, compelling rabbinic leaders to dispute publicly against Christian clergymen, burning and censoring Jewish books, and assisting converts both economically and socially in their transition from one community to another. The foremost scholastic thinkers debated whether Jewish children could be baptized against the will of their parents, while canonists ruled that no matter how much duress entered a particular conversion, the proselyte could never "relapse" to his Judaism.

What may have restrained the Jew from submitting to these variegated pressures, aside from personal religious belief? Anti-Jewish strictures in medieval law often were observed more in the breach than in actual practice. Medieval kings and princes frequently accorded their Jews special rights and privileges as a means of attracting Jewish capital into their domains, thereby stimulating trade, investments, and overall economic development. Catholic rulers came to deem their Jews so valuable an asset that they confiscated the property of Jews who converted to Christianity, a practice which typically elicited vehement objection from ecclesiastical authorities. The glaring contrast between Jewish and Christian values—a society containing only Christians and Jews naturally tended to overlook the similarities—in which Jews too nurtured their children could also militate against apostasy. Christianity embodied all that was dark and evil for the medieval European Jew—the last of the four kingdoms standing in the way of messianic redemption and God's salvation of his people. The stigma which accompanied betrayal to such an enemy was hardly inconsequential. And on a practical level, medieval Jews came to isolate themselves from their Christian neighbors so that all but the essential social and economic contacts were viewed as taboo. Dietary laws, prohibitions against intermarriage, and bans on any participation in the practice of an alien religion underlay such self-imposed segregation and produced inhibitions so deep-seated that proselytizing Christians occasionally had to accommodate them. A seventh-century Visigothic oath of abjuration, prescribed for Jews who elected baptism to avoid a royal decree of expulsion from Spain, permitted the continued abstinence from pork as long as all other ties with Jewish rites were broken.[4] Pope Innocent III similarly allowed converts whose degree of consanguinity would have prevented their marriage under canon law to remain married after their baptism.[5] Traditions which had taken many centuries to mold were not easily discarded. As the church itself could remember, membership in a small, distinctive, persecuted religious minority might generate spiritual zeal just as readily as despondency.

If the factors affecting conversion were so extensive, Jewish apostasy in medieval Christian Europe—apart from that of the Marranos of fourteenth- and fifteenth-century Spain—unfortunately remains a relatively uncharted phenomenon. Rabbinic documents, most of them halakhic responsa, do attest to the various ramifications of apostasy as a social and legal problem for medieval Jewry.[6] What was the status of an apostate vis-à-vis the Jewish community: Could he inherit a Jewish relative? Did he remain tied in some way to his Jewish spouse or widowed sister-in-law? If a member of the priestly clan, did he automatically forfeit his privileged status (*kehunah*)? Could he borrow money from another Jew at interest, indicating that he was now a gentile? Apostasy endangered the sanctity of the most hallowed relationships in the community—between parent and child, husband and wife, rabbi and disciple. The twelfth-century *Sefer Ḥasidim* of Rabbi Judah the Pious indicates that the threat of conversion could gain considerable leverage for a dissatisfied family or community member. In the following story, that the proposed scam was deemed a serious possibility is itself remarkable.

A man desired a certain virgin and sent to her, but neither she nor her relatives wanted him. He said to his father and mother, should they not arrange for the virgin to marry him, he would apostasize. His father and mother told their relatives, "Thus spoke our son; ask a sage if it is permissible to hire two witnesses to testify [i.e., falsely] that she accepted his betrothal in their presence so he will not apostasize."[7]

Nevertheless, the existing primary sources are too scanty to allow for any quantification of medieval Jewish apostasy; the law had to account for the isolated as well as common occurrence, and rabbinic responsa typically deal only with the particular case in point. Even generalizing inferences as to the causes and processes of apostasy are questionable at best, in view of the understandably biased nature of the pertinent documentary material: Christian sources would have tended to highlight conversion on the part of the Jews, Jewish ones to downplay it. Apostates themselves only occasionally made lasting marks on the society and culture of Latin Christendom. Spurned by their former coreligionists, never fully assimilated into the rank and file of the European laity, and often deprived of their property by secular princes, many must have remained on the margins of medieval society, frequently finding their only secure haven in the ranks of the Christian clergy, or hovering indecisively between two hostile religious communities.

Considerations such as these should help to explain why, despite its title, this paper will not offer a profile of the "typical" medieval Jewish apostate, nor will it hazard a psychohistorical analysis of the three illustrious apostates enumerated in its title. Rather, it will attempt a more modest contribution toward the understanding of our subject, demonstrating how Peter Alfonsi, Hermann of Cologne, and Pablo Christiani exemplified three different genera of medieval Jews who voluntarily converted to Christianity, each for different reasons and each undergoing a distinctive sort of conversion.

1

Peter Alfonsi was born Moses the Jew in the Andalusian city of Huesca (Jewish population 250) in 1062, and he proceeded to distinguish himself as one of the intellectual leaders of that Jewish community.[8] After his apostasy, Peter wrote of himself (through the words of an imagined Jewish interlocutor):

I knew that you were once well versed in the writings of the prophets, that from your youth you surpassed all of your peers in the interpretation of the law with the words of our sages, that if ever there were an adversary you took up the shield in defense against him, that you preached to the Jews in the synagogues lest they ever desert their faith, that you instructed your coreligionists, and that you advanced [even] the learned [in their scholarship].⁹

While Moses may not have ranked as an outstanding talmudic scholar in the classic sense, Peter's subsequent writings manifest great sophistication, immersion in the traditions of Hispano-Jewish culture, and considerable expertise in various branches of philosophy and science. In 1096, Huesca fell to the armies of the Aragonese *Reconquista*, and Moses became the court physician of King Alfonso I shortly thereafter. In 1106, Moses converted to Christianity on the festival of Saints Peter and Paul, appropriating the names of the former saint and of his royal patron for his own. He soon completed both his widely translated anthology of Mediterranean folk tales, *Disciplina clericalis*,¹⁰ and his polemical and apologetic *Dialogus Petri et Moysi Iudei*.¹¹ The second decade of the twelfth century found Alfonsi in England, where he instructed English scientists in astronomy, translated Arabic scholarship in the field into Latin, composed his own astronomical treatise, and perhaps served as the royal physician of Henry I. Archival evidence attests that Peter returned to Aragon by 1121, where he died around 1140.

Of all his writings, Alfonsi's *Dialogue* with Moses the Jew—clearly a representation of his Jewish alter ego—bears most directly on our present concern. Peter opens the work with a declaration of his faith in Christianity, a report of his recent conversion, and a description of the Jewish response to his decision:

> When it became known to the Jews who had known me previously and had deemed me well trained in the books of the prophets and teachings of the sages . . . that I had accepted the law and belief of the Christians and was one of them, some of them [i.e., the Jews] thought that I would never have done this unless I had forsaken all sense of shame and despised God and his law. Others asserted that I had done this because I had not understood the words of the prophets and the law properly. Still others ascribed it to vainglory and falsely accused that I had acted for worldly gain, inasmuch as I believed that the Christian people dominated over all others. So that all may understand my intention and hear the rationale, I have thus composed this little book, in which I have first set forth to overcome the credulity of all other peoples and have then concluded [by demonstrating] that the Christian religion is superior to all others. Finally, I have set down all the objections of any opponent of the Christian religion . . . , and I have destroyed them with rational argument and scriptural proof. I have fashioned the entire book as a dialogue, so that the mind of the reader might understand more readily. To defend the arguments of the Christians, I have used the name which I now have as a Christian, to present the arguments of the adversary, the name which I had before baptism.¹²

Responding to the queries of Moses, Peter asserts that as a Christian *he* observes the provisions of divine law more faithfully than do the Jews. In their present condition (i.e., without their Temple and deprived of their land) the Jews are unable to fulfill most of the Mosaic commandments in the literal sense, while they ignore the spiritual, allegorical sense altogether. More important, the Jews' misguided orientation to Scripture leads them into profound doctrinal error—absurd, irrational beliefs which Peter finds totally unpalatable. Christianity, on the other hand, avoids such absurdity but complies with the teachings of the Hebrew Bible nonetheless.

The first, longest, and most original and interesting of the *Dialogue*'s twelve chapters indicts the Jews for their casual interpretation of biblical prophecy and the grievous implications of such error. Peter explains that

> the sayings of the prophets are obscure, and they are not sufficiently clear in every respect. Therefore, when we encounter in the prophets such things whose literal sense would have us deviate from the path of reason, we should interpret them allegorically, so as to return to the rightful course. Necessity compels us to do this, inasmuch as the rationality of the text cannot otherwise be maintained. Your sages, however, have not perceived God as is fitting, and they have erred against him by interpreting the words of the prophets superficially.[13]

Alfonsi supports his claims with a number of talmudic homilies or *aggadot*—e.g., that God wears *tefillin* (phylacteries), that he cries and laments over the dispersion of the Jews, that he is located exclusively in the West, etc.—which "you [Jews] establish not by reason *(ratione)* or scriptural evidence *(auctoritate legis)* but solely through your own disposition...."[14] Any mind that would attribute such anthropomorphic characteristics to God, place limitations on his power, or stray from the teachings of the mathematical and speculative sciences is of questionable sanity at best. How can God be situated in the West if "the West" does not have an absolute, independent existence but varies according to an individual's own frame of reference? How can God weep, if his ability to shed tears would mandate that his actual substance diminish? In his extensive attack on such postbiblical Jewish homilies, Alfonsi surely contributed to a new trend in the anti-Jewish polemic of the high Middle Ages: the denunciation of the beliefs and practices of contemporary rabbinic Judaism, as opposed (or in addition) to the mere contrasting of the "literal" Jewish versus the "spiritual" Christian exegesis of biblical prophecies. Numerous historians have already drawn attention to this innovation in Alfonsi's

25

polemical strategy.[15] But one must emphasize here that Alfonsi's perception of rabbinic Judaism, exemplified by the sort of imaginative or fabulous aggadic homily he adduces in the *Dialogue*, as philosophically unacceptable—"your [presumed] right to affirm any falsehood as the tradition of the ancients"[16]—has in large measure alienated him from the religion of his parents. (As Ch. Merchavya has noted, Alfonsi's refusal to consider that the rabbis might have intended their own homilies figuratively, especially in view of his insistence that the prophets of the Bible did, is indeed curious.)[17]

Other Jewish beliefs next draw Peter's attack. He rejects the Jews' explanation for their present, prolonged, but allegedly temporary state of exile and captivity (chap. 2). Only the rejection of Jesus could have resulted in such divinely wrought affliction; only the acceptance of Christianity will liberate the Jews from it. Peter condemns the rabbinic belief in bodily resurrection (chap. 3) as philosophically untenable, again alluding to the absurdity of talmudic instruction on the subject; and he depicts the Jews' continued observance of Mosaic law as deficient, ineffective, and unpleasing before God (chap. 4). The polemic briefly redirects its attention from Judaism to Islam (chap. 5), a religion spurned (almost abusively) by Peter on the grounds that Muhammad never purged it completely of pagan idolatry, that it focuses predominantly on the carnal in matters of doctrine and practice, and that Muhammad was not a true prophet. Having discredited Judaism and Islam, Peter devotes the remainder of his *Dialogue* to a defense of Christianity, assembling an array of rather standard scriptural proof-texts for beliefs found objectionable by Jews: the Trinity (chap. 6), the Virgin Birth (chap. 7), the Incarnation (chap. 8), Jesus' fulfillment of biblical messianic prophecy (chap. 9), the voluntary nature of his crucifixion (chap. 10), and his resurrection and ascension (chap. 11). A conclusion (chap. 12) reaffirms that Christianity comports well with the Torah of Moses—witness the properly (i.e., christologically) interpreted lessons of the Sabbath, the Passover, and the commandment of circumcision.

Any appraisal of Peter Alfonsi's apostasy should begin with the recognition that minimal change in his career and his values appears to have accompanied his conversion. Both before and after his baptism, Alfonsi was above all else an urbane, erudite devotee of learning, whatever the source of such learning may have been. The *Disciplina clericalis*, although completed after 1106, derives its stories from predominantly Judaic and Muslim sources and displays little allegiance to

Christianity. As an astronomer, Peter is remembered above all for sharing his Andalusian heritage with Christian scientists in England, as teacher, as author, and as translator. The polemical *Dialogue* itself demonstrates continued expertise in classical rabbinic and Islamic lore, just as it capitalizes upon every opportunity to extol the sciences, or Alfonsi's own understanding of them. Conversion hardly appears to have impeded the continuation of Peter's medical career. In other words, Alfonsi's baptism brought little change to his scholarly, intellectual pursuits, and these constituted the most important defining characteristics of his self-image as Jew and as Christian. We recall his account of his own intellectual prowess in the Jewish community, and we may also cite a letter to Christian scholars in France, composed after his conversion, probably during his sojourn in England.

> To all those of the holy mother Church throughout France who are students of Aristotle *(perypateticis)*, otherwise nourished with the milk of philosophy, or diligently engaged in any scientific study—Peter Alfonsi, servant of Jesus Christ, their brother and fellow student, [wishes] salvation and blessing from him who conveys salvation and blessing. Because all who have been given to drink any of the nectar of philosophy should love one another, if any one should have some rare, precious thing useful but unknown to the others, it is right and fair that he freely communicate it to the others so that the knowledge of all may grow and increase over time. Wishing to follow this rule, we have endeavored to investigate carefully if we have some such thing, so that we might present you with something you would find sweet and pleasing.

Attempting to promote an international community of altruistically minded scholars, Peter may have intended to imply that love for learning should transcend even theological frontiers. For although he ostensibly appeals as a Christian to other Christians, he identifies above all with the devotees of Aristotle, of whom there were still few in European Christendom, but a rising number among the sophisticated Jews (and Arabs) of the Iberian peninsula.[18]

Why did a man like Alfonsi convert? Some authorities—Heinz Pflaum, for instance—tend to view him as a "scientific skeptic and deist" who attributed little significance to the differences between Judaism and Christianity and converted out of convenience. The apologetic *Dialogue*, according to this view, intended simply to pay lip service to Peter's new religion, reinforcing a careful and pragmatic "career decision" which he had already made.[19] Other scholars lay greater emphasis on his philosophic doubt, which led him away from Judaism and, given the intellectual climate of his day, perhaps to Christianity as well. Alfonsi's contemporary and sometime co-

religionist Judah ha-Levi, in his noted *Book of the Kuzari*, depicted
Christianity as a faith built on abstract doctrine and asserted the
superiority of Judaism because it derived from the historical traditions
and experiences of a particular people. Perhaps Alfonsi, as Amos
Funkenstein has suggested, agreed with this generic distinction between the two religions but was driven by his rationalist temperament
to prefer Christianity as the only faith which "befits the philosopher."[20]

The available evidence does not allow for a conclusive decision
between these two interpretations, nor are they of necessity mutually
exclusive. In the present context, however, one should appreciate that
Alfonsi's conversion was deliberate, calculated, and, if we may attribute any credibility to the *Dialogue*, the capstone of extended intellectual inquiry. The very composition of this lengthy apologetic tract,
organized around Moses' questions and Peter's answers to them, hints
at precisely the path which a rationalist like Alfonsi might have
followed toward the baptismal font; it suggests that Alfonsi was hardly
the unsuspecting victim of an evangelical missionary or a sudden
transforming experience. (This his former coreligionists well understood—hence their aforecited charges against him which Alfonsi
quotes at the outset.) The *Dialogue* progresses as Alfonsi after the
conversion (Peter) demonstrates step by step to Alfonsi before the
conversion (Moses) the doctrinal problems inherent in his Judaism.
Thus convinced, the sephardic Moses would have expected Peter to
turn to Islam, in view of his experience in an Arabic society, the
burgeoning of medieval philosophy in a Muslim environment, and the
numerous pious observances in Islam, so similar to much within
traditional Judaism. Peter accordingly turns his sights on Muhammad
and Islam.[21] Finally, Peter helps Moses (i.e., himself) to overcome his
qualms concerning Christianity in the order that Moses desires, dealing first with the more taxing beliefs in the Trinity and Virgin, and not
resting without addressing the common Jewish revulsion before the
crucifix and other Christian icons. At every step along the way Moses
demands and Peter provides both rational demonstration and biblical
testimony, but it is clear which takes precedence. In chapter three, for
example, Moses first concedes that Peter has proven his previous
point, concerning the reason for the dispersion of the Jews, "with
irrefutable and most convincing rational arguments." Peter then proceeds against Jewish belief in bodily resurrection, and Moses again
admits,

you have satisfactorily explained philosophically that there is a distinction between bodily spirit and rational soul. But because the depths of subtle reasoning do not penetrate the simple minds of the less learned, I ask that you prove, if you can, the same distinction with testimony from the law or the prophets. Thereby at least authority might establish the faith for those whose minds the weight of profound argumentation will not illuminate. [22]

Alfonsi thus emerges on the enlightened extreme of the Andalusian Jewish community. If more mainstream Jewish thinkers of the early medieval period, most notably Saadya Gaon, accorded philosophic legitimacy to "the truth of reliable tradition" as a valid "root of knowledge" alongside sense perception, reason, and logical inference, Peter Alfonsi rejected it as groundless. [23] Typifying the skeptical adversary in Judah ha-Levi's defense of the faith, Alfonsi foreshadowed many a late medieval Marrano who, given the rising tide of anti-Jewish sentiment, discrimination, and violence in Christian Spain, saw no reason to remain a Jew. [24] We may dub him the intellectually disenchanted apostate.

2

Judah ben David ha-Levi of Cologne became "Hermannus quondam Iudeus" (Hermann the erstwhile Jew) when he approached the baptismal font in 1129 at the age of twenty. He soon became a Premonstratensian canon, rose to the priesthood, and ultimately was chosen abbot of the Premonstratensian cloister at Scheda. Like Peter Alfonsi, Hermann authored a book to explain his apostasy, although his *Opusculum de conversione sua* concerns the events leading up to his conversion rather than the substantive differences between Judaism and Christianity. Hermann's interesting treatise has been termed the most compelling autobiographical account of religious conversion since Augustine's *Confessiones*, and it provides us with the only source for evaluating his departure from the Jewish community. [25]

Hermann reports at the outset that unlike the conversion of many to Christianity, his was prolonged and difficult. At the age of thirteen, he dreamt that the emperor took him into his palace and bedecked him with magnificent gifts; a learned Jewish relative thereupon offered the youth a dissatisfying interpretation of the vision grounded in the pleasures of the flesh ("secundum carnis felicitatem"). Seven years later, while engaged in his family's moneylending business in Mainz, Hermann extended a loan to Bishop Ekbert of Münster without taking any collateral. Apprised of the transaction, his parents compelled him to travel to Münster, accompanied by a guardian, Baruch, and to remain with the bishop for twenty weeks until the debt was paid. At Münster the inner turmoil which culminated in baptism began to surface. There Hermann, inspired by the rationality of Christian scholarship, grew fond of the spiritual, allegorical reading of Scripture; he frequently traveled with Ekbert on his pastoral rounds throughout the diocese; and he was exposed to the proselytizing gestures of numerous Christians, who called upon him to emulate the conversion of Paul. He borrowed Latin books, entered a church out of curiosity, and upset by the sight of the icons, challenged the leading monastic scholar Rupert of Deutz to a debate, in which the abbot ably answered all of his questions. Hermann was favorably impressed by his warm reception at the court and home of the bishop, whose servant Richmar, having expressed a willingness to undergo an ordeal by fire for the sake of Hermann's soul, was restrained only by the prudence of the bishop himself. Accompanying Ekbert to the Premonstratensian cloister at Cappenberg, Hermann realized that its self-sacrificing canons did not merit divine rejection and damnation; perhaps, he concluded, it was the Jews and not the Christians who were to be punished by God—witness the present dispersion and captivity of the former.

Ekbert finally repaid his debt, and Hermann returned home for Passover distraught and perplexed, searching, both inwardly and in frequent conversation with clergymen, for the right path to follow. His tutor Baruch condemned him for excessive fraternization with Christians while at Münster but then succumbed to a fatal fever within days after leveling the accusation. Hermann entreated God for a vision, vainly fasting for three days in order to merit one. Under the threat of excommunication by the now concerned Jewish community, he agreed to marry, but once the honeymoon ended his doubts returned. He eventually became convinced of the validity of Christianity but found intellectual understanding alone, without an accompanying emotional commitment, insufficient to facilitate his total conversion. He began to cross himself, especially as the devil habitually undermined his leaning toward the church. Finally, the piety of two nuns in Cologne induced him to undergo baptism. He fled Cologne, accidentally intercepted letters sent by its Jewish community to that in Mainz calling for his punishment, stopped off in Worms to preach on the shortcomings of Judaism in a synagogue there, kidnapped his younger half-brother from the latter's home in

Mainz, took refuge in various cloisters, and was baptized in Cologne. The treatise concludes with a detailed christological reinterpretation of Hermann's adolescent dream: The emperor represents God, who ushers Hermann into the church and spiritual salvation.

We must approach Hermann's *Opusculum* with due caution. It intends primarily not to polemicize but to publicize among Christians the glorious experience of conversion;[26] written some time after Hermann's baptism, it leaves us at quite a distance from the real world and the world view of young Judah ben David ha-Levi. Despite Hermann's claims to have been esteemed for his learning as a Jew, the *Opusculum* contains no evidence of such accomplishment; his Jewish background is remote indeed, as he even follows the Vulgate when quoting Hebrew Scripture, forsaking the literal meaning of the Masoretic Text when the two versions differ.[27] And as Julius Aronius argued nearly a century ago, there is surely more to the story of the conversion than Hermann would have us believe.[28] The young man would never have offered Ekbert a sizable unsecured loan had the two not known each other previously. How did Hermann's family know in advance that the lad could not be trusted among Christians, so as to dispatch Baruch to Münster along with him?

Nevertheless, the substance of the treatise is instructive for historians on several grounds. First, the *Opusculum* includes a number of precious glimpses into the social history of German Jewry early in the twelfth century: Hermann's remark that "all Jews are engaged in moneylending" manifests the rising concentration of Franco-German Jewry in this one, often hated, sector of the medieval European economy, a trend which gained considerable momentum during the years of Hermann's own life.[29] The self-assurance of Cologne's Jews, who sent letters vilifying Hermann to the Jews of Mainz in the hands of a royal chaplain (a Christian cleric!), testifies to the vitality of this enduring Jewish community which had suffered violent attack during the First Crusade only thirty years earlier.[30] On the other hand, Hermann's attempted evasion of marriage by claiming that he had to travel to France to pursue his studies suggests that in the wake of the Crusade, the French academies of Rashi and his disciples had begun to overshadow the schools of the Rhineland as the superior centers of rabbinic learning.[31]

Second, as a piece of literature the *Opusculum* exemplifies important aspects of twelfth-century Christian spirituality in general and new tendencies in religious piety in particular. Hermann's spiritual restlessness, which ultimately led him to conversion, was shared by many of his contemporaries, in and outside the ranks of the Catholic clergy.[32] He addresses the incompatibility of mundane pursuits with the truly pious life, another typical concern of the age, in a string of glaring contrasts: between his miserly Jewish relatives, preoccupied with worldly glory, and Christians, worried over his soul; between the literal proscription of Mosaic law, that Jews may not eat of animals which do not chew their cuds *(animalia non ruminantia)*, and the urge Hermann felt repeatedly to "chew" over the pleasing words of Ekbert's sermons *(in ventrem memorie sepius mecum ruminanda transmisi)*;[33] between the austere fellowship of the Jewish community and the astoundingly warm reception (hardly befitting a Jew) he received among Christians; between his half-brother's mother who dispatched a posse to retrieve her son and the mother church who bore both brothers into a new, cleansed infancy;[34] and between his wife who threatened his salvation and the nuns of Cologne who effected it. Upon his visit to their convent, Hermann reports

> after no long while, owing to their merits and prayers, the clarity of the Christian faith pervaded my penitent heart so, that it thoroughly purged it of the gloom of its former doubt and ignorance in an altogether fitting exchange: Women sustained with their prayers one who had fallen on account of a woman.[35]

Hermann's preoccupation with the antithesis between Judaism and Christianity echoes a frequent obsession of his contemporaries; as Jaroslav Pelikan notes, the twelfth century gave rise to more treatises of Christian anti-Jewish polemic than any prior medieval century, perhaps as many as the entire medieval period before the Crusades.[36] The repeated insistence that rational argument alone could not produce the inner transformation required of a convert bespeaks the Anselmian dictum of "faith seeking understanding" *(fides quaerens intellectum)*. And Hermann's self-portrait as the blind individual who discovers himself in the collective of Christian religious duplicates the pattern described so eloquently by Caroline Walker Bynum, in her recent work entitled *Jesus as Mother:*

> Twelfth-century religious thinkers stress individual decision, lifestyle, and experience as part of a search for institutions and practices that embody these, and . . . the goal of development to a twelfth-century person is the application to the self of a model that is simultaneously, exactly because it *is* a model, a mechanism for affiliation with a group.[37]

In this age of religious reform and pietistic experimentation, when many rejected or at least sought to improve upon existing institutional opportunities for inner self-perfection, an individual's spiritual solace still depended ultimately on the reinforcing support of an organized community. While the discipline of rabbinic Judaism may have estranged him from family and friends, it is thus hardly surprising that Hermann first sensed the glory of Christianity in the far more structured life of the monastic cloister at Cappenburg.

> Coming to this fellowship of the faithful of Christ, composed of men of varying conditions and different nations, I beheld fulfilled in spirit the prophecy of Isaiah [11.6] concerning the messianic era which I used to think, in support of my error, had yet to be realized in the flesh upon the arrival of the messiah. "The calf," he says, "the lion, and the sheep will graze together, and a small boy will drive them."[38]

Finally, although the typology in Hermann's story might well reinforce our aforementioned doubts as to its accuracy, the *Opusculum* can in fact serve as the basis for a worthwhile appraisal of Hermann's apostasy. That a Jewish youth of early twelfth-century Ashkenaz found himself so attracted to innovative currents in contemporary Christian spirituality itself warrants attention. Moreover, the *Opusculum* does reveal signs of Hermann the individual behind the stereotypes in style and in plot. For instance, we recall that early in his stay in Münster, Hermann challenged the renowned Rupert of Deutz to a debate, at which Hermann complained of Christian hostility toward the Jews, misunderstanding of God's law, and veneration of the crucifix and icons. The *Opusculum* records Rupert's response to the charge of idolatry, to which Hermann adds: "Thus did Rupert, meeting all my objections with the most beautiful rational arguments and the most effective scriptural citations, deflect them with the most illuminating rays of his answers, as if they were the fog of a foul night."[39] Some scholars have consequently assumed that Rupert, himself appropriately a champion of religious life in a twelfth-century Christendom, played an instrumental role in Hermann's conversion.[40] Yet despite his eventual, though not immediate, acquiescence to Rupert's arguments, evidenced by his crossing himself after the debate (but before his formal conversion), Hermann chose for himself a path and a manner different from those of Rupert. Hermann's *Opusculum* lacks the marked anti-Jewish invective and theological polemic characteristic of Rupert's writings; Hermann hardly concerns himself with the issues of the Jewish-Christian debate, so crucial to Rupert the scholar.[41] More important, Hermann after his baptism joined the Premonstratensian canons, a new order signifying current dissatisfaction with the Benedictine monasticism ardently defended by Rupert, and an order which included St. Norbert of Xanten and Bishop Anselm of Havelberg, two of Rupert's staunchest opponents.[42]

What, then, may we conclude about Hermann the individual and his conversion? Bernhard Blumenkranz has pointed to the probable psychological underpinnings of Hermann's apostasy—manifested by his influential dream at the age of thirteen, at the time of his Bar Mitzvah, or Jewish rite of passage into manhood, and experienced shortly after his father's second marriage. (This marriage soon led to the birth of the half-brother whom Hermann would later kidnap and bring with him into the church). "May we not assume that the young Judah, already jarred and emotionally injured by his father's remarriage, placed all his hope in the dramatic change which he expected to accompany his Bar Mitzvah? When this hope remained unfulfilled, his dream-wish came to promise him still greater satisfaction on a different plane."[43] Unfortunately, one learns too little from the *Opusculum* to speculate much further in this direction. Yet one *can* infer from Hermann's treatise that the theological issues dividing Judaism and Christianity did *not* induce him to convert. Although alluding to the misery of the Jews under Christian rule, literal versus allegorical interpretations of Scripture, and the revulsion initially caused by the sight of the crucifix, he worries little over the classic themes of Jewish-Christian controversy: the Trinity, Virgin Birth, Incarnation, messiahship of Jesus—precisely those topics on which Peter Alfonsi had elaborated so strenuously. His own protestations notwithstanding, Hermann does not strike his modern reader as an intellectual or a scholar, but rather as the child of a well-to-do, upper-middle-class, broken home, who was searching for security and meaning in life as his adolescence drew to a close. He never decides, as Peter Alfonsi does, that Judaism is inherently wrong; nor does he ever conclude that Christian doctrine makes sense. His description of his three-day fast, during which he implored God for definitive instructions, evokes both sympathy and scorn; for unable to choose between the two faiths, he observed the fast according to the stringencies of each ritual. (According to Hermann, Jews fasted until evening and then partook of meat, while Christians fasted only until midafternoon but then abstained from meat. Unsure of what to do, Hermann fasted until evening and then ate no meat.)[44] Naïve and impressionable, Hermann clearly fell prey to the subtle means, of which he himself seemed unaware, whereby Bishop Ekbert and his colleagues attempted to win his soul.

They understood their subject well. Neither doctrine nor debate could convert him, but observing the serenity of monastic life or the kindness of an ignorant servant could. Hermann recounts how while staying at Ekbert's residence, the bishop's attendant Richmar graciously invited him to share in his customary repast of bread and water—[45]

> regarding which I was not only overjoyed but greatly astonished, that such a man, whom I then deemed utterly godless and beyond the pale of the law, could be so charitable—especially toward me, whom he too could sooner detest as an enemy of his religion than love, according to the truly lawful warning of the old Law: "Love your friend and hate your enemy."[46] But he, as a follower of the true law of the Gospel, which says, "Love your enemies and reward those who hate you [Matthew 5.44]," knew to behave rightly not only toward his coreligionists but toward all men.

Hermann's was a mentality that beheld everything in stark, cosmic contrasts, in black and white. When he lost his way while fleeing with his half-brother in Mainz, the devil was thwarting him; when he found his way, God had triumphed over the devil; when he forgot the detailed rituals of the baptismal ceremony, it was the devil again; and so on.[47] As a young Jewish layman, to use William James's description of a typical convert, Hermann was "a man living on the ragged edge of his consciousness, pent in to his own sin and want and incompleteness, and consequently inconsolable." Doctrinal theology rarely offers a solution in such emotional crises. In much the same way as evangelical movements and cults attract groping young people in our own time, only the radical antithesis to that which his upbringing had taught him—what James calls "an opposite affection"—could offer Hermann spiritual solace.[48]

3

Originally Saul of Montpellier, Pablo Christiani numbers among the most notorious of medieval Jewish apostates, although in the absence of any extant writings by him, we remain rather ignorant of the details and character of his conversion.[49] After having studied with two noted Provençal rabbis, Eliezer ben Emmanuel of Tarascon and Jacob ben Elijah "of Venice" (formerly of Montpellier), Pablo decided to convert to Christianity probably in the early 1230s; a date of circa 1210 for his birth accordingly appears likely. In the wake of his apostasy, he joined the Order of Preaching Friars (Dominicans) and spent the remainder of his life attacking the Jews and rabbinic liter-

ature in Spain, Provence, and France. This career of missionizing and
inflammatory preaching commenced prior to his prolonged and much
discussed disputation with Moses Nahmanides at the Aragonese court
in Barcelona in July of 1263; the Latin protocol which records the
proceedings of the event indicates that he had previously debated
Nahmanides himself in the latter's residence of Gerona. Following the
disputation, Pablo prevailed upon King James I of Aragon to issue a
series of decrees compelling the Jews of his kingdom to listen to the
proselytizing sermons of Pablo and his Dominican colleagues and to
present their books to a panel of friars (which included Pablo) for
inspection and possible burning. In 1265, Pablo again appeared before
the Aragonese court to protest the leniency with which King James
had reacted to Nahmanides' own written account of the 1263 disputation, a report naturally unfavorable to Pablo and his confreres. Dissatisfied with the ensuing royal exoneration of Nahmanides, the Dominicans appealed to Rome, and Pope Clement IV responded in 1267
with a bull bemoaning the damnable perfidy of the Jews *(Dampnabili
perfidia Iudeorum).* For supervising the eradication of this perfidy, the
pontiff noted that "our beloved son Friar Paul, called Christian, of the
Order of Friars Preachers . . . , is deemed especially capable—both
because he stems from the Jews, ably trained among them in Hebrew,
and knows their language, the old law, and their errors, and because
having been reborn at the baptismal font he embodies the zeal of the
Catholic faith and eruditely presents himself in the faculty of theology."[50] Within a year or two, Pablo crossed the Pyrenees into
northern France, where with the assistance of King Louis IX he
sought to enforce compliance with the Fourth Lateran Council's decree that the Jews wear a distinguishing mark on their clothing, and he
again condemned rabbinic literature and inflicted his sermons upon
the Jews. Before he died in 1274, Pablo had elicited polemical responses from an impressive list of rabbis: Nahmanides, Jacob ben
Elijah of Venice, Mordekhai of Avignon, Samuel ben Abraham of
Dreux, and yet another, anonymous, writer.

Of these details concerning Pablo's life we can be relatively sure.
But recent scholars have attempted, on weaker grounds, to link Pablo
with other developments in the anti-Jewish activity of thirteenth-
century Christendom—conjectures which, in view of the dearth of
knowledge concerning this important friar, deserve mention at least.
Robert Chazan depicts Pablo as the "key figure" in promoting the
compulsory sermon at which Jews had to endure not only an un-

friendly harangue but frequently the wrath of an angry Christian mob that accompanied the preacher into the synagogue. Chazan argues further that Pablo was the "preaching prostitute" *(ha-kadesh ha-doresh)* against whom Meir ben Simeon of Narbonne debates in his *Milḥemet Mitsvah,* and Marc Saperstein believes he also disputed with Rabbi Isaac ben Yedaiah of Beziers. Joseph Shatzmiller suggests that Pablo actually began the practice of disinterring the bodies of Jews who had converted to Christianity but then "relapsed" to their old faith, a practice in which the friar certainly seems to have participated.[51]

The grudge which Pablo bore against the Jewish community throughout his life indicates that for him, as opposed to Peter Alfonsi, conversion to Christianity represented far more than a cool, rational decision—whether undertaken for the sake of convenience or out of conviction. Unlike Hermann of Cologne, Pablo cared about the polemical issues dividing the church and the synagogue; as a Christian he did not seclude himself in the convent—or the school—but took considerable initiative in refining the polemic and attempting to undermine the strength of European Jewry. Pablo obviously left that community infuriated. While the extant sources do not permit a definitive explanation of his apostasy and vendetta against the Jews, three aspects of his career allow for profitable speculation in this direction.

First, Pablo as a Christian was a staunch disciple of Raymond de Peñaforte, Master-General of the Dominican Order from 1238 to 1240, and thirteenth-century Christendom's missionary and anti-heretical ideologue par excellence. Pablo converted not long after Raymond preached against the infidel in southern France at the end of the 1220s;[52] when Raymond returned to Barcelona in 1240, after a decade at the papal curia and at the head of his order, Pablo became his disciple. Raymond organized and presided over Pablo's disputation with Nahmanides in 1263. Acknowledging this initiative, Nahmanides at the opening of the debate requested permission to speak freely from the king and from Friar Raymond. When Pablo invaded the main synagogue in Barcelona to preach to the Jews a week after the disputation, Raymond accompanied him and spoke first.[53] Perhaps not coincidentally, Pablo journeyed to Paris later in the 1260s at precisely the time when Raymond was urging Louis IX to wage a crusade against Muslim Tunisia, and possibly commissioning the composition of Thomas Aquinas's *Summa contra gentiles* as well.[54] Not surprisingly, then, Pablo enthusiastically espoused in his own polemic the goals and methods of Raymond's mission to the Jews, which

Raymond's anonymous fourteenth-century biographer described as follows:

> With his advice and approval, certain friars were thus instructed in the Hebrew language, so that they could overcome the malice and the errors of the Jews, who might no longer, as they had been accustomed to do in the past, audaciously deny the true text and the glosses of their own sages which agree with our own saints in these matters pertaining to the Catholic faith. Moreover, [the friars studied Hebrew] so that the falsehoods and corruptions which they [the Jews] had inserted in many places in the Bible to hide the mysteries of the Passion and other sacraments of the faith, might be revealed through their authentic scriptural texts— which is all meant to confuse them [the Jews] greatly and confirm the Christian faith.[55]

As I have argued elsewhere, Raymond stood at the center of an unprecedented Mendicant effort to convert the Jews, based on the premise that contemporary Judaism had forfeited its rightful place in Christian society. He believed that the Jews had departed from the Old Testament tradition which had hitherto justified their toleration and survival. In a word, to his mind, medieval Judaism had betrayed itself; it was nothing less than heretical.[56]

Our second clue as to Pablo's motivations follows closely upon the first and derives from a seeming inconsistency in his outlook. Pablo's anti-Jewish polemic, as expressed in his disputation with Nahmanides, is distinguished by an innovative attempt to prove that rabbinic *aggadah* bespeaks the truth of Christianity. Pablo's later career, however, suggests a markedly hostile attitude toward talmudic literature: the decrees of James I of Aragon (mentioned above) issued at Pablo's request within weeks after the Barcelona disputation, the bull he solicited from Clement IV condemning the Talmud, and his subsequent pronouncements in northern France. The ostensive contradiction fades if we recall the opinion of Pablo's mentor Raymond de Peñaforte; rabbinic literature had indeed deviated from the traditions of the Old Testament, but from a tactical point of view it could provide the best means for inducing the Jew to accept baptism. If Pablo made such ideology and strategy the core of his attempts to convert other Jews to Christianity, similar considerations may have played a part in his own apostasy. Jewish estimations of Pablo confirm this impression. "You have struck out at the Talmud," Jacob ben Elijah wrote Pablo after his conversion. But Jacob also devotes over a third of his lengthy polemical epistle to defending *Jewish* interpretations of difficult rabbinic homilies against the allegations of Pablo; in the words of another thirteenth-century rabbi, Pablo had been "irreverent *(poker)* toward the *aggadot* of our Talmud."[57] While the friar had rejected talmudic Judaism in general, he remained preoccupied with the vulnerability of the *aggadah* in particular.

The final clue emerges from an impassioned, albeit cryptic, passage in Jacob ben Elijah's polemic linking Pablo's conversion to the conflict between rationalists and antirationalists in the thirteenth-century Provençal Jewish community, a controversy in which both Jacob and Pablo participated. After lauding the piety of Pablo's parents and relatives, Jacob explains:[58]

> Behold, sir, you are Saul *(Sha'ul)*; you were borrowed *(Sha'ul)* from the Lord. You were created with a clear, untainted soul, born in holiness and purity. The soul of your father which did not instill impurity; and your mother, who followed a path of meticulous observance; and your numerous honored relatives—wise, sagacious, compassionate, faithful and Godfearing—who would have believed that a formidable enemy, a stone men strike and stumble over, would have risen from among them? He constantly vexes his coreligionists and has made them the target for his arrows. It was the sin of our youth, secretly hating their brothers, speaking peace but intending malice, when the fire of stormy controversy raged among them and the creditor[59] came to collect both property and souls, that prevented us from finding peace. The slanderers were a brood of sinful men, they assumed leadership[60] and caused division between brothers. They beheld false and fraudulent visions, espoused a foreign faith, and enkindled the fire;[61] children spoke impudently, and the lowly with harshness to the venerable. Accordingly this affliction befell us. When I too was there, I joined in as one of them. And so words fail me; for I am ashamed and reproach myself for the sins of my youth. Most of the controversy resulted from guile and deception. Not the venomous lizard but sin is responsible for death.[62]

Amidst this series of difficult biblical epithets, Jacob here locates the cause for Pablo's apostasy within the context of the Maimonidean controversy, in the betrayal of Maimonides' rationalist books to the Christian Inquisition by fanatical Jews on charges of heresy, and the subsequent burning of those books in Montpellier in 1232. Jacob attributes the strife within the city to a spirit of heresy, in which he himself was then caught up, and which moved the antirationalist slanderers to overturn the sacrosanct structures of communal authority, to usurp leadership themselves, and ultimately to cause the auto-da-fé. The anti-Maimonist heterodoxy, which Jacob subsequently recanted—witness his later commentaries on Maimonides' *Guide of the Perplexed*[63]—precipitated the public tragedy, and it triggered the apostasy of Pablo Christiani as well.

Can these three pieces of evidence illuminate one another? (1)

Raymond de Peñaforte considered rabbinic Judaism heretical and asserted that a proper explication of talmudic texts would lead Jews to become Christians. (2) Pablo Christiani adopted Raymond's anti-talmudic posture, underwent baptism, and, using the *aggadah*, endeavored to persuade others to follow him. (3) Before, during, and after the Maimonidean controversy exploded in Montpellier, charges of heresy were rampant in the Jewish community. Frequently, such charges arose over conflicting approaches to the *aggadah*, a subject which for some time had been exposing Jews to the ridicule of their enemies, whether Karaite, Muslim, or Christian.[64] And Jacob's implication that the crisis degraded Judaism to the delight of the church, making the time ripe for apostasy, is echoed in other recollections of the events. Joseph ben Todros Abulafia, for example, like Jacob an erstwhile anti-Maimonidean, wrote:

> It is not right to turn Israel over to the uncircumcised Gentiles and let our enemies be our judges, they whose word and deed seek to sully our honor and mar our glory, to subject our Torah to false interpretation, and to bundle and hurl us about like a ball . . . , in whose hand the beauty of the Torah decomposes, the flavor of the Torah becomes putrid, and the Torah itself is consigned to the flames.[65]

At the very least, it appears safe to conclude that the issues and strife of the controversy in Montpellier, and somehow the dispute over the *aggadah*, helped to alienate Pablo from the traditional Jewish community. When the smoke cleared, he found himself outside of the fold, attracted by a church and an order which had shown their muscle, and incited by a grudge that governed his energies for the rest of his life. Considering also the somewhat antirationalist temperament of Raymond de Peñaforte,[66] as well as the likelihood that Jacob ben Elijah was Pablo's teacher or comrade in Montpellier while Jacob still numbered among the anti-Maimonideans,[67] one might hazard an additional conjecture: Pablo stood at the radical extreme of the anti-Maimonist camp. His highly literalist orientation to rabbinic literature, when directed toward messianic midrashim in particular, heightened the susceptibility of the *aggadah* to christological interpretation. In the wake of the betrayal of Maimonides' works to the Inquisition, most of the anti-Maimonists realized such a danger in their position and moderated their stance. Pablo, however, did not, and he felt compelled to seek a new outlet for attacking the perceived Jewish heresy of his day. Not lightly did Pablo's anonymous rabbinic opponent label him "one who unveils the secrets of the Torah *(megalleh razei Torah)*."[68]

A champion of conversion to Catholicism in our own century has noted that "the Church is a house with a hundred gates; and no two men enter at exactly the same angle."[69] How much more so during an age when joining the church of Rome entailed emancipation from the second-class status of an alien minority and the assumption of full-fledged membership in the rank and file of society! The scientific intellectual Peter Alfonsi, the groping adolescent Hermann of Cologne, and the vituperative polemicist Pablo Christiani—each for his own reasons could not find fulfillment in the medieval Jewish community. The dynamics of their respective careers and conversions underscore the complexity of Jewish-Christian relations during the Middle Ages and the breadth of the spectrum of influences one European religion could exert upon the members of another. The lives of Peter, Hermann, and Pablo assist in the illustration of an important but obscure chapter in the history of the Jews, our regrettable inability to quantify its significance notwithstanding.

NOTES

1. On medieval European Jewish apostasy in general (prior to that of four-teenth-century Spain), see Jacob Katz, *Exclusiveness and Tolerance: Studies in Jewish-Gentile Relations in Medieval and Modern Times* (1961; repr., New York: Schocken, 1962), pp. 67–76, and "'Though He Sinned, He Remains an Israelite [Hebrew],'" *Tarbiz* 27 (1958): 203–17; Bernhard Blumenkranz, "Jüdische und christliche Konvertiten im jüdisch-christlichen Religionsgespräch des Mittelalters," in *Judentum im Mittelalter: Beiträge zum christlich-jüdischen Gespräch*, ed. Paul Wilpert (Berlin: Walter de Gruyter, 1966), pp. 271–82; Solomon Grayzel, *The Church and the Jews in the XIIIth Century*, rev. ed. (New York: Hermon, 1966), pp. 13–21; and Salo Wittmayer Baron, *A Social and Religious History of the Jews*, 2d ed., 18 vols. (New York: Columbia University Press, 1952–83), vols. 3–8, also, s.v. "conversion," 9:12–24. Informative studies of *meshummadim* not considered below include Franklin J. Pegues, *Lawyers of the Last Capetians* (Princeton: Princeton University Press, 1962), pp. 124–40 (on Philippe de Villepreux); Gilbert Dahan, "Guillaume de Flay et son commentaire du Livre des Juges: Etude et édition," *Recherches augustiniennes* 13 (1978): 37–104; and Dahan's introduction to his edition of Guillaume de Bourges, *Livre des guerres du Seigneur et deux homélies* (Paris: Editions du Cerf, 1981). The available evidence concerning these three additional converts regrettably does not reveal the particulars of their departures from the Jewish community. Cf. also the literature cited in Kenneth R. Stow, "The Church and the Jews: From St. Paul to Paul IV," in *Bibliographical Essays in Medieval Jewish Studies* (New York: Anti-Defamation League of B'nai B'rith, 1976), pp. 145ff.; and in my *The Friars and the Jews: The Evolution of Medieval Anti-Judaism* (Ithaca: Cornell University Press, 1982), s.v. "conversion."

2. Gratian, *Decretum*, D. 45, c. 3.

3. Homily 1 *Against the Jews*, trans. in Wayne A. Meeks and Robert L. Wilken, *Jews and Christians in Antioch in the First Four Centuries of the Common Era* (Missoula: Scholars Press, 1978), p. 97.

4. *Visigothic Code (Forum Judicum)* 12.2.16, trans. Samuel Parsons Scott (Boston: Boston Book Company, 1910), pp. 375–76.

5. See Grayzel, *The Church and the Jews*, pp. 88–89, 100–101.

6. See esp. the works of Jacob Katz, *supra*, n. 1.

7. 1876, ed. Jehudah Wistinetzki and J. Freimann, 2d ed. (Frankfurt am Main: M. A. Wahrmann, 1924), p. 455. In this instance the sage ruled: "Let him convert sooner than have them perjure themselves. Moreover, it is better for him to apostasize than for them to lose a daughter of Israel to such a villain."

8. Alfonsi's life and work are discussed by A. Lukyn Williams, *Adversus Judaeos: A Bird's-Eye View of Christian Apologiae until the Renaissance* (Cambridge: Cambridge University Press, 1935), pp. 233–40; Eliyahu Ashtor, *The Jews of Moslem Spain*, trans. Aaron and Jenny Machlowitz Klein, 3 vols. (Philadelphia: Jewish Publication Society, 1979), 2:272ff., 358; Ch. Merchavya, *The Church versus Talmudic and Midrashic Literature, 500–1248* [Hebrew], (Jerusalem: Mosad Bialik, 1970), pp. 93–127; and Eberhard Hermes' introduction to his German translation of *The Disciplina Clericalis of Petrus Alfonsi*, trans. [to English] P. R. Quarrie (London: Routledge and Kegan Paul, 1977), pp. 3–99. On Alfonsi's scientific career in particular, see Charles Homer Haskins, *Studies in the History of Medieval Science* (Cambridge: Harvard University Press, 1927), pp. 113ff.; and J. M. Millás Vallicrosa, "'Avodato shel Mosheh Sefaradi (Petrus Alfonsus) 'al Ḥokhmat ha-Tekhunah," *Tarbiz* 9 (1937): 55–64, and "La aportación astronomica de Pedro Alfonso," *Sefarad* 3 (1943): 65–105.

9. *Dialogus Petri et Moysi Iudei*, in Migne, *Patrologia latina* (hereafter PL) 157:538–39.

10. PL 157:671–706; critical edition by Hilka and W. Soderhjelm in *Acta Societatis scientiarum fennicae* 37, no. 4 (1911).

11. PL 157:535–672.

12. Ibid., col. 538.

13. Ibid., col. 553.

14. Ibid., col. 542.

15. In addition to the studies of Williams and Merchavya (*supra*, n.8), see Amos Funkenstein, "Changes in the Patterns of Christian Anti-Jewish Polemic in the Twelfth Century [Hebrew]," *Zion*, n.s. 33 (1968): 133–37, and "Basic Types of Christian Anti-Jewish Polemics in the Later Middle Ages," *Viator* 2 (1971): 373ff.; Manfred Kniewasser, "Die antijüdische Polemik des Petrus Alphonsi (getauft 1106) und des Abtes Petrus Venerabilis von Cluny (1156)," *Kairos*, n.s. 22 (1980): 34–49; and my *Friars*, pp. 27–28.

16. PL 157:543: "Cum ad tam irrationabilis conclusionis diffugium vestrum deviet argumentum, per antiquorum successiones omne tibi licebit firmare mendacium."

17. *The Church*, pp. 100–101.

18. The text of Alfonsi's letter appears in Millás, "La aportación," pp. 97ff. On the study of Aristotle (or absence thereof), see, among many others, Etienne Gilson, *History of Christian Philosophy in the Middle Ages* (New York: Random House, 1955), pts. 4ff.; and Julius Guttmann, *Philosophies of Judaism: The History of Jewish Philosophy from Biblical Times to Franz Rosenzweig*, trans. David W. Silverman (1964; repr. New York: Schocken, 1973), esp. pp. 152–274. Noteworthy is Guttmann's observation (p. 152) that although Abraham ibn Daud's *Emunah Ramah*, the first Jewish work of Aristotelian philosophy, was not completed until 1161, "it stands to reason that Judah Halevi [in the *Kuzari* (ca. 1130)] would not have directed his attacks at the Aristotelian system if it had not counted adherents among his contemporaries." Evidence for Aristotelian tendencies among Jews as early as the tenth century is discussed by Shlomo Pines, "A Tenth Century Philosophical Correspondence," *Proceedings of the American Academy for Jewish Research* 24 (1955): 103–36.

19. Heinz Pflaum, "Ein französischer Dichter des 14. Jahrhunderts über Raschi," *Monatsschrift für die Geschichte und Wissenschaft des Judentums* 76 (1932): 580–81; cf. Merchavya, *The Church*, p. 96.

20. Funkenstein, "Changes," pp. 133–37; cf. Ashtor, *The Jews*, 2:273; Blumenkranz, "Jüdische und christliche Konvertiten," p. 274; and Eliezer Schweid, "The Literary Structure of the First Book of the *Kuzari* [Hebrew]," *Tarbiz* 30 (1961): 265ff.

21. PL 157:597ff.

22. Ibid., cols., 581, 586.

23. See Saadya Gaon, *Book of Beliefs and Opinions*, trans. Samuel Rosenblatt, introduction, chap. 5, (New Haven: Yale University Press, 1948), pp. 16ff.

24. Alfonsi's extensive familiarity with the traditions of Hispano-Jewish culture has been demonstrated by Bernard Septimus, "Petrus Alfonsi on the Cult of Mecca," *Speculum* 56 (1981): 517–33; in this regard cf. also Gerson D. Cohen, "The Story of the Four Captives," *Proceedings of the American Academy for Jewish Research* 29 (1960–61): 79–80; and Haim Schwarzbaum, "International Folklore Motifs in Petrus Alphonsi's 'Disciplina clericalis,'" *Sefarad* 21 (1961): 267–99; 22 (1962): 17–59, 321–44; 23 (1963): 54–73. On his debt to Saadya, see Funkenstein, "Changes," pp. 134–35. Typologies of Spanish Jews helpful in appreciating Alfonsi have been advanced by Yitzhak Baer, *A History of the Jews in Christian Spain*, trans. Louis Schoffman et al., 2 vols. (Philadelphia: Jewish Publication Society, 1961–66), 1:1–38; Daniel Jeremy Silver, *Maimonidean Criticism and the Maimonidean Controversy, 1180–1240* (Leiden: Brill, 1965), esp. pp. 190–98; and Bernard Septimus, *Hispano-Jewish Culture in Transition: The Career and Controversies of Ramah* (Cambridge: Harvard University Press, 1982), esp. pp. 75–115.

25. On Hermann and his memoirs, see Julius Aronius, "Hermann der Prä-monstratenser," *Zeitschrift für die Geschichte der Juden in Deutschland* 2 (1888): 217–31; Reinhold Seeberg, *Hermann von Scheda: Ein jüdischer Proselyt des zwölften Jahrhunderts* (Leipzig: Akademische Buchhandlung, 1891); Joseph Greven, "Die Schrift des Hermannus quondam Judaeus 'De conversione sua opusculum,'" *Annalen des historischen Vereins für den Niederrhein* 115 (1929): 111–31; Georg Misch, *Geschichte der Auto-biographie*, 3.1 (Frankfurt am Main: G. Schulte-Bulmke, 1959), pp. 505–22; Gerlinde Niemeyer's thorough introduction to her critical edition of Hermann's *Opusculum de conversione sua* (Weimar: H. Böhlaus Nachfolger, 1963), pp. 1–67; and Arnaldo Momigliano, "A Medieval Jewish Autobiography," in *History and Imagination: Essays in Honour of H. R. Trevor-Roper*, ed. Hugh Lloyd-Jones et al. (London: Duckworth, 1981), pp. 30–36.

26. See Hermann's dedicatory prologue to the *Opusculum*, ed. Niemeyer, pp. 69–70.

27. E.g., the verse cited below at n. 38.

28. "Hermann," p. 227.

29. *Opusculum*, p. 72. On the role of the medieval Jew as moneylender, see among many others Baron, *Social and Religious History*, 12:132–97, 307–40; Grayzel, *The Church and the Jews*, pp. 41–49; and James Parkes, *The Jews in the Medieval Community*, 2d ed. (New York: Hermon, 1976), passim.

30. *Opusculum*, p. 110. On the vitality of Cologne's Jewry during the high Middle Ages, see the essays in Jutta Bohnke-Kollwitz et. al., eds., *Köln und das rheinische Judentum: Festschrift Germania Judaica, 1959–1984* (Cologne: J. P. Bachem, 1984), pp. 17–62, and the literature cited there.

31. *Opusculum*, pp. 98–99; cf. Ephraim E. Urbach, *The Tosaphists: Their History, Writing and Methods* [Hebrew], 4th ed. 2 vols. (Jerusalem: Mosad Bialik, 1980), chaps. 1–4, and Robert Chazan, *Medieval Jewry in Northern France: A Political and Social History* (Baltimore: Johns Hopkins University Press, 1973), chap. 2.

32. On the spiritual climate of the age, see, among others, Marie-Dominique Chenu, "Nature and Man—The Renaissance of the Twelfth Century," in his *Nature, Man, and Society in the Twelfth Century: Essays on New Theological Perspectives in the Latin West*, ed. Jerome Taylor and Lester K. Little (Chicago: University of Chicago Press, 1968), pp. 1–48; Jean Leclercq, François Vandenbroucke, and Louise Bouyer, *The Spirituality of the Middle Ages*, vol. 2 of *A History of Christian Spirituality* (London: Burns and Oates, 1968); and Caroline Walker Bynum, *Jesus as Mother: Studies in the Spir-ituality of the High Middle Ages* (Berkeley: University of California Press, 1982). With specific regard to conversion, see also G. R. Evans, *Old Arts and New Theology: The Beginnings of Theology as an Academic Discipline* (Oxford: Oxford University Press, 1980), pp. 215–21. And for similar tendencies within the German Jewish community itself, cf. Ivan G. Marcus, *Piety and Society: The Jewish Pietists of Medieval Germany* (Leiden: Brill, 1981), and the literature cited therein.

33. *Opusculum*, p. 74.

34. Ibid., p. 120: "Ut igitur per ominia veteribus nova liceat comparare, Naamam Iordanicis septies lotus fluentis a lepra carnis visibiliter est curatus, ego in baptismo per septiformem Spiritus sancti gratiam invisibiliter sum ab anime lepra mundatus. Illius caro detersis elefantie sordibus infantis recepit munditiam; me per lavacrum regenerationis pelle vetustatis exutum in novam peperit ecclesia virgo mater infantiam."

35. Ibid., p. 108; the clear allusion to Adam in "per feminam lapsum" suggests yet an additional measure of conformity to some preexistent pattern.

36. Jaroslav Pelikan, *The Growth of Medieval Theology (600–1300)*, vol. 3 of *The Christian Tradition: A History of the Development of Doctrine* (Chicago: University of Chicago Press, 1978), p. 246.

37. P. 108, emphasis Bynum's.

38. *Opusculum*, pp. 88–89. This interpretation of Isaiah 11 was not original to Hermann; see, for example, Severian (?), *In Genesim sermo*, §1, in Migne, *Patrologia graeca* 56:23. Professor Michael Signer (Hebrew Union College–Jewish Institute of Religion, Los Angeles) informs me that he has written two essays on the spiritual/pietistic typology of Hermann's *Opusculum*. On the failure of medieval autobiography to reflect accurately on the individual, see Karl Joachim Weintraub, *The Value of the Individual: Self and Circumstance in Autobiography* (Chicago: University of Chicago Press, 1978), pp. 49ff., who concluded (p. 60) that in high medieval Christendom, "Self-conscious individuality is not yet to be found." A conflicting perspective, which nevertheless sheds light on Hermann's typology, is that of Chris D. Ferguson, "Autobiography as Therapy: Guibert de Nogent, Peter Abelard, and the Making of Medieval Autobiography," *Journal of Medieval and Renaissance Studies* 13 (1983): 187–212.

39. *Opusculum*, p. 82. On Rupert's interaction with Hermann, cf. also Maria Lodovica Arduini, *Ruperto di Deutz e la controversia tra Christiani ed Ebrei nel secolo XII* (Rome: Istituto storico italiano per il Medio Evo, 1979), esp. pp. 50–57.

40. E.g., Evans, *Old Arts*, p. 229; Hermes' introduction to Peter Alfonsi, *Disciplina clericalis*, p. 44.

41. Arduini, *Ruperto*, passim.

42. On the regular canons and on Rupert's relations with them, see Leclercq et al., *Spirituality*, pp. 137ff.; P. F. Lefèvre, ed., *Les statuts de Prémontré, reformés sur les ordres de Grégoire IX et d'Innocent IV au XIIIᵉ siècle*, Bibliothèque de la *Revue d'histoire ecclésiastique* 23 (Louvain: Bureaux de la Revue, 1946), pp. vii–xxxii; and John H. Van Engen, *Rupert of Deutz* (Berkeley: University of California Press, 1983), pp. 299–334.

43. "Jüdische und christliche Konvertiten," pp. 275f.

44. See *Opusculum*, p. 94: "Eiusdem etiam Danielis secutus exemplum pro huius ardentissimi desiderii mei impetratione triduanum Deo devovi ieiunium. Sciens autem Iudeos et Christianos non eandem ieiunii regulam tenere, cum Christiani diebus ieiunii hora nona vescentes carnium esu abstineant, Iudei vero ad vesperam

usque perdurantes carnibus et quibuscumque eis vesci licitum est utantur, ignarus, quid horum magis Deo placeret, indifferenter utrumque servare decrevi. Itaque et iuxta christianitatis ritum carnibus abstinui, Iudeorum autem more ad vesperam usque ieiunium protrahens modico pane et aqua contentus permansi. Ob nimiam quoque desiderii mei aviditatem solito me maturius sopori tradens, divinam mihi consolationem eo, quo petieram, ordine sperabam affuturam." Cf. Aronius, "Hermann," p. 228.

45. *Opusculum*, pp. 83–84.

46. A rather flagrant corruption of Leviticus 19.18.

47. *Opusculum*, pp. 115, 118, etc.

48. William James, *The Varieties of Religious Experience: A Study in Human Nature* (1902; repr., New York: Collier, 1961), pp. 176–77.

49. On Pablo and his career of anti-Jewish polemic, see my *Friars*, pp. 108–28, and the literature cited on pp. 108–11, nn. 14, 16.

50. Thomas Ripoll, ed., *Bullarium Ordinis Fratrum Praedicatorum*, 1 (Rome: Typographi Hieronymi Mainardi, 1729), 488.

51. Chazan, "Confrontation in the Synagogue of Narbonne: A Christian Sermon and a Jewish Reply," *Harvard Theological Review* 67 (1974): 439f., 445–57; Marc Saperstein, *Decoding the Rabbis: A Thirteenth-Century Commentary on the Aggadah* (Cambridge: Harvard University Press, 1980), pp. 198–99; Joseph Shatzmiller, "Paulus Christiani: Un aspect de son activité anti-juive," in *Hommage à Georges Vajda: Etudes d'histoire et de pensée juives*, ed. Gérard Nahon and Charles Touati (Louvain: Editions Peeters, 1980), pp. 203–17.

52. See Pope Gregory IX's instructions to Raymond in Franciscus Balme and Ceslaus Paben, eds., *Raymundiana*, Monumenta Ordinis Fratrum Praedicatorum historica 6, 2, fascs. (Rome: In Domo Generalitia, 1900), 2:12–13; cf. Williams, *Adversus Judaeos*, p. 244.

53. See Moses ben Nahman, *Kitvei Ramban*, ed. Charles B. Chavel (Jerusalem: Mosad ha-Rav Kook, 1963), 1:302–3, 320.

54. Andre Berthier, "Un maître orientaliste du XIIᵉ siècle: Raymond Martin, O.P.," *Archivum Fratrum Praedicatorum* 6 (1936): 274ff., 299–304; Peter Marc's introduction to Thomas Aquinas, *Liber de veritate catholice fidei contra errores infidelium*, 3 vols. (Turin: Marietta, 1961–67), 1:53–79, 243, 369–71, 468; and Thomas Murphy, "The Date and Purpose of the *Contra Gentiles*," *Heythrop Journal* 10 (1969): 405–15. Marc's explanation (followed by Murphy) for the composition of the *Contra gentiles* has been hotly contested in a review in *Rassegna di letteratura tomistica* 2 (1967): 51–56; and by Alvaro Huerga, "Hipótesis sobre la genesis de la 'Summa contra gentiles' y del 'Pugio fidei,'" *Angelicum* 51 (1974): 533–57.

55. Balme and Paben, *Raymundiana*, 1:32.

56. *The Friars*, pp. 104–8, 163–69.

57. Jacob ben Elijah, "Iggeret," ed. Joseph Kobak, *Jeschurun* 6 (1868): 1–13; Judah M. Rosenthal, ed., "A Religious Disputation between a Jew Called Menahem and the Convert Pablo Christiani [Hebrew]," in *Hagut Ivrit ba'Amerika: Studies in Jewish Themes by Contemporary American Scholars*, ed. Menahem Zohori et al. (Tel Aviv: Brit-Ivrit Olamit, 1974), 3:62.

58. "Iggeret," p. 21. See also the notes of Benzion Dinur, *Israel in the Diaspora* [Hebrew], 2d ed., 2.2 (Tel Aviv: Devir, 1966), pp. 515, 653.

59. Cf. 2 Kings 4.1—perhaps an allusion to the Catholic clergy.

60. Literally "they were those who led out and brought in"—an allusion to the description of David in 1 Chronicles 11.2, that he had exercised authority over Israel even during Saul's lifetime.

61. Cf. Exodus 22.5, and the similar contemporary description of those who burned Maimonides' books by Judah and Abraham ibn Hasdai, leaders of Barcelona Jewry, in Moritz Steinschneider et al., eds., "Milḥemet ha-dat: Kevutsot mikhtavim be-inyenei ha-maḥloket 'al sefer ha-moreh ve-ha-mada im he'arot," *Jeschurun* 8 (1871): 50.

62. Cf. Babylonian Talmud, *Berakhot* 33a.

63. Henri Gross, *Gallia judaica*, trans. Moise Bloch, ed. Simon Schwarzfuchs (Amsterdam: Philo Press, 1969), pp. 264–65.

64. See Saperstein, *Decoding the Rabbis*, pp. 1–20.

65. Steinschneider, "Milḥemet ha-dat," p. 43.

66. Raymond evidently dissuaded the famous Catalan missionary Raymond Lull from pursuing his studies at the University of Paris; see E. Allison Peers, ed., *A Life of Ramon Lull* (London: Burns, Oates and Washbourne, 1927), p. 8.

67. Jacob, "Iggeret," p. 31.

68. Rosenthal, "A Religious Disputation," p. 62.

69. G. K. Chesterton, *The Catholic Church and Conversion* (1926; repr., New York: Macmillan, 1936), p. 30.

2

Seductive Conversion in Berlin, 1770–1809

DEBORAH HERTZ

In 1816, Karl Rothschild complained to his brother James about the difficulty he was having in finding an appropriate Jewish wife. He reminded his brother that he could easily marry "the most beautiful and richest girl in Berlin, which I would not do for all the treasures in the world, because here in Berlin, if she herself has not been converted, then a brother or a sister-in-law has. . . ."[1] Karl Rothschild's perception that Berlin was a hotbed of conversion is definitely confirmed in the published statistics from the same period. Although we do not possess city-by-city statistics, we do know that whereas only 8 percent of Prussian Jewry lived in Brandenburg (the area around Berlin) in the first half of the century, 38 percent of Prussian conversions in these years took place there. While not precisely documenting Berlin's centrality within the region, these numbers do hint at it.[2]

Berlin's reputation as a city where both assimilation and conversion were especially frequent actually began much earlier than Karl Rothschild's lament, as far back as the last decades of the eighteenth

Research for this essay was supported by a grant from the SUNY Binghamton Foundation. Mr. Michael Rocke efficiently coded the conversion records. Professor Otto Pflanze was kind enough to offer a detailed critique of an earlier version of the essay. Other colleagues and friends also made suggestions, and I am grateful to Sarah Elbert, Nancy Fitch, the late Allan Sharlin, Arthur Leibman, Martin Bunzl, Richard Trexler, David Schoenbaum, Benjamin Kedar, Jacob Toury, members of the German Women's History Study Group in New York, and participants in the May 1984 conference on conversion held at Indiana University.

century. In the 1780s, the Berlin *salonnière* Rahel Varnhagen always bragged when traveling abroad that she was "one of Frederick the Great's Jews."[3] This was indeed something to be proud of, for by the last two decades of the century, a small circle among Berlin's Jewish community had attained definite intellectual prominence and had made inroads into social acceptance. Moses Mendelssohn and his friends and students mastered secular languages, published important books in German and enjoyed close friendships with gentile intellectuals. Salons hosted by Jewish women between 1780 and 1806 were a miniature assimilationist utopia, since Jews and gentiles, nobles and commoners, and men and women mixed freely there without any subgroup having a merely "token" representation. Rahel Varnhagen, Henriette Herz, and Mendelssohn's daughter Dorothea Schlegel were the fashionable, daring, sought-after hostesses for many distinguished persons: Alexander and Wilhelm von Humboldt, Friedrich and A. W. Schlegel, a visiting Madame de Staël, even Prince Louis Ferdinand of Prussia.[4] Both the intellectual accomplishments and the social successes of Berlin Jewry were logical, if not necessarily inevitable, consequences of the altogether unique social composition of the community. For Frederick the Great and both of his eighteenth-century successors slavishly obeyed their own maxim: obtain the greatest economic service from the fewest number of Jews. Only extraordinarily wealthy Jewish families—and those who worked for them in their firms, synagogues, and households—were allowed to live in Berlin. One of the smallest Jewish communities in a major German city was also one of the richest.[5]

What astonished observers was not the unusual wealth of Berlin Jewry. That was inevitable, since Jews were able to live in Berlin only at the crown's pleasure and on its terms. What was unprecedented and anomalous about this Jewish colony was that its wealth came to be adorned by intellectual and social success at a time when the state still imposed harsh and humiliating controls over Jewish life.[6] Jewish communities in other German cities where regulations were equally harsh, like Frankfurt am Main and Hamburg, lacked the intellectual and social glamour of Berlin Jewry. And where state regulation was mild in practice, as in London, the Jewish elite did not play the key role in economic, intellectual, or social life that the Jewish elite played in Berlin. In France, where complete political emancipation was already accomplished after 1791, the Jewish elite was not well represented in Paris, and wealthy Jews in the capital city did not play an important intellectual or social role there. Nor could the distinctive composition and accomplishments of eighteenth-century Berlin Jewry be matched in Amsterdam, a city where Sephardic Jews had long been active in local commerce, and where civic emancipation was granted in 1796. But the vast majority of Jews in Amsterdam were impoverished Ashkenazi Jews, and traditional religious themes dominated their cultural world. To be sure, the Sephardic elite in Amsterdam may have resembled the Berlin elite in its economic, cultural, and social achievements. But because it was such a small proportion of Amsterdam Jewry, the elite was not hegemonic in the community, as was the elite of Berlin.[7]

The very intellectual and social success of leading Berlin Jews which made this such a special community tempted them to deepen and solidify their friendships with gentiles by breaking their ties with other Jews. This trend was especially strong among the salon women. The irony was that the closer the Jewish salon women came to being accepted by the cream of Berlin society, the more urgently they felt pressured to convert to Protestantism. It may have been precisely their Jewish qualities that attracted gentiles to them in the first place. Their fathers' wealth, their cultivation in secular high culture, and their darkly "exotic" looks could all be identified as "Jewish" attributes, and were all particularly attractive to the early romantic generation of Berlin intellectuals. Yet their Jewishness had to be eliminated if visitors were to become friends and if courtships were to end in marriages.

Jewish historians have often been impressed by the salon women's mastery of secular culture and by the heterogeneity of the guests they attracted to their homes. But these historians have also usually been dismayed that so many of these same women abandoned their faith. They have admitted that their salons were historically significant, since, in Jacob Katz's words, the salons were "the first time an entire Jewish sector forged real bonds with German society." Indeed, in one rather dramatic, if somewhat exaggerated, formulation, salons "brought Jew and Christian closer" than in any other European setting during the eighteenth century.[8] But few Jewish historians have been able to weigh the salon women's social success dispassionately. The mixing between Jews and gentiles in salons was judged to be "decadent," of an "unwholesome quality." Heinrich Graetz disapproved so strongly of the salon women's behavior that he claimed they actually did Judaism a service by converting.[9] These women were blamed not only for their own departure from the fold, but for the conversion of Berlin Jews not affiliated with salon society. It is these conversions which are the subject of this essay.

Historians have cited contemporary observers who claimed that by 1800 only a small proportion of Berlin's Jewish families had been untouched by the conversion "epidemic." And they have labeled the incidence of conversion in Berlin in the last decades of the eighteenth century a "wave," a "mania," and a "flood" that left Berlin Jewry "bordering on dissolution."[10] It is the purpose of this essay to determine whether these observations are correct, either in accusing the Berlin converts of betraying their religion and their people or in describing the incidence of conversion in eighteenth-century Berlin as a "wave."

In the past, historians have had little statistical evidence with which to substantiate their assertions about the secular trend of Jewish baptisms. Statistical surveys of Jewish conversion compiled by churches, missionary societies, and state agencies simply do not extend back into the eighteenth and early nineteenth centuries. A few twentieth-century historians have attempted to remedy this situation by piecing together fragmentary statistics on conversion during the so-called epidemic era. Abraham Menes attempted this in 1929 because he doubted that Heinrich Graetz could have been correct in claiming that "half" of the Berlin Jewish community converted in this era. Menes believed that conversion statistics for all of Prussia, based upon parish reports to the government, were available only from 1816. The only source Menes located for the earlier years was a Jewish petition from 1811 listing the names of 40 Berlin families who had lost at least one member to Christianity in the preceding "five to eight" years.[11] Since 405 Jewish families reportedly lived in Berlin in the last decades of the eighteenth century, Menes concluded that a tenth, not a half, of the community had left Judaism in these years.

Since Menes's work, two Israeli historians have labored to document the extent of conversion and analyze the motives of converts in Germany in the preindustrial era. Azriel Shohet's main primary source was a missionary institute in Halle established in 1728. Shohet used its reports and other missionary sources to estimate that over three hundred Jews converted in Germany between 1700 and 1750. On the basis of this and other, nonquantitative, evidence, Shohet concluded that in early eighteenth-century Germany, conversion was "a country-wide plague." Shohet's conclusions have recently been challenged by a second Israeli scholar, Benjamin Kedar. Kedar has criticized Shohet's use of the missionary records, and has stressed that the significance of early eighteenth-century conversions can only be judged when a complete series record going back to the seventeenth century has been located. Church records are the most reliable source, in Kedar's opinion. Although he himself has not used primary church records, Kedar has reconstructed secondary reports of Nazi genealogical research to reconstruct some conversion statistics (of unknown geographic location) covering 1640 to 1799. These he uses to critique Shohet's "plague" thesis. Kedar relies mainly on anecdotal reports of individual conversions, however, as the basis for his conclusion that there was a definite broadening of the motives to convert toward the end of the eighteenth century. This postwar Israeli research represents a large step forward in the historiography. The problem is that neither Shohet nor Kedar was able to use a complete series record for any one city (let alone for several cities), a record whose information was extensive enough to utilize for a precise analysis of the changing motives for conversion.[12]

Thus without the precision provided by a truly complete and informative series record, it has been difficult for previous historians to be sure that claims about the social composition of Berlin's eighteenth-century converts gleaned from anecdotal accounts were really accurate. Still, several scholars have been convinced that there was a change in the social origins of the typical convert in the last decades of the eighteenth century. Converts in the seventeenth and early eighteenth centuries, historians have suggested, were typically born into the "lower" or the "socially dejected" classes. But a change was thought to have set in by the close of the century, when "rich" and "learned" Jews began to convert as well.[13] Thus the standard historiography suggests that the rising social position of the converts, as well as the presumed increase in the rate of conversion, contributed to contemporary alarm about the "ominous" rise in the conversions.

The sex of the converts has also been at issue. The few historians who speculated about the converts' gender concurred that those who left the fold in late eighteenth-century Berlin were mainly females. But a mainly female cohort of converts in the eighteenth century would contrast sharply with patterns of conversion in the nineteenth and twentieth centuries, when male converts consistently outnumbered female converts.[14] Nor would a largely female cohort of converts fit the motivations historians have assigned to converts during the era of emancipation: the desire for political equality or better employment.[15] Neither motive could have led a Jewish woman to turn Christian, since Christian women had neither political rights, nor prestigious occupations.

To use the term *wave* to describe the conversions of this era is to imply that the incidence—or at least the proportion—of conversions in Berlin dropped in the subsequent period. But here also evidence has been lacking. Jacob Katz, for instance, claimed that the number of conversions decreased after the Prussian edict of emancipation in 1812. Katz reasoned that the motives for conversion weakened once Jews who could meet the property qualifications were able to receive local (Berlin) citizenship and to take advantage of educational and occupational opportunities previously closed to them.[16] Hannah Arendt reached the opposite conclusion: she suggested that the number of converts actually increased after 1812. Arendt thought that the number of conversions before 1806 had in fact been low. The reason, in her view, was that before 1806 Prussia included numerous poor Polish Jews who had become Prussian subjects in the Polish annexations of 1772, 1793, and 1795. Wealthy Jews in Berlin could be socially accepted in these years without converting because gentiles saw them as pleasing exceptions when compared to the more primitive eastern Jews. According to Arendt's logic, the Berlin Jews lost their token status when Prussia lost her Polish territories in 1806. The result was that after this date Berlin Jews had to convert to gain social acceptance and more did so than in the last decades of the eighteenth century.[17]

The longevity and extent of the discussion about Jewish conversion in Berlin in the late eighteenth and early nineteenth century show how important the problem has become to scholars. But without new sources, the subject of Jewish conversion in Berlin was destined to be one of those tantalizing problems that can never be put to rest.

But the possibility of compiling a rich and complete series record of Jewish conversions does exist after all. Its origin, ironically enough, was in a sinister project undertaken by a regime that sought to remove Judaism and Jewry from the earth. After February 1933, the adoption of the "Aryan clause" by private, public, and Nazi party agencies forced millions of Germans to prove their "Aryan" ancestry at least as far back as their grandparents. The *Reichsstelle für Sippenforschung* ("Agency for Genealogical Research") therefore encouraged and sometimes paid churches in large cities to photograph decrepit parish registers and produce an alphabetical card register for baptisms in order to satisfy the enormous number of requests for genealogical documents.[18] Jewish, Turkish, Gypsy, and "Moorish" converts to Protestantism, who had originally been entered into the parish registers alongside "normal" Christian child baptisms, were catalogued in a separate file called the *Judenkartei*, presumably because the vast majority of converts (or baptized adults) had been Jewish. Since Nazi doctrine defined Jews racially and not religiously, converts out of Judaism needed to be identified as such. The contents of such files could eventually determine life or death. By the terms of the Nuremberg Laws of 1935, not only the number of grandparents born Jewish but the age at which any one of them may have converted out of Judaism dictated whether the grandchild was classified as Aryan or non-Aryan.[19]

In order to locate converts whose descendants lived in Berlin but who themselves had not converted in Berlin, the church officials decided to compile a second card index, which included mixed marriages. More correctly stated, this was a file of marriages between converted Jews and Christians, since before 1846 Prussia did not have civil marriage. While the conversion series covers almost three centuries, from 1645 through 1933, the intermarriage series runs only from 1800 to 1846.[20] The information contained on each of the approximately ten thousand cards (in both the conversion and the intermarriage series) is extensive, including the name, age, sex, and father's occupation of each convert. Moreover, it seems reasonable to conclude that distortion in the data is small and, more importantly, random. Since the clerks who labored at the project had to prove their political loyalty, there is little reason to believe that removal of cards to protect descendants of converts could have resulted in underrepresentation of the real number of converts.[21]

According to statistics derived from analysis of the *Judenkartei*, contemporaries who believed there was a rapid rise in the number of converts in the last decades of the eighteenth century were correct. Between 1700 and 1767, a total of 153 Jews left Judaism in Berlin. As Figure 1 shows, during the first two-thirds of the century the number of Jewish baptisms was steady and small. On the average, only three Jews converted each year. Beginning in 1768, however, the number of baptisms began to climb. In the last third of the century the average number converting each year jumped to eight. Between 1770 and 1779 the number of conversions was 18 percent larger than it had been between 1760 and 1769. The group that converted in the 1780s was, in turn, almost twice as large (by 93 percent) as the cohort of the 1770s. And, in the last decade of the century, the number of converts grew by another 56 percent.

This series of rather sharp increases in the number of conversions during the last three decades of the eighteenth century was not followed, however, by a drop sharp enough to justify applying the term *wave* to the eighteenth-century conversions. Figure 1 shows that the rate of conversion during the first third of the nineteenth century continued upward, despite sporadic declines. Whatever the reasons Arendt cited, she was right—and Katz wrong—about the increase in conversions in the early nineteenth century. The late eighteenth-century curve looks more like the foothills than the peak of a mountain. The steady increase in conversion in the early nineteenth century is still evident even after examining the relative, rather than the absolute, growth in the proportion of Jews who converted. Figure 2 factors out the effect of the changing Jewish population of Berlin by showing the number of converts per 3,000 Jews living in Berlin. (The Jewish population in Berlin was quite stable between 1770 and 1817, hovering around 3,300.)[22] Thus the curve displayed in Figure 2 only begins to slope downward in the third and fourth decades of the nineteenth century, when the Jewish population of the city increased sharply.

But there is reason to doubt that the Jewish population of Berlin alone is in fact the correct denominator to use when calculating the changing proportion of Jews who chose baptism. Authors of contemporary novels and autobiographies as well as historians have stressed that Jews from smaller German towns sometimes came to Berlin in order to be baptized.[23] Unfortunately, it is not known whether such immigrant converts tended to become Berlin residents either before or after their baptism. The geographical designation that appears on some cards is no help at all with this problem, since it is not clear whether the noted location was the convert's place of birth or current residence. In spite of the lack of direct evidence, there are good reasons to believe that before 1812 the number of converts who came to Berlin in order to convert could not have been very large. Before Prussian Jewry was granted freedom of residency in 1812, the government's high wealth requirement for settlement in Berlin made it difficult for any but extremely wealthy Jews to obtain permission to live in Berlin. (Even though it is plausible to argue that the wealth requirement

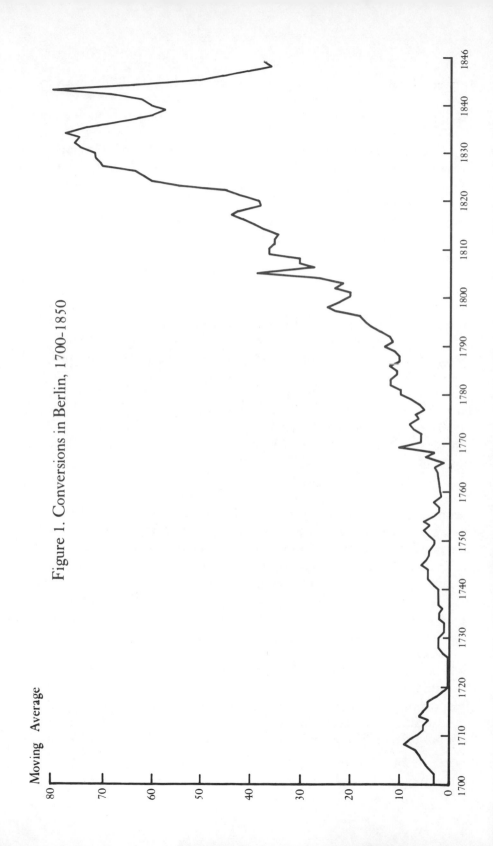

Figure 1. Conversions in Berlin, 1700–1850

Figure 2. Jewish Converts in Berlin 1750-1800 per 3000 Jewish Residents of Berlin

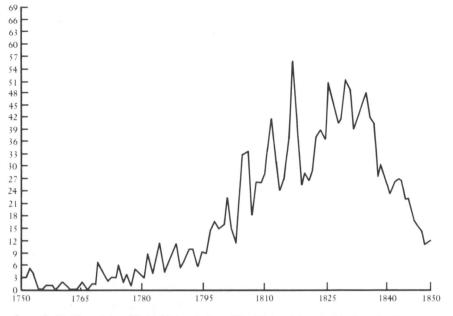

Source for Jewish population of Berlin: Herbert Seeliger, "The Origin and Growth of the Berlin Jewish Community," *Leo Baeck Institute Yearbook* 3 (1958), 159-168.

might not apply to Jews entering Berlin solely to convert, it would seem more likely that such would-be converts would not confess their intentions to the Jewish Elders who aided in monitoring entrance to Jews at the gate where Jews entered the city.) Unlike Vienna, there was not a large number of Jews living illegally in Berlin in this period.[24] Thus it is reasonable to assume that the group of Jews at risk to convert was not significantly greater than the number of Jews registered as living in Berlin. To be sure, although it was difficult to come in to Berlin in order to convert, a few wily individuals might have succeeded. Thus the group at risk to convert may have been somewhat larger than the legally permitted Jewish population of Berlin. By understating the number at risk to convert, using the recorded population as the denominator may result in slightly over-estimating the proportion who did convert.

Unfortunately, questions about the adequacy of the denominator of Jews at risk to convert do not end here. For using the annual population figures as the denominator is still not precise enough to ascertain the exact proportion of Berlin Jewry that converted during any particular cluster of years. Even if there were no Berlin converts who maintained a residence outside the city at all, the recorded Jewish population of Berlin is in fact still not the full number of Jews who were at risk to convert during any specific period. In order to learn this far larger number, it is necessary to know how many persons were alive for how long during this period, not merely the number who were there at its beginning and at its end.[25] To calculate this "person-years" figure, birth, migration, and age-specific death rates for the Jewish community would be required. Unfortunately, none of these numbers are now known, nor can they easily be reconstructed.[26] Since the mean Jewish population of Berlin between 1770 and 1799 was 3,535, all that can safely be concluded for now is that the 249 who converted during these three decades were at maximum 7 percent of those at risk to convert during these years. Since, no doubt, many more than 3,535 Jewish persons were at risk to convert in Berlin during some part of these thirty years, the real denominator was much larger, and thus the real proportion converting was surely far smaller than 7 percent.

There are fewer statistical problems when looking inside the convert population at the age, gender, and social composition of the 249 converts. Almost two-thirds of the converts were children five years old or younger. Most of the rest of the converts were in their twenties. For although converts between twenty and twenty-nine were only a fifth of all 249 converts, this cohort constituted three-quarters of all of the adult converts. As for the gender of the converts, historians who speculated that they were predominantly female were indeed correct. Sixty percent of the converts of all ages were women. As Figure 4 shows, the preponderance of female converts in these three decades contrasts sharply with the gender ratio of the preceding and subsequent decades. During the first two-thirds of the eighteenth century, male and female converts were in roughly equal proportions. Yet from 1770 to 1804 more women than men converted in almost every year. A comparison of the aggregate sex ratios of the emancipation era with later periods highlights the uniqueness of the female predominance in the 1770–1804 period. In these three and one-half decades women were 60 percent of all Jewish converts, whereas in the next half century the proportion of women converting dropped to 43 percent.

The gender of the adult converts very definitely varied with their age. Child and adolescent converts, on the other hand, were equally divided between male and female, and this had a certain logic. They could not have had gender-specific motives for converting, since they probably did not have any motives at all. Their decisions to convert were made for them, most likely by their parents. Although one might speculate that parents might tend to convert boys rather than girls, this cohort of child converts had as many girls as boys. But in contrast, adult men and women tended to convert at quite different ages, as shown in Figure 5. Almost 80 percent of the converts in their twenties were women. But this proportion was reversed among the older converts. A mere 20 percent of the converts over thirty were women.

Age and gender are exceedingly straightforward variables, available for almost all 249 converts, and require no sophisticated classificatory decisions. This is by no means the case with converts' social positions. Only slightly more than half (134) of their fathers' occupations were noted on the cards. And even where the occupation is known, raw occupational titles alone tell little about the social composition of the converts, without a way to classify occupations into classes. This is not because of a paucity of research about the economic life of Berlin Jewry in this era. But none of these economic histories are detailed enough to provide a classificatory schema which could be used to sort the converts' fathers' occupations and to compare them to the occupations of the unconverted.[27] In lieu of such assistance, I have constructed a three-tiered division of the fathers' occupations. Like the social structure of the gentile majority, the Jewish social structure in early modern German cities tended to consist of a small elite and large lower middle and lower classes. The "middle" middle class which evolved with industrialization was largely absent. Here I included large-scale merchants *(Kaufmänner)*, entrepreneurs, bankers, and professionals in the elite; clerks, small-scale traders *(Handelsmänner)*, brokers, peddlers, shopkeepers, and master artisans in the lower middle class; and beggars, servants, day laborers, and apprentice artisans in the lower class.[28]

Forty percent of the converts' fathers belonged to the elite, another 40 percent to the lower middle class, and the remaining 20 percent to the lower class. The large proportion of converts with elite origins indicates that the converts were roughly representative of Berlin's Jewish community at large. The term *elite*, to be sure, is imprecise; current knowledge of the community's social structure consists only of aggregate estimates. Estimates of the proportion of the Jewish community that was "rich" or "wealthy" range from a maximum of two-thirds down to a minimum of 40 percent.[29] Either

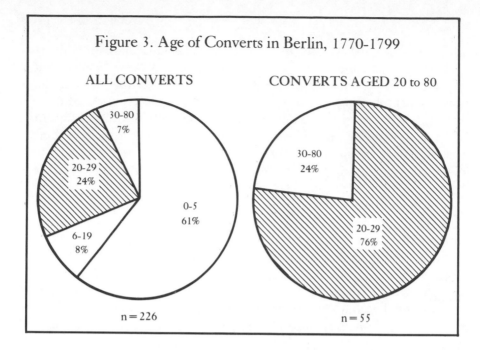

Figure 3. Age of Converts in Berlin, 1770-1799

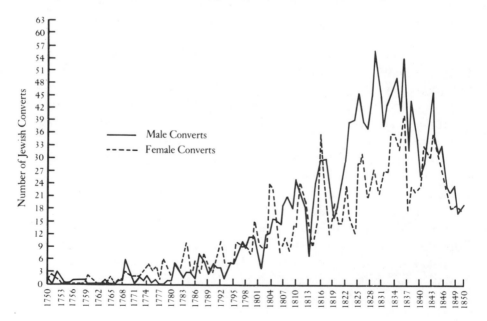

Figure 4. Male and Female Jewish Converts in Berlin, 1750-1850

Figure 5. Age by Gender of Converts in Berlin, 1770-1779

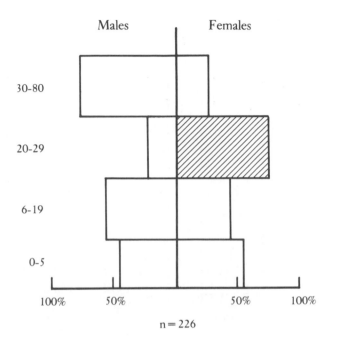

n = 226

estimate, it should be remembered, means that Berlin Jewry had a vastly greater proportion of wealthy persons than any other Jewish community within Germany or Europe at the time. The similarity between the size of the elite among the converted and the unconverted seems to confirm earlier suggestions that the social position of converts was rising over time. Indeed, Figure 6 shows that the convert population's social composition had not always matched that of the community at large. This evidence confirms the frequent speculation that converts before 1780 were Jews who had trouble surviving economically, and saw in baptism a way of improving their material situation. The proportion of converts from the elite only began to equal that of the community as a whole in the 1780s, when their share among the converts began to increase considerably.

Did the social origin of the converts tend to make much difference in the age at which they converted? Not for elite or for lower-middle-class converts, whose age structure closely resembled that of the converts as a whole. But lower class converts were, in contrast, almost all children under five. What about a correlation between the social origin and the sex of the converts? At first glance the answer would

61

Figure 6. Social Origin of Converts by Decade

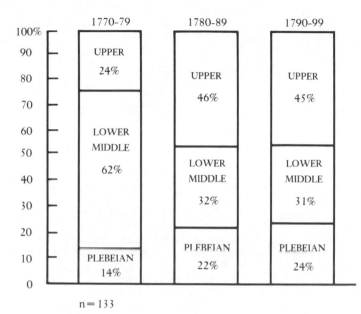

n = 133

have to be no. Within each of the three classes about two-fifths were male and three-fifths female, precisely the same ratio as that of the group as a whole. Yet there is good reason not to be satisfied with this answer, and that is that whatever its advantages, the three-class model used here obscures another useful kind of division among Jewish occupations. Namely, it obscures the distinction between those employed as merchants at various levels of the class hierarchy and those employed as artisans. Divided in this fashion, some differences between the sexes do emerge. As shown in Figure 7, daughters of merchants converted more often (63 percent) than did the daughters of artisans (47 percent). As we shall see shortly, there was a strong correlation between the female rate of conversion and the female rate of intermarriage. Access to the mercantile sector as well as wealth itself may well have been a motive for gentile grooms marrying converted Jewish brides, and thus daughters of men employed in the merchant sectors may have had special incentives to convert in order to intermarry. But to talk here of intermarriage is to get ahead of our story.

Before moving on to inspect the intermarriage records, it is appropriate to pause and look backward once more at the conversion pattern. Child conversion was consistently high throughout the thirty years. More females than males converted. Adult converts were mostly females in their twenties. Although the total exodus from the community in these years clearly did not exceed five percent, the kinds of persons who departed were a significant loss in terms of the community's demographic future and morale. The high numbers of female converts in their twenties undoubtedly made it difficult for Jewish men to find local Jewish wives. Since elite families often found spouses for their children among other elite Jewish families elsewhere in Europe, it might be thought that the loss of elite women in Berlin may not have been so serious. On the other hand, elite women in Berlin who had inherited the right of residence *(Schutzbrief)* were in great demand, since their husbands could then remain in the city. (It was difficult for even the wealthiest families to obtain residency permits for all of their sons.) The loss of Jewish women was not just a demographic one. Moreover, the home and the family are central to Jewish life, and Jewish women have in many times and places played the chief role in nurturing their religious communities.[30] But the

Figure 7. Gender of Converts of Merchant and Artisan Origin

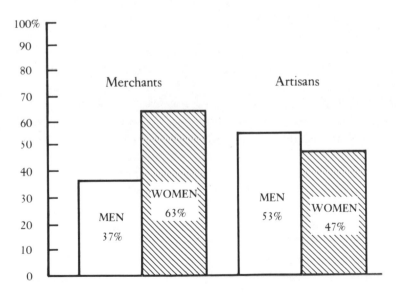

n = 96

impact of these conversions was not just a gender-specific one. The conversion of wealthy members of the community, especially of wealthy men, meant a loss of real and potential political leadership. The richest families in the city had long provided the community with its intermediaries with the Prussian state. The departure of the wealthy also suggests that more and more Jews who may not have had pressing material reasons to convert were finding their Jewishness hard to live with psychologically and socially and thus developed what might be called a "negative Jewish identity." But proving that this particular cohort of obscure individuals converted because they had such a negative Jewish identity is quite difficult.

Ironically enough, statistics may provide a surer guide to this group of converts' motives than the subjective testimonies which are lacking. Our reconstruction of the gender, age, and social composition of the converts has helped somewhat in pinpointing motives, largely by eliminating motives which could only have been held by a certain kind of person. Thanks to the intermarriage records, it is possible to pursue the critical question of motives a bit further. The great value of the intermarriage records is that they allow us to draw parallels between those who converted and those who went on to marry gentiles. It thereby becomes possible to explore a very major question, namely, whether the female converts born into elite merchant families who converted in their twenties did so in order to intermarry.

The conversion records show that the female predominance over male converts which began in the late eighteenth century reversed itself by the third decade of the nineteenth century. As Figure 8 demonstrates, intermarriage records (which only begin in 1800) also show female predominance during the first decade of the nineteenth century. And, as with conversions, the male intermarriage line climbed above the female line during the second decade of the century. Moreover, the extent of the female preponderance among converts and those intermarrying was almost identical. Between 1800 and 1809, converted Jewish females were 69 percent of those who intermarried, whereas between 1811 and 1846 they were only 41 percent.

Beyond the basic fact that more women than men married out, a comparison of the social origin of converted Jewish men and women who married gentiles in the first decade of the nineteenth century shows that they were born on different ranks of the social hierarchy and moved in different directions when they married out. Three-quarters of the (converted) Jewish grooms were from elite families. But

Figure 8. Converted Jewish Outmarriers, 1800-1846

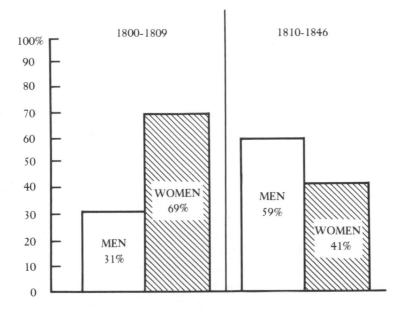

their gentile brides were almost all from lower-middle-class families. In other words, converted Jewish men tended to be born high, but married down socially when they married out religiously. The larger group of (converted) Jewish brides, on the other hand, came twice as frequently from lower-middle-class families and far less often from elite families. (Lower-class Jews were poorly represented among either the brides or the grooms.) Although the brides were less lucky than the converted grooms in their families of birth, they had better luck on the intermarriage market. Roughly half of the brides married down socially, but the other half made horizontal social matches. The Jewish brides' gentile grooms tended to be closer to them in age as well as in social position than the outmarrying men were to their gentile mates. The brides' own mean age was 28, and the mean age of their gentile grooms was 31. The Jewish men who married out, in contrast, were on average, 15 years older than their gentile brides. Their own mean age was 38, and their brides' mean age was 27. Since closeness in age may well have been associated with "companionate" (rather than socially opportunistic) marriages, this pattern suggests that the converted women's intermarriages tended to be more "companionate" than those of the converted men.[31]

Comparing the gender, social position, and ages of those who converted and those who intermarried shows that the female proportion of both groups was similar, and that the reversal in this sex ratio occurred in both groups at roughly the same time. Comparison of the converted men and women who married out shows that the women tended to marry up socially when they married out, and that they were closer in age to their gentile mates than the Jewish men were to their gentile mates. The parallels between the proportion of both groups which was female, the timing of the switch in gender ratios, and the luck that many Jewish women had in marrying gentile men of good social position all suggest that the women's intermarriage prospects were good enough to stimulate what might be called "anticipatory" conversion. Since intermarriage, rather than educational or professional opportunity, was likely to be the way a converted woman made actual the higher status made possible by conversion, preparation for possible intermarriage may have been a frequent motive for female conversion. This was especially telling in an age where there was no civil marriage between unconverted Jews and Christians.

Comparing the intermarriage series to the conversion series in the years when the two series are compatible provides a fourth kind of evidence for the claim that conversion and intermarriage were more closely linked for women than they were for men. These data can be inspected in Figure 9, which shows the ratio of conversion to intermarriage between 1800 and 1846. For every 100 male converts in this period, there were only 13 men who married out. The female conversion/outmarriage ratio was three times as high, since for every 100 female converts there were 39 women who married out. In other words, converted men were less likely to intermarry than converted women. Most likely, this was because employment, rather than the possibility of intermarriage, was what prompted men to convert. This does indeed suggest that although evidence is lacking for the eighteenth century, conversion and intermarriage in Berlin were more closely associated for Jewish women than for Jewish men in the first half of the nineteenth century.

Conversion was, of course, no guarantee that this penultimate act of acculturation would lead to authentic social ties with gentiles. After all, converted families in nineteenth-century central Europe often socialized with and married into other converted families having as few contacts with authentic gentiles as did unconverted Jews.[32] Intermarriage was a much more dramatic stage than conversion was in the

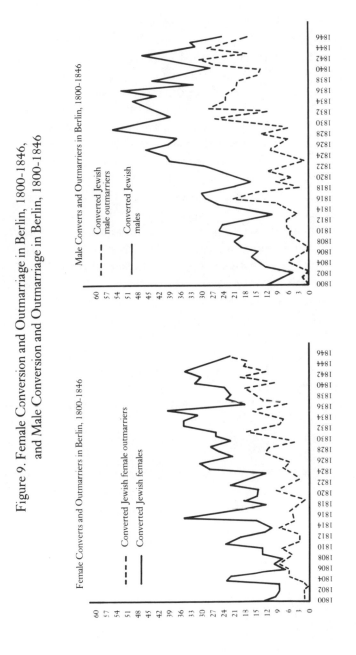

Figure 9. Female Conversion and Outmarriage in Berlin, 1800-1846,
and Male Conversion and Outmarriage in Berlin, 1800-1846

process of social integration. That is why it is important to measure how high the incidence of intermarriage was in this first major chapter of the assimilation story. Owing to the labors of Jacob Jacobson, Berlin Jewry's archivist until 1942, it is possible to answer this question. The Nazi intermarriage records show that 55 converted Jews married gentiles in Berlin between 1800 and 1809. Jacobson's published list of Jewish marriages in Berlin shows that there were 175 marriages between unconverted Jews in Berlin during the same decade.[33] Unfortunately, the mere possession of these two numbers does not provide a simple rate of intermarriage. For there are three rather different ways to calculate the rate of intermarriage, which makes generalization extremely tricky. Using one method, the 55 individuals who intermarried were 14 percent of the 405 individual Jews who married at all in this decade. Using a second method, comparing the intermarriages with the 230 marriages in which a Jew was involved, 24 percent of the marriages were intermarriages. Using a third method, the ratio of mixed (55) to endogamous marriages (175) was 31 to 100. Most published intermarriage statistics use the third denominator (Jewish-Jewish marriages), although the second denominator, all marriages involving a Jew, is also used. But the point here is that by either measure, the 1800–1809 Berlin rate was phenomenally high. This was a threat to the community of far greater dimensions than the conversion rate. The intermarriage rate was twice the rate of intermarriage in the United States before 1840. It was also twice as high as the intermarriage rate in Germany a full century later, in 1901. The Berlin intermarriage rate of 1800–1809 was only 13 percent smaller than the intermarriage rate in Germany in 1933.[34] To be sure, these comparisons are suggestive rather than conclusive. More research is needed to measure the effect of the changing proportion of Berlin Jews who married at all. The state's pre-1812 restrictions on how many and which Jews could marry may well have made the denominator unusually small and therefore the intermarrying proportion during these years artificially large.[35]

The romances between young men and women of different faiths that ended at the altar in Berlin were notorious at the time. These misalliances agitated the memoir, novel, and pamphlet writers of the day, who were angry, delighted, or merely amused that such things could come to pass. Comparisons with subsequent intermarriage patterns suggest that outside as well as inside salon society, the rate at which these romances ended in intermarriage was unusually high. Both contemporary alarm and statistical comparisons raise two burning questions. Why was intermarriage so frequent in Berlin in these years? And why did more Jewish women than men convert and marry out?

Before answering these questions, it needs to be clarified whether the female predominance among those leaving Judaism in Berlin in these years was not in truth a mere statistical artifact. The same state regulations on Jewish settlement and marriage that distorted the social and age structure of the community could well have also distorted the community's sex ratio in an age-specific way. If there were more Jewish women than men in Berlin in the age groups at which Jews converted, this alone might explain the high female rates of conversion and intermarriage. The post-1815 drop in the female rates of conversion and intermarriage might represent nothing more than a return to a normal sex ratio among the age groups from which converts and those marrying out came. Unfortunately, the data necessary to settle this issue are absent. Although the community's birth records have survived, they have not been reconstructed into family units.[36] More importantly, there are no records of the age and gender of those who were forced to leave Berlin in these years because of residence and marriage restrictions.

Although we may never know how the state's restrictions on which children of which families could settle and marry may have affected the community's underlying sex ratio, it is clear how they played a role in determining the social and age composition of the converts. The difficulty of obtaining permission to settle or marry in Berlin gave to poor Jews whose residence in Berlin was either illegal or tenuously legal an incentive to gain exemption from the regulations by ceasing to be Jews. This motive for conversion was especially strong among young female domestic servants who worked for the city's richest families. Sometimes pregnant and often without husbands, they changed their faith to remove obstacles to their continued residence in the city. Their illegitimate children were often given over to orphanages. And if it was indeed the children of these servants who filled the ranks of the child converts, two facts about the convert population would be at least partially explained. First, the servants' children's conversions would account for the lower-class origins of most of the child converts. Second, the servants' own conversions would account in part for the predominance of the females in their twenties among the adult converts. If their seducers were not Jewish, and if they went on to marry their seducers, these female servant converts may well have contributed to the high female intermarriage rate as well.[37]

The domestic servant converts were similar to most converts in the German-Jewish past, insofar as their conversion was caused in some way by their poverty. But the conversion records show that poor women were not the only Jewish women to leave their faith in these years. Why were wealthy young women also so ready to convert, and so lucky on the intermarriage market? To answer this question, it is necessary to shift attention from the anonymous converts, whom we have examined heretofore, to a small group of twenty elite Jewish women who participated in Berlin's salons. (The salon women have an oblique relationship to the women on the conversion and intermarriage cards; none of the salon women who converted or intermarried did so in Berlin in the specific years analyzed here, and so do not show up on the cards.) Because we know more about their lives than we do about the anonymous converts and those who married out, study of the salon women can give insight into the motivations of their more obscure contemporaries.

Of the twenty salon women, at least seventeen converted, and ten married gentiles. Why? Although their formal Jewish education tended to be deficient, so too was the Jewish education of most men from similar families in their generation. And although many salon women managed to master secular languages and disciplines, either with their fathers' help or on their own, so too did many men of their generation. What was distinctive about the salon women's acculturation was not their early education, but rather the social opportunities that became open to them in the 1780s and 1790s. The theater, salons, and reading, discussion, and friendship societies where they made friends with prominent gentile men provided them with a new social universe, a universe which was closed to most Jewish men. It was these social experiences in their years as young adults that gave them both the incentive to master secular skills and the chance to polish those new skills.

But their new social universe also provoked conflict and turmoil in the salon women's lives because by the time they met gentile men most of them were already married to Jewish businessmen. They had had little choice in the matter; the wealth and small size of the community and the state's marriage regulations all contributed to the practice of arranged marriages at an early age. Thus, if the exogamous love affairs that blossomed in salons were to come to pass, first divorce from the Jewish husband and then conversion were necessary. Often, the gentile groom was cash poor, if status rich. Since, as I have shown elsewhere, the brides were either wealthy themselves or had access to wealth, there was a definite economic logic to these intermarriages. [38]

It is therefore clear how, for salon women, the prospect of inter-marriage encouraged conversion. Because it has not been possible to link individuals from the conversion cards to those on the intermar-riage cards, it is difficult to determine whether the same close associa-tion between conversion and intermarriage was true for women on both sets of cards. [39] Nor do we know how closely the social lives of the women on the cards resembled those of the salon women. Still, the parallels between the salon women and the anonymous women on the cards are suggestive. Women in both groups tended to convert in their twenties. And women in both groups tended to marry up or across socially when they married out.

But the prospect of marrying a gentile was not the only incentive for women to convert. The intellectual climate both inside accultu-rated Jewish circles and outside of the Jewish community also encour-aged conversion. This same intellectual climate influenced the deci-sions of Jewish men as well as those of Jewish women and thus helps to explain why wealthy men converted even though they did not seem to have had material or romantic incentives to do so. Deism was the first intellectual influence that favored conversion. Earlier, at midcen-tury, enlightened intellectuals in Prussia had been more theistic than deistic. But toward the end of the century the notion that Judaism and Christianity shared a common set of core assumptions gained ground among Prussian thinkers. There were those who went so far as to hope and plan for the day when the two religions would cease to be separate institutional entities. Just how optimistic Jewish intellectuals had become about this common future was dramatically revealed in an anonymous pamphlet published in 1799 in Berlin. It was an open secret around town that the real author was David Friedländer. Friedländer, a wealthy silk manufacturer, was a friend of Moses Men-delssohn and played a prominent leadership role in the established Jewish community. In this pamphlet Friedländer proposed to William Teller, a leading liberal Protestant minister in Berlin, that the heads of "leading families" of the Jewish community convert en masse to a rationalized form of Christianity. With "dry baptism," Jewish men, at least, would gain the political rights still denied them as Jews, without hypocritically endorsing the nonrational elements of Christianity. Teller unequivocally rejected Friedländer's proposal. He declared it absurd that Friedländer should think that the less rational dimensions of the Christian faith could be separated from what Friedländer, at least, identified as its deistic core. Teller advised Friedländer to give up hope of using "dry baptism" as a shortcut to political emancipation and urged him to work for religious reform within his own faith.[40]

Teller's rejection of Friedländer's proposal suggests that Jewish intellectuals were more optimistic than Christian intellectuals about how soon Judaism and Christianity would cease to be separate religions. Still, the very fact that Friedländer would publicly—if anonymously—propose "dry baptism" was significant in two ways. First, his proposal shows that a prominent Jew could expect a prominent Christian to find "dry baptism" a plausible notion if not necessarily a desirable one. Second, Friedländer's proposal shows that in these years a prominent Jewish leader took leaving Judaism more seriously than reforming it. In the ensuing decades the reform tendency within Judaism would gain strength, both intellectually and institutionally. In part, Reform Judaism's very attraction came from the failure of attempts like Friedländer's to find a third path between traditional Judaism and traditional Christianity. In this way the absence of a reform alternative within Judaism was an internal incentive to convert, just as the fragile deism of Christian intellectuals was an external incentive to convert.

Both the internal and external incentives to convert existed at the intellectual level, and could in theory have influenced Jewish men as well as Jewish women. Insofar as the men may have been socialized to take intellectual matters more seriously than the women did, the absence of a reform alternative and the presence of deistic views may indeed have legitimized conversion more for Jewish men than they did for Jewish women. Yet, at the same time, both the internal and the external incentives to convert affected women in a particular way. A contemporary novel, *Charlotte Sampson*, described the impact of Friedländer's proposal within the Jewish community. The story begins with a group of Jewish elders waiting in suspense for the minister's response to the proposal. When the news comes that the proposal has been rejected, one of the elder's daughters promptly runs off to a small village to convert and then proceeds to marry her gentile lover.

Charlotte Sampson suggests that "dry" baptism was seen not only as a way to make "wet" baptism unnecessary for Jewish men in search of political or occupational advancement, but also as a potentially painless solution for Jewish women on the road to intermarriage.[41]

The external intellectual incentives to convert also affected women in a particular way. By the first years of the nineteenth century, the extreme rationalism and deism of the late enlightenment came under attack by a new generation of young intellectuals. Indeed, it was in the salons that the early romantics formulated and elaborated their critique of the mature rationalist enlightenment. Eventually, the romantic movement would turn quite antisemitic, as it became more mystical, more nationalistic, and more conservative. But in its early years the romantics provided an incentive to convert that was as strong as that provided by the enlightened deism of an older generation. And the incentive to convert provided by the romantics was an especially potent lure for Jewish women. Several romantic intellectuals became personal friends of the Jewish salon women. These men, especially Friedrich Schleiermacher, argued that conversion offered Jewish women a way to achieve personal and intellectual emancipation. (Whether the anonymous women on the cards had similar interpersonal experiences must remain a mystery for now.) The romantics' enthusiasm for the exotic and the foreign was also an incentive for Jewish women to convert, insofar as romanticism disposed intellectual men to wax rhapsodic about dark-haired Jewish women. In this way gentile men, who had more control over their choice of mate than gentile women did, may well have been influenced by romanticism to find Jewish women acceptable, even fashionably desirable, mates.[42] Thus just as deism was fading as an external ideological motive for conversion, early romanticism provided a parallel external ideology that encouraged gentile men to marry Jewish women, in turn causing Jewish women to convert in preparation for intermarriage.

Thus if poor Jewish women had material and legal incentives to convert, wealthy Jewish women had their own set of romantic and ideological incentives to leave their faith. Both poor and rich Jewish women, each in their own way, achieved a kind of emancipation when they converted or married out. For poor Jewish women, the freedom gained was a precondition for survival in the city, a step made necessary by the Prussian state's policies, which kept the Berlin Jewish community small and wealthy. For elite Jewish women, conversion and intermarriage were a reaction—even a protest against—the restricted way of life required of wealthy and privileged Jews in Berlin at this time. In many ways the price for the Jewish elite's economic success was paid by their children, who suffered from the rigid, parentally controlled marriage practices of these families. To be sure, wealthy Jewish families elsewhere in central and western Europe also controlled their daughters' marriages. But the special difficulties of settling children in Berlin, the degree to which Jewish women in Berlin had mastered secular skills, and the deistic, early romantic views which attracted Berlin's gentile intellectual men to wealthy Jewish women all combined to provoke a reaction to these arranged marriages.

The readiness of gentile men to take advantage of the attractions of Jewish women was as much a novelty in the late eighteenth century as were the sophisticated charms of the women they married. The changes on both the Jewish and on the Christian side which encouraged intermarriage made conversion seductively attractive to Jewish women in three ways. First, in the most literal sense, Jewish women converted partly in order to seduce gentile men into marrying them. In addition, Jewish women took other steps to make themselves more desirable wives for gentiles. Memoirs and letters tell the story of many elite Jewish women who changed their names, accents, friends, and interests in a way which facilitated their entry into gentile society. Although this strategy of seducing gentiles by hiding Jewishness was not always successful, it by no means follows that the women's attempts to escape from Judaism were nothing but a crass and opportunistic betrayal of their people. On the contrary, the partners in several well-documented intermarriages were complex adults who chose each other for emotional reasons. So to say that subtle changes in life patterns and mutually complementary economic and status exchanges were required for Jewish women to seduce gentile men to marry them is a decidedly external view, and says nothing about the authentic love involved. To ignore the role of love would be especially wrong for these marriages, whose historical novelty was precisely that the partners were rebelling against a tradition of arranged marriage.

In an altogether different sense, conversion seems to have been a seductive act, insofar as it was tempting in this era for Jews of both sexes to improve their personal situation by changing their faith. More comparative research is required to determine whether the absence of Reform Judaism and the deistic and romantic external inducements which prevailed in this setting combined to render conversion a more

74

innocent act in this era than it was in other times and places. The intellectual and social progress toward religious equality forged in Prussia—especially in its capital city, Berlin—in the last third of the eighteenth century created an especially optimistic mood. Why bother to stay Jewish when both Jewish and gentile intellectuals argued that soon Judaism would cease to be a separate religion, when a leader of the community proposed "dry" baptism for the leading families? Rich and intellectual Jews had every reason to believe that progress toward equality would continue at the same rapid rate. To interpret conversion as "betrayal" presumes the consciousness of belonging to a people and the attachment of a positive value to ethnic solidarity. Yet the rational deism of intellectual circles in Berlin, as well as some Jews' understandable intoxication with their own experiences in cosmopolitan circles, hardly contributed to strengthening their loyalty to the Jewish people. Apostates in the eighteenth century may have felt emotionally guilty for abandoning their still Jewish families and friends. But there does not seem to be evidence that this guilt was exacerbated by those feelings of "bad faith" and self-loathing stemming from a consciousness of escaping from a collective problem which were voiced by converts a century later.[43]

These female conversions can also be called seductive in a third sense, and that is in terms of a specifically female path to upward mobility. Wealthy women in preindustrial estate societies often could move upward with greater ease via marriage than their brothers could via education. Families budgeted accordingly, spending their money on training and decorating their daughters. Some have even argued that the importance of maintaining the virginity of unmarried daughters was rooted in the family's attempt to reserve their (pure) daughters for the highest bidder.[44] Young women's chances of being lifted out of their class, region, or religion by some Prince Charming from a higher status group were thus a seductive possibility. If successful, an upwardly mobile marriage diluted or erased a woman's loyalty to the group into which she was born. And even if the dream of such a husband never materialized, the dreams, hopes, and plans for his arrival might have the very same effect on her relationship to her group. Thus personal emancipation was achieved at the cost of loyalty to the class, region, or religion of her family.

More work with the *Judenkartei* of the successive decades is required to refine and evaluate this interpretation of the conversions between 1770 and 1809. And if it is confirmed, many questions arise about the post-1809 years. Did women's motives for conversion continue to be mainly preparation for intermarriage? Were men's motives for conversion in the nineteenth century mainly preparation for employment? Does the reversal in their rates of conversion and intermarriage in the first third of the nineteenth century represent a decline in women's chances to marry out, simultaneous with an increase in men's incentives to convert for professional reasons? If we learn that women's chances to marry out decreased in the nineteenth century and can learn just why this occurred, the result will be a new, gender-specific history of Jewish conversion in modern Germany. If the last decade's work in the history of women is a good predictive guide in such historiographical matters, a gender-specific reconstruction of the history of conversion will do more than fill a gap in our knowledge. It should make possible a new map of the history, and indeed the meaning, of conversion itself.

NOTES

1. Rothschild's lament is quoted in Anka Muhlstein, *Baron James: The Rise of the French Rothschilds* (New York and Paris: Vendome Press, 1982), p. 75.

2. See Jacob Toury, *Soziale und politische Geschichte der Juden in Deutschland, 1847–1871* (Düsseldorf: Droste, 1977), table 29b, p. 55.

3. The best source in English on Rahel (Levin) Varnhagen is Hannah Arendt, *Rahel Varnhagen: The Life of a Jewess* (London: East and West Press, 1957). Varnhagen's boasts about being a Berlin Jew are cited in Michael Meyer, *The Origins of the Modern Jew: Jewish Identity and European Culture in Germany, 1749–1824* (Detroit: Wayne State University Press, 1967), p. 109.

4. On salon life in Berlin (in English), see also Bertha Meyer, *Salon Sketches* (New York: Bloch Publishing Company, 1938) and Mary Hargrave, *Some German Women and Their Salons* (London: T. W. Laurie, n.d.).

5. See the article by Isaac Eisenstein-Barzilay, who claims that the Berlin Jewish community in the mid eighteenth century was "predominantly wealthy." "The Background of the Berlin Haskalah," in *Essays on Jewish Life and Thought*, ed. Joseph L. Blau et al. (New York: Columbia University Press, 1959), p. 190. Another claim has been made by Stefi Jersch-Wenzel, who described the majority of the community in this period as having "above average" wealth, in her *Jüdische Bürger und kommunale Selbstverwaltung in preussischen Städten, 1808–1848* (Berlin: Walter de Gruyter, 1967), p. 19. Hannah Arendt claimed that "two-thirds" of the 600 Jewish families in Berlin then were "rich": *The Origins of Totalitarianism* (Cleveland: World, 1958), p. 16, n. 6. Raphael Mahler estimated that "45 percent" of 450 Jewish families were either

"fabulously wealthy" or "wealthy." Raphael Mahler, *A History of Modern Jewry, 1780–1815* (London: Vallentine, Mitchell, 1971), p. 127. It needs to be noted that Jacob Toury's "Der Eintritt der Juden ins deutsche Bürgertum" (pp. 144–45), table 1, does not show Berlin to have had an unusually wealthy Jewish community in the first half of the nineteenth century. However, the absolute numbers for some cities on the table are tiny, and it also has limited relevance for the eighteenth-century situation. The article can be found in Hans Liebeschütz and Arnold Paucker, eds., *Das Judentum in der deutschen Umwelt* (Tübingen: J. C. B. Mohr, 1977), pp. 139–242.

6. The fullest account of these restrictions on immigration into Berlin can be found in Selma Stern, *Der preussische Staat und die Juden*, part 3, *Die Zeit Friedrichs des Grossen*, section 1 (Tübingen: J. C. B. Mohr, 1971), chap. 5. Henri Brunschwig thought that a lax implementation of official regulations helps to explain Jewish accomplishments in Prussia then; see his *Enlightenment and Romanticism in Eighteenth-Century Prussia* (Chicago: University of Chicago Press, 1974), appendix, "The Struggle for the Emancipation of the Jews in Prussia."

7. On Hamburg Jewry, see Helga Krohn, *Die Juden im Hamburg, 1800–1850* (Frankfurt am Main: Europäische Verlagsanstalt, 1967); on Frankfurt am Main, see Isidor Kracauer, *Geschichte der Juden im Frankfurt a.M., 1150–1824* (Frankfurt am Main: I. Kauffmann, 1927); on English Jewry, see Todd M. Endelman, *The Jews of Georgian England* (Philadelphia: Jewish Publication Society, 1979); on French Jewry in this era, see Arthur Hertzberg, *The French Enlightenment and the Jews* (New York: Columbia University Press, 1968). On Amsterdam Jewry, see the article on Amsterdam in *Encyclopedia Judaica*, vol. 2 (Jerusalem: Keter Press, 1972), pp. 893–906, and H. Bloom, *The Economic Activities of the Jews of Amsterdam in the Seventeenth and Eighteenth Centuries* (Williamsport, Pa.: Bayard Press, 1937).

8. This claim is made by Adolf Leschnitzer, *The Magic Background of Modern Anti-Semitism: An Analysis of the German-Jewish Relationship* (New York: International Universities Press, 1956), p. 14.

9. The two quotes in the previous sentence come from Raphael Mahler, *A History of Modern Jewry*, p. xxi, and H. G. Adler, *The Jews in Germany from the Enlightenment to National Socialism* (Notre Dame: University of Notre Dame Press, 1969), p. 53. H. Graetz's condemnation can be found in his *History of the Jews* (Philadelphia: Jewish Publication Society, 1894), 4:425.

10. See S. M. Dubnow, *Die neueste Geschichte des jüdischen Volkes* (Berlin: Jüdischer Verlag, 1920), 1:197 and 202; Mahler, *A History of Modern Jewry*, p. 150; Heinz Mosche Graupe, *Die Entstehung des modernen Judentums: Geistesgeschichte der deutschen Juden 1650–1942* (Hamburg: Leibniz Verlag, 1969), p. 155; Arthur Ruppin, *The Jews in the Modern World* (London, 1934; rept., New York: Arno Press, 1973), p. 328; N. Samter, *Judentaufen im neunzehnten Jahrhundert* (Berlin: M. Poppelauer, 1906), p. 4; Adler, *The Jews in Germany*, p. 24.

11. Abraham Menes, "The Conversion Movement in Prussia During the First Half of the Nineteenth Century," *YIVO Annual of Jewish Social Science* 6 (1951): 187. Another scholar skeptical about Graetz's claim that "half" of the Berlin community converted was Eugen Wolbe, *Geschichte der Juden in Berlin und in der Mark Brandenburg*

(Berlin: Kedem, 1937), p. 231. Even recent scholars seem to have accepted a version of Graetz's extreme estimate. The author of the "Apostasy" article in the 1972 *Encyclopedia Judaica* states that in late eighteenth-century Berlin, "more than half of the descendants of old patrician Jewish families converted" (3:206). A copy of the petitions, including the names of the families, can be found in Ismar Freund, *Die Emanzipation der Juden in Preussen* (Berlin: M. Poppelauer, 1912), vol. 2; the original petition is in the Central Archives for the History of the Jewish People, Jerusalem.

12. A summary in English of Shohet's thesis can be found in Jacob Katz, *Out of the Ghetto: The Social Background of Jewish Emancipation, 1770–1870* (New York: Schocken, 1973), pp. 34–36. Shohet's phrase, "a country-wide plague," is cited in B. Z. Kedar, "Continuity and Change in Jewish Conversions to Christianity in Eighteenth-Century Germany" (Hebrew), in *Studies in the History of Jewish Society in the Middle Ages and in the Modern Period Presented to Jacob Katz*, ed. E. Etkes and Y. Salmon (Jerusalem: Magnes Press, 1980).

13. Gerhard Kessler, *Judentaufen und judenchristliche Familien in Ostpreussen*, in *Familiengeschichtliche Blätter/Deutsche Herold*, vol. 36 (Leipzig, 1938), p. 51; Barrie M. Ratcliffe, "Crisis and Identity: Gustave d'Eichthal and Judaism in the Emancipation Period," *Jewish Social Studies* 37 (1975): 122; Katz, *Out of the Ghetto*, pp. 105 and 122. Friedrich Schleiermacher's 1799 statement that hitherto converts had been "ruined individuals" who were "close to desperation" suggests that there were still nonelite converts in the last few decades of the century. Schleiermacher's quotation appears in Alfred D. Low, *Jews in the Eyes of the Germans* (Philadelphia: Institute for the Study of Human Issues, 1979), p. 179.

14. The tendency of Jewish men to marry gentile mates more often than Jewish women did in these two centuries is discussed in Ernest-Ludwig Ehrlich, "Emanzipation und christlicher Staat," in Wolf-Dieter Marsch and Karl Thieme, eds., *Christen und Juden: Ihr Gegenüber von Apostelkonzil bis heute* (Mainz: Matthias-Grünewald-Verlag, 1961), p. 155; Max L. Margolis and Alexander Marx, *A History of the Jewish People* (Philadelphia: Jewish Publication Society, 1927), p. 622; N. Samter, *Judentaufen*, p. 78; Dubnow, *Die neueste Geschichte*, 1:193; Wolbe, *Geschichte der Juden*, p. 231. For the specific rates at which men married out, see Uriah Zevi Engelman, "Intermarriage among Jews in Germany, U.S.S.R., and Switzerland," *Jewish Social Studies* 2 (1940): 165; Leonard J. Fein, "Some Consequences of Jewish Intermarriage," *Jewish Social Studies* 33 (1971): 45; Bernard Lazerwitz, "Intermarriage and Conversion: A Guide for Future Research," *Jewish Journal of Sociology* 13 (1971): 42; W. Hanauer, "Die jüdisch-christlichen Mischehen," *Allgemeines Statistisches Archiv* 17 (1928): 519; Marion A. Kaplan, "Tradition and Transition: The Acculturation, Assimilation and Integration of Jews in Imperial Germany: A Gender Analysis," *Leo Baeck Institute Year Book* 27 (1982).

15. For example, see Dubnow, *Die neueste Geschichte*, 1:204, or Ludwig Geiger, "Vor hundert Jahren: Mitteilungen aus der Geschichte der Juden Berlins," *Zeitschrift für die Geschichte der Juden in Deutschland* 3 (1899): 233. One scholar who found a majority of female converts in the late eighteenth century and a female-specific aim for conversion, namely, intermarriage, is Ehrlich in his "Emanzipation und christlicher Staat," p. 154.

16. For a highly unscientific approach to the "wave" question, see Solomon Liptzin, *Germany's Stepchildren* (Philadelphia: Jewish Publication Society, 1944), p. 26. Wolbe, *Geschichte der Juden in Berlin*, p. 231, claimed that a high rate of conversion continued up until the third decade of the nineteenth century. For Katz's analysis, see his *Out of the Ghetto*, p. 122.

17. Arendt, *The Origins of Totalitarianism*, p. 59.

18. The Reichsstelle für Sippenforschung (R.S.F.) was a state office under the administration of the Ministry of the Interior; it was later called the Reichssippenamt. See Fhr. von Ulmenstein, *Der Abstammungsnachweis* (Berlin: Verlag für Standesamtswesen, 1938), pp. 12ff. For a useful summary in English of the adoption of the Aryan clause and the "professional" genealogists who profited from the clause's implementation, see Karl A. Schleunes, *The Twisted Road to Auschwitz: Nazi Policy Toward German Jews, 1933–39* (Urbana: University of Illinois Press, 1970), p. 130.

19. The tendency for a local church to produce a *Judenkartei* seems to have varied with the size of the city. For a discussion of how the date of a grandparent's conversion could affect the racial status of the grandchild, see von Ulmenstein, *Der Abstammungsnachweis*, p. 33.

20. The conversion and the intermarriage cards are in the Evangelisches Zentralarchiv (Protestant church archive) in West Berlin.

21. Officials directing this genealogy bureaucracy were concerned with the removal of cards to protect the descendants of converts. An advertisement for the files used stressed how the cards are *"zuverlässig aufbewahrt"* ("dependably deposited") in this particular file: the advertisement is in File 577 of the Reichssippenamt (R.S.F.) files (R39) in the Bundesarchiv in Koblenz, West Germany. Dr. Kurt Mayer, Director of the R.S.F., described his firing of a Herr Fahrenhorst for falsifying records in his *"Begründung"* document of 18 March 1935, file 2, R39, Bundesarchiv. A case of "mass" falsification by a "band" in Hungary in 1938 is summarized in a clipping of 2 July 1938 from *Angriff am Abend*, file 567, R39, Bundesarchiv.

22. My source for the changing Jewish population of Berlin is Herbert Seelinger, "Origin and Growth of the Berlin Jewish Community," *Leo Baeck Institute Year Book* 3 (1958): 159–69.

23. *Charlotte Sampson oder Geschichte eines jüdischen Hausvaters, der mit seiner Familie dem Glauben Seiner Väter entsagte* (Berlin: Johann Friedrich Unger, 1800), the anonymously published story of a young Jewish woman who leaves Berlin to convert and intermarry, but runs into difficulties at the village church. Another, but real-life, tale of this sort can be found in *Salomon Maimon: An Autobiography*, ed. Moses Hadas (New York: Schocken Books, 1967), chap. 21. Another real-life conversion in a small town succeeded; see Julius Fürst, ed., *Henriette Herz: Ihr Leben und ihre Erinnerungen* (Berlin: W. Hertz, 1858), pp. 55, 58, and 65.

24. On the proportion of Jews without a *Schutzbrief* ("letter of protection") who managed to live in Vienna in this period, see Hans Tietze, *Die Juden Wiens* (Leipzig: E. P. Tal, 1933), p. 127, and Hans Jäger-Sunstenau, "Die geadelten Judenfamilien im vormärzlichen Wien" (diss., University of Vienna, 1950), p. 63.

25. The tendency to think of the conversion rate solely in reference to the recorded population can be seen in the stimulating unpublished manuscript by Ivar Oxaal, "The Jews of Pre-1914 Vienna: Two Working Papers," Department of Sociology and Social Anthropology, University of Hull, England, pp. 95–97.

26. The Jewish community's birth records (in German using Hebrew script) are a part of the Jacob Jacobson Collection (AR 7002) in the Archive of the Leo Baeck Institute in New York City. It is not yet known whether death and migration information is also contained in these files. Linking families by use of common surnames will be difficult, since the practice of taking on surnames was new then and most irregular.

27. The most detailed occupational division of the Jewish community can be found in Stefi Jersch-Wenzel, *Juden und 'Franzosen' in der Wirtschaft des Raumes Berlin/ Brandenburg* (Berlin: Colloquium, 1978), table D, p. 260. Jersch-Wenzel's source for her useful tables is Jacob Jacobson's published marriage lists [*Jüdische Trauungen in Berlin, 1723–1859* (Berlin: Walter de Gruyter, 1968)]. Since marriage was so restricted by the state, use of his work may have led to a distortion in favor of the rich in Jersch-Wenzel's tables. A more severe problem in adapting this profile for my purpose here is that since it clumps persons into *Handel* (trade) and *Gewerbe* (industry), it cannot be easily used to establish a social hierarchy of rich and poor.

28. For some comparative occupational classifications, see Paula Hyman, "Jewish Fertility in Nineteenth-Century France," and Steven M. Lowenstein, "Voluntary and Involuntary Limitations of Fertility in Nineteenth-Century Bavarian Jewry," in *Modern Jewish Fertility*, ed. Paul Ritterband (Leiden: E. J. Brill, 1981).

29. For the sources for these estimates, see note 5 above.

30. For some comparative perspectives, see Elizabeth Koltun, ed., *The Jewish Woman: New Perspectives* (New York: Schocken, 1976), and Charlotte Baum, Paula Hyman, and Sonya Michel, *The Jewish Woman in America* (New York: New American Library, 1975), chap. 2. Marion Kaplan, in *The Jewish Feminist Movement in Germany* (Westport, Conn.: Greenwood Press, 1979), chap. 1, argues that early twentieth-century Jewish women in Germany tended to stay more loyal to family and faith than did many Jewish men.

31. On companionate marriage in eighteenth-century Germany, see Heidi Rosenbaum, *Formen der Familie* (Frankfurt am Main: Suhrkamp, 1982), pp. 285–87. On the debate about when Jewish marriages began to follow this pattern, see David Biale, "Love, Marriage, and the Modernization of the Jews," in *Approaches to Modern Judaism* (Chico, Calif.: Scholars Press, 1983), ed. M. L. Raphael.

32. See Marsha Rozenblitt, "Assimilation and Identity: The Urbanization of the Jews of Vienna 1880–1914" (Ph.D. diss., Columbia University, 1980), p. 345, for discussion of this phenomenon in Vienna; Rozenblitt's revised thesis has appeared as a book: *The Jews of Vienna, 1867–1914* (Albany: SUNY Press, 1983).

33. Jacobson was the Director of the Gesamtarchiv der deutschen Juden until 1943; his papers are at the Archive of the Leo Baeck Institute (AR 7002) in New York

City. Jacobson's compilation of primary marriage records is *Jüdische Trauungen in Berlin, 1723–1859*, as cited in note 27.

34. For a more detailed description of this problem and a formula for transforming one rate into another rate, see Hyman Rodman, "A Technical Note on Two Rates of Mixed Marriage," *American Sociological Review* 30 (1965): 776–78. For further technical discussion of intermarriage computations, see C. A. Price and J. Zubrzycki, "The Use of Intermarriage Statistics as an Index of Assimilation," *Population Studies* 16 (1962): 58–69. Statistics using as the denominator the number of endogamous Jewish marriages (for which the Berlin 1800–1809 rate was 31 percent) include Germany, 1933, 44 percent [I. Gordon, *Intermarriage: Interfaith, Interracial, Interethnic* (Boston: Beacon Press, 1964), p. 179] and Germany, 1901, 16.9 percent [Uriah Zevi Engelman, "Intermarriage among Jews in Germany, U.S.S.R., and Switzerland," *Jewish Social Studies* 2 (1940): 157]. Statistics using the total number of marriages in which a Jew participated (the Boston rate being 24 percent) include the United States, mideighteenth century, 10 percent, and the United States, pre-1840, 16 percent [Gordon, p. 179]. No comparative statistics using as the denominator all individual Jews who married have been found. (In all these comparisons I equate converted Jews with Jews, since no civil marriage was possible in Berlin at this time.) Some sources use as the denominator all Jews; see Hanauer, "Die jüdisch-christlichen Mischehen," p. 518.

35. Jacob Jacobson observed that the numerous conversions and intermarriages of this era were a result of the state's limitation on Jewish marriages. *Die Judenbürgerbücher der Stadt Berlin 1800–1851*, (Berlin: Walter de Gruyter, 1962), p. xxxiii.

36. See note 26 above.

37. This finding is consistent with Jacob Jacobson's claim that the high number of children converted were the "key" to understanding the conversion "movement" of the period. *Die Judenbürgerbücher*, p. xxxiii. For a summary in English of this volume, see Jacobson's "Some Observations on the Jewish Citizens' Books of the City of Berlin," *Leo Baeck Institute Year Book* 1 (1955): 317–31.

38. The analysis summarized here can be found in my "Intermarriage in the Berlin Salons," *Central European History* 16 (1983): 303–46.

39. One reason this linkage has been difficult is that the intermarriage series begins only in 1800. Another reason is that even if one individual converted and intermarried, he did not necessarily do both in the same city.

40. The publication appeared anonymously with the *Sendschreiben an Hochwürden Herrn Oberconsistorialrat und Probst Teller zu Berlin von einigen Hausvatern jüdischer Religion* (Berlin: August Mylius, 1799). Whether there actually were other authors or not and if so, who they were, has not come to light. Although many knew of Friedländer's authorship at the time, he did not publicly admit it until 1819. For discussion, see Ellen Littmann, "David Friedländers Sendschreiben an Probst Teller und sein Echo," *Zeitschrift für die Geschichte der Juden in Deutschland* 6 (1935): 92–112, and Immanuel Heinrich Ritter, *Geschichte der jüdischen Reformation*, part 2, *David Friedländer, sein Leben und sein Wirken* (Berlin: W. J. Peiser, 1861). Reference to the derisive term "dry" baptism is made by Low, *Jews in the Eyes of the Germans*, p. 178.

41. See note 23 above.

42. See Charlene A. Lea, *Emancipation, Assimilation and Stereotype: The Image of the Jew in German and Austrian Drama, 1800–1850* (Bonn: Bouvier, 1978), chap. 4. On gentile men's power over intermarriage decisions, see John E. Mayer, "Jewish-Gentile Intermarriage Patterns: A Hypothesis," *Sociology and Social Research* 45 (1961): 188–95, and Mayer's *Jewish-Gentile Courtships: An Exploratory Study of a Social Process* (New York: Free Press, 1961).

43. For personal statements which reveal these feelings, see Werner Sombart et al., *Judentaufen* (Munich: G. Müller, 1912). See also Rozenblitt's thesis, "Assimilation and Identity," p. 324.

44. See Sherry Ortner, "The Virgin and the State," *Feminist Studies* 4 (1978): 19–36; Pierre Bourdieu, "Marriage Strategies as Strategies of Social Reproduction," in *Family and Society: Selections from the Annales*, ed. Robert Forster and Orest Ranum (Baltimore and London: Johns Hopkins University Press, 1976), pp. 117–44. Also useful were Lucy Mair, *Marriage* (Harmondsworth, Middlesex: Penguin, 1971), and Robin Fox, *Kinship and Marriage: An Anthropological Perspective* (Harmondsworth, Middlesex: Penguin, 1967), p. 202.

3

The Social and Political Context of Conversion in Germany and England, 1870–1914

TODD M. ENDELMAN

IN the medieval and early modern periods Christian efforts to convert Jews were largely unsuccessful. Neither learned polemics nor coercion and persecution significantly weakened Jewish loyalties. To be sure, from time to time individuals and even whole families embraced Christianity—for both spiritual and material reasons—but these isolated instances of defection had little impact on the overall fabric of Jewish communal life. Only in the Iberian peninsula, at the end of the medieval period, did apostasy assume epidemic proportions, as tens of thousands of Jews converted, many from inner conviction, others out of necessity, such as those forcibly baptized in Portugal in 1497.

With the exception of the Iberian experience, however, large-scale conversion from Judaism to Christianity did not occur until the last decades of the nineteenth century—ironically, just at the time when the churches in western Europe were losing their hold on much of the gentile population. With a handful of exceptions, those who left Judaism in the period 1870–1914 were not attracted by the spiritual truths or ethical values of Christianity. They were, on the whole, indifferent to religious practices and doctrines. Most had been raised

I wish to express my gratitude to the National Endowment for the Humanities and the Memorial Foundation for Jewish Culture for supporting this research and to the Oxford Centre for Postgraduate Hebrew Studies and its president David Patterson for providing me with a home while I was working in England. I am also grateful to James Turner and Jack Rakove for their helpful comments and suggestions.

in homes in which Jewish customs and symbols were absent or in which Judaism had become a pallid, diluted version of its former self. Others abandoned Jewish tradition early in life, at school or university, or at the start of a career, believing it to be an unnecessary burden or an embarrassing atavism. At the baptismal font, they ceased being nominal Jews and became nominal Christians instead. Their reasons for changing religious allegiance were secular and opportunistic. Some sought to improve their social status by escaping the stigma attached to Jewishness. Others wished to make careers outside the usual range of Jewish occupations and bought their ticket of admission, in the memorable phrase of Heinrich Heine, with baptism. Still others, having already mixed in non-Jewish social circles, passed out of the community through intermarriage, which frequently but not always was accompanied by conversion.

Although defection was a hallmark of modern Jewish life everywhere in the West, the flow out of Judaism was not uniform, equally strong in all countries and among all strata of Jewish society. Characteristic patterns of apostasy emerged in each country bearing the impress of larger political and social conditions. The temptation to abandon Judaism increased in the period 1870–1914, when the character of Jewish integration into state and society was called into question with unprecedented vehemence by the renewal of anti-semitism. In England and Germany, states with markedly dissimilar political cultures and social systems, Jews responded to the temptation in ways reflecting these larger dissimilarities—so much so that a comparative treatment of Jewish apostasy in these two settings illuminates the history of state and society as much as the inner history of the Jewish communities there. For the willingness—or refusal—of a state to admit unconverted Jews to elite circles and prestigious posts testifies to the self-confidence of its ruling class and the flexibility of its social structure.

At the very outset of this discussion, it is critical to note that in the case of England it is impossible to know the number of Jews who formally separated from Judaism and hence impossible to compare apostasy in the two communities statistically. In England, membership in a religious body was voluntary and an individual's religious affiliation a matter of indifference to the state. Thus, there are no official statistics on conversion. Indeed, the very boundaries of the Jewish community were not well defined.[1] In Germany, on the other hand, with its centralized bureaucratic traditions, religious affiliation and civil status were linked. The state monitored religious life closely and required those persons moving from one community to another to register the change officially. However, even the quantitative evidence about the German case is flawed—first, because the conversions of Jewish children under fourteen by their parents were not considered conversions and hence not recorded with the authorities, and second, because an unknown number of converted adults did not bother to register their change in status, despite the legal obligation to do so.[2] Nonetheless, the problems of documenting apostasy are not so formidable as to preclude a comparison of the phenomenon in English and German Jewry in the half century or so before World War I, for there is an abundance of other kinds of evidence to fill in the gaps left by the absence of statistical information. Memoirs, sermons, newspaper and journal articles, communal reports, personal correspondence, and even novels provide sufficient information to reconstruct the general character and extent of apostasy and permit a fruitful comparison between the German and English experiences.

The most immediately apparent dissimilarity between apostasy in the two communities in this period is that of magnitude. In Germany conversion was a pervasive feature of Jewish life, an item on the public agenda of communal organizations, a subject for journalistic inquiry, a topic of concern to Jews of various outlooks as well as to their critics and enemies. In the early 1880s, there were at least two hundred conversions a year; twenty years later, over five hundred. In relative terms, this means that in the 1880s there was one conversion a year for every 2,200 Jews in Germany; in the early 1900s, one for every 1,100 Jews. More significantly, in Berlin, the center of gravity of German Jewry, the ratios were much higher: about one for every 600 to 650 Jews in the period 1882 to 1908.[3] (In reality, the number of Jews leaving Judaism was much greater still, since these figures do not include converts to Catholicism and children baptized by their parents. Felix Theilhaber estimated that at the turn of the century German Jewry was losing at least one thousand persons a year.)[4] On the eve of World War I, alongside Germany's Jewish population of 620,000, there may have been as many as 100,000 converts and children and grandchildren of converts.[5]

Moreover, the number of converts in Germany would have been much higher had not many religiously indifferent Jews felt that baptism was, in the words of Gershom Scholem's father, "an unprincipled and servile act" at a time when antisemitism was on the rise. Walther

Rathenau, who loathed his origins and officially withdrew from the organized Jewish community in 1895, refrained from embracing Christianity, since he felt that conversion for opportunistic reasons was degrading and also an implicit endorsement of Prussia's discriminatory Jewish policy. As the sociologist Arthur Ruppin noted at the turn of the century, "If numbers of men and women cannot decide to be baptised, it is not so much because of their love of Judaism as of their unwillingness to face the reproach of cowardice and treachery by deserting a minority which is in danger, and is being attacked on all sides."[6]

One sign of the scope of apostasy in German Jewry was the vehemence with which communal leaders denounced it. The Centralverein deutscher Staatsbürger jüdischen Glaubens, the chief defense organization and most representative body of liberal assimilationist opinion, mounted a scathing polemic against the *Taufjuden*, who were, in its eyes, traitorous cowards, "renegades who sacrifice their honor and conviction to win recognition." Committed to fostering pride and self-respect among acculturated middle-class Jews, the Centralverein denounced apostates as the most dangerous enemies of Jewish survival in Germany, not only because they depleted the ranks of the community, but also because they substantiated the antisemitic canard that Jews were unscrupulous opportunists. Moreover, the Centralverein leadership believed that the willingness of some Jews to convert in order to obtain official posts delayed the attainment of full emancipation, since the government could claim that Jews were not being denied access to public employment at all. To counter the rising tide of baptisms, the Centralverein emphasized in its publications the positive values of Judaism and the importance of the Jews as its bearers, and simultaneously, how little Jews would gain by converting. In 1910, the organization became sufficiently alarmed that it even began sponsoring mass meetings to denounce conversion, one of which attracted several thousand persons.[7]

In England, by contrast, conversion—at least among the native community, as distinct from the immigrant community—was not a matter of communal concern before World War I. Cries of alarm about declining synagogue attendance, neglect of the dietary laws, indifference to Jewish education, and even increasing intermarriage were heard in sermons and editorials, but outright apostasy was not mentioned as a threat. In 1887, Oswald John Simon told a missionary that while, before emancipation, some English Jews had been baptized in order to attend university or enter Parliament, now, when being a Jew involved "no inconvenience to anybody," English Jews with ambitions no longer converted: "the most pious, the most learned, the most cultivated, and the most enlightened remain honourably by the Covenant." The only converts in England, he explained, were recent immigrants from Germany, Russia, and Poland, where Jews grew up under a set of influences different from those with which English Jews were familiar. Ten years later, when interviewed for Charles Booth's survey *Life and Labour of the People in London*, Chief Rabbi Hermann Adler discussed the character and extent of intermarriage but said not a word about conversion, an issue he surely would have raised if it had been a pressing concern.[8]

In his sermons Hermann Gollancz, rabbi of the Bayswater Synagogue, frequently lamented the tendency of some wealthy Jews to discard "what they regard as the weight of their former surroundings" and "to withdraw from the circle of their own people, in order, as they fondly imagine, to enable them to rise yet higher in the social scale." But it is clear from the context of his remarks that he was referring not to Jews who formally became Christians, but rather to Jews who achieved prominence in English society and then ceased to identify with the Anglo-Jewish community. In fact, Gollancz did not explicitly raise the question of apostasy in his sermons until 1911, when he denounced Jews who "leave the brotherhood to which they belong, and label themselves with a religious connexion in which they cannot possibly have any faith." Yet, in surveying the progress of assimilation in Anglo-Jewry in the *Nineteenth Century* the following year, Lewis S. Benjamin stated confidently that "the number of Jewish converts is so small as to be immaterial."[9] Clearly, while conversions did take place in the years before World War I, they were not considered a threat to communal solidarity, certainly not in the way they were in Germany, where rabbis and lay leaders publicly bemoaned their increase.

The pervasive character of conversion in Germany is best viewed against the backdrop of the illiberalism of the imperial period, especially the growth of antisemitism from the mid-1870s and the willingness of the state to ignore constitutional guarantees of equality and tolerate widespread occupational discrimination in the public sector. The impact of this defamation and discrimination on the consciousness and behavior of German Jews cannot be overemphasized. Neither affluence nor intellect could spare them the pain of knowing that Jews and Judaism were viewed with contempt and disdain. Walther Rathenau, who belonged to the most privileged stratum of German Jewry and thus was sheltered from the taunts of street-corner antisemites, nevertheless experienced antisemitism in an immediate, personal way. As he wrote in 1911, "In the years of his youth there is a painful moment for every German Jew that he remembers for the whole of his life—when he is struck for the first time by the consciousness that he has entered the world as a second-class citizen and that no ability and no merit can liberate him from this situation." For Theodor Lessing, who grew up without any con-sciousness of his ethnic origins, this moment came one day in school when he joined his classmates in taunting the other Jewish students only to be rudely told that he was one himself. He later recalled that he had become convinced that being Jewish was something evil because he had absorbed all the religious prejudices of his schoolmates and had no training at home to counterbalance them. He became a Protestant at age twenty-three, although later, under the influence of Zionism, he reembraced his Jewish origins.[10]

Most converts in Germany were young persons whose nominal attachment to Judaism imposed obstacles, immediate or potential, to their social and professional advancement. Men intending to enter occupations outside those in which Jews had traditionally been con-centrated were more likely to convert than those who followed their fathers' footsteps into business. This was particularly the case in the public sector, where discrimination was rife. In Berlin, for example, in the period 1873–1906, university students constituted 36 percent of converts of known occupation.[11] Indeed, in some Jewish families in imperial Germany, the son interested in a career in the university or the civil service converted, while the son entering the family business remained Jewish.[12] In many cases, young men deserted Judaism before encountering specific obstacles to their advancement. They acted instead on the reasonable expectation that whatever career path they chose they would find greater success and perhaps greater hap-piness as Christians than as Jews. Richard Lichtheim, a prominent figure in the Zionist movement in the first part of this century, recalled how, when he was fourteen, his father, a prosperous Berlin grain broker, had asked him one day if he wanted to convert. Most of his father's relatives had become Christians—some had been so for two generations—but his father had himself rejected conversion as undig-nified. By the turn of the century, however, when he was less sanguine about the future than he had once been, his diminishing sense of security led him to propose baptism to his son, who, after all, might want to become a lawyer rather than a grain merchant.[13]

In many instances parents who remained Jewish baptized their children at an early age, without regard to their future prospects, simply to spare them any unnecessary unpleasantness later in life. Felix Theilhaber estimated that between 1 and 2 percent of all Jewish children born in Germany in any year in the period 1880–1910 were baptized. The *Allgemeine Israelitische Wochenschrift* reported in 1898, for example, that of the ten or so Jewish professors at the University of Strasbourg—none of whom was himself baptized—not one had failed to baptize his children. They, like other German Jewish parents, sought to protect their children—boys and girls alike—from humiliation and insult as they grew up and to ease their way later when, as adults, they made their way in the world. In Heinrich Graetz's "Correspondence of an English Lady on Judaism and Semitism" (1883), a Jewish mother who urges Jews to baptize their children asks in anguish, "Should we expose them to the ridicule of their classmates and to the spiteful allusions of teachers who fancy themselves comic with their Jewish intonation? Should our sons be barked at in the army by some coarse sergeant or some insolent boor of a second lieutenant simply because they are Jews? Should they fulfill their military service conscientiously only to be discriminated against? Should our daughters who attend a public ball, even if graced with physical and spiritual charm and impeccably and modestly dressed, be scorned by geese with crosses on their breasts, avoided by men and forced into a gloomy corner?"[14]

In some instances Jewish men already launched on their careers were required to convert in order to obtain posts that would otherwise have remained closed to them. Conversions of this kind were especially common in academic life. Government and university officials made it quite clear to Jewish *Privatdozenten* that promotion without baptism was nearly impossible. The organic chemist and Nobel laureate Richard Willstätter recalled that his mentor Adolf von Baeyer repeatedly urged him after his *Habilitation* to get himself baptized in order to advance his career. He refused because he thought that conversion for personal advantage, without religious reasons, was improper.[15] When *Privatdozent* Harry Bresslau, a medieval historian, complained to Leopold von Ranke that his religion was hindering his career, Ranke flatly advised him to become a Christian. Bresslau rejected the advice but succeeded, nevertheless, in eventually obtaining a professorship in 1890—not at an old German university, however, but at Strasbourg, which was professionally and geographically on the periphery of German academic life. Like the other unconverted Jewish professors there, Bresslau baptized his children (one of whom later married Albert Schweitzer) in the hope of sparing them the anguish he had endured.[16]

Bresslau's ascent was unusual. In general, unconverted Jews became full professors less often than the *Getaufte*. At the University of Berlin, in the academic year 1909–10, there were 70 Jews, 31 baptized Jews, and 147 Christians at the rank of *Privatdozent*, for example, while at the rank of full professor, there were no unconverted Jews, 5 baptized Jews, and 80 Christians. The career of the theoretical physicist Felix Auerbach well illustrates the burden that Jewishness posed in university life. Auerbach spent the first ten years of his academic career as a *Privatdozent* at Breslau, where his work brought him considerable attention. When the University of Jena established an associate professorship in theoretical physics in 1889, he was a candidate. His sponsors, concerned that antisemites might block the appointment, took extra measures to gather supporting materials. Auerbach received the appointment, but then was repeatedly passed over for promotion to full professor until 1923. It took him forty-four years after his *Habilitation* to reach a position that the average full professor gained in less than half the time.[17]

Patterns of apostasy among Jewish women in Germany were different from those among men since the latter were more likely to have careers and thus run head-on into discrimination. Most women, at least before the First World War, remained enclosed in a private network of family and close friends, cut off from the social and occupational temptations that led to conversion. However, there were some groups of women whose lives took them beyond these confines and who chose to leave Judaism in order to avoid antisemitism. Women in the lower middle class increasingly entered into paid employment in the late nineteenth and early twentieth centuries—as clerks, teachers, domestics, and dressmakers—and they frequently found that conversion aided them in finding a position. Thus in Berlin the share of women in the total number of conversions rose considerably during this period. In the decade 1873–82, women accounted for only 7 percent of those converting; by 1908, 37 percent; and by 1912, 40 percent. (Since 84 percent of female converts in Berlin in the period 1873–1906 were from the lowest income groups, the increase in the share of women in the total number of conversions was clearly due to greater numbers of women from the lower middle class leaving Judaism.)[18]

At the other extreme of the social scale, women from the wealthiest German Jewish families were also likely to be tempted to leave the community. Here the yearning for social advancement frequently led parents to marry their daughters to Christian noblemen.[19] These nuptials, remarked the English novelist Cecily Sidgwick, who was herself of German Jewish stock and an astute observer of the German scene, "are just as business-like as if the *Schadchan* had arranged them and received his commission. The Graf or the Major gets the gold he lacks, and the rich Jewess gets social prestige or the nearest approach to it possible in a Jew-baiting land."[20] (Mixed marriages such as these, however, were not so frequent as cartoons and anecdotes would lead one to believe.)[21] When such matches occurred, inevitably it was the Jewish partner who converted, for aristocratic society was too intolerant to permit the wife to retain even a nominal Jewish affiliation. (In England, by contrast, the daughters of the Rothschilds and other Jewish banking families married into titled families without converting.)[22] Parents who arranged such matches were convinced that they could do little to improve their own social standing—their Jewish background and milieu, as well as their ties to commerce and finance, were simply too obvious. Instead, they hoped to enhance their daughters' chances for success by acquiring for them high-ranking husbands of the Christian faith.

This longing for integration into the feudalized ruling class was most intense at the very summit of German Jewish society. There, Sidgwick noted, "you have the spectacle . . . of Jews seeking Christian society instead of avoiding it; and you hear them boast quite artlessly of their *christlicher Umgang.*"[23] Young men and women whose families had arrived at the top a generation or two earlier usually abandoned Judaism. Perhaps the most notable example in the imperial period of this process of radical social assimilation can be found in the three generations of the Bleichröder family. The founder of the family banking firm, Samuel Bleichröder, embarked on the road to fortune as a money changer and lottery agent in Berlin during the Napoleonic wars, expanding only a few years later into merchant banking. Success and prosperity came his way after he became the principal agent in Berlin for the Rothschilds in the 1830s. His son Gerson, who became senior partner in the bank on the death of Samuel in 1855, built the firm into one of the richest and most important in Germany, largely due to his personal ties to Bismarck. When Gerson died in 1893, he was the richest man in Berlin and perhaps in Germany, his only rival for the title being Alfred Krupp. Where Samuel's energies and ambitions had been focused almost entirely on the family business, Gerson's were divided. Unlike his father, he had aspirations to a world beyond the Jewish and banking communities, Yet, while Gerson took little active interest in communal affairs, he remained a Jew. From time to time, reports appeared in the press that he was about to convert, but there was no truth to the rumor. For however strongly he craved entrée to aristocratic society, he had sense enough to realize that even as a Christian he would still be regarded as a parvenu Jewish banker. His children, on the other hand, who had moved in gilded circles from their youth and been exposed to wider horizons than their father, aspired to positions of the highest status: exclusive dueling fraternities, elegant army regiments, smart casinos and clubs, membership in the landed aristocracy. All of Gerson's children became Protestants and married non-Jews. His three sons, whom he had taken into the business, inherited none of their father's financial acumen and ended up as layabouts and playboys—decadent, debauched, useless.[24]

Those groups within German Jewry in which conversion was least common were those with little desire or opportunity for intensive contacts outside Jewish circles. Jewish grain merchants and garment trade entrepreneurs, whose closest associates were Jewish businessmen like themselves, were, thus, less likely to leave the community than Jewish journalists or civil servants. The latter not only mixed in gentile company to a far greater degree than the former but also were more exposed to antisemitic discrimination and defamation. Similarly, university-educated, upper-middle-class Berliners were more likely to cut their ties to Judaism than provincial shopkeepers and merchants with more limited social horizons. In his memoirs, Richard Willstätter highlighted this distinction in contrasting his own attitude toward conversion with that of his teacher, Adolf von Baeyer, whose mother was the daughter of a prominent converted Jew. Baeyer, he pointed out, "stemmed from the exceptional environment in Berlin in which, favored by the government, a mingling of Jews and Christians took place to a considerable extent during the last century." He "represented the principle of assimilation, the absorption of established and more highly developed Jewry into the State religion and the leading stratum of society." In contrast, Willstätter, whose father was a textile merchant in Karlsruhe, "came from a smaller, socially limited provincial circle which was liberal in religion but conservative in its adherence to Judaism." In his circle, the accepted escape from anti-semitism for persons desiring "freer and greater development" was not conversion but emigration to the United States or Great Britain.[25] Here local standards, as well as social expectations and aspirations, influenced patterns of apostasy.

Whatever their social background, almost all converts in Germany were motivated by worldly considerations: a desire to improve their social standing, advance their careers, or escape the psychological burden of belonging to a besieged minority. In all but a handful of cases, spiritual issues were irrelevant. Nominal Jews became nominal Christians. As Fritz Mauthner noted, while it was not impossible that a Jew might become a Christian out of conviction, he, for one, had never seen such a case. In his experience, expediency brought the overwhelming majority of adult converts to profess their belief in Christianity. However, because both antisemites and loyal Jews accused converts of opportunism and careerism, a few of them, mostly intellectuals, went out of their way to attribute their conversions to loftier, though essentially nonreligious, grounds. Maximilian Harden (né Felix Ernst Witkowski) claimed that he had adopted Christianity because it had seemed to him "the way of life corresponding to the higher culture." The Nobel laureate chemist Fritz Haber also claimed that his conversion, while a student, was essentially a matter of demonstrating his cultural allegiance to the German people. He felt thoroughly German and was alienated from Jewish practices and beliefs; since Christianity in Germany was, in his view, no more than a cultural community and his formal attachment to Judaism the last barrier separating him from other Germans, he became a Christian.[26] Claims such as these are, of course, difficult to evaluate. Without doubt, Harden, Haber, and others sincerely preferred *Deutschtum* to *Judentum* and were convinced that they were not motivated by ambition, greed, or cowardice. At the same time, however, it is difficult to suppress the feeling that beneath the intellectual rationales they advanced there lurked more pragmatic needs (which at a conscious level they may not have been able to confront). In any case, they must have known that, whatever motives they cited, baptism would bring in its wake certain concrete advantages.

In Anglo-Jewry in this period there are no parallels to the patterns of apostasy that developed in Germany. As we have seen, conversion from Judaism to Christianity among native English Jewry was infrequent. It would be convenient to attribute this to the superior moral character of English Jews, who, by comparison with their German brethren, appear less opportunistic and more steadfast in their loyalties. However, there is no reason to believe that English Jews were any less eager to get on in the world than German Jews. What was different was the set of social and political circumstances in which they strove to do so.

In Britain, there was far less violent antipathy to Jews than in Germany and consequently less reason to abandon Judaism. As I have argued elsewhere, the Jewish Question occupied a much less prominent place in political and cultural life, in public affairs and social arrangements, in schooling and careers, although in the last ten years or so before the outbreak of World War I this was beginning to change. (In 1913, for example, Claude Montefiore felt that it was less easy for Jews to get into certain clubs than it had been six or seven years earlier.) However, for most of the period 1870–1914, British Jews by and large were spared the pervasive and constant disparagement of everything Jewish that so unsettled their coreligionists in Germany.[27]

This is not to say that antipathy to Jews in England was negligible. Expressions of suspicion and hostility could be felt at all levels of society. Caricaturists, novelists, and dramatists employed unflattering stereotypes of Jews in their work; preachers, politicians, and journalists disparaged Jews as sharpers and cheats, aliens and outsiders, and even as the traditional blaspheming enemies of Christianity. Jewish schoolboys at Eton and Harrow were made aware that they were indeed different from their schoolmates. Jawaharlal Nehru, who entered Harrow in 1905, recalled that although the Jews there "got on fairly well . . . there was always a background of anti-Semitic feeling." They were "the damned Jews." Charles de Rothschild, who was at Harrow a decade earlier, looked back on his years there with much unhappiness. As he later told a friend, "If I ever have a son he will be instructed in boxing and jiu-jitsu before he enters school, as Jew hunts such as I experienced are a very one-sided amusement, and there is apt to be a lack of sympathy between the hunters and hunted." In less exclusive circles, as well, Jews encountered prejudice. A young Jewish journalist in Leonard Merrick's novel *Violet Moses* (1891) admits that "there *is* a difficulty about admitting oneself a Jew" because "one is always afraid the genial faces will harden, and the cheery smiles grow chilly, and fade away—we have seen it so often." Christians might aver that their prejudice had disappeared and Jews might try to persuade themselves that indeed it had, but, in the view of Merrick's Jewish journalist, "it is all rubbish."[28]

In comparison with anti-Jewish hostility in Germany, however, English prejudice was a minor irritant rather than a cancerous growth. This was certainly the perception of contemporary observers who compared the lot of Jews in both countries. In 1908, Cecily Sidgwick noted that "the social crusade against Jews is carried on in Germany to an extent we do not dream of here" in England. "The Christian clubs and hostels exclude them, Christian families avoid them, and Christian insults are offered to them from the day of their birth." German girls who wanted to ask a Jewish schoolmate to a dance "discovered that their Christian friends flatly refused to meet anyone of her race." On the other hand, wrote Sir John Foster Fraser in 1915, "Nowhere does the Jew receive better treatment than in Great Britain." Englishmen were hardly free of prejudices, but they did not feel strongly enough about them to translate them into a system of defamation and discrimination. As a contemporary Jewish observer explained, "the Anglo-Saxon has a more robust confidence than the German in his powers and destiny, and does not feel the need of bolstering up his self-esteem by running down the Jews."[29]

Moreover, not only were social barriers and unflattering caricatures less pervasive in Britain than in Germany, they also lacked political resonance. Prejudice against Jews was not linked to more profound or potentially divisive political questions about the basic structure of state and society. It did not breed antisemitic political parties and pressure groups nor erupt into public campaigns to reverse the tide of integration into the mainstream of society, as happened in Germany, where the Jewish presence was problematical in a way totally foreign to England. As Fraser explained, while it was not unusual to hear harsh opinions about "the way Jews are laying their hands on the commercial direction of London and other cities" and while "there is an occasional shrug of the shoulder at the position of Jews in society," these represented "individual opinion" and not any "movement of antagonism against the race."[30] Ideological antisemitism, such as it was, remained on the periphery of national political life.

A significant indicator of the absence of pervasive antisemitism in England is the infrequency with which one encounters intense cases of Jewish self-hatred there. To some extent, Jews everywhere in the West who distanced themselves from synagogue and communal life usually expressed feelings of contempt for the society they had rejected, even if they did not go so far as to renounce formally their ties to Judaism. In certain circles of German Jews—intellectuals, the haute bourgeoisie, students, artists, writers, and musicians—self-loathing was a particularly common personality trait. In fleeing their Jewishness, many of these Jews absorbed the antisemitic hostility of the gentile world they aspired to join. Theodor Lessing found sufficient evidence of this psychological trait in German-speaking Europe to devote an entire volume to it, *Die jüdische Selbsthass* (1930). It would be difficult to compile a similar volume for Anglo-Jewry. There were Jews in England who ceased to identify themselves as Jews and became indistinguishable from other Englishmen in similar walks of life, but their passage from one community to another was less likely to be accompanied by the urge to disparage the group they were leaving behind. One only has to compare the sentiments of a Walther Rathenau on these matters with those of an Edwin Montagu or a Leonard Woolf to realize that Montagu's and Woolf's discomfort about their Jewishness was a pale imitation of the full-blown self-hatred that flourished in imperial Germany.[31]

The relatively mild character of antisemitism in Britain does not alone account for the low level of apostasy in Anglo-Jewry. The occupational structure of the community also contributed to reducing the pressure for conversion. With some exceptions, native English Jews were to be found in commerce and finance, not in the professions, the civil service, the universities, and the arts (although more Jews were entering these fields from year to year).[32] The small number of Jews in these areas was not primarily the result of obstacles to their entry, but rather of the absence of incentives to abandon the activities they had customarily pursued.[33] (Earlier, in the mid-Victorian years, when English Jews attempted to enter fields from which they were barred by christological oaths, such as the bar or the universities, they found that resistance to their entry was either easily overcome or conveniently circumvented.) Commerce and finance in England did not suffer from the same opprobrium that they did in Germany, where capitalism and Jewry, which were consistently linked in the public mind, were held responsible for all the ills of the modern world. In the absence of this anticapitalist ethos, Anglo-Jewish sons tended to follow the occupational paths of their fathers and grandfathers. The acquisition of wealth in the City did not preclude social respectability.

There was no massive "hemorrhage of ability," in Martin Wiener's phrase,[34] out of commerce and finance in pursuit of occupations considered more prestigious in other national contexts. Thus, most young Jewish men remained in occupations where their closest associates in the day-to-day routine of business were very likely Jews. In such circumstances, not only would conversion have been of little utility, it would have been a distinct liability.

Because most Jewish men remained within the orbit of traditional Jewish occupations, few sought or received a university education before the turn of the century. When the future geneticist Redcliffe Salaman was an undergraduate at Cambridge in the mid-1890s, he later recalled, there were at most a dozen Jewish students, all sons of well-to-do and generally long-established families. In 1906, the head of Christ Church, Oxford, estimated that there had not been more than half a dozen Jews at the college in the previous ten years. And six years later, according to Basil Henriques, there were only thirty Jewish undergraduates in all the Oxford colleges.[35] This indifference to higher education stemmed from the absence of any significant material or social benefits to be gained from attendance at university. (In general, Oxford and Cambridge were less significant socially than public schools at this time; most public school boys did not go on to university.) A university degree not only did not prepare English Jews for careers they were likely to follow, it also did not confer status in the way that a degree did in Germany. There the university degree was a passport into the mainstream of national life for young Jewish men, not only because it was a prerequisite for many high-status bureaucratic and professional positions, but also because it witnessed their devotion to and mastery of German culture and science. Since English universities did not perform these functions, the sons of the Anglo-Jewish middle class, with a few exceptions,[36] were spared exposure to cultural and social influences that could have weakened their communal loyalty.

If conversion from Judaism to Christianity was rare in Anglo-Jewry, marriages between Jews and Christians (that is, with neither partner converting) were much less so. Although no figures are available, it is clear from other kinds of evidence that intermarriages were increasing throughout this period at several levels of Anglo-Jewry. *Jewish Society*, a London weekly that appeared for nine months in 1890, printed a number of articles and a stream of letters on the causes of intermarriage during its short life. In its first number, it observed that

Jewish parents had become so terrified about their daughters marrying Christians that they were offering enormous dowries to secure them Jewish husbands. In 1895 Hermann Gollancz deplored the increase of mixed marriages in a Sabbath sermon devoted to that theme, and in another sermon three years later denounced wealthy Jews who identified themselves so slightly with the Jewish community that their children married out while their parents were still alive.[37] Marriages between Jews and Christians are a central feature in novels from the period, such as Julia Frankau's *Dr. Phillips* (1887), Leonard Merrick's *Violet Moses* (1891), and Leonard Woolf's *The Wise Virgins* (1914). Describing Leopold Moses's marriage to Violet Dyas, Leonard Merrick comments: "Religious scruples did not weigh with him an atom, nor social ones. Maida Vale [an area of middle-class Jewish settlement in northwest London, less exclusive than Bayswater or Kensington] was growing used to mixed marriages."[38]

Communal leaders considered such marriages as a form of apostasy, since the offspring of these unions were usually reared within the majority faith and eventually merged into the English mainstream. Although such marriages resulted in the loss to Judaism of the children and hence might seem to resemble instances in which Jewish couples baptized their children, as frequently occurred in Germany, the circumstances surrounding these two types of radical assimilation differed significantly. In the former instance, intermarriage was the outcome of a high degree of prior social contact between Jews and gentiles. Generally such unions were not arranged by parents, but were rather the natural consequence of unregulated social mixing—at dances, in drawing rooms, at seaside resorts, and so on. Indeed, one contemporary quipped that it was only in mixed marriages that romance played any part—it was only then that "Israel worships at the feet of Venus."[39] In the latter case, the decision to baptize the children was the result of the absence of successful social integration. As Christians, it was hoped, the children would find fewer obstacles to success when they had to make their way in a society actively hostile to Jews. To put the comparison crudely, Jews were ceasing to be Jewish in England because resistance to their incorporation into society was weak; in Germany, their ties to Judaism were being sundered because the resistance was strong.

Yet it would be misleading to suggest that there were no similarities between Jewish behavior in the two countries. Although less numerous than in Germany, there were at various levels of the Anglo-

Jewish middle class religiously indifferent persons eager to move beyond their own community who believed that their Jewishness retarded their social ascent. Simeon Singer, rabbi of the fashionable New West End Synagogue, described such persons in a Sabbath sermon in 1905. They were "those who measure their success in life by the distance to which they are able to withdraw themselves from all Jewish associations, and by the force with which they can attach themselves to those who are not of their own people. . . . The highest rung in the ladder of their ambition is reached when they are able to say that they have rid themselves of all Jewish consciousness, and are merged body and soul among the Gentiles, by whom they are surrounded."[40] In these instances, it was not the existence of specific barriers that prompted the flight from Jewishness but rather the belief that Jewishness was a burden not worth bearing as long as Jews were viewed with suspicion or contempt by some Englishmen. In other words, there were persons whose social aspirations or psychological constitution could not tolerate even the low levels of hostility directed toward Jews in England. For example, the stockbroker Edward William Meyerstein and his wife, who were not practicing Jews and had raised their children as members of the Church of England, formally converted the children when their son was about to enter Harrow, although such a step was not necessary for admission—the sons of several prominent Jewish families were students there at the time. In fact, young Meyerstein's status as a convert made his years at Harrow more unbearable than if he had remained unconverted. Much later he recalled that while a Jewish boy who was proud of his religion and confident that he was as good as his schoolmates could get through school successfully, one who had been baptized, especially if he had a German name, was "due for hell." Boys, he concluded, "like to know what a thing is."[41]

Conversions such as these were more likely to occur in families of German origin that had settled in England in the course of the Victorian period than in families whose roots in England went back to the eighteenth or early nineteenth centuries. German Jews who migrated to England came primarily to escape the hostility and discrimination that embittered Jewish life there, especially before the bestowal of full emancipation in 1871. These immigrants carried with them a set of attitudes regarding Judaism and Jewishness that bore the impress of German conditions. They were thus more likely than native English Jews to regard their Jewishness as a burden or a misfortune, since antisemitism was so much more acute in the land of their birth. Once settled in England, they acted, so to speak, as if they were still living in Germany, where conversion was a frequent response to antisemitism. They failed to realize that economic and social advancement were obtainable in England without conversion. In the booming industrial cities of the North and the Midlands, as well as in London, scores of prosperous German Jews cut themselves off completely from any association with Judaism and converted to Christianity. In the provinces, many of them, perhaps the majority, joined Unitarian congregations, whose antitrinitarianism was more appealing, for obvious reasons, than the doctrines of other Christian groups. In addition, in manufacturing cities like Manchester and Bradford, Unitarians were the most dynamic, well-educated, and culturally active group and hence served as the reference group for upwardly mobile Jews in the way that Anglicans did in London.[42]

The one other section of Anglo-Jewry in which conversion was more than negligible during this period was the rapidly growing eastern European immigrant community. The motives for conversion among recent immigrants were largely unrelated to the willingness or refusal of the host society to absorb Jews, as was the case with the native community. When immigrants or their English-born children embraced Christianity—and they did so by the hundreds during this period—it was poverty above all that formed the background to their conversions. Christian missions to the Jews were devoted exclusively to the evangelization of the very poorest stratum of Anglo-Jewry. (Middle-class Jews and poor Jews whose families had lived in England for many years were beyond the reach of the conversionists; the former could not be visited in their homes, and the latter could not be induced to come to any sort of meeting in a church or mission hall.)[43] More than a dozen missionary organizations operated in the East End of London, for example, offering a wide range of free social services to the newcomers—medical care, reading rooms, vocational training, youth clubs, country holidays, as well as food, clothing, and even help with the rent in some cases—with the aim, of course, of luring them to Christianity.[44]

Thousands of immigrants took advantage of the conversionists' largesse because the relief and services provided by agencies of the native Jewish community were inadequate. The free library offered them "a comfortable, cheerfully warmed and lighted room" stocked with newspapers in Yiddish and other languages, as well as abundant conversionist literature, and was "presided over by quondam [i.e., former] professors of Judaism, who are always at hand and ready to assist 'enquirers.'" At the medical mission, they were given prompt attention and not kept waiting for hours; they could speak directly to doctors who understood them and dispensed medicines plentifully and without cost.[45] Most of those who availed themselves of this aid remained Jewish; some, however, became Christians, although whether they remained Christians is difficult to say. There were, clearly, immigrants who changed their religion with the intention of obtaining aid and then returning to Judaism at a later date. A handful even supported themselves in a fashion by repeatedly converting or expressing the intention to do so, such as one unnamed Jew who was described in 1894 by the Rev. J. M. Eppstein (himself a convert) as "an out-and-out rascal" for running away from the Wanderers' Home for Enquiring and Relieving Jews in Bristol on Christmas Day "after enjoying a good dinner and taking with him his Christmas presents."[46]

In Germany, interestingly, Christian missionizing among immigrant Jews was minimal. In part, this was due to the weakness of the missionary impulse there. The Berlin theologian Paulus Cassel, a former Jew, thought that the majority of Christians in the German capital were heathens, without any sense of religion. German pastors, he told a group of visiting English clergymen in 1886, had no interest in missions to the Jews. They were happy to preach in favor of their conversion but unwilling to exert themselves in any other way. A representative from the London Society for Promoting Christianity among the Jews who surveyed the state of missionary interest in Germany four years later also concluded that "German Christians as a whole can hardly be said to take a warm interest in the conversion of the Jews." He further noted that the German Evangelical Church employed only four missionaries to work among Jews and two of them were not so much actual missionaries as agents and secretaries attempting to arouse public interest in the work. The mission at Hamburg, for example, a major port of embarkation for immigrants to the United States, was operated by Irish Presbyterians.[47]

Public apathy about Jewish missions also reflected the absence of a large immigrant community—such as developed in Britain—although, in fact, Germany was better suited economically and geographically to receive migrants from eastern Europe. However, the German authorities took active measures to prevent the growth of an immigrant Jewish community, for if they considered Jews born in Germany to be unassimilable, how much the more so Jews born in the half-civilized Slavic East! Accordingly, the imperial and state governments acted to prevent large numbers of Jewish aliens from settling permanently in the country. By discriminating against Jewish applicants for residence permits and naturalization, by harassing immigrants for real and imagined offenses, and finally by periodically expelling so-called burdensome Jews, Germany reduced the numbers who attempted to settle there while simultaneously discouraging others from even thinking of doing so.[48] Thus, the absence of an impoverished immigrant community, ripe for missionizing, was in fact linked to the wave of conversions among native Jewry, the connecting thread being the pervasive Judeophobia of German ministers, politicians, and bureaucrats.

The larger contrasts in the patterns of apostasy that developed in Germany and England grew out of profound differences in the respective positions of Jews in those lands. As we have seen, conversion in Germany was a response to the failure of emancipation and the resurgence of ideological and social antisemitism after 1870. In England, on the other hand, relatively few Jews took this path to radical assimilation, largely owing to the more benign conditions there. The success of emancipation in England and its ultimately tragic failure in Germany were not, of course, isolated, unconnected events in the histories of these two states. Their willingness or unwillingness to permit a distinctive minority to retain its group identity while its members simultaneously pursued success in the mainstream was part and parcel of a more general orientation to state, society, and nation. In politically illiberal Germany, unsure of its own national identity and unhappy about the passing of an older social and economic order, there was no room for cultural and religious pluralism, particularly when those who wished to be tolerated had lived previously as degraded outsiders and were now competing successfully for wealth, status, and honors. In England, by contrast, a mature industrial society well before 1870, the values of liberal individualism were sufficiently enshrined and a sense of national confidence sufficiently established that Jewish integration into the mainstream hardly appeared threatening to the national well-being, even if it was not always welcomed with great enthusiasm.

NOTES

1. Missionary organizations in Britain occasionally published figures on the number of persons they had converted, but these figures are of limited use. First, conversionist groups tended to inflate the number of souls they had saved. Many of the Jews who accepted Jesus under their auspices returned to the Jewish community once they had received the material assistance offered them at the time of their baptism. Second, these groups worked only among the Jewish poor, and thus the figures they reported do not include cases of apostasy at more respectable levels of Jewish society, which were probably more numerous than those at the bottom of the social ladder.

The German conversionist J. F. A. de le Roi estimated that 23,500 Jews were baptized in Great Britain in the nineteenth century, but, as I explained in note 6 to the "Introduction," this is not a trustworthy estimate. *Judentaufen im 19. Jahrhundert: Ein statistischer Versuch*, Schriften des Institutum Judaicum in Berlin, no. 27 (Leipzig: J. C. Hinrichsche Buchhandlung, 1899), p. 23.

2. Jacob Lestschinsky, "Ha-shemad be-aratsot shonot" [Apostasy in Different Lands], *Ha-Olam* 5, no. 8 (1911): 5; Nathan Samter, *Judentaufen im neunzehnten Jahrhundert* (Berlin: M. Poppelauer, 1906), p. 74; Arthur Ruppin, *The Jews of Today*, trans. Margery Bentwich (London: G. Bell and Sons, 1913), p. 190. According to Lestschinsky, in some instances a Jewish community would be notified of a member's conversion only after his or her death. In general, he found that the figures on Jewish converts published annually in the church journal *Allgemeines Kirchenblatt für das evangelische Deutschland* were higher than those published by the Jewish communities, even though the former did not include, of course, converts to Catholicism or Jews declaring themselves *religionslos*.

3. Lestschinsky, "Ha-shemad be-aratsot shonot," *Ha-Olam* 5, no. 8 (1911): 5–6; no. 10 (1911): 6.

4. Felix A. Theilhaber, *Der Untergang der deutschen Juden: Eine volkswirtschaftliche Studie*, 2d ed. (Berlin: Jüdischer Verlag, 1921), p. 117.

5. Gershom Scholem, "On the Social Psychology of the Jews in Germany, 1900–1933," in *Jews and Germans from 1860 to 1933: The Problematic Symbiosis*, ed. David Bronsen (Heidelberg: Carl Winter Universitätsverlag, 1979).

6. Gershom Scholem, *From Berlin to Jerusalem*, trans. Harry Zohn (New York: Schocken Books, 1980), p. 11; Ismar Schorsch, *Jewish Reactions to German Anti-Semitism, 1870–1914* (New York: Columbia University Press, 1972), pp. 145–46; Ruppin, *The Jews of Today*, p. 194.

7. Schorsch, *Jewish Reactions to German Anti-Semitism*, pp. 139–42; Jehuda Reinharz, *Fatherland or Promised Land: The Dilemma of the German Jew, 1893–1914* (Ann Arbor: University of Michigan Press, 1975), p. 83.

8. *Correspondence between Mr. Oswald John Simon and the Dean of Litchfield, Rev. George Margoliouth, and Rev. A. E. Suffrin, on Parochial Missions to the Jews* (London: The Jewish World, 1887), pp. 15–16, 25; interview with Hermann Adler, file B197, p. 17,

Charles Booth Collection, Manuscript Room, British Library of Political and Economic Science, London School of Economics.

9. Hermann Gollancz, *Sermons and Addresses*, 1st ser. (London: Unwin Brothers, 1909), p. 190; idem, *Sermons and Addresses*, 2d ser. (London: Chapman & Hall, 1916), p. 108; Lewis S. Benjamin, "The Passing of the English Jew," *Nineteenth Century* 72 (1912): 502.

10. Walther Rathenau, "Staat and Judentum: Eine Polemik," in *Gesammelte Schriften*, 5 vols. (Berlin: S. Fischer Verlag, 1925), 1: 188–89; Lawrence Baron, "Theodor Lessing: Between Jewish Self-Hatred and Zionism," *Leo Baeck Institute Year Book* 26 (1981): 325–26.

11. Ruppin, *The Jews of Today*, p. 194.

12. Abraham A. Fraenkel, *Lebenskreise: Aus der Erinnerungen eines jüdischen Mathematikers* (Stuttgart: Deutsche Verlags-Anstalt, 1967), p. 97; Leonard Baker, *Days of Sorrow and Pain: Leo Baeck and the Berlin Jews* (New York: Oxford University Press, 1980), p. 96.

13. Richard Lichtheim, *She'ar yashuv: zikhronot tsiyyoni mi-Germanyah* [A Remnant Shall Return: Memoirs of a Zionist from Germany] (Jerusalem: Ha-sifriyyah ha-tsiyyonit, 1953), p. 19.

14. Theilhaber, *Untergang der deutschen Juden*, p. 118; *Allgemeine israelitische Wochenschrift*, quoted in Samter, *Judentaufen*, p. 80; Heinrich Graetz, "The Correspondence of an English Lady on Judaism and Semitism," in *The Structure of Jewish History and Other Essays*, trans. and ed. Ismar Schorsch (New York: The Jewish Theological Seminary, 1975), p. 192.

15. Richard Willstätter, *From My Life: The Memoirs of Richard Willstätter*, trans. Lilli S. Hornig, ed. Arthur Stoll (New York: W. A. Benjamin, 1965), pp. 83–84.

16. Friedrich Meinecke, *Strassburg, Freiburg, Berlin, 1901–1919* (Stuttgart: K. F. Koehler Verlag, 1949), p. 27; James Brabazon, *Alfred Schweitzer: A Biography* (New York: G. P. Putnam's Sons, 1975), p. 153. A granddaughter of Bresslau told Brabazon that he himself might have become a Christian, but "his pride and dignity would never let him take a step which might seem to have been motivated by expediency."

17. David L. Preston, "The German Jews in Secular Education, University Teaching and Science: A Preliminary Inquiry," *Jewish Social Studies* 38 (1976): 109–10.

18. Lestschinsky, "Ha-shemad be-aratsot shonot," *Ha-Olam* 5, no. 11 (1911): 6; Marion A. Kaplan, "Tradition and Transition—The Acculturation, Assimilation, and Integration of Jews in Imperial Germany—A Gender Analysis," *Leo Baeck Institute Year Book* 27 (1982): 18.

19. For some examples of such marriages, see Lamar Cecil, "Jew and Junker in Imperial Berlin," *Leo Baeck Institute Year Book* 20 (1975): 49, and the sources cited there.

20. Cecily Sidgwick, *Home Life in Germany* (London: Methuen & Co., 1908), p. 80. Sidgwick was the daughter of a German Jew who settled in England in 1848, married a Christian, and raised his children in the Church of England.

21. Kaplan, "Tradition and Transition," p. 16.

22. Todd M. Endelman, "Communal Solidarity and Family Loyalty among the Jewish Elite of Victorian London," *Victorian Studies* 28 (1985): 509–14.

23. Sidgwick, *Home Life in Germany*, p. 320.

24. Fritz Stern, *Gold and Iron: Bismarck, Bleichröder, and the Building of the German Empire* (New York: Alfred A. Knopf, 1977); David S. Landes, "Bleichröders and Rothschilds: The Problem of Continuity in the Family Firm," in *The Family in History*, ed. Charles E. Rosenberg (Philadelphia: University of Pennsylvania Press, 1975), pp. 75–114.

25. Willstätter, *From My Life*, pp. 18, 83.

26. Fritz Mauthner, in *Judentaufen*, ed. Arthur Landsberger (Munich: Georg Müller Verlag, 1912), p. 76; Harry F. Young, *Maximilian Harden: Censor Germaniae* (The Hague: Martinus Nijhoff, 1959), p. 12; Rudolf A. Stern, "Fritz Haber: Personal Recollections," *Leo Baeck Institute Year Book* 8 (1963): 88.

27. Montefiore, who was not quick to acknowledge antisemitism in English society, made this remark at an annual meeting of the Anglo-Jewish Association following a lecture by Morris Joseph on antisemitic tendencies in England. *Jewish Chronicle*, 4 July 1913.
The failure of a significant "Jewish Question" to emerge in Victorian England is critical to the argument set forth in this essay, yet to introduce at this point a discussion of that issue would lead us too far afield and would require an essay in itself. On the absence of a full-blown *Judenfrage* in modern England, see Todd M. Endelman, "Comparative Perspectives on Anti-Semitism in the Modern West," in *History and Hate: The Dimensions of Anti-Semitism*, ed. David Berger (Philadelphia: Jewish Publication Society, 1986) and "The Englishness of Jewish Modernity in England," in *Toward Modernity: The European Jewish Model*, ed. Jacob Katz (New Brunswick, N. J.: Transaction Books, 1986).

28. Jawaharlal Nehru, *Jawaharlal Nehru: An Autobiography* (London: John Lane, Bodley Head, 1936), p. 18; Charles de Rothschild to Hugh Birrell, quoted in Miriam Rothschild, *Dear Lord Rothschild: Birds, Butterflies and History* (Philadelphia: Balaban Publishers, 1983), p. 90; Leonard Merrick, *Violet Moses*, 3 vols. (London: Richard Bentley and Son, 1891), 1: 151.

29. Sidgwick, *Home Life in Germany*, p. 319; John Foster Fraser, *The Conquering Jew* (New York: Funk & Wagnalls, 1915), p. 114; M. Simon, "Anti-Semitism in England," *Jewish Review* 2 (1911): 298.
See also Sidgwick's story "The Powder Blue Baron" in her collection *Scenes of Jewish Life* (London: Edward Arnold, 1904), in which one of the Jewish characters remarks, "In London, no one cares, socially speaking, whether you are a Christian or a Jew" (p. 5). In this story, when the beautiful young English Jewess Esther Schon attends a concert with her German aunt and uncle in their home town, a small diamond brooch she is wearing elicits antisemitic remarks. Her German cousin Rosalie explains to her, "Diamonds are considered very Jewish," to which Esther

responds: "In London they are considered pretty. We don't attach a faith to them" (p. 8).

30. Fraser, *The Conquering Jew*, p. 114.

31. For Rathenau's views, see his notorious polemic "Höre, Israel," *Zukunft* 18 (16 March 1897): 454–62; Solomon Liptzin, *Germany's Stepchildren* (Philadelphia: Jewish Publication Society, 1944), pp. 139–51; Peter Loewenberg, *Walther Rathenau and Henry Kissinger: The Jew as a Modern Statesman in Two Political Cultures*, The Leo Baeck Memorial Lecture 24 (New York: Leo Baeck Institute, 1980), pp. 7–14. For Montagu's feelings, see H. H. Asquith, *Letters to Venetia Stanley*, ed. Michael Brock and Eleanor Brock (Oxford: Oxford University Press, 1982), p. 576, and Sigismund David Waley, *Edwin Montagu: A Memoir and an Account of His Visits to India* (New York: Asia Publishing House, 1964), pp. 4–5, 7–8, 11, 58. On Woolf, see his autobiographical novel *The Wise Virgins* and Freema Gottlieb, "Leonard Woolf's Attitudes to His Jewish Background and to Judaism," *Transactions of the Jewish Historical Society of England* 25 (1977): 25–37.

32. Harold Pollins, *Economic History of the Jews in England* (Rutherford, N. J.: Fairleigh Dickinson University Press, 1982), chap. 11.

33. The only historian to argue that Jews were excluded from positions of prestige in English society at this time is Peter Pulzer, who, in comparing the character of antisemitism in Germany and Britain, cites two examples of alleged discrimination. First, he points out that no Jews served in the Foreign Office before 1914. This is probably true, but it does not prove that a policy of systematic exclusion was at work. I cannot recall one complaint in sermons, memoirs, letters, and newspapers from the period about anti-Jewish sentiment in the Foreign Office keeping Jews from finding employment there. In fact, very few Jews were interested in making careers in any branch of the civil service. Second, Pulzer believes that being a Jew was an obstacle to gaining a fellowship at an Oxbridge college but supports his contention solely with the story of Sir Lewis Namier's failure to win a fellowship at All Souls in 1911. This is a weak example, for Namier, in addition to being a Jew, was also a Pole who spoke heavily accented English and was, by all accounts, a difficult and frequently unpleasant man. Of course, had there been as many Jews in England intent on making academic careers as there were in Germany, they probably would have encountered obstacles. The weakness in Pulzer's argument derives from his tendency to view the English scene through central European spectacles. Peter Pulzer, "Why was there a Jewish Question in Imperial Germany?" *Leo Baeck Institute Year Book* 25 (1980): 145.

34. Martin J. Wiener, *English Culture and the Decline of the Industrial Spirit, 1850–1980* (Cambridge: Cambridge University Press, 1981), p. 145.

35. Redcliffe N. Salaman, *Whither Lucien Wolf's Anglo-Jewish Community?*, The Lucien Wolf Memorial Lecture, 1953 (London: Jewish Historical Society of England, 1954), p. 17; Israel Rubinowitz to Herbert Bentwich, 17 December 1906, A100/7 aleph/20, Herbert Bentwich Collection, Central Zionist Archives, Jerusalem; Rose Henriques, unpublished biography of Basil Henriques, chap. 8, Basil Henriques

Papers, AJ/195, Anglo-Jewish Archives, Mocatta Library, University College, London.

36. The few Jews who studied at Oxford and Cambridge before World War I encountered a broader world of learning and socializing than they were accustomed to at home, and some of them became estranged from Judaism as a result. See Endelman, "Communal Solidarity among the Jewish Elite of Victorian London," p. 521.

37. *Jewish Society*, 31 January 1890; Gollancz, *Sermons and Addresses*, 1st ser., pp. 99, 190.

38. Merrick, *Violet Moses*, 2: 79.

39. *Jewish Society*, 10 September 1890.

40. Simeon Singer, *The Literary Remains of the Rev. Simeon Singer*, ed. Israel Abrahams, 3 vols. (London: George Routledge & Sons, 1908), 1: 254–55.

41. E. H. W. Meyerstein, *Some Letters of E. H. W. Meyerstein*, ed. Rowland Watson (London: Neville Spearman, 1959), pp. 240–41.

42. For a fuller discussion of the radical assimilation of German Jews in Victorian Britain, see Endelman, "Communal Solidarity among the Jewish Elite of Victorian London," pp. 522–25.

43. "Das Evangelium unter den Juden in England," *Nathanael* 4 (1888): 107–8.

44. Michael D. Sherman, "Christian Missions to the Jews in East London, 1870–1914" (M. A. thesis, Yeshiva University, 1983).

45. Simeon Singer, *Conversionist Activity and Its Perils* (London: Jewish Chronicle, 1903), p. 4.

46. J. M. Eppstein to Lukyn A. Williams, 29 December 1894, letters of inquiry from Jews to the head of the London mission, 1890–95, Dep. CMJ c.107, Church Mission to the Jews Collection, Bodleian Library, Oxford.

47. W. Ord-Mackenzie and Thomas Chaplin, *Report of Visit to Continental Missions, August & September 1886* (London: Alexander and Shepherd, n.d.), pp. 10, 13; Thomas Chaplin, Memorandum with Reference to German Societies for Promoting Christianity amongst the Jews, 23 January 1891, Dep. CMJ d.45, Church Mission to the Jews Collection, Bodleian Library, Oxford. See also the comments of de le Roi on the weakness of the missionary impulse in nineteenth-century Germany, *Judentaufen im 19. Jahrhundert*, p. 22.

48. Jack L. Wertheimer, "German Policy and Jewish Politics: The Absorption of Eastern European Jews in Germany (1863–1914)," (Ph.D. diss., Columbia University, 1978), chap. 1.

4

The Heine-Disraeli Syndrome among the Palgraves of Victorian England

BENJAMIN BRAUDE

Two of the most eminent Jewish converts to Christianity in the nineteenth century were Heinrich Heine and Benjamin Disraeli. Their achievements in German letters and British politics earned them recognition in gentile society, even as they prompted some Jews to try to claim them for the pantheon of Jewish contributors to civilization. This attempt was not without justification, since for both Jewishness became something of an obsession in their lives.

Heinrich Heine was born Chaim Heine in Düsseldorf in 1797 to a family long settled in northern Germany.[1] Although his ancestors included successful men of commerce and finance, his father, Samson, did not match this record. Young Chaim proved as financially incompetent as his father—in 1819 he plunged the family firm into bankruptcy—and eventually was sent off to university where he could do

Research for this article was funded by grants from Boston College (Summer 1980 and 1982), the American Philosophical Society, the American Council of Learned Societies, and the Dillaway, Kennedy, and Smith fellowships of Harvard University. Particular thanks are due to two generations of the Palgraves, the late Geoffrey Palgrave Barker, his wife, Mary, and his sons and their families, who generously made available their papers and their hospitality without which this essay could not have been written. I thank Professor Raphael Loewe for allowing access to his family papers and for his help in many other ways. The archivists of the Public Record Office and the Quai d'Orsay deserve thanks, as does Father Edmond Lamalle, S.J., archivist of the Society of Jesus, Rome, who provided copies of correspondence by and about Gifford Palgrave. I thank professor Ira Robinson of Concordia University for first providing a forum to discuss the ideas in this essay. Lois Dubin, as always, has been my first, last, and best critic.

no further harm to their business. Now away from the milieu of his birth, he sought companionship among Jewish and gentile intellectuals in Berlin. He became a disciple of the philosopher Georg Wilhelm Friedrich Hegel, as well as an officer of the *Verein für Kultur und Wissenschaft der Juden*, which included among its members the talented scholar Leopold Zunz. When this society disbanded, Heine found himself adrift. As his Jewishness became an obstacle to his advancement, he abandoned it to gain a doctorate from Göttingen and what he hoped would be an academic career. In 1825 he was baptized a Lutheran and christened Christian Johann Heinrich Heine, an act he later referred to as his entry ticket to European culture. Although he paid the price, the ticket never gained him the entry he expected. Neither Jews nor Christians accepted him. In the reactionary aftermath of European restoration Heine's radical politics made him suspect and the career he sought was denied him. He turned increasingly to writing, first as a journalist and then as a poet and essayist. Even here he found no relief, for soon he was embroiled in controversies with antisemitic opponents in a hostile Germany. In Paris where he sought refuge in 1831 he was befriended by a circle of artists, Jews and non-Jews, who sustained him. There he settled for the rest of his life. In 1856 he was buried without religious rites in a Montmartre cemetery.

As is well known, Jewish elements continuously recurred throughout his writings, both before and after his conversion. He used his novel *Der Rabbi von Bacharach* to denounce the libel of ritual murder and to introduce the kind of Jew he wished he could be, the cynical and freethinking Don Isaac Abarbanel. Apostasy was a subject reserved for his most bitter words. In *Einem Abtrünnigen*, a poem which was published after the conversion of his former *Verein* colleague, Edward Gans, and which may have been written after he himself took that same step, he condemned the turncoat's "crawling to the cross." Later he tried to rationalize his own acceptance of Protestantism, first by claiming that unlike Catholicism it implied no faith in Jesus' divinity, and then by arguing that both Judaism and Christianity were really one spiritual faith, "Nazarenism." On another occasion he wrote, "I make no secret of my Judaism, to which I have not returned, because I never left it."

In fact, Heine's beliefs, for much of his life, were influenced by the optimistic expectations of human deliverance which had been first aroused by the French Revolution. In his youth he had been intoxicated by hero-worship for Napoleon, and later the refuge which France furnished him confirmed that this land, and the ideals he felt it represented, were the only real faith he had. But in 1840 an event occurred, the so-called Damascus affair, which shook that faith and turned Heine back to explore the Jewish roots he never honestly knew. An accusation was made that the Jews of Damascus had murdered a Catholic priest and used his blood for ritual purposes, the ancient blood libel. Far from denouncing this calumny, France, which had considerable diplomatic influence in the region, aided and abetted it. In fact the French consul in Damascus soon emerged as the principal instigator of the attack. Heine, in turn, denounced this policy and sought to arouse public protest against the government. In the aftermath Heine started to read works of Jewish history and began to look upon the Bible as "an imperishable treasure," a "portable fatherland" of the Jewish people. It was under the influence of this reading that Heine composed his nostalgic *Hebräische Melodien*. In *Romanzero*, a late work, he wrote this series of Hebrew melodies which included *Prinzessin Sabbat*, a paean to the world of the Jewish Sabbath, *Jehuda ben Halevy*, a tribute to the great Spanish Jewish philosopher-poet, and *König David*.

While his work contained much that was sentimental and sympathetic about Jews and Jewishness, Heine was also ready to denounce and repudiate Judaism, which he once described as an affliction worse than poverty and sickness. He also internalized some of the radical anticapitalist accusations of the antisemites. Notwithstanding his conversion, Heine remained a writer obsessed with Jewishness. In many respects he might be called the first modern Jewish writer, driven as he was by that mixture of awe and self-hatred—self-hatred as both Jew and gentile—and that mixture of biting wit combined with ignorance of, and fascination with, matters Jewish that characterizes such writers of our own day as Philip Roth and Mordecai Richler. Though Heine tried, he never escaped his Jewishness, because neither he nor his Christian brethren ever allowed him to forget it. And in the end, with all the ambiguity that has been mentioned, he reveled in, even as he reviled, his Jewish origins.

Benjamin Disraeli's obsession with his Jewishness was of a different sort.[2] As befits a politician—albeit a politician with literary pretensions to be sure—he was not driven by the guilt and self-doubt which afflicted Heine. Son of the anecdotal anthologist Isaac D'Israeli, of an Italian Jewish family generations resident in England, Benjamin was born in 1804, baptized at thirteen and buried with Anglican rites in 1881. Since his conversion was the father's decision, rather than his own, he did not bear the guilt of choosing baptism. His Jewishness was accordingly less complicated. As a number of recent studies have shown, his attitude toward his origins changed over time, but unlike Heine he seems not to have held several contradictory impulses at one and the same time. Consistently he was alienated from Judaism, even as he came to glory in the past of the Jews. Publicly he expressed his feelings differently over the course of his career and the reasons for this evolution—political expediency, psychological need, or personal experience—need not detain us here. What is clear is his exaggerated notion, almost theatrical, of Jewish power and influence, a trait preserved through the racial purity of the Jews. These notions he expounded systematically in 1852 in a biography of a Tory political colleague, where, in a chapter remarkable for its irrelevance to the book's subject, he argued that the Semitic race was superior to others and the Jews the elite of the Semites. It was Jewish spirituality which made them superior to the materialism characteristic of the northern races. And it was Christianity which was the quintessence of this spirituality. As he had written a few years earlier in *Tancred*, "Christianity is Judaism for the multitude, but still it is Judaism." Such beliefs also emerge in his other novels, particularly *Alroy* and *Coningsby*, which may be seen as "the secret history" of his feelings. Taken together they present a confused mélange of political posturing, imperialist rumination, and messianic fantasy. Jewishness of a most peculiar and idiosyncratic kind is what Disraeli had to offer. In these works and toward the end of his political career Disraeli unabashedly gloried in his Jewish origins as he romanticized and invented them. Disraeli's flaunting of his Jewishness was certainly part of the theatrical extravagance that made him the most enchanting of Victoria's prime ministers; at the same time it reflected a continuing and deep source of identity.

For both Heine and Disraeli, Jewishness was not an identity easily shed. Their experience represents a recurring malady of adjustment, an obsession with their past, which afflicted other apostates as well. This syndrome specifically describes the phenomenon whereby a Jewish convert to Christianity retains a certain pride, perverse perhaps, but pride nonetheless in his Jewish origins accompanied by a residual, if ambiguous, sympathy for Jews and Judaism. Indeed an element of the convert's identity is still rooted in his Jewish past. Although encouraged by social pressures, such conversions were by no means forced, and thus this lingering attachment to Jewishness should be clearly distinguished from the phenomenon of Marranism, that is, the crypto-Judaism of those Jews of Iberia who were forcibly converted to Christianity at the end of the fifteenth century. The Heine-Disraeli syndrome also differs from the example of Paul, the early follower of Jesus, whose conversion was complete, and accompanied by rejection of Judaism, particularly Jewish law, and hostility to any judaizing impulses on the part of his new community. So the Heine-Disraeli syndrome represents a phenomenon clearly to be distinguished from the tension between the outward Christianity and inward Judaism of the Marranos as well as from the embrace of Christianity and scorn for Judaism of Paul, that is, from Marrano crypto-Judaism and Pauline rejection of Judaism. The Heine-Disraeli syndrome partakes of both, but is more nuanced and subtle than either.

Heine's and Disraeli's well-known obsessions with their Jewish past are a phenomenon worth comparing to other instances of the syndrome, which have attracted much less attention, that is, among the Palgraves of Victorian England.[3] They represented in many ways the success story of conversion and rapid social assimilation into the British literary, intellectual, and political establishment, almost to the center of power itself. The founder of the family was born Francis Ephraim Cohen, the only son of Meyer Cohen and Rachel Levien Cohen, in London in 1788. Meyer, despite some earlier business failures, had by this time become a wealthy member of the London stock exchange, maintaining a fine home in Kentish Town. His family were of Ashkenazi origin. Along with his brothers Jacob and Joseph, who were also merchants in London, he was a member of the Hambro synagogue.[4] Francis Ephraim was privately tutored in French, Italian, and the classics. He also seems to have acquired the rudiments of a Hebrew education, though this fact is not discussed in his biographies. In 1805, at the age of sixteen, he started clerking in the law firm of Loggin & Smith. A few years later the ease and wealth in which he had been raised were shattered by the stock exchange slump of 1810, which bankrupted his father—an interesting parallel to Heine's experience. By this time he had become an attorney in a firm of solicitors and the next year he was appointed managing clerk. Through the remaining years of his parents' lives—his mother died in 1815, his father in 1831—he supported them. From 1814 on he started to write for the major literary journals of the age, the *Edinburgh* and *Quarterly* reviews. He was befriended by Sir Walter Scott and Isaac D'Israeli. He also began what was to be his life work, research in the records of medieval England. During these years of self-support and independence he had gradually moved away from his family and Judaism. The final break and his Christian baptism came sometime between 1815 and 1821. In November of that last year, in recognition of his various publications, notably a collection of medieval chansons which appeared in 1818, he was admitted to fellowship in the Royal Society.[5] His sponsors included William Sotheby, a writer and classical scholar, Peter Mark Roget of *Thesaurus* fame, and Dawson Turner, his future father-in-law.

Dawson, and his wife, Mary Palgrave Turner, were of old East Anglian stock. Though an Anglican, he was a partner like his father in the Quaker-owned Gurney Bank, which he first joined in Great Yarmouth, his birthplace. His uncle had been Master of Pembroke College, Cambridge, where he had intended to prepare for holy orders. However, his father's death in 1796, when Dawson was just twenty-one, forced him to abandon the cloth for the counting-table. Business did not eclipse his other interests. He was a lifelong patron of the local artist John Sell Cotman. He was a first-rate amateur botanist. He was devoted to the antiquities of Norfolk. And he became one of the great collectors of books, manuscripts, and autograph letters in the nineteenth century. His education at Cambridge had prepared him in Greek and Latin, as well as Hebrew, which he learned well enough to teach his second wife some sixty years later.[6]

It was through Dawson's old friend and business partner, Hudson Gurney, who employed Loggin & Smith as solicitors, that the future father- and son-in-law first met, but it was their shared passion for subjects antiquarian that turned this contact into a close intellectual partnership. Francis Cohen was invited to the Turner home in Yarmouth to help Dawson complete his book, *A Tour in Normandy*. During his stay he fell in love with Elizabeth Turner, whom he married in 1823, some three years later.

Their courtship was a long and uneasy one. Although the family correspondence does not dwell upon it, clearly his Jewish origins were a source of discomfort. Hudson Gurney wrote to Dawson Turner of Cohen's ambitious and impatient temperament—which might be seen as a coded antisemitic comment. But Mrs. Turner was relieved to learn that he had been baptized into the Church of England and she was even more pleased to learn that he had accepted the family's offer that he change Cohen to Palgrave, her maiden name, and be inscribed on the Palgrave pedigree in the College of Arms. Her husband was delighted and bestowed upon his son-in-law not only a marriage settlement of £3,000, but also a credit note at Barclays Bank in London which refunded what Francis had paid in order to change his name. He added that this change "was done on account of my family, & it is only right I should bear the expense."[7] Although Francis had advanced very far on his own before joining his new family, it is clear that the ties they offered moved him forward even more rapidly. He was now brother-in-law to William Jackson Hooker, who was to found the Royal Botanic Gardens at Kew. In the next decade he was to gain the bishop of Chester, William Jacobson, as a second in-law. His entry ticket, indeed a first-class seat, had been duly purchased.

In 1821, two years before his marriage, Francis Cohen left Loggin & Smith after being denied a partnership and took chambers on his own at King's Bench Walk in the Temple. He applied, without success, to become Keeper of Records in the Tower of London. However, he did succeed in gaining an appointment, albeit without compensation, as a subcommissioner on a board investigating the state of England's archives. His proposal to consolidate all of the nation's archives into one building was to result decades later in the establishment of the Public Record Office in Chancery Lane. Ironically, this was located on the very same site as the *Domus Conversorum*, an establishment founded some six centuries earlier by Henry III to shelter and support Jewish converts to Christianity. After his marriage his prospects grew much brighter. In 1827 he was admitted to the bar—as a Jew he had been barred—and began a successful practice specializing in peerage cases. His proposal to publish a series of parliamentary rolls and writs had previously been accepted, and gradually that brought in an income as well. Subsequently he obtained an appointment to work on a bill to reform municipal corporations. In recognition of his service to reform, in 1832 he gained a knighthood and the friendship of Lord John Russell, the Liberal leader. Two years later he finally obtained a regular appointment as an archivist, Keeper of Records at the Chapter House, Westminster Abbey. In 1838 he, at last, was rewarded with a post in the institution that he had first proposed nearly two decades earlier, first Deputy Keeper of the newly created Public Record Office, a position he held until his death in 1861.

Sir Francis Palgrave's talents were not restricted to records and the law. Throughout these years he continued to pursue the literary and historical studies which had first won him recognition while only a twenty-six-year-old Jew. His principal works were the four-volume *History of Normandy and of England* (1, 1851; 2, 1857; 3, 1920; 4, 1921). *The History of the Anglo-Saxons* (1837), and *The Rise and Progress of the English Commonwealth* (1832), but he also wrote several dozen articles as well as volumes of historical fiction and a historical guide, *Handbook for Northern Italy*. When just after World War I his last surviving son collected and published most of his historical writings in a handsome edition from Cambridge University Press, they filled ten weighty volumes.[8]

If anything, his four sons were even more accomplished. The eldest, Francis Turner Palgrave (1824–97), was assistant private secretary to William E. Gladstone—the family's connections with the Liberal Party continued in this generation. Frank Palgrave, as he was known in the family, was also one of the great art and literary critics of his age. He was a friend of Alfred Tennyson, elected Professor of Poetry at Oxford, and the compiler of the most popular anthology of poetry ever published in the English language, *The Golden Treasury*. William Gifford Palgrave (1826–88) was a diplomat and one of the great literary travelers of the nineteenth century. Until the publication of T. E. Lawrence's *Seven Pillars of Wisdom* after the Great War, Gifford Palgrave's *Narrative of a Year's Journey through Central and Eastern Arabia* was the most widely read book about the Arabs. Sir Robert Harry Inglis Palgrave (1827–1919) was a leading banker and scholar of economics—among his admirers was John Maynard Keynes; he was also for a time editor of the *Economist*. It was he who edited his father's writings for Cambridge. The youngest, Sir Reginald Francis Douce Palgrave (1829–1904), was the Clerk of the House of Commons, as well as author of several books on parliamentary procedures, customs, and traditions. This band of remarkable sons achieved positions of eminence in fields as diverse as literature and the arts, politics, government, foreign affairs, business, and education. Few families of Jewish origin could match such a record. By any definition this clearly was success.

But what of their father's conversion and what of the syndrome? For otherwise than with Heine and Disraeli, here the evidence of a residual Jewish identity seems absent. Indeed, in such reference works as the *Dictionary of National Biography* or the *Encyclopedia Judaica*, or in Todd M. Endelman's *Jews of Georgian England*, there are few hints of the Palgraves' inability to shed their Jewishness. Endelman presents Sir Francis Palgrave as an example of another common phenomenon, the desire to participate in an intellectual culture outside the commercial confines of Anglo-Jewish life:

> Having been given the education of an English gentleman by an indulgent and proud father, and having responded to this education with enthusiasm and ability, he had to look, as a consequence, beyond his family's friends and acquaintances for social and intellectual companionship. For within the Jewish community there were no secular intellectual coteries.[9]

This desire was clearly at work in his early friendships with Isaac D'Israeli and the Judeophile Scott, who were figures capable of easing the transition from one community to another. But the question of Sir Francis's attitudes toward his Jewish origins remains. The initial evidence is neither abundant nor indicative of the syndrome. Shortly after his death in 1861 one of his sisters-in-law wrote to Inglis, the third son, reminiscing about the letter her mother had written to her future son-in-law expressing the hope that he had been properly baptized. Francis Cohen's reply

> was short but reverent and earnest—speaking in a few simple words of the *strong* motives which alone could have impelled him to such a step, and adding that he was baptized by the Rev. Mr. Routledge (I think), Librarian of the Temple Library. . . . But *when* this baptism took place or what or who were the means of leading your dear f's mind to this change, I never heard. Certainly it was long before he knew Anna Gurney [Hudson's half-sister whom Francis met in 1818]. . . . But to us, and for upwards of 30 years of his married life he never alluded to his own previous name or religion. I well remember the first time of his withdrawing the curtain which hid that part from our view, his speaking of that elderly cousin (Miss Levien) and of his father and his own name (which signified Priest) and of his being of the tribe of Levi.[10]

To his own wife he was a bit more open. He told her that the irreverences and the indifference of the Jews and their irreligion had convinced him of their hypocrisy. This was the reason he decided to leave them.[11] Indeed, to all intents and purposes he was a pious and devout Anglican. Regular church attendance was the family's routine. Their children went to church on weekdays, and on Sundays, besides attending two services at the local parish church, in the evening they would walk the distance from their Hampstead home to Albany Street to attend Christ Church. Both Francis and his wife Elizabeth were "accustomed constantly to bring forward matters of religion to bear upon the occupations and amusement of their children."[12] Deeply concerned about the issues of church doctrine and ritual that were intensely debated in these decades, they were all much influenced by the Tractarian movement, which sought to combat distasteful elements of authority and doctrine introduced by latitudinarian churchmen, by reviving the life of prayer and worship of the pre-Reformation church. Francis was an early correspondent of the most famous Tractarian, John Henry Newman, and the eldest sons in particular were much influenced by him.[13]

Behind this facade of High Church propriety, however, there lurked a more complicated reality. The distinguished American historian and man of letters Henry Adams, who knew the family very well, alluded to this when he wrote in his autobiography, "Old Sir Francis . . . had been much the greatest of all historians of early England, the only one who was un-English; and the reason of his superiority lay in his name, which was Cohen, and his mind which was Cohen also, or at least not English."[14] Adams was probably the most imaginative medievalist in America—his *Mont-Saint-Michel and Chartres* is still worth reading—and his comments about Palgrave should be taken seriously, even though he had a tendency to see Jews anywhere and everywhere.[15] What was there about Palgrave's work that led Adams to stress his Jewishness? Certainly not the subjects of his research, for Palgrave devoted himself to the Roman and Anglo-Saxon origins of the English constitution. His work rarely touched upon Jews.[16] However, there was a distinct character to his approach to English history which may have been linked in some way with his origins. As George Peabody Gooch claimed, Palgrave gave an entirely new construction to Anglo-Saxon history. He challenged the prevailing view that the study of political events must precede the study of institutions and the law. He came to this conclusion independently of the great Prussian founder of the historical school of jurisprudence, Friedrich Karl von Savigny. "The history of law," he argued, "is the most satisfactory clue to the political history of England," for "the character of the People mainly depends on their Laws. And it is utterly impossible to obtain a correct view of the general administration of the State, unless we fully understand the spirit of the institutions which pervade the community and regulate the daily actings and doings of mankind." His attitude toward the law was imbued with deep reverence: "The function of the lawgiver is the highest exercised by man. Legislation is a duty involving the most fearful responsibility which can devolve on any human being."[17]

The obvious source for his approach was the legal training he received at Loggin & Smith. There is a second source—reinforcing the first—which might explain the Jewish link in Adams's mind. Palgrave's exalted view of the law is curiously reminiscent of the view of law held by traditional Jewish learning. For Judaism, *halakhah*, that is, "the way," is in fact the essence of belief and practice, for it is the divine blueprint for human thought and behavior. Study of *halakhah* was exalted as the highest form of human activity. It is not unreasonable to suggest that something of this attitude may have influenced this bright and sensitive young man during the first three decades of his life, before he abandoned Judaism. Palgrave may have been rejecting the Judaism of the Anglo-Jewish community, but elements of the Jewish tradition may still have influenced him.

It may appear that this latter claim is an exaggeration, resting on insubstantial evidence and unsound speculation. Perhaps the points of convergence between Palgrave's historiography and traditional Jewish scholarship are mere coincidence. But there is more to the argument than this parallel. Palgrave was a great book collector. When Sotheby's auctioned his library after his death, in addition to the works that one would expect to find in the collection of an English antiquarian, it included a surprising amount of Judaica for someone who, according to his sister-in-law, "never alluded to his previous name or religion." The library was sold over eight days in 2,647 lots, totaling at least 4,000 titles.[18] Judaica comprised a very small part, less than 3 percent, some 73 lots, yielding 113 titles. A good number of these titles—32— were Hebrew Bibles, grammars, and dictionaries. Though his Biblica included some nineteenth-century Jewish translations and commentaries, for the most part these were works which, in kind, if not in quantity and bibliographic rarity, might be found in the collection of a well-educated Anglican divine. The bulk of the Judaica collection, however, was of a different character. He had a number of classic works which had been published in Hebrew with translations by Christian Hebraists. These included the early mystical work *Sefer Yetsirah*; two editions of the chronology *Seder Olam Rabba*, traditionally attributed to the Palestinian rabbi Yose ben Halafta; and Jedaiah Bedersi's early fourteenth-century ethical treatise, *Beḥinat Olam*. In addition there were a number of titles by and about Moses Maimonides, one complete set of *Mishnah* with commentaries by Maimonides and Obadiah Bartinoro, as well as a set of mishnaic extracts, a Hebrew-German edition of the ethical tractate *Derech Erets Zuta*, and a number of editions and translations of *Pirkei Avot*. He also owned two rare works of opposing character, Johann Andreas Eisenmenger's *Entdecktes Judenthum*, and Isaac Cardoso's *Las excelencias de los hebreos*. More remarkably, he had acquired a prayer book for the Jewish New Year published in 5586, that is, 1825/6, after his conversion, his name change, and his marriage. He had acquired as well contemporary Jewish scholarship, such as Isaak Markus Jost's multivolume *Geschichte der Israeliten*, Zunz's latest publications, and Michael Sachs's book on Jewish religious poetry in Spain. He seemed to be particularly interested in the work of Leopold Dukes, a former disciple of the Hatam Sofer (Rabbi Moses Sofer, leader of Orthodox Jewry), for he owned at least five of his books, including one in duplicate. In this list of 113 are 17 works whose titles were not provided in the catalogue—for the most part these were Hebrew books without Latin-lettered title page—thus the full range of his interests cannot be assessed, but based on what is available it is clear that in addition to works on Jewish law, he paid attention to two particular areas of Judaica: ethical works—13 titles—and Hebrew literature, especially poetry—10 titles.

What is the significance of these tomes? A bibliophile may of course acquire without reading. Moreover, with one exception as mentioned above, his published work gives no evidence that he consulted any of this Judaica. Were the collection restricted to the Christian Hebraist imprints of seventeenth-century Basle and Paris, the claim that the Judaica was merely bibliomania might hold, but the amount of *Wissenschaft* scholarship he acquired suggests that Sir Francis had a continuing interest in the world of Jewish learning and that he regarded Judaism and the Jews as not merely an ancient relic to be ignored, but as a living and evolving entity whose scholarship he approached with respectful curiosity. As for his published indifference to the Jews, that is consistent with the persona he sincerely adopted. The interior reality was indeed complex.

However, there is more than the mute testimony of book titles to reveal the lingering Jewishness hidden behind Sir Francis Palgrave's Anglican exterior. Evidence of a more substantive kind is provided by a letter which Sir Moses Montefiore wrote to his secretary, Louis Loewe, on 10 April 5616 [1856]:

Dear Doctor
    I have had the pleasure to receive the enclosed Note from Sir
F   P   with Ten Pounds to remit to those who devote themselves "to the
study of the Law at Tiberias" *his Name must not be made known* But I will thank you to
send with the remittance to Tiberias the form of the receipt they should transmit to
me to forward to Sir Fr   P
it should be written well on a handsome sheet of Paper signed and sealed by some of
the heads of the several Congregations at Tiberias Sir F   P   wishes to
have the receipt, pray let it express the sense of gratitude felt to their unknown
benefactor for his consideration towards them.[19]

There is no doubt as to the identity of the mysterious benefactor, Sir
Fr P ; adjoining the text in the letter book is a separate sheet in
Montefiore's hand which supplies the missing letters, Francis Pal-
grave.

    This evidence is striking proof of the abiding hold that Jewish
identity—particularly the respect for Jewish law and scholarship—
had on Palgrave and certainly justifies citing him as an example of the
Heine-Disraeli Syndrome. In some respects, however, the case of
Palgrave père was different from those of Heine and Disraeli. On the
surface Sir Francis's assimilation was the most complete. He married
well and thereby acquired a new name and identity. Neither Heine
nor Disraeli matched that success; in fact their marriages were by
comparison misalliances. Unlike Heine, he got extremely good value
for the price of his entry ticket. Given the rewards he had achieved
and the discreet way he had earned them, he had no reason to indulge
in the kind of behavior which marked these fellow apostates. He had
no reason to be wracked—as far as we know—by the doubt and guilt
which tormented Heine. Cohen had made it as Palgrave; the others
were still Heine and Disraeli. Thus Palgrave père avoided the public
identification with Jewishness which delighted Disraeli and which,
significantly, he could in no way avoid. However, in the next generation of the Palgrave family there arose a case which was as bizarre and
flamboyant an example of this syndrome as anything that Disraeli
himself could have imagined.

    The second of Sir Francis's four sons had a career which could
have been lifted from the pages of *Tancred*. William Gifford Palgrave
was the exotic man out among the four. In 1847 he gained a First Class
degree at Oxford, but shunned the promise of a brilliant career at
home to seek his fortune in India as an officer in the Bombay Native
Infantry. His military career lasted only two years, long enough for
him to decide that the life of the cloth was preferable to that of the

sword. He converted to Catholicism and resigned his commission—a delayed response to the conversion of his idol, John Henry Newman, which took place during Gifford's years at Oxford.[20] Now Gifford took the further step of joining the Jesuits in Madras, in the south of India. There and in Rome he studied, readying himself for a priestly mission to the Levant. In 1855 he reached Lebanon, the center of Jesuit activities in the Middle East. He spent the next five years studying, teaching, traveling, and preaching. He also mastered Arabic to the point that he became the leading Catholic preacher in Beirut. In 1860 a squabble that started as a peasant revolt in a district of Mount Lebanon burst into a civil war between the Maronites and the Druze. In the midst of the conflagration he and his fellow Jesuits fled to France. It was during this exile from the East that he conceived a gradiose scheme for Arabia.

In France he worked diligently to gain adherents for an imaginative political-religious project. Through well-connected superiors, he reminded Emperor Napoleon III that his uncle, Napoleon I, had sent a spy to Arabia to organize an auxiliary force against the Ottomans in 1798. Encouraged by this example, the Jesuits believed that the Ottomans, who still nominally ruled the region, could be routed and an Arab regime established under French tutelage if the dissident bedouins of the desert were to revolt—a scheme which anticipated T. E. Lawrence's own adventures by one half-century. Among these dissidents was the Wahhabiya, a movement for the revival of Islam led by the Saudi family and based in central Arabia. Decades earlier they had attacked and occupied Mecca. For the Ottomans this had been a profound challenge to their *raison d'être* as protectors of the Holy City, Islam's most sacred shrine. They branded the Wahhabiya a heretical enemy of Islam. Ottoman discomfort was seen as European opportunity. The Jesuits saw this movement as "pure deism," Islam shorn of its oriental sensuality, fertile ground for the spread of Christianity.[21] Napoleon III endorsed the plot to the sum of 10,000 francs. Pius IX and the head of the Jesuits blessed the proposal to bring the light of the gospel to the heart of Arabia. In 1861 Gifford returned to the East.

With a trusted assistant, Butrus Jerajiri, he entered Arabia, disguised as a Syrian doctor. Then he acquired a new conspirator, Talal ibn Rashid, an emir restive under Saudi control. But in the Wahhabi capital, Riyadh, he failed. Rather than the simple deism he had expected, he discovered a dour and devout society presided over by Wahhabi divines fiercely dedicated to preserving and spreading their own brand of Islam. They attacked him as a Christian spy and revolutionary and he fled for his life. After more adventures along the pirate coasts of the Persian Gulf and in Iraq, he finally reached Beirut in 1863.

Almost immediately the Ottomans uncovered the plot. The papal representative, heeding their protests, dispatched the frustrated conspirator Romeward. He was never to return to the Middle East as a Jesuit. Profoundly discouraged, he abandoned Catholicism for Protestantism. Eventually he married and joined the British Foreign Office, serving in Trabzon, St. Thomas, Manila, Sofia, Bangkok, and Montevideo, where he died.

Never again did his career match the high adventure of his Arabian journey. Although a political and religious failure, it did prove a literary inspiration; his book was a best seller in three languages, but problems remained. He had completed *Narrative of a Year's Journey through Central and Eastern Arabia* in 1865 as he was abandoning his commitment to Rome. Suppressing the Napoleonic and Jesuit intrigue, he filled the pages with adventure, pedantry, and coy hints at some great plot. The *Arabian Nights* style and rumors about the author provoked both popularity and skepticism. But the most severe criticism came from a rival explorer a half-century later. Harry B. St. John Philby claimed that the book was a fraud, written by a master spy who never set foot in Arabia.

Recently uncovered letters, however, have proven that Palgrave made his journey.[22] As to how accurately he reported it, one can only quote his trusted assistant, later patriarch of the Melkite Catholic Church, "Don't believe everything that is written there."[23] But why did he so distort his account? Parallel to the *Journey through . . . Arabia* was a more complex and equally dangerous spiritual journey from Catholic back to Protestant. To survive this second voyage Palgrave had to forget much of the first. What the book cloaked then was not so much espionage as the search for a new identity. *Journey through . . . Arabia* has provoked among generations of critics a profound unease. Although the pretexts for their criticisms have varied, the ultimate source of their discontent was the shifting identity of the author. Gifford Palgrave had no bedrock of identity. He and his work seemed to float upon the shifting sands of deserts he so eloquently described.

Not only had Gifford journeyed from lay Anglican to Jesuit priest and back, he had also traveled back and forth over much of the same spiritual and psychological terrain as his father. For many of his

Jesuit years he resurrected his Jewish origins by calling himself Cohen, under circumstances we shall explore. No hint of this occurs in his published writings, although unlike his father's they do contain abundant references to Jews.[24] Also in contrast to his father's secretive behavior, Gifford's judaizing was flamboyantly public, but it was public only outside of England. The earliest evidence of the syndrome dates from a letter he wrote to his father in 1854 from the Jesuit college in Rome. At the time he was twenty-eight, about the same age as when his father had abandoned Judaism. Unfortunately the letter in question has not survived, but we have a witty reference to it in a second letter, dated April of that year, written by one brother, Reginald Francis Douce Palgrave to another, Robert Harry Inglis Palgrave:

> You will see from Gifford's letter to my Father—how much his mind runs upon the Judaic extraction & so I suppose he would take pleasure in the phiz of a Mosaic lawyer, the contour of whose face I have tried to do justice to down there. By taking Disraeli as a type I have arrived at a very correct appreciation of the peculiarities of our brethren's countenances—The shape of the forehead is as typical as the nose—I am not scientific eno' to say what is signified thereby—but it is very delicate—Dizzy has it in almost exaggerated form—[25]

Note the reference to Disraeli and the sketch (unfortunately not reproduced here) which Reginald penned in the letter; it was undoubtedly a drawing from life by a House of Commons clerk who often watched him in action. But beneath the good humor of Reginald's caricature there lay another slumbering fear. It was as if he were saying to his brother—Beware! Giffie is stirring up our Jewish past; if we be not careful we too will be seen as blatantly Semitic as Disraeli and all our father's efforts to intermarry and pass as a gentile will be for nought. As if to reinforce that last point Reginald ended his letter with a second caricature, contrasting "our brethren's" countenance with a drawing of one of their gentile uncles. Dizzy's lacked "strength of character"; Reginald added, "it is very different from the clifflike form of [Uncle Thomas] Brightwen's for instance."

Another of Gifford's letters from this period conveys again a Judaic preoccupation—specifically with his wandering forefathers—mixed with sincere devotion to his new faith and eagerness to pursue his mission in the lands of his origin:

> For me, what with so frequent change of abode, companions, language &c. I feel equally at home (or, if you wish, equally a stranger and a sojourner, as my fathers were) everywhere. . . . At any rate this is well for me, as this will probably be my

lot henceforth. At present I am in my 1st year, as we call it of theology, four years of study are generally required, and during this time, d.v. I shall receive the Priesthood to be ready to return to Asia, please God, at a moment's notice. And I shall be very glad to do so as this seems to be the field alotted me by the Master.[26]

In 1855, the following year, he fulfilled this earnest desire, a posting to the Jesuit establishment closest to the Holy Land, the Syrian mission, with its headquarters near Beirut. Subsequently his family seems to have lost touch with him—there is no correspondence in the extant archives—and in February 1857 Sir Francis Palgrave wrote to the British consul-general in that city, Noel T. Moore, inquiring after his son, whom he identified as "l'Abbé Giffard [*sic*] Palgrave." Consul Moore discovered and reported to the Foreign Office, and presumably to the father, that this son of "Palgrave of the Rolls Court" was none other than Père Michel Cohen, S.J., who had become a thorn in the consul's side with his "vituperating" comments about the English in general and British Indian policy during the Great Mutiny in particular. Moore's discomfort grew because Palgrave-Cohen was "a most popular preacher in this place, in fact, the only preacher of any note amongst the Native Roman Catholic Community." Moore added that "Father Michael has made it known in this country that he is of Jewish origin from India; he has studiously repudiated his British nationality. Upon asking him the name of his family he said it was that of the 'Cohen'"—no explanation is provided for Michel. Through the French consul (for as a Jesuit he came under that protection), superiors in the Society of Jesus, and finally Lord Cowley, the British ambassador in Paris, Moore made attempts to silence or expel Father Michael, but all failed. In the end Her Majesty's Government decided that he was not worth the effort to notice. But the episode remained to haunt Gifford Palgrave for the rest of his life. The question of Gifford's origins and identity—was he an Indian-born Jew, as he was allegedly claiming and as some records stated?—was discussed and debated at the Quai d'Orsay in Paris and the Jesuit curia in Rome. No one was quite sure who he was.[27]

Some months after this international incident, on 24 February 1858, Gifford wrote his father a letter which began with a description of his mission activities in Syria and concluded with the most explicitly Judaic and Hebraic passages of all his extant correspondence. A close reading suggests the bizarre strains of identity and association which ran through his mind at the time. He viewed the confrontation with the British consul in biblical terms as a struggle between Consul

Haman and Father Mordechai. At a later point someone in the family tried to obliterate that passage, but it and the letter can still be deciphered:

Dearest Father

. . . But to return to Beyrout. In addition to the work of preaching &c of which I have spoken, I have also in hand the superintendance of our day schools, where about forty lads learn French, and eighty more or less, Arab [*sic*—he is clearly translating from the French *l'Arabe*. French and Arabic were the two languages of his daily discourse]. Besides Christians of all rites, Greek, Maronite, &c we have Mahometans and Jews, the latter in great number since that I am become superintendant, by a sort of attraction they belong to the best Hebrew families of the town. During a visit which I paid to one some days since, the conversation fell on Monte-Fiore[*sic*] who visited Jerusalem and passed by Beyrout some time since. He is, if I mistake not, somehow related to us [perhaps through Lady Montefiore whose maiden name was Cohen. However this would have been a very distant connection, simply the family of the descendants of Aaron, but it suggests the way that Gifford's mind was running to his ancestral roots.]: What is his personal name? Should he come here again I should claim his acquaintance, perhaps he would even aid our school [There seems no awareness of the father's donation less than a year earlier, but Gifford had been thousands of miles away at the time.], the only one for the Hebrews here, and the more so because I push them to the study of Hebrew, and do all that I can to maintain them in the patriarchal way of thinking. This indeed I do with respect to all in common, whence I am become great friend with the Arabs in general [Note his combining of Arab and Hebrew, *arav* and *ivri*—doubtless the same in his mind.], and a perfect Paria for the Europeans, [Here begins the crossing out.] *especially for my old acquaintances the English so much so that the British Consul thought himself obliged* [?unclear] *to write to his government complaining of the harm I do them by word and deed. Poor fellow, please God, I will do them yet much more.* [Here it ends.] Meanwhile as I have put myself long before under French protection I laughed at the complaining consul, and with a note to the French Government silenced the English plaints. If it ever happened that you had official dealings with me it is to the French Consul and not to the English with whom I have nothing to do, not even a bow of civility that you should write, for I am the *MORDECHAI* [written in block Hebrew letters] of this latter. Now that I have given you my news, I renew my heart-felt thanks to you, my dearest Father, and to brothers for your joint letters. All together it seems that your health is fairly good, may God prolong it as well as your strength according to this His holy will. Reggie deserves congratulation and praise for his *HATUNAH* [written in block Hebrew letters] [wedding]. I wish that his elders would follow his example. I hope that the blow which commerce has received in these days has not caused any of you loss; God has broken the *EGEL* [written in block Hebrew letters] [calf] of gold which all the world worshipped. Here at Beyrout Christians, Jews and Mahometans are weeping [over] the fragments. It is most true, as you say, that faith is everywhere diminishing. Let us do our best to maintain with God's help what one can of the sacred fire for the *OLAT TAMID* [written in block Hebrew letters] [burnt offering] which must be offered till the end. Whatever way one regards this world, one sees little to comfort much to sorrow over, grief and sin, sickness and death. Such should be the land of pilgrimage and valley of tears, lest we should mistake it for the country. Farewell, dearest Father. I beg very humbly your prayers and blessing for myself and what I have in hand. Best love to Brothers &c.

Your truly affectionate and respectful son[28]

The attraction to the local Jews, the claim about a would-be relative, the biblical references, the Hebrew words scattered across the text (a favorite habit, incidentally, of Heine) all make perfectly clear how deeply committed Gifford had become to his peculiar form of Jewish identity. As this commitment grew it started to assume more and more normatively Jewish forms. His Jesuit colleagues were astounded that he would eat no meat at their table. His knowledge of Hebrew surprised them, but even more shocking was the fact that as he was effortlessly reading aloud a Hebrew manuscript brought for his perusal he stopped in midcourse and refused to pronounce the name of God, the tetragrammaton that pious Jews treat as ineffable.[29]

The adoption of Cohen as his last name was the most public and flamboyant of his judaizing behavior. Since such changes are an obvious indicator of identity this is worth some attention. Until he reached Lebanon in 1855 he had been content with Palgrave, but subsequently he started calling himself Michael Sohail.[30] Sohail is the Arabic for the constellation Canopus. Although there has been speculation about this choice, there is no satisfactory explanation.[31] He may have chosen an Arab name for the convenience of his flock, who would have found Palgrave unpronounceable. The earliest use of his Hebrew name seems to date from 1857, the year of his ordination as a Catholic priest. To be priest by vocation, and by descent as a cohen, might have prompted him to make the change. Calling himself Cohen was one peculiar way of publicly asserting the appropriateness of his new status. However he was inconsistent about this name. In 1857, when he revived his father's name, he did not immediately abandon Sohail. In correspondence with his family and with his Jesuit superiors he continued to use it. Not until his pilgrimage to Palestine in 1859 did he consistently start to call himself Cohen. The first letter so signed was written from Nazareth.[32] Thus it was after establishing a tie with his ancestral land that he publicly proclaimed his ancestral name—a curious parallel to the apparent influence of a voyage to Palestine upon the young Disraeli.[33] Subsequently he used his Jewish name in all his dealings with the Jesuits, as well as the French and papal authorities. With his family he was less consistent, using either

Cohen or Palgrave or both. Significantly it was as Cohen that he conceived and pursued his grandiose political and religious scheme for Arabia.

He also changed his first names. Why abandon William Gifford for Michael? Again the ease of pronouncing a Semitic name might explain it. But perhaps there is more, admittedly speculative. Michael was the name of the archangel, the one charged with casting Lucifer out of heaven.[34] Gifford Palgrave proposed to throw the infidel Turks out of the holy lands of the East. He may also have pondered the question which the words *mi cha-el* ask in Hebrew, who is like unto God? His eventual answer was, a priest, Cohen.

Gifford Palgrave's apparent ruminations about the divine were not limited to the heavens. In his correspondence he furnished continual evidence of his concern for what would happen in the end of days, his insistence that "the *olat tamid* be offered till the end." His awareness of how transitory this world is and how imminent the next appeared even more strongly in the following letter to his father:

> . . . as the Temple remained, in spite of all wars, troubles, schisms and defections till the Messiah came, so the Catholic Church, its continuation and successor will remain till he returns. Would to God I could see all mine counted therein: perhaps they will be one day in God's memory; it is my daily and nightly prayer. Nor can I now imagine what d[amnation awaits??] them without. As for me I have found herein true and unvarying happiness, in sure hope and confide[nce in ?] His Name. Nor do I see without the Ark except a drowning deluge. But enough of this for the present. . . The country is quiet in the main for the moment, but if we have not wars we have rumours of wars; it seems probable that the Egyptian dynasty will ere long swallow up Syria again; so much the better; this Turkish government is worst than nought. Robberies, murders, all kinds of injustice abound; and the Turk does nothing to redress he is even himself the greatest robber. Besides the influence of the European consuls aids the troubles of the land, too many cooks spoil the broth. And as for Religion it looses [*sic*] rather than gains; the very Mahometans become free-thinkers, a bad change; and the Isrealites [*sic*] here are learning to shave like those in Europe.[35]

This last letter presents a strange combination of realpolitik, personal salvation, and perhaps messianic hints—the darkness and the mist before the coming of the light—as we shall see below. Such a mixture of the religious and the political was at the heart of the Arabian mission he started to plan in 1860. Through his own peculiar syncretistic religion and through his own person, a Christ-like notion, Palgrave had already brought together what John Henry Newman in an influential book called the Church of the Fathers,[36] that is, the

Church of Rome, with the church (i.e., synagogue) of his own fathers by becoming Father Cohen, a priest by descent and vocation. The next task was to bring his Muslim brethren into his union as well. The journey through the desert to convert and unite the Arabs grew out of his conviction that as one son of Abraham he was uniquely qualified to bring the truth of the New Israel to the other offspring of Abraham, the children of Hagar. The reference in his long letter of 1858 to "the patriarchal way of thinking," coupled with his combining of Arab and Hebrew, reveals his particular ethno-religious vision. Like most of his contemporaries—not just Heine and Disraeli—Gifford Palgrave was convinced of the unity of Abrahamic descent. Ultimately all were Semites, all of the desert, and all worshiped one God. In a lengthy memorandum he prepared for the Society of Jesus on the eve of his departure for the East in 1861, *Eclaircissement sur la nation arabe, la manière d'y implanter le Christianisme. . . ,*[37] he wrote that the Arabs of central Arabia—whose Wahhabi inhabitants were the prime object of his mission—were the purest of the Arabs, descendants for the most part of Ishmael, though mixed with some children of Abraham by Keturah as well as some of Esau's offspring. They had succeeded the best in preserving "the traditions of patriarchal life, its attitudes and its customs." Among them nomadic life was preferred to life in the cities and they gloried in deprivation and strain rather than wealth and rest. He recognized, however, that other influences were present in the peninsula as well. The inhabitants of western Arabia, the Hejaz, were also descendants of Ishmael. But here they were intermingled with numerous Jewish tribes who gave them a peculiar character. Thence came the Judaic element in "Mohammedanism." Craftier than the highlanders of central Arabia, of a more civilized spirit, they were also more malicious. Their possession of the sacred precinct of Mecca gave them a strong moral influence over the Arab nation, despite their numerical inferiority. Devout pagans and opinionated Jews converted to Islam centuries earlier and became zealous apostles who in less than fifty years brought all of the Arabian peninsula under the rule of the chiefs of the Hejaz. Palgrave had wished to maintain "the patriarchal way of thinking" among his Hebrew flock in Beirut, but only "with respect to all in common." However much of a judaizer he had become, there were limits. The attitudes toward Jews in this document composed for his Jesuit brethren is remarkably different from that expressed to his family. Here they are the pejorative "juifs opiniâtres," malicious and crafty. There they were Hebrews and Israelites, the polite and positive designations of the nineteenth century. Clearly each audience required a different tone, but which was his sincere expression? Like Heine's internally contradictory attitudes and Disraeli's distinction between people and religion, Palgrave's feelings about his origin also were mixed. However, a personal letter should be regarded as a more candid indicator of attitudes than a policy memorandum. In addressing his superiors he had to use language which would appeal to their prejudices so that his risky and unorthodox proposal would be supported. It would be useful to compare Gifford's tone here to what he was writing at the same time to his father. Unfortunately none of those letters has survived. The memorandum was composed in June 1861. His father died in July (his mother, who has played little role in this account, had died nine years earlier). With Sir Francis's death Gifford had lost his only Jewish correspondent.

The proof texts, cited, though not quoted, in an earlier memorandum, *Possibilité de la conversion des Arabes de l'Asie, et manière de l'opérer*,[38] clarify the messianic hopes he held. His mission to the Arabs, their political unification and religious conversion, was surely a step in the second coming. Isaiah 60 supported his claim:

> Arise, be enlightened, O Jerusalem; for thy light is come, and the glory of the Lord is risen upon thee. For behold darkness shall cover the earth, and a mist the people; but the Lord shall rise upon thee. And the Gentiles shall walk in thy light, and kings in the brightness of thy rising. . . . The multitude of camels shall cover thee, the dromedaries of Madian and Epha: all they from Saba shall come, bringing gold and frankincense, and showing forth praise to the Lord. All the flocks of Cedar [Kedar] shall be gathered unto thee. . . .

So also did the prophecy of Psalm 72 (71 in the Vulgate):

> . . . the kings of the Arabians and of Saba shall bring gifts and all the kings of the earth shall adore him [Christ], all nations shall serve him. . . . Therefore he shall live and they shall give to him the gold of Arabia. . . .[39]

To make certain his biblical references were not lost, he ended his note with the words of Isaiah (60:6) taken from the mass of the day, "Inundatio camelorum operiet te, dromedarii Madian et Epha; omnes de Saba venient aurum et thus deferentes et laudem Domino annuntiantes."

Although Gifford Palgrave wrote numerous precise and businesslike proposals covering the practical and religious issues of his mission, such as the question of rite, the matter of episcopal organization, and the formation of native priests, one still wonders what ultimate religious vision possessed this wildly eccentric man. These sober memorandums seem strangely inappropriate.[40] They clearly address ecclesiastically vital matters, but they seem forced. His heart was not in them. And in fact as soon as he was away from Rome, and on his own, he proceeded to ignore almost everything which he previously accepted, particularly concerning the proper conduct of a priest alone on such a dangerous mission. Moreover, he pretended to be a Muslim. One could speculate that in fact he had an even more breathtaking plan, which he kept hidden from his superiors and in a certain sense from himself, one more consistent with his eccentricity. The new political constellation of Arab and Semitic unity which he was about to create in the East through the leadership of the Wahhabis would hasten the second coming of the messiah, who is like unto God, and end the Catholic Church which remains only "till he returns." In its place Father Mi cha-el Cohen, S.J., would hasten the advent of a new faith unifying all three. This kind of vision is consistent with the syncretism of his own religious practice as well as with an impulse common to other converts, that is, the desire to found a new religion which will encompass both the old and the new community. There is some evidence to hint that such a vision was in his mind.[41]

When his plot to organize an Arab revolt was uncovered by the Ottomans in 1863 and he was barred from the East by his Jesuit superiors, his vision and faith were lost.[42] He had returned to being a Cohen by returning to his ancestral home of Palestine, but once he was forced into exile again to be "a stranger and a sojourner, as my fathers were," as he wrote in his letter of March 1854, he could no longer be either a Jewish priest or a Catholic Cohen.

The circumstances of his leaving the Jesuits and returning to Protestantism need not detain us here, but it is worth noting that in his new career as a Foreign Office official, the fact that he was an ex-Catholic, Jesuit, and agent for Napoleon III was more troubling than that he was of Jewish origin. There were some antisemitic outbursts by a former colleague and rival, but that was an exception.[43]

Despite all his judaizing and despite his varied religious experimentation—he dabbled in Islam, Shintoism, Eastern Orthodoxy, and Buddhism and before his death returned to Catholicism—he never actually became a Jew, perhaps because, like Heine, he always regarded himself as a kind of Jew. Indeed Father Cohen's restless soul and ever-wandering religious vision were clearly shaped by an idiosyncratic sense of his Jewish past. And it is this sense of Jewishness lost that helps us find the key to the mysteries of his bizarre life. Gifford Palgrave's life demonstrates that conversion and assimilation, however successful on the surface, could still create inner tensions over two generations of new Christians in Victorian England. His brothers, for whatever reasons, seem not to have been troubled by these concerns, but Gifford clearly was. The constancy of his religious quest illustrates the spiritual rootlessness that conversion could foster. With all the estrangement attendant upon conversion, both generations still retained a certain identity, curiosity, and pride in their stock which was made manifest through intellectual curiosity and, in one case, spiritual neediness.

The curious path that Gifford Palgrave followed to judaizing, from Anglicanism to Catholicism, and then to his Jewish period, illustrates a phenomenon at work in upper-class English society. The Tractarian movement, with its emphasis on tradition, ritual, and dogma, the attempt to return the Church of England to a character consistent with its authentic past, was consonant with a certain romantic temper prevalent in the midnineteenth century.[44] The logic of the movement, particularly its insistent desire to confront the present church with its ancestral pre-Reformation origins, brought many of its exponents and followers first to try to make over the Anglican church into an Anglo-Catholic church, and when not satisfied with that to take the next step and return to Catholicism itself, for clearly the roots of their church were in Rome. This same logic had a highly confusing effect on Jewish converts to Anglicanism who took their new faith seriously. If they were to confront the Church of England with the faith, traditions, ritual, and dogma of their own ancestors—which the Tractarians were urging as the true test of authenticity for the church in general—then they would risk rejecting the new faith they had just accepted. Socially and practically such a step was impossible, but there were other ways of maintaining authenticity. Disraeli did so, paradoxically enough, by inventing his own glorious Jewish past. Sir Francis Palgrave did so in a much more private and less flamboyant way by acquiring and supporting Jewish scholarship. And Gifford Palgrave did so by pursuing a peculiar path through each step of its logical course, like Newman from Canterbury to Rome, then back to the temple in Jerusalem as a Cohen of the New Israel, and then like his forefather Abraham as a wanderer in the desert.

There is another larger point to be drawn from this story. Clearly it must be seen against the background of Jewish emancipation, the movement that brought Jews out of the self-contained legally autonomous community of the ghetto into the modern world as individuals, citizens of the newly invented nation-state, free and equal, tremulous and insecure. The challenge that all who came through this process faced was, in Sir Isaiah Berlin's words, how "to replant themselves in some new and no less secure and nourishing soil." For some, like Disraeli, with his image of the Jew as the true aristocrat at the head of the English aristocracy, and Gifford Palgrave, with his scheme for religious convergence and national independence—the Arabs, after all, were no less than "Jews on horseback" in Disraeli's phrase—there was a need for firm moorings and "since they were not born with them, [they] invented them. They did this only at a price of ignoring a good deal of reality seen by less agonised, more ordinary, but saner men"[45]—how else could Disraeli and Palgrave have conceived their plots, Dizzy in his novels and Giffie in his life?

The context of emancipation helps us to understand the essential differences between the Heine-Disraeli syndrome and earlier types of conversion, Marrano or Pauline for example. The Heine-Disraeli syndrome is not known before this period. In ancient and medieval times converts from Judaism, whatever their motives, abandoned both faith and community. Of course the Marrano entered a kind of way-station that was neither completely Christian nor completely Jewish, but he could no longer return openly and publicly to the company, let alone the practices, of Jews without risking the inquisitorial charge of judaizing. With emancipation, community was willy-nilly abandoned. Converted and unconverted, consciously or not, many now existed in a state of *anomie*. Paradoxically it was thus both easier and harder to cease to be Jewish. The elements of Jewish identity—at least in terms of the external notions of Jewishness—were much less certain and could be slipped on and off with fewer constraints. While conversion had become much more accessible, it had also become much less complete.

APPENDIX:
Sir Francis Palgrave's Hebraica and Judaica

The following list is taken from the *Catalogue of the Extensive and Valuable Library of the Late Sir Francis Palgrave* (London: S. Leigh Sotheby & John Wilkinson, 1862). The bibliographical information is presented exactly and in the same order as in the original catalogue. The numbers indicate the lot number in the sale of these 113 titles.

20. Alexander (L.) Hebrew Ritual, 1819

Levi (D.) Ceremonies of the Jews, n.d.

and 1 other

28. Michaelis (J.D.) Anfangs Gründe der Hebräischen Accentuation, Halle, 1753

44. Apocrypha Hebraice emissit Seckel Isaac Fraenkel, Lips., 1830

116. Benjamin of Tudela (Rabbi) Itinerary in Hebrew and English, translated and edited by A. Asher, with notes and Essays, 2 vol., Berlin, 1840–1841

130. Biblia Hebraica sine Punctis, Amsterdam, 1630

131. Biblia Hebraica, in 5 parts

and 4 others, Hebrew [!]

186. Abrahamae Patriarchae Liber Jezirah cum Commentario Rabi Abraham, Heb. et Lat. cum notis J.S. Rittangelii, Amsterdam, 1642

194. Atias (Ishac) Tesoro de Preceptos, Venecia, 1627

347. Decius (Br.) Die Hebräischen Mysterien oder die älteste religiöse Freymaurerey, Leipzig, 1788

363. Buxtorfi (J.) Florilegium Hebraicum et Grammatica Chaldaica et Syriaca, 2 vol. in 1, Basileae, 1648–1650

364. Buxtorfi (J.) de Abbreviaturis Hebraicis Liber et Bibliotheca Rabbinica, Herbornae, 1708

Abrahami Ben Dior Commemoratio Rerum Romanarum ad Tempora Muchammedis, Heb. et Lat. cum Notis A.C. Zelleri, Stutgardiae, 1724

Buxtorfi (J.) Thesaurus Grammaticis Linguae Hebraeae, Basileae, 1629

Bythneri (V.) Lyra Prophetica Davidis, Tiguri, 1676

Psalmi, Hebraice, cum Notis A. Hulsii, Lugd, Bat., 1650

Leopold (E.F.) Lexicon Hebraicum et Chaldaicum, Lipsiae, 1832

485. Decalogus cum Commentario Rabbi Aben Ezra, Heb. et Lat. cura S. Munsteri, Basileae, 1527

Seder Olam Rabba (Chronologia major) Heb. et Lat. cura G. Genebrardi, ib., 1580

507. Dessauer (J.H.) Leschon Rabbananm oder Aramäisch-Chaldäisch-Rabbinisch-Deutsches Wörterbuch, interleaved, Erlangen, 1849

Auswahl historischer Stücke aus Hebräischen Schriftstellern mit Uebersetzung, Berlin, 1840

Corve (C.J.) Chrestomathia Rabbinica cum Versione Latina et Vitis Scriptorum, ib. 1844

568. Biblia Hebraica eleganti Charactere (cum Punctis) impressa ex Recensione Menasseh Ben Israel, Amsterdam, 1635

569. Biblia Hebraica, 2 vol.

and 5 others [!], Hebrew

683. Dukes (L.) Zur Kenntniss der Neuhebräischen religiösen Poesie, Frankfurt, 1842, (2 copies, the second bound with)

684. Munk (S.) Sur Abou'l-Walid Merwan Ibn Djana'h et sur quelques autres Grammairiens Hebreux du Xe et du XIe Siecle, Paris, 1851

685. Dukes (L.) Rabbinsche Blumenlese, mit Glossarium, Leipzig, 1844

701. Edelman (H.) and L. Dukes, Treasures of Oxford, containing Poetical Compositions by ancient Jewish Authors in Spain, in Hebrew, with English Translation by M.H. Breslau, Part 1, 1851

Nachal Kedumim, Heb. von L. Dukes, 1853

and 3 others [!]

703. Edrehi (M.) Historical Account of the Ten Tribes settled beyond the Sambatyon, portrait and map, 1836

728. Ewald (G.H.A.) Kritische Grammatik der Hebräischen Sprache, Leipzig, 1827

733. Fabricii (J.A.) Pseudepigraphis Veteris Testamenti, 2 vol., Hamburg, 1713

755. Fleury (C.) Moeurs des Israelites et des Chretiens, Paris, 1766

774. Friedrich (C.W.) Unterricht in der Judensprache und Schrift, Prentzlow, 1784

792. Genesis in Hebrew and English, with notes by Rev. D.A. De Sola, J.L. Lindenthal, and Rev. M.J. Raphall, 1844

793. Genesis and Exodus, in Hebrew, with a new Translation and a historical and critical Commentary by M.M. Kalisch, 2 vol. MS. notes, 1858–1855 [sic]

795. Gesenii (G.) Lexicon manuale Hebraicum et Chaldaicum, Lipsiae, 1833

796. Gesenius (W.) Lehrgebaeude der Hebräischen Sprache, Leipzig, 1817

Gesenius (W.) Hebräische Grammatik, Halle, 1831

797. Gesenius (W.) Hebräisches and Chaldäisches Wörterbuch, Leipzig, 1828

803. Giles (J.A.) Heathen Records to the Jewish Scripture History collected and translated, with original text, 1856

856. Cardoso (Yshak) Las Excelencias (y Calunias) de los Hebreos, Amsterdam, 1679

***A very curious work, in which is to be found the refutation of the calumny of the Jews murdering young children. On the title-page Sir Francis Palgrave has written 'Very rare. F.P.'"

881. Gosri Liber continens Colloquium de Religione inter Regem Cosareorum et R. Isaacum Sangarum Heb. et Lat. cum Notis J. Buxtorfi, MS notes, Basileae, 1660

1105. Hurwitz (H.) Elements of the Hebrew Language, 1829

1123. Jedaia (Rabbi Jacob) Bachinas Olim [sic], on Examen du Monde en Hebreu et Francois; Sentences morales des anciens Hebreux en Heb. Fr. et Italien; et les treize Modes desquelles ils se servoient pour interpreter la Bible en Heb. et Latin. Traduicts par P. d'Aquin, 3 vol. in 1, Paris, 1629

1127. Jobi Liber Heb. et Lat. cum Notis R. Grey, 1742

Second Lessons for the Morning Service in Hebrew, edited by Rev. R. Caddick, 1798

Ben Ezra (Rabbi A.) Jesod Mora sive Fundamentum Pietatis Heb. et Lat. curante M. Creizenach, Francof, 1840

Trattato Morale Heb. et Ital. da S. Calimani e J. Saravel

1131. Jost (J.M.) Geschichte der Israeliten seit der Zeit der Maccabär bis auf unsere Tage, 9 vol. in 5, Berlin, 1820–1828

1144. Kennicott (B.) State of the printed Hebrew Text of the Old Testament considered, 2 vol. Oxford, 1753–1759

1154. Koegleri (I.) Notitiae SS. Bibliorum Judaeorum in Imperio Sinensi. Seriem chronologicam atque Diatriben de Sinicis SS. Bibliorum Versionibus addidit C.T. de Murr, Halae ad Salam, 1805

1177. Eisenmenger (J.A.) Entdecktes Judenthum, 2 vol. in 1, Königsberg, 1711

1281. Psalterium Quadruplex, being the Psalter in Hebrew and Greek, with the Vulgate Latin Version and St. Jerome's Translation [sic] Basileae, 1516

1302. Josephi (Flavii) Opera Gr. and Lat. cum Notis J. Hudsoni, 2 vol. Oxford, 1743

1340. Levi (D.) Lingua Sacra (Hebrew Grammar and Dictionary) 5 vol., 1803

1407. Maimonides (Rabbi) Laws of the Hebrews relating to the Poor and the Stranger, with notes by J.W. Peppercorne, 1850

Maimonides (Rabbi) Creed and Ethics of the Jews, with notes by H.H. Bernard, Cambridge, 1832

and three others respecting Maimonides [!]

1424. Manasseh ben Israel, the Conciliator, with notes by H. Lindo, 2 vol. 1842

1449. Menasseh [sic] ben Israel de Fragilitate humana ex Lapsu Adami, Amsterdam, 1642

————, Problemata de Creatione, ib., 1635

————, Spes Israelis, ib. 1650

1473. Milman (Rev. H.) History of the Jews, 3 vol. 1829

1482. Mishna, Eighteen Treatises from, translated by Rev. D.A. De Sola and Rev. M.J. Raphall, 1845

1483. Mishna. Pirke Aboth oder Sprüche der Väter, Heb. und Deutsch von Dr. P. Ewald, Erlangen, 1825

Dessauer (J.H.) Paradigmen, Erlangen 1838

1498. Montefiore (Lady) Notes from a private Journal of a Visit to Egypt and Palestine by Way of Italy and the Mediterranean, privately printed, presentation copy, 1844

1506. Mosaica Praecepta DCXIII cum Rabbinorum Expositione, Heb. et Lat. Cura S. Munsteri. Henry VIIIth's copy, Basileac, n.d.

1538. Jehuda ha-Levi Das Buch Kusari, Hebräisch and Deutsch herausgeben von Dr. D. Cassel, Leipzig, 1853

1543. Jose Ben Chelpheta de Tzippuri (Rabbi) Seder Olam Rabba et Seder Olam Zuta Auctore R. Joseph Toboh Elam sive Chronicon Hebraeorum Majus et Minus Heb. et Lat. cum Commentario perpetuo illustravit J. Meyer, Amsterdam, 1706

1544. Josephus Gorionides sive Josephus Hebraicus, Heb. et Lat. cum notis J.F. Breithaupti, Gotha, 1707

1548. Kabbala denudata cum Libro Sohar et Porta Coelorum (Auctore C. Knorr a Rosenroth) 4 vol., Sulzbachi, 1677 et Francof., 1684

1608. Maimonidis (Mosis) Mora Nevochim, cum Commentario, Hebraice, Jesnitz, 1742

and one other in Hebrew [!]

1651. Moses Ben Esra aus Granada. Darstellung seines Lebens und literarischen Wirkens nebst Hebräischen Beylagen und Deutschen Uebersetzungen von L. Dukes, Altona, 1839

Dukes (L.) Ehrensaeulen und Denksteine zu einem kunftigen Pantheon Hebräischer Dichter und Dichtungen mit Hebräischen Beylagen und Deutschen Uebersetzungen, Wien, 1837

Massecheth Derech Erez Sutta, Heb. und Deutsch von J. Harburger, Bayreuth, 1839

1661. Munsteri (S.) Compendium Hebraicae Grammaticae, Basileae, 1529

Eliae Levitae Capitula Cantici, Specierum, Proprietatum et Officiorum Hebraice cum Versione Latina S. Munsteri, ib., 1527

Eliae Levitae [?] Grammatica Hebraica cum Versione Latina S. Munsteri, ib. 1525

136

1824. Powell (Rev. B) On Christianity without Judaism, 1857

1826. Prayers (Form of) for the New Year, Hebrew and English, 5586 [1826]

1831. Psalms in Hebrew, with a Commentary by Rev. G. Phillips, 2 vol. in 1, 1846

1833. Psalmorum Liber, Hebraice, curante C.G.G. Theile 3 copies, Lipsiae, 1851

1856. Maimonides (R. Moses) de Fundamentis Legis, Heb. et Lat., Amsterdam, 1638

1857. Maimonidis [sic] (R. Mosis) More Nevochim, Latine, cura J. Buxtorfi, Basileae, 1629

Abravenel (R. Isaac) de Capite Fidei, translatus per G. Vorstium, Amsterdam, 1638

1858. Maimonides (R. Moses) de Jure Pauperis et Peregrini apud Judaeos, Heb. et Lat. cum notis H. Prideaux, Oxford, 1679

1880. Mischna sive totius Hebraeorum Juris, Rituum, Antiquitatum ac Legum Oralium Systema, cum Commentariis Maimonidis et Bartenorae, Hebraice, 6 vol. in 2, Berlin, 1832

2088. Sachs (Dr. M.) Die religiöse Poesie der Juden in Spanien, with Hebrew specimens at end, Berlin, 1845

2095. Philon Juif ses Oeuvres, translatees par P. Bellier, Paris, 1612

2168. Spinoza (B.) Oeuvres, traduites par E. Saisset, 2 vol., Paris, 1842

2515. Zunz (Dr.) Zur Geschichte und Literatur, Erster Band, Berlin, 1845

2516. Zunz (Dr.) Die synagogale Poesie des Mittelalters, Berlin, 1855

Zunz (Dr.) Die Gottesdienstlichen Vorträge der Juden historisch entwickelt, 2 vol., Berlin, 1832

2562. Toovey (D'Blossiers) Anglia Judaica, Oxford, 1738

2610. Thomassin (L.) Glossarium universale Hebraicum, Paris, 1697

NOTES

1. This discussion of Heine is drawn from *Encyclopedia Judaica*, s.v. "Heinrich Heine," and Siegbert S. Prawer, *Heine's Jewish Comedy: A Study of His Portraits of Jews and Judaism* (Oxford: Clarendon Press, 1983).

2. The most useful discussion of Disraeli is Todd M. Endelman, "Disraeli's Jewishness Reconsidered," *Modern Judaism* 5 (1985): 109–23.

3. Details on the Palgraves are drawn from my "The Spiritual Quest of William Gifford Palgrave: A Jesuit Mission to Arabia" (B. A. thesis, Harvard University, 1967)

and "Bedouins and Priests, Napoleon III's Middle East Adventure" (graduate seminar paper, Harvard University, 1968), as well as Mea Allan, *Palgrave of Arabia* (London: Macmillan, 1972).

4. Hambro Synagogue records, entries for 1785–92 and 1795, Archives of the United Synagogue, London. For the Cohen business failures, see the *Gentleman's Magazine* 28 (1758): 453; 37 (1767): 528; 40 (1770): 280.

5. *Chanson moult pitoyable des grievouses Oppressions qe la povre Commune de Engleterre souffre soubz la Cruelte des Justices de Trayllbastun. Le Flabel du Jongleur de Ely e de Monseignour le Roy de Engletere. Chaunt de fust fet sur la mort de Symon de Mountfort nadgweres Cuens de Leycestre (de la Bataile de Eowesham)*, London, 1818.

6. A. N. L. Munby, "Dawson Turner of Yarmouth" (lecture delivered at London University, 22 November 1960).

7. Quoted in Allan, *Palgrave*, p. 44.

8. Sir R. H. Inglis Palgrave, ed., *The Collected Historical Works of Sir Francis Palgrave, K. H.*, 10 vols. (Cambridge: Cambridge University Press, 1919–22).

9. Todd M. Endelman, *The Jews of Georgian England, 1714–1830: Tradition and Change in a Liberal Society* (Philadelphia: Jewish Publication Society, 1979), p. 260.

10. Lewis Edwards, "A Remarkable Family: The Palgraves," in *Remember the Days: Essays on Anglo-Jewish History Presented to Cecil Roth* (London: Jewish Historical Society of England, 1966), p. 298.

11. Allan, *Palgrave*, p. 43. This book furnishes no references; however it is based on thorough use of the Palgrave family papers.

12. Gwenllian F. Palgrave, *Francis Turner Palgrave: His Journals and Memories of his Life* (London, New York, and Bombay: Longmans, Green and Co., 1899), p. 2.

13. On this see Braude, "Spiritual Quest," pp. 20–24; Palgrave, *Francis Turner Palgrave*, p. 211; as well as excerpts from the following letters by William Gifford Palgrave to his mother Elizabeth Turner Palgrave:

> At Rouenne we [Sir Francis and Giffie] made acquaintance with a very good-tempered Padre, who after some conversation, opened a whole battery of controversy in a most catechetical style. "Que pensez vous de—&c. &c." I declined giving my definitions in a language of which I was so little master; and then we discussed faith; and he was very inquisitive about "Dr. Pusea" [E. B. Pusey, one of the early Tractarians], whose name he knew well. But as for Mr. Newman, he had never heard anything about him, so much further do words go than things; and I thought that it would be vain to mention the Author of the Ideal. (21–26 August 1844)

and "We have read our service, and Dr. Newman today. . . ." 24 August 1844, both Palgrave Family Archives, London.

14. *The Education of Henry Adams: An Autobiography* (Boston and New York: Houghton Mifflin Co., 1930), p. 214.

15. Robert Mane, *Henry Adams on the Road to Chartres* (Cambridge: Harvard

University Press, 1971); *The Letters of Henry Adams, 1858–1892*, ed. Jacob Claver Levenson et al., 3 vols. (Cambridge: Harvard University Press, 1982) 2: 511–12.

16. *Collected Historical Works*, 4: 322 and 10: 105–6, for example. The former reference suggests a certain degree of sympathy for the Jewish plight during the Crusades. The latter reference is the only published suggestion that he knew Hebrew, ironically in discussing the etymology of Yule or Christmas day.

17. G. P. Gooch, *History and Historians in the Nineteenth Century* (Boston: Beacon Press, 1968), pp. 268–71; *Collected Historical Works*, 6: iii–v.

18. See Appendix, Sir Francis Palgrave's Hebraica and Judaica.

19. Montefiore Letter Book, Loewe Family Archives, London.

20. For a sense of the Tractarian influence at Trinity College, Oxford, when Gifford Palgrave studied there, see William R. W. Stephens, *The Life and Letters of Edward A. Freeman* (London and New York: Macmillan and Co., 1895), 1: 43–46.

21. Pierre Martin, S.J., "Lettre de Mallakah, 3 avril 1863," *Messager du Sacré Coeur* 4 (1863): 36–37.

22. Benjamin Braude, "Palgrave and His Critics, the Origins and Implications of a Controversy: Part One, the Nineteenth Century—the Abyssinian Imbroglio," *Arabian Studies* 7 (1985): 97–138; for an assessment of Palgrave's explorations in the context of other Arabian travelers, see Benjamin Braude, "The Explorers," in *The History of Transportation in Arabia*, ed. Milbry Polk (Cambridge: Cambridge University Press, forthcoming).

23. Michel Jullien, S. J., *Histoire de la nouvelle mission de la cie. de Jésus en Syrie. Notes et additions confidentielles . . .* (Tours, 1898), p. 13.

24. William Gifford Palgrave, *Narrative of a Year's Journey through Central and Eastern Arabia* (London and Cambridge: Macmillan, 1865), 1: 22–23, 35, 119, 130, 193–94, 240–41, 250, 266, 465; 2: 73, 216, 263, 365–66, 377; and *Ulysses* (London: Macmillan, 1887), p. 209.

25. R. F. D. Palgrave to R. H. I. Palgrave, 20[?] April 1854, Palgrave Family Archives, London.

26. W. G. Palgrave to R. H. I. Palgrave, 25 March 1854, Palgrave Family Archives.

27. Braude, "Palgrave and His Critics I," pp. 98–99; C. Sommervogel, *Bibliothèque de la Compagnie de Jésus* (Brussels and Paris, 1891), 2: 1271; and statement of André de Damas, S. J., Procurator of the Jesuit mission in Mount Lebanon to Thouvenel, Minister of Foreign Affairs, 8 March 1860, Archives du Ministère des affaires étrangères, Mémoires et Documents, Turquie, 122, no. 31, fols, 367–68.

28. W. G. Palgrave to Sir F. Palgrave, 24 February 1858, Palgrave Family Archives.

29. Jullien, *Notes*, p. 13; "I gave the North Star the name which in the Hebrew

Bible [note: not the Old Testament] in the Book of Exodus, is attributed as the uncommunicable title of God, the well-known name composed of the letters JAH. . . . I only repeat what they say; for God forbid that anyone should make anything like an improper allusion to the very name by which God revealed Himself to Moses in sacred history." Gifford Palgrave, S. J., "Notes of a Journey from Gaza, through the interior of Arabia, to El Khatif on the Persian Gulf, and thence to Oman, in 1862–63," *Proceedings of the Royal Geographical Society* 8(1863–64): 80.

30. Miscellanea Epistolae P. Cohen (= Sohail = Palgrave), Missio Syriae, 1848–60, Syr. 3, fasc. VII, Archivum Romanum Societatis Iesu.

31. Mea Allan suggested that Canopus may have been his star, *Palgrave*, p. 133. There is no evidence to corroborate her second assertion that Sohail was a common name among Jews. Among the bedouin of the Sinai and the Negev, the constellation Sohail has the reputation of a proverbial inconstant, an indecisive person. However, we do not know if this lore reached Syria where Palgrave could have come to learn it. Furthermore, it would seem unlikely that he would have chosen such a prophetically critical name for himself at this stage in his life. Clinton Bailey, "Bedouin Star-Lore in Sinai and the Negev," *Bulletin of the School of Oriental and African Studies* 37 (1974): 583. I thank Dr. Frank Stewart for calling this proverb to my attention.

32. Michael Cohen, S.J., to Father General Pieter Beckx, Nazareth, 2 May 1859, Syr. 3. VII, 9, Archivum Romanum Societatis Iesu.

33. Robert Blake, *Disraeli's Grand Tour: Benjamin Disraeli and the Holy Land, 1830–31* (New York: Oxford University Press, 1982), p. 106, quoted in Endelman, "Disraeli's Jewishness," p. 120.

34. I thank Prof. James Michael Weiss for calling Michael's role to my attention.

35. Michael Cohen, S.J., to Sir Francis Palgrave, 5 November 1859, Palgrave Family Archives, London.

36. G. F. Palgrave, *Francis Turner Palgrave*, p. 34.

37. Michel-Xavier Cohen, S.I., Rome, 19 June 1861, Syr. 4. VIII, 7, Archivum Romanum Societatis Iesu.

38. 10 January 1861, Syr. 4. VIII, 1, Archivum Romanum Societatis Iesu.

39. These translations are taken from the Douay version, translated from the Vulgate, the particlar edition is New York: Catholic Book Publishing Company, 1949–50. The verses from Isaiah were included as a special reading, a proper for the Octave of the Epiphany, the festival commemorating the manifestation of Christ to the gentiles, in the persons of the Magi. I thank Prof. Paul Russell for this explanation.

40. For example, *Annotationes quae ad pleniorem Missionis Arabicae intelligentiam*, Syr. 4. VIII, 5; and *Sur la question si dans le premier voyage on doit prendre avec soi un Père Jesuit pour compagnon ou non*, Syr. 4. VIII, 6, Archivum Romanum Societatis Iesu.

41. Most particularly in his judaizing behavior while a member of the Jesuit mission in Syria. Jullien, *Histoire*, p. 13.

42. Giuseppe Valerga to Cardinal Alessandro Barnabo, 15 September 1863, Scritture Riferite nei Congressi Siria, 1860–73, 1, 353, Archivio dalla sacra congregazione "de Propaganda Fidei."

43. Braude, "Palgrave and His Critics," particularly pp. 110 and 130.

44. For an example of a similar obsession with origins among other Victorians, see Braude, "Explorers," section on Doughty.

45. Isaiah Berlin, *Against the Current: Essays in the History of Ideas*, ed. Henry Hardy (London: Hogarth Press, 1979), p. 284.

5

Jewish Conversion in Hungary in Modern Times

WILLIAM O. McCAGG, Jr.

IN most European countries and in the United States in the past two or
three centuries there have been conversions from Judaism to Christianity. This has happened in Hungary too. In most countries, however, such conversions have occurred in fairly small numbers and have
not resulted in new demographic categories with special names, such
as the "Marranos" in the sixteenth and seventeenth centuries. In
Hungary by contrast conversions occurred in large numbers and
converts came to form precisely such a demographic category. According to the Hungarian census of 1941, there were 61,548 people in the
country's population who were called "Christians of Jewish Descent."[1]
In that same year a new "Jewish Law" (the third of its kind) redefined
Jewishness to include not just people who had converted since 1919,
but also all people who had at least two grandparents born as members
of a Jewish community. This meant that the "Christian Jew" census
figure had to be expanded to about 80,000. After 1941 the "Christian
Jew" category continued to grow because of conversions: by 1944,
according to postwar estimates, there were at least 100,000 "Christian
Jews" in Hungary.[2] At the end of the catastrophic summer of that
year, there were some 80,000 bearers of conversion documents (often
forged) just in Budapest, the only part of Hungary where Jews still
survived.[3]

   How can one account for this phenomenon? This is the basic
question of this paper. In answering it, we will touch on questions of
population, of law, and of sociology; but basically our approach will be

historical, for explanations are to be found not just in immediate circumstances, but deep in the two-centuries-long record of modern Hungarian Jewry.[4]

It is useful to begin with matters of demography. According to Ruppin's familiar survey of world Jewry in 1938, the Hungarian Jewish community was the fourth largest in Europe and the fifth largest in the world.[5] It numbered 440,000 people, and gave place only to the vast Jewish populations of the United States, the Soviet Union, and Poland, and to the 800,000 Jews in Rumania. The Hungarian community was then about double the size of the one in France, four times as large as the historic community in Holland, a third again as large as the community in Britain, and almost as large as the Jewry of pre-Hitler Germany. Hungarian Jewry comprised 5.1 percent of the general population: only in Poland, the Ukraine, and Belo-Russia was the proportion higher. In western Europe the Jewish proportion of the general population nowhere even approached that figure.

To review the population situation only a few years earlier or later than 1938 is to gain an even greater sense of the size of Hungarian Jewry. In 1910, in the last Austro-Hungarian census, there had been 932,458 Jews in Greater Hungary, comprising 4.5 percent of the population. Hungarian Jewry had then been the third largest Jewish community in the world.[6] Only a few years after 1938 Hitler returned to tiny interwar Hungary some of the territories she had lost by the peace treaty of 1919–20 and thus radically diminished the number of Jews in Rumania. As a result, by January 1941 there were 725,007 Jews in Hungary, the fourth largest Jewish community in the world.

These numbers serve to put the "Christian Jew" phenomenon of the interwar period into context. Even in 1941 "Christian Jews" were equal to only about 10 percent of the entire Hungarian Jewish population (61,000 to 80,000 out of 725,000). Considering the circumstances, it is surprising that it was not a much higher proportion. A comparison between conversion rates in Hungary and those in other countries also reveals how relatively small the per capita rate of defection was. According to a recent study of Bohemian Jews by Michael Riff, about 90 persons left Judaism annually in Bohemia in the 1890s and early 1900s—about 0.1 percent of the total Jewish population each year. The corresponding figure for the city of Vienna was 573 annually, or 0.4 percent.[7] In Hungary, by contrast, the 476 who seceded in 1900 represented about 0.05 percent. Even in the thirties the conversion rate in Hungary was per capita no more than in neighboring lands. In Prague, the average annual rate of secession in the middle thirties was 185, or 0.46 percent of the city's Jewish population; in Vienna in 1936 there were 647 secessions, or 0.38 percent;[8] yet in Budapest in 1935, with the figures skyrocketing to 890, the percentage was only 0.43 percent.[9]

Demography regards not only the size of populations, but popular migration. This is a subject of great importance in Hungarian Jewish history, and in fact leads to some first explanations of the numerous conversions there. In the early eighteenth century probably only some 4,000 Jews lived in Hungary, half the number in the city of Prague. By the end of the eighteenth century, however, there were 80,000. This was double the number of Jews in France at the time, about the same number as in the Bohemian Crownlands, and about a third of the number counted then in all of Austrian Poland. Most of the increment was due to immigration from Bohemia and Moravia, where Jews were then prevented by law from freely marrying. Thereupon, in the wake of the final agonies of the Polish state, a vast new immigration of Jews to Hungary began, this time from the north. For three quarters of a century after 1795 the Jewish population of Hungary jumped by some 40 percent every twenty years, with the result that in 1869, shortly after the Austro-Hungarian compromise, there were half a million or more Jews in the country, nearly as many as in Galicia whence so many of them had come. They already comprised 4 percent of the population.[10]

To refer thus to the migratory history of the Jews in Hungary is not to suggest that migration leads directly to conversion. Mention of the migrations suggests, however, the weakness of the Jewish community structure of Hungary, and that does relate to the conversion problem. The Jewish community structure in Hungary largely lacked a past. It was developed on the whole ad hoc in the nineteenth century as the Jewish population grew and spread; and though there were periodic attempts to strengthen it, it was fragile in proportion to its newness.[11] It lacked staying power; it lacked the hold that might have ensured religious stability in the face of an onslaught of "modernism."

In Poland, to cite a contrast, Jewry was anchored, until its destruction in the 1940s, in its past. Though there had been some movement over the decades into modern cities such as Warsaw, most Polish Jews still lived on the eve of the Holocaust in close propinquity to orthodoxy. Much the same might be said of prerevolutionary Russian Jews, who were on the whole confined until 1917 to a "Pale of

Settlement" where orthodoxy was ubiquitous and strong. They were not what the sociologists call "mobilized" (albeit "mobilization" in common parlance need not refer just to physical uprooting, but also to cultural, economic, or political detachment from a past environment).[12] In Poland and Russia also the decaying structure of the ancient Jewish communal organizations remained in place in the nineteenth century, and vigorous new community ties were introduced by Hasidism. All this inhibited the impact of Jewish "modernism" in Poland, where in any case it came late.

In Hungary the onslaught of "modernism" commenced early, and far more powerfully than in Poland. It is important to remember that the mobilization of nineteenth-century Hungarian Jewry was not only geographical, from rural Bohemia/Moravia or rural Galicia into rural Hungary, but also cultural, from one style of life to another. At home the immigrants had lived in villages or at best in small towns where community elders could oversee rather strictly the preservation of the old ways. Perhaps the first stopping place in Hungary was similar, whether it was a small town "Jew-street" along the western frontier of old Hungary or an impoverished Ruthenian village in the Carpatho-Ukraine. But increasingly over the century newly arrived Jews remained at such settlements for only a short time, often less than a generation. Then they picked up and moved on again, this time to a larger, less insulated town, and very often to the metropolis of Budapest. Until Joseph II's day, Budapest consisted of three separate small cities, Pest, Buda, and Óbuda (Altofen). Jews were not allowed in the first two, and only some one hundred families could live in the third. Joseph forced the closed gates open, and by 1825 there were some 8,000 Jews in the three cities, 8.8 percent of their population; by 1850 there were 17,000, 11.1 percent of their population. By 1910 Budapest was Europe's most rapidly growing city. Now administratively united, it contained 880,000 persons, of whom 204,000 were Jews—23 percent of the population.[13]

All told, one may perceive behind modern Hungarian Jewry's demographic growth and migrations a virtual "modernization miracle." This was one of the major instances of eastern European Jewry's entry into the world of today, and some contrasts suggest its importance. It occurred without an agonizing and dangerous overseas migration (as to the United States), without the brutalities of a revolution (as in post-1917 Russia), and without the Holocaust (as before the establishment of Israel).

Obviously the hold of a Jewish community—or any kind of religious community—on its flock is more tenuous in the face of big-city temptations than it is in the village. One need not be surprised, therefore, that prior to 1938 most of the Jewish conversions in Hungary took place in Budapest. In 1941 the "Christian Jews" were 17.5 percent of the quarter-million Jews resident in the capital, whereas in the provincial cities that had been part of interwar Hungary the figure was nearer 10 percent, and in the towns recovered from Czechoslovakia and Rumania, where Jewish orthodoxy was strong and the anti-Jewish laws had not yet been applied, it was under 5 percent.[14]

Let us now continue our search for an understanding of why Jews became Christians in Hungary by turning to some important early individual cases. As Guido Kisch has suggested in his study of Jewish conversions in Germany, it is difficult to document exactly the psychology of most historical conversions. In some cases there may always be doubt about whether individuals were "opportunistic" or "sincere."[15] But one can legitimately point to the general sociological and cultural factors affecting prominent converts, without any pretense to having the last word. And there is quite enough evidence to show that in Hungary during the modern period there was a very strong atmosphere favoring conversion, indeed almost a tradition of it.

In its first stages, this story differs little from the story of Jewish conversions elsewhere in central Europe. As in the other Habsburg lands one finds cases in the eighteenth century of the forced baptism of Jewish children by their peasant nurses, for example.[16] There was a case also of a military contractor from the Reich who waxed wealthy in Hungary, feeding the army and exploiting tax farms, and then in the 1780s converted so as to settle more comfortably in Vienna and marry off his daughters to penniless title holders.[17] There was a leading Pest trader who converted about 1810, when his nephew, an inventor who had married well in Vienna, wanted to escape the restrictions on Jewish industrial enterprise.[18] In none of this was there anything particularly Hungarian. The reason was that Hungary, no less than the other Habsburg dominions, was then rather wild and under-developed, a fallow land as a famous Magyar nationalist called it. Her largest city, in some ways her only city, was the non-Hungarian city of Vienna, directly across the Austrian frontier. Her enlightenment came from Maria Theresa and Joseph II in more or less exactly the same ways as it came to the Bohemian and Alpine Crownlands, albeit a little later and with tougher going. And her Jews came from the Bohemian lands, with which they retained close ties.

But then in 1822 an odd event occurred. In that year Moses Ullmann, the chairman of the then-new Jewish community at Pest, abruptly became a Catholic, allegedly because of quarrels with his colleagues.[19] Ullmann was a wealthy produce trader, and in the years after his conversion he became Hungary's outstanding capitalist entrepreneur. By the 1840s he was a banker with international contacts and with notably modern attitudes, a builder of railroads, bridges, and hotels, an organizer of shipping on the Danube. It is easy to speculate, therefore, that he converted in part to liberate some unusual business acumen within him. It is notable, in addition, that Ullmann's conversion roughly coincided with the conversion of several leading Hungarian Jewish business families in Vienna, with their acquisition of estates and ennoblement. Since he himself followed that path and was ennobled in 1825, one may presume he converted in part to gain status and buy land.[20] But there is also a mystery here. It is known, for example, that Ullmann's conversion was instructed by an intellectual, Karl Kohlmann, who had been the first German Jewish schoolteacher in Pest until his conversion in 1816. Kohlmann was peculiar in that after his conversion he remained in touch with Jewish circles all through his long life.[21] Legend has it that Ullmann himself did the same, remaining somehow Jewish in behavior and continuing to patronize Jewish causes. This suggests the possibility of some sort of arrière-pensée in what he did.[22]

All the more does an unusual éclat of Ullmann's conversion catch the eye. It was common enough for Jewish rich people and entrepreneurs to convert in central Europe in Ullmann's day, but often there was an effort at concealment, or at minimizing the insult to the ancestral faith. There appears to have been no other case prior to the twentieth century when the chairman of a community undertook to convert. (David Friedländer, who in 1800 proposed from a position of social prominence the conversion of the Berlin community, insisted on conditions and consequently failed to carry his project through.) Yet in Hungary, even in Ullmann's lifetime there was another case of a Pest community elder suddenly converting, that of Samuel Wodianer,[23] and in 1848, as we shall see, the Pest community chairman again converted.

Some peculiarities of the Danubian Jewish Enlightenment may

have contributed to these flamboyant Hungarian conversions. The first was intellectual emphasis different from that in the north of Germany. The Jewish Enlightenment everywhere involved a melting, as it were, of the intellectual walls around Jewry in the warmth of perceived "higher" and non-Jewish ideas; but in the Habsburg lands this melting took place at once more from within, and on a less articulately philosophical level than in the north. Suffice it to contrast Moses Mendelssohn's clear philosophical defiance of the demands that he convert, with the leadership of the famed Rabbi Ezekiel Landau of Prague, the central figure in Habsburg Jewry in Mendelssohn's day. In 1781, in the name of Jewry, Landau hailed Joseph II's reforms and welcomed the establishment at Prague of a modern Jewish school. A few years later he even sanctified the start of conscription of Jews into the Habsburg army. From these acts one might deduce he was decidedly enlightened. Yet actually he was no such thing, and indeed expressed strong misgivings in the 1780s about Mendelssohn's translation of the Torah. The point is that he was a much more "Jewish" Jewish leader than Mendelssohn. He was obliged by his office to underwrite initiatives by the Christian state, which Mendelssohn as an individual could take on their merits. Yet Landau as a rabbi presumably never had to come to grips with the problem of conversion, which faced Mendelssohn more than once.[24]

These differences in emphasis between the Jewish enlightenments in northern and southern central Europe were flanked by the special image of the convert Jew in the south. It is useful to remember, for example, that the Danubian equivalent of Mendelssohn, the Jewish philosophe who rejected conversion, was the Habsburg civil servant Josef von Sonnenfels, a well-rewarded neophyte.[25] Further, at Vienna in the Napoleonic era, there emerged a great Catholic proselytizer of Jews, Clemens Hofbauer, who was eventually sainted for his efforts, and who made Jewish conversion seem distinctly respectable in the decades after Sonnenfels ceased to do so.[26] The result of such different models was surely a certain fogginess among Danubian Jews all through the nineteenth century about conversion. When one recalls that Mendelssohn's clarity of mind and personal example failed completely to prevent conversions in northern Germany, even in his own family, one may guess the attitudes of people like Moritz Ullmann in the south.

There were also differences between north and south regarding, as it were, the size of the stakes. When Mendelssohn at Berlin thought to bring Enlightenment to the Jews he thought above all of the German Jews, of whom there were not many, and of whom many were already enlightened. Jews on the Danube in his day could not think of such limited goals. In Bohemia and Hungary alone in the eighteenth century there were more Jews than in all the German states, and they were far less affected by the early Enlightenment. Later, when the collapse of Poland brought Prussia a large contingent of eastern Jews, it brought Austria an even larger one. Consequently, whereas from Berlin one could contemplate the "Jewish Question" without being overwhelmed by the sheer numbers and poverty of the eastern Jews, at Prague, Vienna, or Pest the numbers were inescapable. By Moritz Ullmann's day, perhaps insuperable too. In the Habsburg Empire by then the great conflict between Jewish reform and Jewish tradition had erupted as violently as anywhere else in Europe. The Jewish schools at Pozsony, Hungary's capital, had shortly after 1800 become, under the famed teacher the Hatam Sofer, the center of eastern Jewry's rejection of the Enlightenment; and in Ullmann's time there were conservative rabbis at Buda and Obuda who were incessantly fulminating against the modern-minded Jews across the river at Pest.[27] Small wonder, perhaps, that in these circumstances, a modern-minded man like Ullmann should have suddenly sought to give up his Jewishness altogether. It was entirely human in Danubian circumstances that abruptly the sheer numbers of Jewry and the obduracy of Judaism should cause despair.

A final distinction of the Danubian Jewish Enlightenment derived from the presence of Jakob Frank, the flamboyant Podolian-born false messiah who in the 1750s sought to save Jewry by converting, first to Islam, then to Christianity; who then encouraged his followers to acquire land by getting themselves ennobled in Poland; and who later still, from 1773 until 1785, maintained a crypto-Jewish court at Brno in Moravia from which he launched further schemes that may be termed national in their attitude, if not in their scope.[28] Not much is known today of Frank's activities in Austria. The documents were apparently collected in the 1830s by his followers, and then destroyed. But it is known that even in his Polish period he had influence in the Habsburg dominions. In 1763, for example, an eighty-one-year-old rabbi in Nagyvarad (Oradea Mare), approached the Capuchin monks with an offer to convert, and they considered him both a Frankist and not a rare case.[29] Later when Frank was resident at Brno, some Jews associated with him sought ennoblement in Austria—indeed they became the first "Austrian Jewish nobles."[30] In the early 1780s Frank apparently stood behind a well-known attempt at Vienna to gain Jews admission into freemasonry.[31] In the 1790s Frankists were among the founders of the famed cohort of Jewish textile factories at Prague.[32] In 1798 the Prague Jewish community literally exploded under the impact of a Frankist millennarial prediction.[33] In the 1820s some of the wealthy Jews of Vienna, men of Bohemian origin who had extensive business interests in Hungary, may have especially prized ennoblement because of a notion, suggestive of Frank, that Jewish nobles might soon replace the "bagatelle" gentries of the Habsburg Crownlands to form a modern-minded pillar for a reconstructed Habsburg state.[34]

Frank did not start a conversion movement in Habsburg Jewry, as he did in Poland. Here, so far as we can tell, only a few of his followers converted.[35] But his impact was clearly widespread in Jewish modernizing circles, and acted as leaven to encourage individuals to break with traditional behavior patterns. For want of documents today's historian can only speculate about his influence. Still, it seems significant that Moritz Ullmann, whose family was from Bohemia, was an industrial entrepreneur like the Frankists of Prague; that he sought ennoblement like those of Poland and Vienna; and that he had a Prague-trained intellectual at his side.[36] There is absolutely no evidence that either Ullmann or Kohlmann was a Frankist, but better say it than leave it out. Their behavior suggests that alongside the different intellectual emphases and practical grimness of the Danubian Jewish Enlightenment, a memory of Frankism informed this first incidence of flamboyant apostasy in Hungary.

During the 1840s there were further incidents on which it is worth dwelling here, and among these the most interesting was that of Moritz Bloch in 1843. Bloch was born in the northeastern part of Hungary in 1815—in other words he was presumably of Galician origin—and his parents were very poor, though apparently the father knew enough of the Talmud to start his son on the path to higher learning.[37] Moritz's early training was entirely Jewish, and in the early 1830s he seemed directed to a career as a teacher of Jewish subjects in the then arch-traditional ghetto world of the west Hungarian towns. Somewhere, however, he discovered not only the German language, then the universal tongue of the Danubian Jewish Enlightenment, but also Greek, Latin, French, and finally the Magyar of the then infant reform movement of the Great Hungarian noble intelligentsia. In 1837 he came to Pest, already a talented linguist, to study "Christian subjects" such as mathematics. To support himself he began to write for German and Magyar newspapers, and consequently became involved with the political leaders of the Magyar language movement, especially with Baron Joszef Eötvös, the movement's intellectual leader.

At Pest, as a Jew, Bloch could obtain no university degree, so in 1839 he departed to study in Paris. But by then he had made himself the chosen publicist of the Magyar cause among the Jews. The Liberal leaders of the Magyar cause were then incorporating Jewish emancipation as a plank in their reform platform, and in 1840, as they prepared to demand it in the Diet, Eötvös commissioned Bloch first to compose an encomium advocating Jewish magyarization and then to translate the Torah into Magyar. Bloch responded ardently. In a widely distributed pamphlet he called on the Jews of Hungary to cleave in every way to the Magyars—not just to "deserve" emancipation, but also to convert themselves into Magyars by making the Magyar tongue the vehicle of their innermost thoughts.[38] Then in extraordinarily short order he produced a magyarized Torah. The Magyars could not reward him with emancipation, because the Liberals had been unable to carry the Diet, but in 1841 Eötvös did obtain for him (when he was only twenty-six) an invitation to join the Hungarian Academy of Sciences. As the first Jew to be so honored, he gained huge repute among reform-minded Jews in the country. In 1842 he left Hungary once more, this time to study linguistics at the Theological Faculty of Tübingen University in Protestant Württemberg, and in 1843, just before the award of his degree, he converted to Lutheranism. This did not affect his credit among the Magyars. They made him a professor. In return, he magyarized his name to Mór Ballagi, fought with the Magyars in 1848, suffered for them a while in the 1850s, and then spent a long career as the most eminent of Hungarian linguists and a leading spokesman of Hungarian Protestantism. But among the Jews his defection was like a bomb. Their Magyar Mendelssohn, who had been imploring them to cleave to the Magyars to obtain emancipation, had left the community, and worse, was urging them all to do the same so that they too could become proper Magyars.[39]

Even more shattering was the defection of Jonas Kunewalder in 1848. Kunewalder was chairman of the Pest Jewish community, Ullmann's successor, in many respects the leading lay spokesman for Hungarian Jewry.[40] He was from a family long settled in the country,

151

decidedly wealthy, dedicated to the cause of Jewish emancipation and Jewish reform. In the fall of 1847, when the Diet opened for the first time in some years and emancipation seemed no longer postponable, Kunewalder published a long and detailed complaint about the injustice and unreason of relegating the Jews, with all their talents, their readiness to serve the Magyar cause, and their sheer dedication, to second-class status.[41] When the revolution broke out in February 1848, he again published a call for Magyar action on Jewish equality. On both occasions he wrote with a boldness wholly befitting a Jewish national leader, demanding emancipation as by right. But then late in March 1848 he led a delegation from Pest to the Diet at Pozsony, talked to the Liberal political leaders, and discovered that some of them were openly saying the Jews could never be assimilated because of their religious separatism. Coincidentally the entire Magyar reform leadership backed away from Jewish emancipation because of widespread Judeophobic riots organized by the German townsmen of many Hungarian cities. Kunewalder came back to Pest dismayed. He issued an appeal to his coreligionists as passionate as Bloch/Ballagi's had been eight years earlier, imploring them to reform their religious and social practices with all possible vigor, to make themselves as soon as possible Magyars of the purest hue. And then without further warning, he converted to the Roman Catholic Church and spread rumors that all the Jews in Hungary were about to follow him in his self-sacrificing dedication to the Magyar cause.[42]

In both these cases, far more clearly than in Ullmann's, one can identify why the conversion took place. Ballagi was a young intellectual in an age when all over Europe intellectuals were being produced in far greater numbers than society could absorb.[43] Everywhere the likes of him were searching for sustenance, becoming journalists, selling their pen for what they could get in order to eat. In central Europe, where for demographic and cultural reasons Jews were disproportionately numerous among them, there was an added problem. Not only were there fewer jobs, but most university faculties were closed to Jews. Consequently conversion out of Judaism offered modern-minded youths the only way they could make a living with their minds, and over and over again they took this option.[44] Such conversions were certainly motivated by careerism, but they involved also an element of desperation that should not be despised.

Beyond this, for both Bloch/Ballagi and Kunewalder, conversion was a matter of dedication to Magyar nationalism. To comprehend the

significance of this, one should recall that at the start of the Enlightenment period, central European Jews had not spoken the tongues of the
lands in which they lived: they had spoken Hebrew and Yiddish, and
then as a first step toward Europeanization had universally adopted
modern German. The German language had in fact assumed an
almost holy status in their eyes because it had been the vehicle of their
conversion to enlightened ways. This meant that when, as in Hungary
in the 1830s and 1840s, enlightened Jews became involved with the
romantic revivals of the eastern European nationalities, they had to
convert, so to speak, for a second time. Magyarization was for the
Blochs and Kunewalders a soul-rending experience, a shaking of their
identity far greater than the discovery of national consciousness was
for any Christian.[45] When these men wrote passionately to their
fellow Jews about the need to become in mind and practice pure
Magyars, and thereby to win emancipation, they were advocating
something very close to religious conversion, a transformation in
which a formal religious switch to Christianity might easily seem
excusable.

In some degree these neophytes of the 1840s in Hungary imitated
precisely the flamboyant conversion model of Moritz Ullmann. From
the same position of leadership, they committed the same act of
seeming betrayal that he had committed. But they did so for entirely
different reasons. They made the model their own, adjusting it to the
fresh needs of the Jewish people inside Hungary. And with this
adjustment one may speak of a tradition of Jewish conversion in that
country. By the 1850s flamboyant conversion by Jews there had
already for two entirely different sets of reasons seemed an appropriate
resolution of the problems of modernization.

There is no space in this short paper to document the further
metamorphoses of the convert model in Jewish Hungary. Suffice it to
mention briefly that in later metamorphoses the model itself was
modified. This happened even in 1848, when virtually no one at Pest
followed Kunewalder's model. Instead, the more radically magyarized
members of the community, some of them young but many of them
older, founded a radical reform synagogue. They were the only Danubian Jews to imitate the radical reform that was emerging in Berlin (in
fact, they sent an envoy to Berlin to find out how to do it), and until
the Austrians suppressed them in 1852 they not only had an organ and
Magyar-language prayers in their temple, but also celebrated the
sabbath on Sunday. Though individuals among them later converted,

the group conversion advocated by Bloch and Kunewalder was evidently too much for them.[46] One might cite also, as a latter-day metamorphosis of the Ullmann model, Theodor Herzl's famous dream in which he saw himself presiding over the mass conversion of Viennese Jewry at Saint Stephen's Cathedral.[47] As Andrew Handler has emphasized just recently, the future Zionist grew up and received all his lower schooling in the magyarizing environment of post-*Ausgleich* Hungary.[48] His dream suggests that the lesson of Kunewalder's fate was learnt. Now in the 1890s the Jewish hero himself no longer converted: only the Jewish masses did so!

It was not flamboyant tradition which dominantly shaped Jewish attitudes toward conversion in late-nineteenth-century Hungary, however. The most important fact now comes out clearly in a patriotic essay published in the yearbook of the Magyar Jewish Literary Society in 1908. The author first waxed enthusiastic:

> Oh, how different is Jewry's appearance today from what it was before the emancipation! Confidently we can boast that we've become not just more Magyar but more Jewish!

Then he faced the question: "And what about the largish number of conversions?" In responding he showed a tendency to pooh-pooh it.

> Let people who worry about them recall that conversion has been an old old phenomenon among Jews! . . . One other matter speaks with incontrovertible force alongside the great increase in Jewish religious enthusiasm among us since the emancipation. We can state boldly that today no Jew converts out of conviction any more.

As in Herzl's dream, so here, clearly enough, conversions shouldn't be taken too seriously, albeit gentlemanly Jews don't convert. But in the midst of the apology the author raised a critical matter:

> Let them recall also that the emancipation law is incomplete. The State rewards converts. Anyone who seems unacceptable for a given office simply because he is a Jew is perfectly acceptable if he converts.[49]

To explain this cryptic remark, let us look now at the legal situation of religion in Hungary in the modern period.

In the German states and in the Habsburgs' Austrian lands alike, the final legal break with the old discriminatory laws against Jews took place in 1868, when new Liberal laws not only made the Jewish religion equal with others, but also permitted an individual to declare himself *konfessionslos*.[50] After that it was possible to simply back away from Judaism without accepting another religion; and for this reason the number of declared "Christian Jews" remained in the German-speaking lands rather low. In Prague for example about one third of the people who seceded from the Jewish faith in the pre-1914 decade remained without a new confession. In that same city in the middle thirties over three quarters of the secessionists remained without a new confession.[51]

In Hungary the legal situation was different. Hungarian Jews won their emancipation in 1868, but Catholicism remained the religion of the state, mixed marriages remained impossible and no "confessionless" status emerged. In fact those Jews and Christian Liberals who in the German lands would have been most eager for the establishment of such a category came in Hungary to favor its opposite—universal religious enrollment. The development is worth a brief recounting because Hungarian Jews and Hungarian Liberals at midcentury were not very different from those of Germany and Austria who won the introduction of "confessionlessness."[52]

The divergence began in 1868 itself when it became clear that the Hungarian Parliament was very different from the new Liberal-dominated parliaments in Berlin and Vienna. In Budapest the lower house was malleable, as in those other capitals, and could be persuaded to vote both for the emancipation of the Jews and for religious toleration; but there was an upper house which had a strong contingent of ecclesiastical princes, who were not prepared to demolish the powers of the church. Hungarian Liberals backed away from confrontation, therefore, and the act that emancipated the Jews simply abolished legal discrimination based on religion. It did not define in positive terms, as in a *Rechtsstaat* it should have, the new status of the various religious groups. The consequences were most unsatisfactory for religious Jews, for indifferent Jews, and for members of non-Catholic Christian faiths alike. Not only did state funding go almost exclusively to the Catholic Church, but because that church was in control of Catholic marriages and birth certification, there was considerable abuse in matters regarding infants and orphans.

In the 1890s the religious question once more became a burning political issue in Hungary. The issue was not, however, as it was in that decade in France, whether or not to evict religious groups altogether from civic affairs. The issue in Hungary was whether or not to give Protestantism and Judaism a standing in civic affairs equal to that of the Catholic Church. The struggle was arduous and long, and, just as in France, set the forces of modernity and of religious indifference against Catholic bigotry. The battle was won in 1895 when the government forced the House of Lords to approve the Protestant and Jewish faiths as religions officially "received" by the state. But once again compromises were made. The Lords insisted that Catholicism should remain first among the received religions. In fact, at the final vote they expunged from the new law a paragraph specifically authorizing conversions not just from Judaism into Christianity, but also the other way around. This, they protested, was incompatible with Christian dogma. Hereupon the government consented to a substitute paragraph that required every Hungarian citizen to register with a religious faith. It was hoped that such registration would stop Catholic poaching of Protestant and Jewish infants, but by backing it the Hungarian Liberals themselves renewed the ban in Hungary on "confessionlessness." Subsequent legislation made it legal to stand outside the "received" religions once one became an adult, but until 1945 all children under eighteen not only had to be registered with a "received" religion, but also had to receive appropriate religious instruction while in school. A "confessionless" adult could not spare his children a Jewish religious label or a Jewish education unless he had them baptized.[53]

The laws of 1868 and 1895 are not the only explanation of why there were so many "Christian Jews" in Hungary by the end of the Liberal era. In that period throughout the western world religious indifference was becoming widespread. There were large numbers of people who felt no inclination any longer to obey the Jewish (or Christian) dietary laws, to worship regularly according to the old rules, or even to pay a community tax; and the desire for civic status, professorship, or advantageous marriage was more powerful than ever. In addition, one may recall that Liberal Hungary made itself very attractive to Jews.[54] The governing parties repressed the modern political antisemitism that seemed to be running wild in the country early in the 1880s. By the middle 1890s, when the antisemite Karl Lueger became mayor of Vienna, antisemitism was virtually silent in Hungary, which was one of the reasons he labeled Budapest "Judapest." Another reason was the economic power which the Magyar leadership allowed to Jews, and the high positions in Hungarian culture and society to which they had access. In the years before 1914 Jews even became government ministers in Hungary. In this situation, a real sense of gratitude underlay the careerism of Jews who converted to accept some sort of office. Nonetheless, it was basic to the phenomenon of Jewish conversion, in both the Liberal era and the interwar period that followed it, that the law forced one's hand. Individuals who wished simply to free their children from Judaism had to carry through their secession from the old faith with adherence to a new one. The regularly rising number of conversions in Hungary after 1895 shows how strong the pressure was. The annual average went up from 323 in the years just before 1900 to 505 in the years just before the war. It has been estimated that by 1918 there had been twenty thousand Jewish conversions in Hungary since 1867.[55]

In the final periods of modern Hungarian history it was inarguably persecution that led to the emergence of "Christian Jews." One may observe this first in the three years at the end of the war, when there were 9,898 conversions. (See table.) There was, moreover, a change in the gender composition of the converts: whereas before the war more women than men had converted, reflecting a predominance of mixed-marriage conversions, now the males exceeded the females by 10 percent.[56] The reason, all too evidently, was an explosion of antisemitism touched off by the loss of the war and compounded by the establishment of a socialist republic and its suppression by virulently antisemitic counterrevolutionary forces. A few Jews may have converted to a disassociate themselves from the leftist Jews who had appeared in the leadership of the republic, and a few may have wished to avoid the law of 1920 that established a *numerus clausus* against Jewish university students.[57] But the sheer physical brutality of the new antisemitism was clearly the prime factor, because once law and order were restored in 1921 and after, the rate of conversion fell back to the prewar level and even below.

With the advent of the Great Depression, the rise of Hitlerism in Germany, and a renewed outbreak of political antisemitism in Hungary, now much better organized, the pace of conversion advanced again. By 1938, when the first Hungarian "Jewish Law" was passed, there had been 6,543 conversions in just five years, and in that year alone there were 8,584 more.[58] Christian missionaries were eagerly helping,[59] but obviously fear accounts for the extent of the wave; and now we encounter another unique aspect of the Hungarian "Christian Jewish" experience. In most of Europe after 1938 conversion was too slow a path—or an altogether ineffectual path—for Jews who wanted to escape, or else it was altogether interdicted by the war. But in Hungary, which remained at peace until 1941, and fairly isolated from the front until 1944, conversions were still logical. Indeed, the Chris-

WILLIAM O. McCAGG, JR.

CONVERSIONS IN HUNGARY, 1896–1938

	Jews becoming Christian	Jews becoming Cultless	Christians becoming Jews
1896–1900	323	13	89
1901–1905	476	17	81
1906–1910	490	24	109
1911–1914	505	37	121
1915–1917	527	33	81
1918	?	?	?
1919	7146	23	137
1920	1925	9	168
1921	827	7	243
1922	499	6	340
1923	458	7	326
1924	433	0	315
1925	412	6	311
1926	451	5	271
1927	412	11	279
1928	517	6	199
1929	588	4	204
1930	655	11	184
1931	636	14	170
1932	688	11	144
1933	909	11	147
1934	1128	11	192
1935	1261	6	197
1936	1647	8	144
1937	1598	8	142
1938	8584	2	98

MStSz, vol. 17, no. 10, p. 1115. Figures for 1896–1917 are annual averages for the years indicated.

tian churches welcomed them, and since the Jewish laws of 1938, 1939, and 1941 caused great hardship among poorer Jews, there now occurred a mass rush to convert. The available statistics reflect the changed social complexion of the wartime converts. Whereas earlier the bulk of the conversions was in wealthy Budapest, even in 1938 provincial Jews accounted for one third of the total. The stream of impoverished converts was so great that during the war years the churches found it necessary to organize special welfare societies to care for them.[60]

Finally, in 1944 the German occupation of Hungary lent impetus to the conversion movement. In the catastrophic circumstances of that year one's religious affiliation was often a life-or-death matter. The people in the "Christian Jew" category were not guaranteed exemption from deportation to the extermination camps. Alas, there was no

158

guarantee of anything then in Hungary; and during May and June 1944 Eichmann and his cohorts shipped off the converts in provincial Hungary along with the rest. But this convert category did touch the conscience of the authorities in the Christian camp, and in the summer of 1944 when Regent Horthy suspended the deportations, he took the "Christian Jews" under his protection. Many people converted in 1944 to get precisely this sort of protection. A great many of the converts were able to survive the war, although we do not know whether their survival may be attributed to this reason.[61]

In historical perspective the "Christian Jews" of interwar Hungary seem neither so startlingly numerous as they did at first sight, nor so inexplicable. In the very large reservoir that Hungarian Jewry was until 1944, the numbers who had converted were not relatively greater than the convert numbers in other parts of Europe; in fact in some measure they were proportionately low. Furthermore, it can be seen that an extraordinary mass mobilization and modernization of eastern Jews lay behind the conversion rate in Hungary. For a century and more the atmosphere in Hungary and the pressures on the wealthier strata of Hungarian Jewry had favored conversion. Hungary's religious laws of the emancipation period did the same; so did the persecutions that specifically led to the emergence of the "Christian Jewish" demographic category.

Our effort in this paper has been not just to point to this record, but also to explain and evaluate it. In approaching an explanation we have observed the advantage of abandoning the view that conversion is just the product of opportunism, and of adopting a broad, comparative, and problem-oriented attitude toward the history of Jewish conversion in modern times. This attitude has brought us to perceive conversion as a special difficulty, or point of frustration, faced by modernizing Jews that modernizing Christian Europeans did not have to face. All Europeans had in some measure to deny their old "selves" under the impact of the rational, scientific, and democratic ideas of the modern period—of the Enlightenment. They all had to cut out their old theological identity. Most of them, however, could rather easily devise a new identity by reinforcing or creating secular national symbols. The Jews could not do that, in part because they possessed no land or modern state, in part because their pre-Enlightenment identity was overwhelmingly theological. This meant already that in the Jewish Enlightenment modernists were faced far more than their Christian counterparts with the need to deny their "self." In addition there was a moral stigma. In other nations, when an individual decided to move somewhere else, to learn a new language, or otherwise to change identity, there was very little stigma, especially if he rose socially in the process. But among the Jews exactly the same sort of effort ran into the moral bar against conversion.

This perception leads to our main judgment, which is that the Jews of Hungary showed, over a century and more face to face with the "self"-denial possibility, a remarkable degree of resistance. Despite their numbers, the temptations they faced and growing external pressures, the conversion rate remained low. The Ullmann model simply did not catch on, even in the excitement of the revolution of 1848; nor did the liberalism and Jewish laxity of Hungary in the Dualistic Era lead to mass conversions. Only the radical persecutions of 1919–20, and then the new laws of 1938–41 and the Hitlerite persecutions, induced large numbers of Hungarian Jews to deny their faith.

NOTES

1. See *Magyar Statisztikai Szemle* 19 (1941): 772–73 (hereafter cited as *MStSz*). Previous studies of the "Christian Jews" in Hungary are Alajos Dolányi (Kovács), "A keresztény vallású de zsidó szarmazású népesség a népszámlás szerint," *MStSz* 22 (1944): 95–103; Ze'ev Rotics, "Beshulei ha-netunim ha-statistiim al hamerot ha-dat ḥekerev yehudei Hungaria beshanim 1900–1941," in *Dapim le-ḥeker tekufat ha-shoah* (Tel Aviv: Hakibbutz hameuchad Publishing House, 1978), 1:223–28; and Victor Karady and István Kemény, "Antisémitisme universitaire et concurrence de classe," *Actes de la Recherche en Sciences Sociales* no. 34 (Sept. 1980): 67–96. I am indebted to Prof. Michael Rubner of Michigan State University for a translation of the Rotics article. Karady, "Antisémitisme universitaire," p. 94, promises a much more detailed sociological study of the conversion problem.

2. See Randolph L. Braham, *The Politics of Genocide*, 2 vols. (New York: Columbia University Press, 1981), 1:77.

3. See Jenö Lévai, *Fekete könyv a magyar zsidó szenvedéseiröl* (Budapest: Officina, 1946), p. 190; Braham, *Politics of Genocide*, 2:814.

4. The standard work on modern Hungarian Jewry is Lajos Venetianer, *A magyar zsidóság története* (Budapest: Fövárosi nyomda, 1922), hereafter cited as *MZsT*; but see also the following recent works: William McCagg, *Jewish Nobles and Geniuses in Modern Hungary* (Boulder, Colo. and New York: East European Quarterly, 1972); Victor Karady and István Kemény, "Les juifs dans la structure des classes en Hongrie," *Actes de la Recherche en Sciences Sociales* no. 22 (June 1978): 25–59; György Szalai, "A hazai zsidóság magyarosodása 1849-ig," *Világosság* 15 (1974): 216–23; Ká-

roly Vörös, "Ungarns Judentum vor der bürgerlichen Revolution," *Studies in East European Social History* 2 (1981): 139–56; George Barany, "Magyar Jew or Jewish Magyar," *Canadian American Slavic Studies* 8 (1974): 1–44; and the relevant sections of Andrew Janos, *The Politics of Backwardness in Hungary* (Princeton: Princeton University Press, 1982).

5. See Arthur Ruppin, *The Jewish Fate and Future* (London: Macmillan, 1940), pp. 30–33. For interwar statistics on Hungarian Jewry see Alajos Kovács, *A csonkamagyarországi zsidóság a statisztika tükrében* (Budapest: Held János könyvnyomdája, 1938), pp. 58ff.

6. See Alajos Kovács, *A zsidóság térfoglalása magyarországon* (Budapest: A szerzö, 1922), pp. 10ff. (hereafter cited as *ZsTMO*). For comparative pre-1914 statistics on world Jewry, see Arthur Ruppin, *Soziologie der Juden*, 2 vols. (Berlin: Jüdischer Verlag, 1930), vol. 1, chaps. 5, 6.

7. See Michael A. Riff, "Assimilation and Conversion in Bohemia," *Leo Baeck Institute Year Book* 22 (1981): 78–79; and Jakob Thon, *Die Juden in Oesterreich* (Berlin: Louis Lamm, 1908), p. 70.

8. See Ruppin, *The Jewish Fate*, pp. 287–88; and Jan Heřman, "The Development of Bohemian and Moravian Jewry, 1918–1938," in *Papers in Jewish Demography, 1969–70*, ed. V. O. Schmelz, P. Glikson, and S. Della Pergola (Jerusalem, 1973), pp. 191–206.

9. See *MStSz* 17 (1939): 1118.

10. On the mobility of the Hungarian Jews, see Kovács, *ZsTMO*, pp. 10ff.; Venetianer, *MZsT*, passim; and Erno Laszlo, "Hungarian Jewry: Settlement and Demography," *Hungarian Jewish Studies* 1 (1966): 61–137. Both Venetianer, a convinced assimilationist, and Kovács, an equally convinced antisemite, accept the basic premise that Hungarian Jewry derived from a core community that had always been in the country, and that in the nineteenth century there was simply an increment because of the Galician immigration. Laszlo, a convinced Zionist, challenges this view, claiming that as early as 1800 the "old Hungarian" contingent was but a drop in the bucket, and that modern Hungarian Jewry has been body and soul "Galician," and thus more "Jewish" than Hungarian.

11. See Venetianer, *MZsT*, pt. 2, chaps. 2, 3; and his *A zsidóság szervezete az europai államokban* (Budapest: MIOT, 1901), pp. 478–533.

12. See Celia S. Heller, *On the Edge of Destruction* (New York: Columbia University Press, 1977), chap. 6.

13. See Kovács, *ZsTMO*, pp. 61–63.

14. See Dolányi, *MStSz* 22 (1944): 102.

15. See Kisch's long essay on the (originally Hungarian) Viennese convert juridicist, Josef Unger, in his *Judentaufen* (Berlin: Colloquium Verlag, 1973), chap. 6.

16. See for many examples Gerson Wolf, *Judentaufen in Österreich* (Vienna: Herzfeld-Bauer, 1863).

17. Case of Ferdinand Arenfeld: see Heinrich Schnee, *Die Hoffinanz und der moderne Staat*, 4 vols. (Berlin: Duncker & Homblot, 1953–67), 4:320–21.

18. Case of Abraham Offenheimer: see Hanns Jaeger-Sunstenau, "Die geadelten Judenfamilien im vormärzlichen Wien" (diss., University of Vienna, 1950), pp. 160–61.

19. There are conflicting accounts of Ullmann's conversion in Sigmund Mayer, *Die Wiener Juden* (Vienna: Löwit, 1917), pp. 140–41; and in an article by Bernát Mándi in the newspaper *Egyenlöség*, 9 April 1921, pp. 10–11. In my *Jewish Nobles and Geniuses in Modern Hungary*, pp. 59–61, I followed Mándi's account, which seemed better researched, but it now appears that the conversion date he provided, 1826, is impossible: see Peter Üvári, ed., *Magyar Zsidó Lexikon* (Budapest: private, 1929), p. 494 (hereafter cited as *MZsL*). Further data about Ullmann's family experience is in Béla Kempelen, *Magyarországi zsidó és zsidóeredetü családok*, 3 vols. (Budapest: A szerzü, 1939) 1:96–102.

20. Cases of the Leidesdorfer/Neuwall, Lippmann/Liebenberg, and Kaan families, all noted seriatim in Jaeger-Sunstenau, "Geadelte Judenfamilien."

21. On Kohlmann, see *MZsL*, p. 494, and Kempelen, *Családok*, 2:37–38.

22. See Kempelen, *Családok* 2:96ff.

23. On Wodianer, see McCagg, *Jewish Nobles*, pp. 55–56. The exact date of Samuel Wodianer's conversion is not clear. His son, a towering Vienna business-world figure, converted in 1830, but the father was still a Jew in 1839 when he joined a Jewish delegation from Pest to the Hungarian Diet: see Béla Bernstein, *A negyvennyolcas magyar szabadságharc és a zsidók* (Budapest: 1898), p. 9. In any case the Wodianer conversion must have been prior to 1844, when both father and son were ennobled.

24. See Salomon Wind, "Ezekiel Landau," in *Jewish Leaders*, ed. Leo Jung (New York: Bloch, 1953), pp. 77–98; and Ruth Kestenberg-Gladstein, *Neuere Geschichte der Juden in den böhmischen Ländern* (Tübingen: Mohr, 1969), pp. 84ff.

25. A recent summary of the vast literature on Sonnenfels is Josef Karniel, "Josef von Sonnenfels," *Jahrbuch des Instituts für deutsche Geschichte* 7 (1978): 111–58. For Sonnenfels's influence in Hungary, see Miksa Grünwald, *Zsidó Biedermeier* (Pécs: Egyetemi Könyvnyomda, 1937), p. 49.

26. See Rudolf Till, *Hofbauer und sein Kreis* (Vienna: Herold, 1951), chap. 5.

27. See Sándor Büchler, *A zsidók története Budapesten* (Budapest: IMIT, 1901), pt. 2, chaps. 3, 4.

28. Frank is one of the more controversial figures in Jewish history. An older but convenient nationalist interpretation is in Israel Zinberg, *A History of Jewish Literature*, 12 vols. (New York: Ktav, 1972–78), 9:3–26. Polarized modern interpretations are in Gershom Scholem, "Redemption Through Sin," in his *Messianic Idea in Judaism* (New York: Schocken, 1971), pp. 78–141; and Bernard Weinryb, *The Jews of Poland* (Philadelphia: Jewish Publication Society, 1972), chap. 11.

29. See Grünwald, *Zsidó Biedermeier*, p. 63, citing older literature.

30. This will be shown in my forthcoming "Assimilation on the Danube: Habsburg Jewry, 1670–1918," chap. 3.

31. See Jacob Katz, *Jews and Freemasons* (Cambridge: Harvard University Press, 1970), pp. 222ff.

32. See Kestenberg-Gladstein, *Neuere Geschichte*, p. 111, and other indexed references to Moses Porges.

33. See V. Žáček, "Dva příspěvky k dějinám frankismu v českých zemích," *Jahrbuch der Gesellschaft für die Geschichte der Juden in der Tschechoslowakei* 9 (1939): 343–410.

34. See Hermann Broch, *Hofmannsthal und seine Zeit* (Zurich: Suhrkamp, 1974), p. 73.

35. See Abraham Duker, "Polish Frankism's Survival," *Jewish Social Studies* 25 (1963): 289.

36. It may be noted that the two most prominent rabbis of early nineteenth-century Hungary, Aaron Chorin and Josef Bach, both encountered Frankists while receiving their training in late eighteenth-century Prague: see Leopold Loew [Dr. Weil], *Aron Chorin* (Szeged: Sigmund Burger, 1863), chap. 3; and Buchler, *A zsidók története Budapesten*, pp. 403–5.

37. On Bloch/Ballagi, see especially Imre Sándor's memorial in *Akadémiai Emlékbeszédek* (Budapest: Akademia, 1893).

38. "A zsidókról" (Budapest, 1840).

39. For the impact of the conversion and Bloch's further appeal to the Jews, see Venetianer, *MZsT*, p. 149; and Zsigmond Grosszmann, *A magyar zsidók V Ferdinand alatt* (Budapest: 1916), p. 15.

40. On the Kunewalder affair, see Bernstein, *A negyvennyolcas magyar szabadságharc és a zsidók*, chap. 2.

41. The documents are cited at length by Venetianer, *MZsT*, pp. 157–59, 168; and in J. Zsoldos, ed., *1848–1849 a magyar zsidóság életében* (Budapest: Neuwalt Illés, 1948), pp. 59–60, 71.

42. See the eyewitness account of the impact of the conversion in J. Einhorn, *Die Revolution und die Juden in Ungarn* (Leipzig: Carl Geibel, 1851), p. 81. Cf. S. Baron, "The Revolution of 1848 and Jewish Scholarship," *Proceedings of the American Academy for Jewish Research* 19 (1951): 88.

43. See Lenore O'Boyle, "The Problem of an Excess of Educated Men in Western Europe, 1800–1850," *Journal of Modern History* 42 (1970): 471–95.

44. The distinguished Hungarian Jewish intellectuals who converted before the emancipation range from Max Falk to Arminius Vámbéry: see Grünwald, *Zsidó Biedermeier*, chap. 19; and the articles about various academic professions in *MZsL*.

45. On this subject see especially Barany, "Magyar Jew or Jewish Magyar," and

WILLIAM O. McCAGG, JR.

the same author's "Hungary," in *Nationalism in Eastern Europe*, ed. Peter F. Sugar and Ivo Lederer (Seattle: University of Washington Press, 1969), pp. 259–86.

46. See Büchler, *A zsidók története Budapesten*, pt. 3, chap. 6.

47. See *Theodor Herzls Tagebücher*, 3 vols. (Berlin: Jüdischer Verlag, 1923), 1:7–8.

48. Andrew Handler, *Dori* (University, Ala.: University of Alabama Press, 1983).

49. See *Az Izraelita Magyar Irodalmi Társulat. Évkönyv* 25 (1908): 310.

50. See in general Guido Kisch, *Judentaufen*, chap. 3.

51. See Riff, "Assimilation and Conversion in Bohemia," p. 77; and Ruppin, *The Jewish Fate*, p. 287.

52. For reasonable statements of the legal position of religion in late nineteenth- and early twentieth-century Hungary, see *Révai Nagy Lexikona*, 2:268 (s.v. "Áttérés más vallásra"); 7:300 (s.v. "Felekezeten kivüliek"); and 8:165 (s.v. "Vallásszabadság"). For the emancipation, see Venetianer, *MZsT*, pt. 2, chap. 8.

53. Venetianer, *MZsT*, pt. 3, p.5.

54. For the record, see my *Jewish Nobles and Geniuses*, passim, esp. chap. 6.

55. See the *Egyenlöség*, 11 Feb. 1937; and Kempelen, *Családok*, 2:83–85.

56. See J. Asztalos, "Áttérési mozgalom és felekezetnélküliség az 1919–1924 években," *MStSz* 6 (1926): 183–91.

57. On the Jewish Bolsheviks, see William McCagg, "Jews in Revolutions: The Hungarian Experience," *Journal of Social History* 22 (1972): 78–105. On the *numerus clausus* and its small effect in bringing about conversions, see Karady-Kemény, "Anti-sémitisme universitaire," esp. p. 94.

58. See Lévai, *Fekete könyv*, p. 74.

59. See Braham, *Politics of Genoicide*, vol. 2, chap. 30; and the interesting contemporary booklet by Viktor Rojkó, *Katolikus lettem* (Kiskunfélegyháza: A szerzö, 1935).

60. See Lévai, *Fekete könyv*, p. 190; and Braham, *Politics of Genocide*, 2:814, n. 86.

61. See Braham, *Politics of Genocide*, vol. 2, chap. 25.

6

The Orthodox Rabbinate and Apostasy in Nineteenth-Century Germany and Hungary

DAVID ELLENSON

WITHIN the corporate structure of the medieval body politic, the Jewish community was distinguished by a common ethos and enjoyed a semiautonomous political status. The rabbis, as the dominant cultural and at times political class within the community, not only articulated a religious ideology which legitimated their position, but were also empowered with police authority to punish deviations from the norms they established. They often employed bans of excommunication to suppress dissent and ensure discipline within their communities. Such power was, as Salo Baron describes it, "the most effective punishment and method of enforcement wielded by Jewish communal organs,"[1] since it both removed the offending individual and his family from the synagogue and forced them to endure economic, social, religious, and educational boycott.

In such an undifferentiated world, where religious and civil life were virtually one, the rabbis were able to construct a broad definition of apostasy. This definition, as codified in the authoritative legal work of Joseph Caro, the *Shulḥan Arukh* (1564), *Oraḥ Ḥayyim*, 385:3, held that apostates were not only persons who abandoned Judaism to embrace another religion, but Jews who publicly violated rabbinic proscriptions concerning the Sabbath. This view of apostasy reflects a world where the life of the individual Jew was coextensive with the life of the community itself, so that a violation of a rabbinic edict could be seen as tantamount to heresy.

With the transformation of Jewish life ushered in by events in

Europe at the end of the eighteenth century, such communal unity, despite the efforts of the rabbinate, was impossible to maintain. Jewish stirrings toward cultural and social integration into non-Jewish European society meant that the idea of communal solidarity no longer possessed sufficient potency to dissuade individuals from either ignoring rabbinic teachings or leaving the community altogether. Furthermore, with the rise of the modern nation-state and its attendant notions of individual citizenship, rabbinic authorities were stripped of their coercive powers and individual Jews were permitted to aspire to and attain political emancipation. These conditions of cultural openness and political freedom combined to create a situation in which the leaders of the Jewish community, in their efforts to maintain Jewish continuity and identity, had to confront a secularized and differentiated central European setting where religious pluralism flourished and apostasy from the community was an ever-increasing reality. Reform and Positive-Historical trends within Liberal Judaism arose, and 45,000 Jews in Austria Hungary and 22,500 more in Germany converted to Christianity.[2] These numbers, even if not altogether accurate, reveal that apostasy and religious pluralism were not isolated phenomena confined to a few individuals, but developments characteristic of the nineteenth-century European world.

While leaders of all elements within Judaism had to acknowledge and struggle with these changes, it was the Orthodox segment of that leadership which experienced a special degree of trauma in dealing with the novel dimensions of the modern situation. After all, Orthodoxy was absolutely committed to a belief in the divine sanction for Jewish law, a belief most Jews in the modern setting no longer affirmed. In addition, the political autonomy of the community that formerly supported the administration of the Jewish legal system no longer existed. Finally, the Orthodox had to contend with a definition of apostasy that seemingly made no distinction between those Jews who converted to Christianity and those Liberal or secular Jews who remained within the bounds of the nineteenth-century community despite their failure to observe the strictures of Sabbath laws. In short, the demands of a transformed modern European world challenged Orthodoxy to respond in distinctive and original ways if it was to adapt both legitimately and effectively to this radically altered setting. An analysis of the Orthodox approaches taken to the issue of apostasy will thus provide important insights into how the traditionally oriented segment of the nineteenth-century central European Jewish community's leadership accommodated and traversed the distance between "medievalism" and "modernity."

The pathways and directions this journey followed will be illuminated in this paper by examining the attitudes of representative groups of Hungarian and German Orthodox rabbis toward this issue of apostasy and apostates. One group, the "traditionalists," includes three generations of the Sofer family of Pressburg—the Hatam Sofer, Rabbi Moses Schreiber (1762–1839); the Ktav Sofer, Rabbi Abraham Samuel Benjamin Wolf (1815–71); and the Shevet Sofer, Rabbi Simha Bunem (1842–1906). Also numbered among this group are rabbis Akiva Eger (1761–1837) of Posen; Zvi Hirsch Chajes (1805–55) of Zolkiew; and Judah Aszod (1794–1866) of Dunaszerdahely. These men, who are commonly labeled "traditionalists" because of their rejection of modern western culture, typify one major trend in the Orthodox world of the nineteenth century. The other circle of leaders—rabbis Samson Raphael Hirsch (1808–88) and Marcus Horovitz (1844–1910) of Frankfurt; and Esriel Hildesheimer (1820–99) and David Hoffmann (1843–1921) of Berlin—are representatives of the "modernists" in the Orthodox camp. This elite, in contradistinction to the "traditionalists," enthusiastically embraced modern culture and the benefits it offered Jews of the post-Enlightenment era. Taken together, their writings present a balanced picture of the Orthodox response to this issue.

The principal sources employed in this paper are rabbinic responsa—authoritative renderings of Jewish law issued by leading rabbis to rabbinic colleagues for application and, sometimes, public dissemination in individual cases. Responsa are elite, technical documents—case discussions and their "holdings" in modern western jurisprudential nomenclature—and rabbis throughout the ages have used them to apply the insights, meanings, norms, and precedents provided by the literary and legal texts of the Jewish past to the pressing and often novel issues of a contemporary age.[3] As Orthodox Jews, the rabbis considered in this paper were totally wedded to this system of Jewish legal hermeneutics. Consquently, these writings provide a particularly fruitful, albeit often neglected, way of assessing the reactions of these men to the novel dimensions presented by the issue of apostasy in the nineteenth century. They also indicate why these men, as traditionalists guided by the precedents of the past, approached and defined the problem in the manner they did. In this particular instance, the responsa are also employed because they are the only sources that deal in depth with the topic under discussion. While some letters and portions of speeches and journal articles dealing with apostasy are cited, they are conspicuous by their paucity. Research into the Orthodox journals of the age did not uncover a single programmatic article concerning this problem.[4] A suggestion as to why this is so will be forthcoming in the course of the paper. For now, suffice it to say that the responsa are the most authoritative and classical mode of Orthodox expression and positions extrapolated from them allow a view to emerge of how nineteenth-century central European Orthodoxy dealt with this dilemma.

At the outset of the century rabbinic views of apostasy and apostates were tied very closely to rabbinic attitudes toward religious reformers in the community. As Jacob Katz, in speaking about Orthodox reactions to apostasy at this time, observes:

> Of course, Orthodox Jews deplored the defection of great numbers of Jews to Christianity, but, observing that conversion in most cases was preceded by abandonment of the traditional way of life, their wrath fell upon the heads of those whom they held responsible for the disloyalty of Jews to their tradition . . . the religious reformers.[5]

Indeed, an analysis of central European Orthodox responses to apostasy in the first half of the nineteenth century supports Katz's view that the Orthodox regarded apostasy as simply another point, perhaps more extreme, along a continuum of dissolution and desertion thrust upon the Jewish community by enthusiasts of the *haskalah* and Reform some years earlier.

The Hatam Sofer, undisputed leader and architect of traditionalist Orthodoxy in Hungary during the early nineteenth century, forcefully articulated this view in 1819 at the time of the Hamburg Temple controversy. In his contribution to *These Are the Words of the Covenant*, a pamphlet condemning the "pernicious" deeds of the founders of this early Reform temple, Sofer stated that traditional rabbis would be duty-bound, if they possessed the power, to excommunicate reformers from the Jewish community. In his view, the reformers, by denying the divinity and transgressing the authority of the Oral Law, were persons of no religion. Consequently, to excommunicate them would simply be putting distance between them and the community, a policy they themselves had already established by their refusal to accept traditional religious doctrine.[6] Sofer, keenly aware of modern political conditions in Hamburg, knew that such action could not be taken. His attitudes, however, were clearly shaped by legal judgments taken from the Jewish past, which viewed violations of rabbinic law as equivalent to heresy. It is for this reason that Sofer failed to distinguish between Jews who converted to another religion and those who simply left the Orthodox fold. More significantly, no theoretical position was advanced in this document that might have allowed others to make this actual distinction. Thus, at the outset of the century, "apostasy" was defined in a widely circulated pamphlet by the outstanding leader of the Orthodox community in such a way that it focused not on persons who converted to Christianity, but on Jews who openly rebelled against rabbinic authority. Moreover, the disabilities attached to these reformers, as "apostates," were, as will be enumerated below, considerable.

Sofer's views, because of his unparalleled eminence in central European Orthodoxy, influenced many Orthodox leaders at the time and continued to do so for several decades. Typical of those whose thinking was shaped by Sofer's position was Rabbi Zvi Hirsch Chajes (1805–55) of Zolkiew, one of the foremost rabbinic scholars of the nineteenth century. Chajes issued a blistering polemic, *Minḥat Kena'ot*, against the Reformers in 1845 and added an excursus to this work in 1849. Focusing on the Reform rabbinical conferences that met in Germany from 1844 to 1846, Chajes attacked the Reformers as *maddiḥim* (those who lead astray)[7] and *mumarim* (open opponents of Jewish law, apostates),[8] terms traditionally reserved for apostates in medieval rabbinic literature. Chajes was particularly agitated by the debates concerning the issue of mixed marriage that took place at the 1844 Brunswick conference. While the assembled rabbis rejected a motion that stated that "marriages between Jews and Christians, in fact, marriages with monotheists in general, are not forbidden," they did agree to the following motion: "Members of monotheistic religions in general are not forbidden to marry if the parents are permitted by the laws of the state to bring up children from such wedlock in the Jewish religion."[9] To Chajes such a resolution was a serious and unforgiveable breach of Jewish tradition. He contended that it was a holy duty for the Orthodox to separate themselves from these people on account of such deviations and perversions of tradition. He not only proscribed marriages between Orthodox and non-Orthodox Jews, but even forbade Orthodox Jews to visit the non-Orthodox in their homes. Testimony offered by Reform Jews was not to be considered valid in a

Jewish court of law and Orthodox Jews were neither to mourn nor eulogize reformers at their deaths. Moreover, Chajes declared the children of these people to be *mamzerim* (illegitimate) because of their refusal to obey the laws of family purity. The polemic Chajes undertook against the reformers represents something more than a midnineteenth-century attempt by an Orthodox leader to combat Reform. It reveals conclusively that the Orthodox regarded reformers as apostates.[10]

Chajes' book also contains a proposal for the most appropriate way to respond to the changes then transforming the nature of Jewish religious life. In an excursus to the 1849 edition, Chajes observed that the reformers claimed that the Talmud empowered the authorities in every age to make whatever changes were necessary in their eyes concerning the order and structure of the liturgy. Consequently, the reformers believed they were authorized to introduce innovations such as Sabbath worship on Sunday for those who had to work for economic reasons on Saturday. Chajes pointed out that Ludwig Philippson, one of the leaders of Reform, hoped that this innovation would allow these persons to have a Sabbath worship experience. Such concessions to social reality, in Chajes's opinion, were totally unwarranted. Whatever authority contemporary rabbinic leaders did possess could not contravene, as this change did, even a single dictum in the *Shulḥan Arukh*. Chajes therefore wrote, "We do not need to attempt to aid one who profanes the Sabbath publicly . . . as the Holy One, Blessed be He, needs neither him nor his prayer." Here Chajes was asserting that the Orthodox had to be vigilant in their defense of Jewish law, even if this meant that some would leave the Jewish fold as a result. In his view, no compromise with God's law was to be tolerated.[11]

This view of Reform, associating it with apostasy, also appears in the pages of *Der Zionswaechter*, a journal of traditionalist thought edited by Rabbi Jacob Ettlinger (1798–1871) of Altona. In 1846 one writer claimed that the reformers could not be retained within the community. It was forbidden to eat in their homes and to marry their daughters. "No common religious bonds exist between us. . . . They must be viewed as any other religious confession."[12] Solomon Eger (1786–1852) of Posen urged Ettlinger to heed a decree issued by the rabbis of Posen to ban the reformers from the community. The Orthodox were obligated, Eger wrote, "to separate them from Israel for in no wise are they to be considered as belonging to the people

Israel."[13] Ettlinger, despite his vociferous attacks upon Reform in the pages of his journal, refused Eger's request. In his view, these people, whatever their sins, remained Jews. The seeds for another Orthodox attitude toward apostasy, one that distinguished between religious reform and conversion to Christianity, are here apparent. The struggle between these two views of apostasy remained an active one in the Orthodox world as the community approached midcentury.

Rabbi Mattathias Levian of Halberstadt issued a responsum in 1847 that underscored the opinion that Reform was a form of apostasy and that the reformers were to be treated as apostates. Levian, a traditional Orthodox rabbi, was responding to the first manifestations of Reform in his bailiwick. On 3 March 1847, a law was passed permitting Jews to petition "to secede from the community to which they are attached." With passage of this bill, eight Jewish citizens appeared before the city officials and requested permission to leave the Orthodox-controlled Jewish community. Levian, in responding to these men, wrote that they were "apostates [*mumarim*] to the entire Torah." They had decided to sever their ties to the community, he charged, because they intended to convert to Christianity and thereby gain more rights than other Jewish citizens of Halberstadt. Moreover, Levian held that even if they did not formally convert to Christianity, they were, by virtue of their rejection of the Oral Law and traditional rabbinic authority, "like gentiles." Consequently, Levian held that these men were to be treated as apostates. They were not to be married in a Jewish wedding ceremony, counted as Jews for the purpose of a prayer quorum, or receive a Jewish burial. In addition, they were not to be called to a public reading of the Torah and they were not to be allowed to recite the mourner's prayer on behalf of deceased relatives. Here again the Orthodox tendency to equate religious reform with apostasy is evident.[14]

At the time Levian wrote his responsum, the university-educated Esriel Hildesheimer, who was destined, in 1874, to establish and head the Orthodox *Rabbinerseminar* in Berlin, also served the Halberstadt community. It is interesting, therefore, to contrast the responsum issued by Hildesheimer on this matter with that of his senior colleague Levian. Hildesheimer recognized that a decision to reject the traditional basis of Jewish faith need not be accompanied by a desire to convert to Christianity. He observed that those who wished to secede from the community cited as their motive that they disagreed with a majority of the community on matters of faith. As they did not speak of converting to Christianity, Hildesheimer did not charge them with "apostasy." He contended that the reformers' desire to secede was not an effort "to destroy God's covenant with Israel at Sinai." As "Deists," these reformers were not "apostates to the entire Torah." Rather, they were ones "who separated themselves from the ways of the community," a lesser offense. Hildesheimer thus employed categories taken from the tradition to distinguish between religously "unfaithful" Jews and Jews who actually converted to Christianity. A student of Jacob Ettlinger's, Hildesheimer obviously adopted his teacher's position that these persons remained Jews. Nevertheless, Hildesheimer felt that their violations were serious enough to warrant virtually the same proscriptions Levian had laid down. He ruled that these men were not to be included in a Jewish prayer quorum or be buried in a Jewish cemetery. They were not to be called to a public reading of the Torah nor to be permitted to recite the traditional mourner's prayer on behalf of deceased relatives, unless there was no one else to do so. Hildesheimer did not address the question of whether these men might be married in a Jewish wedding ceremony.[15] While these edicts undoubtedly outraged the reformers, the whole issue became moot when the secular authorities of Halberstadt, for a variety of reasons, refused to allow the group to secede.[16] The particular episode aside, the critical point at this juncture is that Hildesheimer, in his responsum, made a distinction between Reform Jews and apostates to Christianity. On the other hand, the practical prohibitions he issued against them were similar to those of the Ḥatam Sofer, Eger, Chajes, and Levian.

The ambivalent posture that Hildesheimer adopted in this instance reflects the dilemma in which midnineteenth-century Orthodox leaders found themselves on the question of apostasy. Social reality clearly indicated to these men that the reformers were not beyond the bounds of the contemporary community. However, the language of the legal tradition to which they were committed did not easily provide for a distinction between these persons and actual apostates, that is, converts to Christianity.[17] This inability of the legal tradition to do so and the subsequent framework it established for the approach these leaders adopted to the problem, as well as their simultaneous recognition that it was inadequate to cope with the parameters of the modern situation, are evidenced elsewhere in the writings of Hildesheimer and his colleague Samson Raphael Hirsch. In an 1873 responsum concerning Zacharias Frankel's *Darkhei Ha-Mishnah* (1859),

Hildesheimer began with the words, "Therefore, concerning the book of the *meshummad* [apostate] Frankel. . . ."[18] Lest it be supposed that the use of this term was either accidental or hyperbolic, Hildesheimer continued by noting explicitly that the term *meshummad* identified the individual as a graver heretic than if he were labeled an *apikoris*, a simple unbeliever.[19]

Hildesheimer's reference to Frankel as a *meshummad* is an outgrowth of the canons he inherited from the tradition. After all, Frankel, the head of the Jewish Theological Seminary in Breslau, was a strictly observant Jew and an active leader in communal matters. He was hardly, by any reasonable definition, beyond the bounds of the community. In his *Darkhei Ha-Mishnah*, however, he expressed the view that the *Mishnah*, the earliest code of the Oral Law, had developed in history. He also maintained that the talmudic phrase "*halakhah le-Moshe mi-Sinai*" referred to a law of such great antiquity that it was *as if* it had been revealed to Moses at Sinai.[20] This was in direct opposition to the ahistorical approach the Orthodox leadership of his day took to the issue of revelation. They believed that Jewish law had been delivered in its totality to Moses at Sinai and savagely attacked Frankel in the Orthodox press for his deviation from this dogma.[21] They contended that the phrase "*halakhah le-Moshe mi-Sinai*" could only be understood in its literal sense, "as a law given to Moses at Sinai." Frankel's rejection of these views and his insistence that Jewish law had developed over time were sufficient to allow Hildesheimer to label him a *meshummad*. Frankel, as a non-Orthodox Jew in matters of belief, had, in the eyes of the Orthodox, somehow stepped beyond the boundaries of the Jewish religious community. As late as 1873 an Orthodox leader thus felt constrained to utilize a term of apostasy to describe the leader of another Jewish religious viewpoint. Hildesheimer's use of *meshummad* to characterize Frankel is a direct result of the legacy he received from his medieval rabbinic forebears on this issue. As such, it reveals the limitations inherent in this approach, even from the perspective of a Hildesheimer, in the changed circumstances of the nineteenth century.

Hildesheimer's own ability to draw a distinction between "heretics" who did not leave the fold and those who actually became Christians is apparent in an exchange of letters he had with Rabbi Hirsch, the great ideologue of nineteenth century German Orthodoxy and rabbi of the Orthodox *Austrittsgemeinde* in Frankfurt. Hildesheimer, Hirsch discovered, was an active member of the *Alliance*

Israélite Universelle, a Paris-based charitable and educational organization. Non-Orthodox Jews, including graduates of the Breslau Seminary, were active members of the group, and not only was its Paris head, Adolphe Crémieux, not Orthodox, but his wife had had their children baptized! [22] Hirsch wrote to Hildesheimer:

> I have absolutely no connection with the *Alliance*. . . . I fail to see how a man imbued with proper Jewish thought can attach himself to a group founded for the sake of a Jewish task when its founder and head are completely removed from genuine religious Judaism. . . . It is very painful for me to see an honored name like Dr. Hildesheimer united with the *Alliance* and the men of the Breslau Seminary. [23]

In a manner reminiscent of other Orthodox rabbinical leaders, Hirsch concluded by stating that this was not the way of the pious men of old who separated themselves from heretics such as these for the sake of preserving Judaism. He clearly felt that no distinction was to be made between the graduates of the Breslau Seminary, Crémieux, and actual converts to Christianity. The former group, as "bad Jews" who transformed "apostasy into priesthood," posed a threat to the survival of Judaism equal to that posed by the latter group of "baptized Jews."[24]

Hildesheimer disagreed. He recognized that there was a great difference between graduates of Frankel's seminary and apostates to Christianity. The prestige of the Orthodox, he argued, was injured by the adoption of this isolationist position vis-à-vis other elements in the community on matters of common charitable concern. Despite the fact that he labeled Frankel a *meshummad*, had issued proscriptions earlier in his career against Reform segments of the community on certain practical matters, and obviously deplored Crémieux's ability to tolerate his wife's baptism of their children, there is no doubt that Hildesheimer viewed converts to Christianity differently than he did Jews who left the Orthodox fold. Another incident supports this interpretation.

In May 1881, a Dr. Staadecker from Mannheim wrote Hildesheimer asking him what the relationship of the Orthodox ought to be to the general Jewish community of that city. Staadecker reported that conversions to Christianity were frequent in the community; in fact, the daughter of the head of the community was baptized and married to a non-Jew. Hildesheimer responded to Staadecker in exceedingly bitter tones. He told him that these converts to Christianity upset him deeply and referred to them as "cowardly opportunists" with weak ideals who mouthed the most banal platitudes. "Because we live in such bitter times, all the more so is the Jew commanded to hold his head high." Angrily, Hildesheimer added, "It is a holy and pressing duty to bring such vile desertions into the open."[25]

Hildesheimer, by the last quarter of the century, reflected the changes that were beginning to mark Orthodox attitudes toward apostasy. While no programmatic statement concerning this issue was forthcoming, the attacks upon Reform Jews as "apostates" had almost disappeared. Undoubtedly, the rise of antisemitism in Germany after 1870 contributed to this transformation in Orthodox policy. Hildesheimer and others in his camp recognized that antisemitism posed a threat to the entire Jewish community and that sectarian divisions that caused the Orthodox to brand religious liberals as apostates could no longer be tolerated. Unlike Hirsch and his devotees, Hildesheimer eagerly joined forces with non-Orthodox Jews in combating this menace.[26] The bitter battles of the midnineteenth century between the Orthodox and the Liberals were, by this point, already a thing of the past. This is not to say that Orthodoxy either embraced or approved any variety of liberal Judaism. However, the struggle for hegemony in the community was over. Each side had staked out its own territory and Orthodoxy was increasingly content to strengthen commitment to the observance of Torah among its own adherents.[27] In short, the diferentiated conditions of modern life caused an important segment of the Orthodox rabbinate's leadership to acknowledge and accept the reality of a denominationally divided community. An affirmation of non-Orthodox Judaism did not necessarily constitute, in the eyes of a leader like Hildesheimer, a decision to abandon Jewish identity. This posture, seen in nascent form in Ettlinger's decision to reject Eger's demand that the Orthodox ban the liberals from the community, was to be articulated more fully, as will be discussed below, in the writings of Hildesheimer's students, Horovitz and Hoffmann. By 1881, though, the desire to do battle with Reform was clearly on the wane and the assessment of Reform more sober.

On the eastern periphery of central Europe the threat of apostasy was still seen from a more medieval perspective, though even there responsa issued by leading Hungarian rabbinical authorities of the midnineteenth century reflect differences in attitude and policy toward this issue. The Ktav Sofer, successor to his father Moses Schreiber as head of the famed Pressburg *yeshivah*, was certainly one of the most influential Orthodox rabbis in Hungary during his day. In 1848 Sofer was asked whether it was permissible to sell a Torah scroll to an apostate. This apostate, according to the rabbi who sent the question to Sofer, still observed Jewish dietary laws and went to the synagogue during the High Holidays, despite having changed his religion. Unfortunately, there is no information about what motivated this man to become a Christian. It is only reported that the individual desired to purchase the Torah in order "to read from it." Sofer, in a brief responsum, ruled that it was clearly forbidden to sell the Torah scroll to a *mumar* such as this, even if he "walks in the ways of Israel." This man was not, in Sofer's opinion, "a proper Jew," and his children, who would certainly be raised as gentiles, would be unlikely to accord the Torah scroll the honor and respect due it. Acceptance of Jesus as the messiah placed one beyond the boundaries of the Jewish world.[28]

Another midcentury responsum of Sofer reveals his attitude toward apostasy and its relationship to the Jewish community more completely. In this case, a man had committed adultery with his uncle's wife and subsequently married her. Both these acts were in clear violation of rabbinic law. As there was no civil marriage in the Austro-Hungarian empire, the rabbi who sent Sofer the question reported that he could go to the secular authorities in the community to have the marriage dissolved. However, if he did so, he feared that the people would apostasize. Civil law did not give the rabbi absolute authority over persons born into the community in these areas. If an individual chose to convert formally to Christianity, then the rabbi's power over the individual, as in the medieval past, was abrogated. The key difference was that now the rabbi was compelled to recognize that commitment to traditional Jewish norms in matters of marriage and divorce had attenuated to the point that a couple's decision to convert to Christianity in order to evade the requirements of Jewish matrimonial law could not be seen as an unusual one. This case reflected an all too common occurrence, not an isolated event, in the life of the midnineteenth-century central European Jewish community. The decision rendered here, Sofer realized, would have important implications for the Orthodox world's definitions of and attitudes toward apostasy.

Sofer began his response by noting the famous ruling of Rabbi Moses Isserles in the *Shulḥan Arukh, Yoreh Deah* 334:1, "Excommunication is imposed upon one who deserves it, even if there is no reason to assume that this will cause his defection from the fold." He observed that his father, Moses Schreiber, had permitted Isserles's ruling to guide him in analogous cases earlier in the century. Adhering to a definition of apostasy that drew no distinctions between Jews who converted to Christianity and those who violated rabbinic injunctions, the Ḥatam Sofer had held that it was proper for a court to attempt to compel "transgressors" to comply with rabbinic law regardless of the consequences. No exceptions were to be made. The younger Sofer, mindful of his father's teachings, acknowledged that stringency in the case before him might well provide an example to others that Judaism, in its war for survival in the contemporary world, would sanction no compromises with Jewish law. A strict decision in this case, one that would define apostasy as a violation of rabbinic law, would demonstrate to all Jews both the seriousness of the couple's offense and the determination of the Orthodox rabbinate to preserve Judaism in the modern era.

The Ktav Sofer, despite all these considerations, decided that this course was not the wisest one for the community to pursue in the present situation. His reasoning was twofold, based on both reason and talmudic precedent. From the standpoint of Jewish law, Sofer cited the commentary of the *TaZ*, the famed seventeenth-century legal authority Samuel Halevi, to the Isserles passage quoted above. In that commentary Halevi maintained that it was unthinkable that Jewish law would sanction an action likely to drive a Jew to apostasy. As the couple already had children, Sofer drew upon the warrant from the *TaZ* and suggested that "perhaps we need to show mercy to the children so that they will not assimilate among the nations." He also noted that a talmudic passage (*B.T. Kiddushin* 81a) stated that an individual suspected of adultery was not to be punished if there was fear that slander concerning the legitimacy of his offspring would result. If this were so in a case involving illegitimacy, then, Sofer reasoned, it should be all the more so in an instance which would lead to the apostasy of the children. He contended, "What reason is there for me to correct others [i.e., the parents] and lose these children by forcing them to change their religion so that they would be lost from the community of God?"

Sofer continued by setting out the direction he felt the Orthodox community ought to take in this instance. The community, in his view, should do everything in its power to preserve these children for the Jewish people and its religion. He wrote, "These sheep, what is their sin, their transgression, that we should push them away from the inheritance of the Lord so that they will be lost forever?" If the rabbinic court chose to exercise its authority and call the parents to task for their admittedly sinful actions, then the community at large would view the parents as having been pushed out of the community and the children as having been forced to convert to Christianity, developments Sofer wanted to avoid. He thus concluded, "Certainly, it is better for us to hold back our hands [in this instance]."[29]

Sofer's approach to this question was sensitive and, perhaps, even accommodating to the realities of the apostasy. Jewish law possessed lenient precedents that, in his opinion, ought to be applied to certain aspects of this problem. It is the evolution of Orthodox attitudes toward this issue that is of crucial import here. A traditionalist Hungarian rabbinical leader, the son of the Hatam Sofer, drawing solely upon precedents taken from the legal tradition, forged a definition of apostasy by the midnineteenth century that distinguished between Jews who converted to Christianity and those who violated rabbinic law. The latter group, whatever their transgressions and however detestable in Sofer's eyes, still remained within the boundaries of the community. The Ktav Sofer had reversed his father's policies on this matter and, in so doing, demonstrated that Hungarian Orthodox attitudes toward the issue of apostasy were very much in transition by midcentury.

The legal writings of Sofer's colleague Judah Aszod display a different sensibility on the matter and demonstrate that Orthodox attitudes were hardly uniform or settled on this question. A prominent rabbinic scholar, Aszod shared the disdain of many Hungarian rabbinic figures for secular culture.[30] In 1864, for example, he led a delegation of Orthodox rabbis to the Habsburg emperor to request that funds not be appropriated, as some circles wanted, for the establishment of a modern rabbinical seminary, either Orthodox or Neolog. A rabbi trained in anything other than traditional rabbinic texts was an anathema to him.

In one telling responsum, Aszod revealed his own positon on the issue of apostasy. Rabbi Moses Samuel Jellinek of Vienna had sent a query to Aszod concerning the marriage of a *cohen* (a man of priestly descent) to a *halutsah* (a woman who has been released from the obligation of levirate marriage), a union forbidden by Jewish law. The couple, Jellinek reported, were deeply in love, and since the *"mesitim* [troublemakers]*[31] had greatly increased in Vienna," Jellinek feared that the couple would apostasize if he refused to grant them permission to marry. Thus, Jellinek wanted to know if "we are able to overlook [*l'hatir*] the prohibition [*issur*] forbidding the marriage of a *ḥalutsah* to a *cohen*, which is a rabbinical prohibition, in order to prevent the couple from transgressing the entire Torah through apostasy, God forbid." Jellinek, in framing the question as he did, clearly distinguished between Jews who converted to Christianity and those, like the couple in this case, who did not obey rabbinic law. Aszod made no such distinction.[32]

Aszod was astonished by Jellinek's suggestion. If a permission was granted in this case, then all "wayward people" who wanted "to fulfill their desires" would threaten to leave the community unless certain rabbinic prohibitions were relaxed. Thus, Aszod feared, all rabbinic ordinances which were constructed as "hedges to the Law" would be overturned. In order to preserve Judaism from the threat of dissolution posed by such Jews, no "leniency" could be shown in this instance. Unlike the Ktav Sofer, Aszod approvingly quoted Isserles, who had ruled that a rabbinic court was obligated to excommunicate individuals who merited the ban, even if it meant that they would apostasize. After all, Aszod reasoned, "the responsibility is not ours" if "this fool and sinner" consciously chooses to ignore the proscriptions of rabbinic law. Aszod stated, "His blood will be on his head . . . and we and all Israel will be clean." In concluding, he held that the rabbinic court would "sin" were it to permit this transgression of rabbinic law, for they would set a negative example for the community. Unlike the Ktav Sofer, Aszod felt that Jewry and Judaism could be preserved in the modern era only by the application of the strictest interpretation of Jewish law on the part of the rabbis. To rule leniently, as Sofer suggested, was to invite destruction. Aszod defined and viewed apostasy and apostates in accord with the all-encompassing vision derived from the medieval rabbinic tradition, and his attitudes, as reflected in this responsum, indicate that Hungarian rabbinic opinion was far from uniform on this issue at this juncture in time.

It remained for the Ktav Sofer's son, the Shevet Sofer, to deal with this issue, and his responsum on the subject reveals something of the Hungarian Orthodox community's attitudes toward this issue at the end of the century. Abraham Gruenbaum, rabbi in Hesse, wanted to know if the relatives of an apostate who had not actually died had to engage in mourning rituals for him, as was the custom in some traditional circles. The family saw apostasy as akin to death and had the psychological need to observe a mourning rite. Sofer acknowledged that there was some precedent for this practice, but felt that mourning observances in such an instance should be seen as tokens of sadness, not as lamentations in the face of death itself. For there was the possibility that "the son will return in repentance" and "thus no [need] to engage in genuine mourning, as it is not comparable to a [real] death." Conscious of the father's psychological state, Sofer said it would be fitting for this man "to sit in sadness and tears." He should not, however, engage in other acts of mourning, for as the apostate is "still alive, there is yet hope that he will return." The other members of the family should not perform even these acts of mourning. Although he saw apostasy as a genuine tragedy, the Shevet Sofer, like his father, was primarily concerned that the family deal with the crisis in such a way that the possibility of the apostate's return not be blocked.[33] The reasoned posture Sofer assumed in this case demonstrates how far the position of the Hungarian Orthodox rabbinate had evolved on this issue from the days of the Hatam Sofer's blistering attacks upon the reformers.

In light of this, it is interesting to return to Germany to see the attitudes exhibited by the Orthodox rabbinate of that country toward this issue at the end of the century. Marcus Horovitz, *orthodoxer Gemeinderabbiner* in Frankfurt from 1878 until his death in 1910, mentioned apostates and apostasy as relevant considerations in several of his responsa. In one case from 1891, Horovitz ruled that it was not only permissible, but a commandment for a Jew to contribute to the construction of a Catholic church.[34] If *meshummadim*, Jewish apostates, were members of the church, then Horovitz ruled that it was forbidden to do so. Conversion to Christianity clearly defined an individual as an apostate. In another responsum, Horovitz was asked to decide whether it was permissible and/or desirable for children born to gentile mothers and Jewish fathers to be ritually circumcised by a *mohel* as the first step in a process leading to their conversion to Judaism. In discussing this question, Horovitz related what he had done in two previous cases.[35] Once, Horovitz reported, he forbade the *mohel* to perform the circumcision because the father told him he did not plan to raise the child "according to the ways of Torah" and, moreover, threatened to abandon Judaism if Horovitz did not permit the circumcision. Therefore, wrote Horovitz, "I decided that if the father wanted to change his religion, why should I bring his son into the community of Israel?" The threat of apostasy obviously aroused Horovitz's ire and steeled his resolution to preserve the religious character of the Jewish community. In the second case, the father said he wanted to raise his son "according to the religion of Moses and Israel," but Horovitz heard that there "were heretics in the man's family who wanted to persuade him to convert to his wife's faith." Since the man seemed determined to reject their advice and since Horovitz feared that if he forbade the circumcision, the man would yield to their entreaties, he permitted the circumcision. He did not want to cause a Jew to "deny the God of Israel publicly." Horovitz's position, then, was similar to that of the Ktav Sofer in all of these instances.

In a third responsum, this from 1905, Horovitz fully articulated his attitude toward apostasy and Jewish communal policy. A Rabbi Rosenthal of Cologne asked Horovitz whether an individual who had converted several years earlier but was now an observant Jew and who had joined the synagogue and paid communal taxes could be called to the Torah.[36] The problem, in Rosenthal's opinion, was that this man, at the time he had returned to Judaism, had neither been ritually immersed nor formally received before a court of three as prescribed in the *Shulḥan Arukh, Yoreh Deah* 268:9.

Horovitz responded by asserting that these rituals were matters of custom, not law, in Judaism. Moreover, the purpose of these rituals was to indicate that the penitent, like a convert to Judaism, "was as a new-born babe." They also served to mark the former apostate's resolve to observe the commandments. As this man had already conducted himself as a Jew for a long period of time, "there was no ground for telling him that he should now immerse himself." In addition, Horovitz observed, "In this epoch [one] can neither expect nor wait for him to be a totally pious man." It would be enough if he were to lead a simple life observing the Sabbath and Jewish dietary laws. To expect more of him and to insist upon his fulfillment of the ritualistic requirements asked of a repentant apostate would, at this juncture, only be counterproductive. Why remind the man of his past deeds? "In my humble opinion, we are not free to do something which we know, from the outset, is not a remedy, but, perhaps, God forbid, a stumbling block for this man." In conclusion, Horovitz observed that the community should "not intimidate [former apostates] when they come to return in repentance." His accommodationist posture on this matter was akin to that of both the Ktav Sofer and Shevet Sofer, and reflects a new attitude that had developed in the community by the end of the nineteenth century.

Not all German Orthodox rabbis adopted the same position.

Horovitz's colleague and close personal friend, David Hoffmann, believed that the community had to adopt a stringent policy concerning these persons in order to protect itself from destruction. Hoffmann, initially an instructor in rabbinics, and later Hildesheimer's successor as head of the *Rabbinerseminar*, was a great scholar of *jüdische Wissenschaft*. He was also the outstanding legal authority for Orthodox Jewry in Germany during his day. In one case, Hoffmann related that a Jew had written to the secular authorities in his city and asked to be designated, in the eyes of the law, as *konfessionslos* (a citizen of no religion).[37] In this way he could formally cut his ties to Judaism without having to convert to Christianity and could also avoid the burden of paying Jewish communal taxes. The man now regretted his decision and wanted to return publicly to Judaism. The question posed for Hoffmann was twofold. First, should this man who, after all, had not formally converted to Christianity, be considered an apostate? And, if so, should he, in accordance with Jewish law, be ritually immersed and openly admonished before a court of three? Hoffmann's response to the first question was direct. The man was an apostate: "For, in any event, he left the *community and religion* of Israel." Hoffmann pointed out that there was nothing explicit in either earlier or later rabbinic writings to distinguish between " a *mumar* who turned to another religion and a *mumar* who left the community of Israel and yet did not accept another religion." The first category of apostasy, wherein the individual publicly acknowledged belief in another religion, was, of course, "complete idolatry." However, the label of idolater also applied, Hoffmann maintained, "to one who departs from the community of Israel even if he does not accept another religion. For, in any event, he, too, confesses openly that he denies the Torah of Moses," the basis of Jewish faith. "And, if this is so, he is comparable to an idolater and identical to one who apostasizes to another religion." Therefore, the man must receive ritual immersion before being allowed to return to the Jewish fold.

Hoffmann bolstered his argument for stringency with another consideration. He emphasized that many of those who declared themselves *konfessionslos* did so in order to avoid paying communal taxes. Yet, they still identified themselves socially as Jews and married Jewish women. Moreover, they themselves claimed that they were not apostates. "Thus if we are lenient with them when they return and do not reckon them as apostates . . . we are extending a hand to these sinners in the performance of their alien deeds." In order to erect "a necessary fence" against these persons, it was essential to deal stringently with them. Otherwise the boundaries of the community would become blurred and dissolution would ensue.

While the unyielding tone of Hoffmann's responsum placed him at odds with Horovitz, the actual definition he offered of apostasy reveals how far Orthodox opinion on this subject had been altered during the course of the century. Hoffmann's broad criterion for apostasy, a public denial of the divinity and binding authority of Mosaic and rabbinic law, was clearly derived from rabbinic tradition and without a doubt could have been interpreted, as it was by the Hatam Sofer and others, to include Reform. Hoffmann seems to have employed an additional standard as well in arriving at his definition. For him, the decision to officially leave the *Gemeinde*, not lack of belief or failure to observe the Torah of Moses alone, marked one as an apostate. This does not mean that Hoffmann approved of Liberal Judaism. In fact, he attacked it strongly in other responsa, labeling reformers as *meharsim* (destroyers).[38] Nevertheless, in other legal decisions, Hoffmann ruled that these non-Orthodox Jews *were* members of the community and thus, by logical extension, not "apostates." He therefore allowed them to be included in a prayer quorum, to be called to a public reading of the Torah, and to be married in a Jewish wedding ceremony.[39] All the disabilities the Hatam Sofer, Levian, Chajes, Hildesheimer, and others had issued against the reformers at the beginning of the century had now been removed.

This paper has shown that neither a shared "modernity" nor "traditionalism" nor similar geographic circumstances prevented rabbis like Hoffmann and Horovitz on the one hand and Judah Aszod and the Ktav Sofer on the other from developing different viewpoints on the issue of apostates and apostasy. This indicates that even when persons share a common theological and cultural perspective on the world, they will not respond to social reality in the same way. This does not mean that social environment and cultural outlook have no impact on the decisions of a jurist and religious leader. Rather, it means that the stratagems a rabbi employs to respond to contemporary problems depend as much upon his personal predilections as they do upon any other factor. The framework of Jewish law provided clear boundaries for these men in formulating their positions. However, the decision to employ either "lenient" or "stringent" precedents to justify either this or that stance suggests that personal visions of what would most likely benefit the community were as, if not more, crucial than other variables in formulating Orthodox policy on this issue. Locale and cultural outlook, while undoubtedly significant, were not determinative in this matter.

Virtually the entire leadership of the central European Orthodox community, Hungarian and German, "modern" and "traditional," responded with a single voice to the problem and definition of apostasy and apostates in the first half of the century. The inheritors of a medieval rabbinic traditionalism that made no distinctions between the religious and civic life of the community, they were given a definition of apostasy that failed to differentiate between Jews who violated rabbinic law and Jews who converted to another religion. Given this definition, as well as their observation "that conversion in most cases was preceded by abandonment of the traditional way of life," it is possible to understand why the Orthodox centered their wrath upon the religious reformers and not upon persons who actually converted to Christianity at this time. Their decision to accord the same treatment to Reform as they would have to actual apostasy to another religion demonstrates the powerful force the received religious tradition exerted upon them. The definitions and attitudes these men displayed toward the issue of apostates and apostasy not only reflect the contours of a past they honored and cherished, but indicate how significant this past was in shaping them. The potency of this heritage is further evidenced in the fact that these attitudes and definitions continued to exercise an influence throughout the course of the century. Traces of them, for example, can be found in the writings of Hoffmann and Aszod.

The novel political, cultural, and social situation of the nineteenth century central European Jewish community did not allow these positions to remain unchallenged and unaltered. By midcentury significant Orthodox opinion began to emerge that distinguished between religious reformers who remained in the community and apostates who actually left it. By the end of the nineteenth century this evolution was complete and many rabbis advocated that the community adopt a lenient and accommodationist stance toward apostates. Nearly all rabbis now differentiated between Jewish religious liberals and apostates who abandoned the community, whether through formal conversion or adoption of the status *konfessionslos*. Reformers, though viewed by the Orthodox as "sinners," were nevertheless considered legitimate members of the Jewish community rather than apostates.

This analysis of central European Orthodox attitudes toward apostates and apostasy in the nineteenth century has shown how the received canon of Jewish religious tradition clashed with the realities of the modern setting over this issue. By tracing the development of Orthodox opinion on this matter, it has demonstrated that the Orthodox refocused elements of the tradition to reduce the dissonance that existed between the conditions of the past and the actualities of the present. It thus possesses a significance beyond the issue of apostasy itself, for in viewing this issue through an Orthodox lens, this paper has provided a barometer for measuring how even the most traditionalist segment of the Jewish community succeeded in transplanting itself from the medieval to the modern world. As such, it is an important chapter in modern Jewish intellectual and religious history.

NOTES

1. Salo W. Baron, *The Jewish Community*, 3 vols. (Philadelphia: Jewish Publication Society, 1941), 2:228.

2. *Jüdisches Lexikon*, s.v. "Taufjudentum."

3. For a full description of the nature of the responsa literature, see David Ellenson, "Jewish Legal Interpretation: Literary, Scriptural, Social, and Ethical Perspectives," *Semeia* 34 (1985): 93–114.

4. Two colleagues who are experts in this literature, Professor Mordechai Eliav of Bar-Ilan University and Professor Steven Lowenstein of the University of Judaism, have told me that they know of no Orthodox statement in the Jewish press of the day that deals specifically with this issue. They are not responsible, of course, for conducting an extensive investigation into this area, but as my own research was unable to uncover any such piece, their observation confirms the impression that no programmatic article on the issue of apostasy appeared in the German Orthodox press of this period.

5. Jacob Katz, "Religion as a Uniting and Dividing Force in Modern Jewish History," in *The Role of Religion in Modern Jewish History*, ed. Jacob Katz (Cambridge: Association for Jewish Studies, 1975), p. 10.

6. Ibid., p. 11. For further information on Sofer, see Jacob Katz, "Kavim le-biographiyah shel ha-Ḥatam Sofer" [Contributions toward a Biography of the Ḥatam Sofer], in *Studies in Mysticism and Religion Presented to Gershom G. Scholem*, ed. E. E.

DAVID ELLENSON

Urbach, R. J. Zwi Werblowsky, and Ch. Wirszubski (Jerusalem: Magnes Press, 1967), pp. 115–61. The views of Sofer related in this paragraph are drawn from Katz's article.

7. This term stems from Deuteronomy 13. In verse 7 it states, "If your brother, your own mother's son, or your son or daughter, or the wife of your bosom, or your closest friend, entices you in secret, saying, 'Come, let us worship other gods. . . .'" This is followed in verse 11 by the admonition, "Stone him to death, for he sought *to make you stray* from the Lord your God, who brought you out of the land of Egypt, out of the house of bondage." Also see verse 14 in the same chapter.

8. Marcus Jastrow, *A Dictionary of the Targumim, the Talmud Babli and Yerushalmi, and the Midrashic Literature*, s.v. "Mumar."

9. W. Gunther Plaut, *The Rise of Reform Judaism* (New York: World Union for Progressive Judaism, 1963), p. 222.

10. Zvi Hirsch Chajes, *Minhat Kena'ot*, in *Kol Sifrei Maharaz Chajes*, 2 vols. [All the Writings of Zvi Hirsch Chajes] (Jerusalem: 1958), 2:1008–9 and 1013.

11. Ibid. pp. 1003 and 1007.

12. *Der Zionswaechter* 2 (1846): 50, cited in Robert Liberles, *Religious Conflict in Social Context: The Resurgence of Orthodox Judaism in Frankfurt am Main, 1838–1877* (Westport, Conn.: Greenwood Press, 1985), p. 79.

13. *Iggerot Soferim* [Letters of the Sofers] 4 parts, ed. S. Sofer (Tel Aviv: Sinai, 1970), 1:84.

14. Levian's responsum is printed in Esriel Hildesheimer, *The Responsa of Rabbi Esriel, Orah Hayyim*, no. 7.

15. Ibid.

16. For a full account of this episode, see David Ellenson, "Rabbi Esriel Hildesheimer and the Quest for Religious Authority," *Modern Judaism* 1 1981) : 279–97.

17. I am indebted to my friend Rabbi Daniel Landes, a professor of Talmud at Yeshiva University in Los Angeles, for this insight and formulation, which provides the direction for this essay.

18. It is interesting to note that Hildesheimer uses the German word *Buch* in this text instead of the Hebrew word for book, *sefer*. Obviously, the term *sefer* possessed religious connotations for Hildesheimer which the word *Buch* did not. As he did not want to ascribe any religious worth to Frankel's book, he purposefully chose to employ the German and not the Hebrew word to designate this work. In any event, the transliterated use of *Buch* stands out in the otherwise Hebrew text.

19. *The Responsa of Rabbi Esriel, Yoreh Deah*, no. 238.

20. An excellent synopsis of Frankel's position on this issue can be found in Seymour Siegel, "The Meaning of Jewish Law in Conservative Judaism," in *Conservative Judaism and Jewish Law*, ed. Seymour Siegel (New York: Ktav, 1977), p. xvi.

21. See, for example, Hirsch's letter on this matter in *Jeschurun* (1861): 297. An English summary of the debate between the Orthodox and Frankel, as well as the

references to the relevant German literature on this affair, can be found in Noah Rosenbloom, *Tradition in an Age of Reform* (Philadelphia: Jewish Publication Society, 1976), pp. 107–8 and 425.

22. On the baptism of Crémieux's children and the disappointing consequences it had for his life, see. S. Posener, *Adolphe Crémieux: A Biography*, trans. Eugene Golob (Philadelphia: Jewish Publication Society, 1941), pp. 88–89.

23. Azriel Hildesheimer, "Hiluf mikhtavim bein Ezriel Hildesheimer u'vein ha-rav Shimshon Rafael Hirsch b'inyanei erets yisrael" [An Exchange of Letters Between Esriel Hildesheimer and Rabbi Samson Raphael Hirsch on Matters Relating to the Land of Israel] *Ha-Maayan* (Tishrei, 5714): 48–49.

24. Samson Raphael Hirsch, "Religion Allied to Progress," in *The Jew in the Modern World*, ed. Paul R. Mendes-Flohr and Jehuda Reinharz (New York and Oxford: Oxford University Press, 1980), pp. 177–78.

25. *Rabbiner Esriel Hildesheimer Briefe*, ed. Mordechai Eliav (Jerusalem: Verlag Rubin Mass, 1965), letter 54.

26. For a description of the distinction between the Hirsch and Hildesheimer camps, see Sanford Ragins, *Jewish Responses to Anti-Semitism in Germany* (Cincinnati: Hebrew Union College Press, 1980), pp. 88–103.

27. See M. A. Shulvass, "The *Rabbinerseminar* of Berlin," in *Mosedot torah be-eiropah* [Jewish Institutions of Higher Learning in Europe], ed. Samuel Mirsky (New York: Ogen, 1956), p. 695.

28. *Responsa of the Ktav Sofer, Yoreh Deah*, vol. 2, no. 133.

29. Ibid., no. 168.

30. It is interesting to note, in light of Aszod's general approach to western culture, that he chose to send his son to the yeshivah of Esriel Hildesheimer in Eisenstadt. This yeshivah introduced secular subjects into the curriculum of the school, a highly controversial innovation in the eyes of many of the Hungarian Orthodox. A description of the Hildesheimer yeshivah in Eisenstadt is found in Mordechai Eliav, "Torah-'im-derekh-erets be-hungariyah" [Torah-'im-derekh-erets in Hungary], *Sinai* 51 (Iyaar-Sivan, 5722-1962): 127–42.

31. This term stems from Deuteronomy 13:7. It literally means "enticers" and is often employed in Jewish literature to refer to missionaries. It is not clear here whether Aszod is referring to missionaries or apostate Jews. For this reason I have left the Hebrew word in the text.

32. Judah Aszod, *Yehudah Ya'aleh*, no. 140.

33. *Responsa of the Shevet Sofer, Yoreh Deah*, no. 108.

34. Marcus Horovitz, *Matte Levi, Yoreh Deah*, no. 28. For an analysis of this responsum see David Ellenson, "Jewish Covenant and Christian Trinitarianism," in *Jewish Civilization: Essays and Studies*, 3 vols., ed. Ronald Brauner (Philadelphia: Reconstructionist Rabbinical College, 1985), 3:85–100.

187

35. Horovitz, *Matte Levi, Yoreh Deah*, no. 54. There is a discussion of this responsum in David Ellenson, "Accommodation, Resistance, and the Halakhic Process," in *Jewish Civilization: Essays and Studies* 2 (1981) : 83–100.

36. Horovitz, *Matte Levi, Oraḥ Ḥayyim*, no. 5.

37. David Hoffmann, *Melammed Leho'il, Yoreh Deah*, no. 84.

38. Ibid., no. 16, sec. 1.

39. Ibid., *Yoreh Deah*, no. 79, and *Orah Hayyim*, no. 29.

7

Jewish Apostasy in Russia: A Tentative Typology

MICHAEL STANISLAWSKI

In the spring of 1905, frantic political turmoil in Russia forced the government of Tsar Nicholas II to issue a series of laws and concessions that attempted to stem the tide of revolution in the land. One of these palliative measures was the "Law on Religious Toleration" of 17 April, a noble, if ultimately vain, stab at institutionalizing freedom of belief and religious pluralism in the beleaguered and fractious empire. Among the unprecedented provisions of this law was the granting of permission to Jews who had converted to Christianity to return to Judaism. Petitions of redress soon began to flood the Ministry of the Interior, as hundreds of former Jews demonstrated their desire to return to their erstwhile faith. Very soon thereafter, as the dream of political and confessional liberty receded in the wake of pogrom and reaction, the number of returnees dwindled, and was soon overwhelmed by a new wave of applicants for baptism.[1]

Who were the Russian Jews on either side of the font?

Unfortunately, a definitive answer to this question—as to countless other questions more central to the history of the Jews in Russia—is far from available at this stage of our knowledge and access to archival materials. The historiography on the subject is extremely limited, highlighted by two fascinating collections of anecdotal biographies of apostates—Shmuel Leib Tsitron's *Meshumodim: tipn un siluetn fun noentn over* [Apostates: Types and Silhouettes from the Recent Past] and Shaul Ginzburg's *Meshumodim in tsarishn rusland* [Apostates in Tsarist Russia].[2]

189

These quasi-moralistic biographical accounts were written by extremely talented raconteurs in a highly melodramatic style appropriate to the popular Yiddish press of the 1920s, in which they were originally published.[3] Although they contain a wealth of intriguing and beguiling stories, these sketches are severely limited as historical sources, since they provide no documentation for the facts, incidents, and conversations they relate, and detail the conversion of only several dozen famous (or mostly infamous) Russian Jews.

It is clear, however, that in the nineteenth century more Jews converted to Christianity in the Russian Empire than anywhere else in Europe; this is not too surprising, of course, since Russian Jewry was by far the largest Jewish community in the world. The most reliable extant statistics—which, like all other numbers referring to Russian Jews in the nineteenth century, must be treated with a healthy dose of skepticism—were published by the Russian Holy Synod itself, and establish that 69,400 Russian Jews were baptized in the Russian Orthodox Church during the nineteenth century.[4] Western historians of Jewish apostasy have claimed in addition that some 12,000 Jews, most probably in the Polish provinces, converted to Roman Catholicism, and 3,100 to various forms of Protestantism, especially Lutheranism. In total, these historians assert, the 84,500 Russian Jews represented 41 percent of all Jewish converts to Christianity in nineteenth-century Europe.[5]

While the numerical extent of Russian-Jewish apostasy cannot be ascertained with any precision, its chronology seems roughly to have paralleled the course of the political status of the Jews in tsarist Russia. In the early years of the century there were very few converts, despite the interest of Tsar Alexander I in the baptism of the Jews—at his direction, a Society of Israelitish Christians was established to grant extensive privileges and landholdings to apostates, but it never converted even one Jew and was disbanded in the next reign. From 1827 to 1855, the number rose sharply, as a result of the baptism of large numbers of Jews in the army of Nicholas I—a subject to which we shall return; this period witnessed the largest proportion of conversions over the century, the highest yearly averages, and the greatest number in one year, 1854, in which 4,439 Jews were baptized. But the converted soldiers did not constitute the entire total of Jewish apostates even in the Russia of Nicholas I, and they accounted for only approximately 30 percent of the total for the century as a whole. In the more liberal reign of Alexander II, from 1855 to 1881, the number of converts dropped considerably as more avenues of hope were opened to Russian Jews. The crash of these hopes in the last decades of tsarism, however, led to a renewed flight to Christianity, especially after the introduction, in the late 1880s and early 1890s, of admission quotas in institutions of higher learning and restrictions on the practice of law and medicine by Jews. While the heady years of 1905–6 saw the number of converts decline, and the astonishing return to Judaism of recalcitrant apostates, between 1907 and 1917 a new, and even larger, wave of baptism was reported to have swept Russian Jewry.[6]

While the nexus between political repression and apostasy seems unimpeachable, it does not provide us with sufficient information about the nature of Jewish apostasy in tsarist Russia. Precisely who were the Jews who resorted to this extreme measure? What can be said about their motivations, their social and economic status, their personalities? Generalization from anecdote distorts eastern European Jewish historiography more than most other fields, and so sensitive a topic as conversion to Christianity is even more susceptible to subjective and apologetic treatment. This difficulty is partially resolved by the discovery of an impressive body of archival data on Jewish apostates in Russia: the files of the Lithuanian Consistory of the Russian Orthodox Church, which surfaced in the archives of the YIVO Institute in New York in the 1970s. The materials relating to the reign of Nicholas I were analyzed and published in a previous study; this paper continues that investigation, reporting on the entire collection, which consists of 192 files detailing the conversion to the Russian Orthodox Church of 244 Russian Jews from 1819 to 1911 (as well as 13 who began the process but for one reason or another were not baptized in the end).[7]

The Lithuanian Consistory archives, to be sure, elucidate only a tiny fraction of the total number of Jewish converts in the Russian Empire. Moreover, since the population of Lithuania was (and remains) overwhelmingly Catholic, these archives undoubtedly reflect only a partial picture of Jewish apostasy even within that region. Nonetheless, if used with caution and care, these materials can provide an interesting sample of a phenomenon previously unstudied: the conversion to Christianity of ordinary Russian Jews otherwise unknown to history. On the basis of this new data, it seems possible to posit a tentative typology of Jewish apostasy in Russia in the nineteenth century.

Before proceeding with the typology, it is necessary briefly to summarize the legal context of Jewish conversion to Christianity in tsarist Russia. The Imperial Code of Laws, in its various redactions through the nineteenth century, guaranteed freedom of religion to all subjects of the realm; even in the midst of great repression, the law specifically stated that Jews as well as all Christians enjoyed freedom of religion and worship, protected by the agencies of state. Of course, the official religion of the Empire was Russian Orthodoxy, and only the Russian Orthodox Church had the right to seek converts. Other Christian denominations as well as Judaism and Islam were strictly forbidden to engage in any sort of proselytizing; Protestants, Catholics, or Jews engaged in missionary work were subject to severe punishment in the civil courts. If an adherent of another church or faith desired to become Russian Orthodox, no one had the right to interfere with that decision. Only in exceptional circumstances, however, could a Christian join a non-Orthodox denomination of Christianity.[8] On the other hand, Jews were permitted to convert to any tolerated variety of Christianity; in all cases, though, the conversion had to follow an intensive course of study of the dogmas and practices of the faith. Moreover, in accord with canon law, all baptisms had to be performed in public, without the hint of secrecy or subversion—in urban churches, preferably on a Sunday or holy day. Baptisms in village churches or private homes were strictly forbidden (except in the case of the mortally ill or soldiers).[9]

From time to time, these canonical regulations regarding the conversion of Jews may well have been ignored by zealous missionaries or state officials intent on satisfying the clear desire of the government to encourage the conversion to Russian Orthodoxy of as many Jews as possible. The government's attitude toward Jews joining other Christian denominations, however, was far less straightforward: Jews were forbidden to join the Old Belief, and foreign Protestant missions to the Jews were either denied permission to work in Russia or were closely controlled. Thus, throughout the nineteenth century, the London Society for the Promotion of Christianity among the Jews was intermittently permitted to operate its missions only in Congress Poland, never in the Pale of Settlement proper.[10] Clearly, the risk of spreading Protestantism to the Russian Orthodox faithful outweighed the benefit of converting a few Jews; in Poland, the worst that could happen was the conversion of Catholics. Even in regard to the admission of Jews into the Russian Orthodox Church, there was a minor strain of ambivalence to be detected in the government's position—an ambivalence that was most pronounced in a remarkable law promulgated in 1850, stipulating that upon baptism, a former Jew would receive a Christian first name but could not change his family name. In fact, this statute was not enforced very rigorously. But in theory, alone in Christendom after the abolition of the *limpieza de sangre* decrees in Portugal and Spain, the Russian state required that the descendants of Jews bear their Jewish surnames forever, as a mark of their tainted origin.[11]

The Lithuanian Consistory of the Russian Orthodox Church, based in Vilna with branches in other major cities, was scrupulous about all the laws regarding the conversion of Jews. Its archives faithfully preserve the documentation and correspondence relating to Jews who had applied for baptism in its jurisdiction. A complete file includes the original petition of the Jew, penned either by the applicant or the priest in charge of the case; a report by the priest to his superior; a questionnaire addressed to the prospective convert regarding his name, age, place of birth, religion, sect, parents' names and occupations, judicial and military status, and profession. Many files contain follow-up reports about the actual baptism and the life of the new Christian.

In attempting to order these data into a typology of apostates, the first distinction that emerges is between involuntary and voluntary converts. In the category of involuntary apostates belong first and foremost the soldiers forcibly converted in the army of Nicholas I—of whom thirteen are represented in the consistory files. These converted soldiers—most of whom were children recruits, known as Cantonists—are part of that most famous (and often misunderstood) episode of Russian-Jewish history that is too long and complicated to be recapitulated here.[12] For our purposes, three points will suffice about the Cantonist episode: on the basis of the published conscription records of the Russian army and archival material analyzed by Shaul Ginzburg, I have estimated elsewhere that approximately 70,000 Jews were drafted from 1827 to 1855 into the army of Nicholas I. Of these 70,000 about 50,000 were under the age of eighteen. These children recruits, it must be understood, were chosen by the Jewish communities themselves: although the Russian authorities undoubtedly preferred underage conscripts—as more susceptible to missionizing—the actual choice of recruits was the responsibility of the Jewish communal authorities. There is no evidence that the government applied any specific pressure on the Jewish officials to comply with its preference for underage recruits; that the leaders of the Jews did comply was one of the most significant occurrences in Russian-Jewish history. About half of these underage soldiers, i.e., some 25,000 Jewish children, were baptized into the Russian Orthodox Church. There is some indication that these Jews constituted a distinct social grouping within the army and, upon release, in Russian society at large; they may have exhibited a significant degree of endogamy and similar economic behavior. In any event, the *nikolaevskii soldat*, estranged from Jewish life but not completely integrated into Russian life, became a standard figure of Russian society in the second half of the century and a stock character of Jewish literature.[13]

To the category of involuntary apostates must be added a second group: children baptized by parents who may or may not have themselves converted. In the history of Russian Jewry, perhaps the most famous of such converts was Vladimir Medem, the leader of the Bund, the Jewish socialist party. Medem was born in Minsk in 1879 to upwardly mobile Jewish parents who had him baptized at birth in the Russian church. As he explained in his memoirs:

> I was the first Christian in our family despite the fact that I was the very youngest—the "baby." At the time of my birth (in July 1879), my parents made the decision: "We've suffered enough on account of our Jewishness; let at least our youngest son be spared the hardships!" And they had me baptized in an Orthodox church a few days after birth just as if I had been born into a Russian Orthodox family. They themselves were still Jews, and were to remain Jews for a long time.[14]

Later, Medem's siblings converted to Lutheranism; finally, in response to legal restrictions on Jewish professional activities, the older Medems joined their children in the Protestant faith.

Medem's case was not typical, at least inasmuch as he ultimately returned to the Jewish community; without many more such accounts, it is impossible to extrapolate how prevalent was the rationale that he ascribed to his conversion or that of his family. But the Lithuanian consistory documents do demonstrate that his baptism was not of unique ilk: of the 244 apostates, 29 (or 12 percent) were under the age of fifteen; 18 were converted along with their parents, 8 were baptized alone with the permission of their parents, and 3 were illegitimate children born of Jewish mothers and non-Jewish fathers. (Thus, for example, in 1873, Feige Kazrielev of Vilna had her son, born out of wedlock, baptized as Dmitrii, while she remained Jewish.)[15]

The vast majority of Jewish converts in Russia, however, cannot be consigned to the category of forced apostates. The second major rubric of our typology, therefore, is voluntary converts, who can further be divided into five distinct groupings: (1) those seeking educational or professional advancement (whether or not they ever attained it); (2) the haute bourgeoisie; (3) the criminals; (4) the believers; and (5) the destitute and the desperate. In the popular studies by Tsitron and Ginzburg, only the first two types were included, for rather obvious reasons: first, the professors and the industrialists were well known and of interest to readers; moreover, given the populist slant of the Yiddish press, the apostasy of large numbers of working-class Jews was an uncomfortable fact of life better left unmentioned. In general, both the historiography and the popular press have preferred apotheosizing the "laboring classes and dangerous classes" of eastern European Jewry as the vanguard of the revolution rather than rigorously studying their social, demographic, and political profile. Finally, it was assumed as given by all students of Russian-Jewish apostasy that all protestations of belief in Christianity on the part of baptized Jews were spurious and self-serving; the possibility that some of the converts truly believed in the Christian faith was not even considered.

The first type, those seeking educational or professional advancement, were the converts most studied by Tsitron and Ginzburg. Among these were the famous censors, high government officials, and university professors whose names were broadly known to the Jewish public. Perhaps the best known apostate of this type was Daniel Chwolson, the Vilna Jew who converted in 1855 to become professor of Semitics at St. Petersburg University and later publicly disputed the charges of ritual murder periodically brought against Russian Jews. Chwolson achieved legendary status among the Jewish masses for his activities in defense of Jewish honor, as well as for his quip about apostasy: When asked what he believed in that accounted for his conversion, Chwolson is reputed to have responded: "I believed that it is better to be a professor in St. Petersburg than a *melamed* in Eyshishok."[16] But not all the apostates for professional advancement retained warm ties to their former coreligionists; on the contrary, more often than not they displayed the hatred of Jews typical of apostates throughout Jewish history. Almost as well-known as Chwolson, and probably much more influential, was Jacob Brafman, the most successful anti-Jewish propagandist in nineteenth-century Russia. In a series of pamphlets and widely read books alleging a first-hand knowledge of secret Hebrew and Aramaic sources, Brafman claimed first, that the Talmud mandates hatred of Christianity and Christians, and second, that on the basis of the talmudic teachings, there exists a universal Jewish conspiracy aimed at seizing control of the whole world. Ultimately, Brafman's calumnies against Judaism and the Jews formed the basis for much of the spurious material included in the *Protocols of the Elders of Zion*.[17]

In the Lithuanian Consistory materials, this type of convert appears in only a small number of cases: four gymnasium or university students, two teachers, two pharmacists, one doctor, and one dentist. Typical of this group is Sima Keller, a single woman who was graduated from the women's gymnasium in Odessa in 1900 with a teaching certificate, and at age twenty-seven was baptized as Serafima in order to obtain a position.[18] Or the case of Moshe Volkoveiskii of Vilna: "an immense passion for learning," he reported, led him to the government-sponsored Vilna Rabbinical Seminary, which was the hothouse of Jewish modernism in Lithuania. There, he claimed, he not only learned Russian and secular studies but also became estranged from the Jewish faith and convinced of the eternal verity of Christianity. Thereafter, he studied to become a pharmacist (a popular profession among "enlightened" Russian Jews, and one which vouchsafed residence throughout the empire.) In 1870, able to support himself, Moshe petitioned to join the Orthodox Church.[19] Perhaps also in the category of those converting for careerist reasons can be placed the two hitherto unknown missionaries who emerge from the Consistory files: one Aleksandr Shkafel, born in Vilna in 1848, who graduated from the Lithuanian Church Seminary in 1871 and was assigned to Brest-Litovsk in 1877 to induct Jewish children into Christianity;[20] the other, Yosef/Pavel Dreyzin, a graduate of the government-sponsored rabbinical seminary in Zhitomir, who served as rabbi of several towns in the Pale of Settlement during the 1880s, and in 1891, at the age of forty-eight, was baptized, along with his three children, Leyb/Lev age nine, Sure/Maria, seven, and Hirshl/Grigorii, three. (Their mother, Fruma, thirty two, did not want to convert.) Dreyzin completed a translation of the New Testament and various saints' lives into Yiddish, and at least for a time made a decent wage as a missionary and translator.[21]

The second category of voluntary convert—dubbed here the haut-bourgeois apostate—is closely related to the first, except that this group converted after having already achieved significant economic mobility and success. In the consistory materials there are only four such converts, three members of the merchant elite of various Lithuanian towns and one Honorary Citizen (a seminoble title betokening high social and economic status.) It seems logical to assume that this type of convert represented a greater proportion in the total number of apostates than in these lists; undoubtedly, were data available on Jewish converts in St. Petersburg and Moscow, the major seats of the Jewish upper classes, this type of apostate would abound. Still, this phenomenon does not seem to have been as common in Russia as in the West, or for that matter in Poland, where the upper ranks of society attracted far more converted Jews. Although the cause of this disparity between Poland and Russia remains to be studied, it is most likely to be found in the differing processes of Jewish embourgeoisement in the two societies: the Polish upper middle class seems at once to have been more receptive to the infusion of Jewish capital and Jewish entrepreneurs (and Jewish marriage partners) and more insistent on a conversion to Catholicism of the Jews involved; the Russian haute bourgeosie, conversely, appears in general to have been far less welcoming to Jews, yet paradoxically more pluralistic in regard to their national and religious status. Russia was, after all, a multinational empire, and its leading circles included many non-Orthodox politicians and businessmen with foreign names and connections. In sharp contrast, the intimate connection between Polishness and Catholicism need not be elaborated in this context. In any event, a comparison between the economic elites of Russian and Polish Jewries remains a major scholarly desideratum.[22]

At the opposite end of the social spectrum, and specific to Russia, was the third type of voluntary converts—the criminals. Until 1862, any Jew convicted of a crime in a Russian court could have his sentence automatically reduced or entirely rescinded upon baptism. In our sample, nine Jews, guilty of offenses ranging from loitering to fraud and theft, entered Russian Orthodoxy under such conditions. Such was the story of Shmuel Porembskii of Volkovysk, born in 1789, who compiled a long record of criminal offenses through his adult years. Finally, in 1844, at the age of fifty-five, recently divorced from his wife Sorka and estranged from his one daughter, Shmuel was charged with the crime of contraband and decided to join the Orthodox Church rather than face sentencing.[23]

The spiritual concerns of this type of convert were marginal at best, but that was not true of the fourth group of converts—the true believers in Christianity. This type is perhaps the most difficult to identify, given the nature of the documentation. Almost every file contains a formal declaration of faith in Jesus Christ, the Trinity, and the dogmas of the one, true, Orthodox Church, as well as a statement that the petitioner had long secretly yearned for salvation through Christianity. But from time to time the confession takes on a personal cast with details and phrases that strike a note of authenticity and sincerity. It is intriguing to note that at least in the Lithuanian materials, the only true believers appear to be women; the men who converted always seem to have had blatant pragmatic motives. Three cases were very clear-cut: two women on their deathbeds called for priests and requested conversion and the last rites, and one eighteen-year-old woman, Esther Izabelinskaia, remained after her baptism as a nun at the monastery where she had studied for conversion.[24] Other cases are less obvious, but still convincing: Sheyna Khodos, born in 1882 in a small Jewish community in Vilna province, related in 1901 that she had decided a year earlier to seek baptism in the Russian Church, but her parents found out about her plan and kept her under strict surveillance for the entire year. Finally, she escaped to Vilna and applied for quick baptism, afraid that her parents would catch her. She was converted under the name of Aleksandra.[25] Similarly, nineteen-year-old Masha Teitelboym, clearly the child of a highly integrated Russian-Jewish family, wrote in elegant Russian:

> I was born and raised in the city of Lida, where I was educated in schools alongside Russian Orthodox Christians, with whom I was very friendly, and from whom I slowly became acquainted with the faith and teaching of Christ in the Gospels, which I frequently read in secret. I sometimes even attended church, becoming slowly convinced that faith in Christ was the only means to salvation. This conviction forced me to abandon the Jewish faith and to accept Holy Baptism according to the Orthodox rite, for which I have been steadily preparing. As a literate person, I already know many prayers and symbols of the Orthodox faith. I therefore request of Your Holiness to teach me all that is necessary to complete my conversion, and if such permission is granted, to have me baptized as quickly as possible, as I am being sought and followed.[26]

Masha soon thereafter became Anna.

One case in the Consistory records raises unanswerable questions about the receptivity of church officials to Jewish converts not displaying, or at least affecting, Christian piety: Kasper Berman, an eighteen-year-old student at the Vilna gymnasium in 1834, applied for conversion on the grounds that he was "enlightened by his studies and

convinced of the fallacy of Judaism and the veracity of Christianity."
He asked to be baptized in the Russian Orthodox Church and incidentally mentioned that he wanted to study medicine. The archi-
mandrite was skeptical: Kasper never appeared in catechism class and
did not study the dogmas of the Church. He obviously was not
sincere, the prelate concluded: "Knowing his inconstancy and poor
character, which will not be of honor to our religion, I see no good in
him." Kasper's petition was repeatedly denied, with the proviso that
he could apply again after he completed gymnasium.[27] It is not clear
how many other Russian Orthodox priests were so fastidious about
whom they would admit into the state of grace—the incentive of
saving Jewish souls may have been too great. However, in half a dozen
cases in the Lithuanian consistory records, desperate petitions of
Jewish parents whose children applied for baptism without their
knowledge were acceded to, and the underage applicants were sent
home. After 1862, indeed, the law of the land stipulated that children
under the age of fourteen could not be baptized without parental
consent.[28] In several other cases, the Jews themselves were rather
shocked to find that the priests or monks required of potential converts
a rather intensive period of preparation and study before baptism, and
the disappointed applicants slipped out the back door of the church
without accomplishing their missions.

These, of course, were exceptional cases; most applicants met
with success. The vast majority of these belonged to the last, and
largest, class in the typology: the destitute and the desperate. To this
group belong 177 of the 244 converts, or fully 72.5 percent. The
numbers permit some statistical analysis: all of these Jews save two
were members of the broad urban class, the *meshchantsvo*, in which
most Russian Jews were registered; the two exceptions, farmers,
belonged to the agriculturist estate. The greatest part of these Jews
lived in urban centers or small towns, with only a handful coming
from villages. Since the consistory in question was based in Vilna, it
baptized Jews mostly from Lithuania and Belorussia, the strongholds
of traditional rabbinic Jewish culture in eastern Europe. Thus, the
hometowns of these apostates resonate with irony: we encounter Jews
not only from Vilna and Kovno and Minsk and Brest-Litovsk, but also
from Volozhin, Mir, Kotsk, and Liubavich—all sacred names in eastern European Jewish culture.

As seems logical—and consistent with patterns of apostasy in
western Europe—almost all of these converts were young: 94 percent

of those for whom ages were recorded were between 16 and 30 years old; of these, 43 percent were between the ages of 16 and 21. The median age for women was 18, for men 21. This overwhelmingly young population, taken as a whole, was almost neatly divided by gender: 58 percent men, 42 percent women. But it is noteworthy that the proportion of women rose steadily through the decades from 0 percent in the 1830s to 12 percent in the 1840s, 33.3 percent in the 1850s, 57 percent in the 1860s, 54 percent in the 1870s, 53 percent in the 1890s, 65 percent from 1900 to 1911. Once more, given the small nature of this sample, it is difficult to assert with any degree of certainty that this startling increase in the proportion of women converts was typical of the entire population of Jewish apostates in nineteenth-century Russia; yet a tantalizing hypothesis does assert itself: that as Russian-Jewish society underwent the dramatic revolutions of the nineteenth century, its female members were less able successfully to adjust to the new social, economic, political, and cultural conditions than their brothers, husbands, and sons; therefore, more women than men made their way to the baptismal font.

The social complexion of the Lithuanian Jewish converts is apparent as well from their marital status: three-quarters of all the converts were unmarried. Extremely interesting is the fact that single women far outnumbered single men: almost twice as many of the male converts were married. Half a dozen Jewish girls converted in order to marry peasant men; only one Jewish male in this group was baptized for love. Almost half of the files contain information on the literacy of the apostates: two-thirds of these Jews were literate (in the minimal sense that they could sign their names), and perhaps surprisingly, nine out of ten of those who could sign their names did so in Russian, not in Hebrew. Not one woman signed her name in Hebrew—perhaps yet another indication that the breakdown of the traditional Jewish order in eastern Europe affected women more adversely than men.

A few examples may illustrate this type of convert better than the statistics. Itsik-Yankl Pass was born in a village in the Vilna province in 1858. His father was a laborer in a local plant, but Itsik-Yankl was still able to receive a good *ḥeder* education, as his beautiful Hebrew penmanship attests. By the age of 16, in 1874, he had learned to speak Russian and was teaching himself how to write in Cyrillic. At the same time, he started frequenting the new railroad station located not far from his home, and he became friendly with the local station-master, Ivan Ivanovich Minestvin, who took a paternal interest in the boy and awakened in him the desire to become a Christian. Itsik-Yankl then entered a monastery in Vilna and applied for courses leading to baptism. Two weeks later his parents came to town, and he went home with them.[29]

More satisfactory to the record-keeper of the Vilna Consistory was the case of Zadik-Leyb Shakhovich, born in 1835 in a small town near Kovno, at least according to his internal passport: Zadik-Leyb didn't know where he was born, nor could he answer the question of which sect of Jews he belonged to, or sign his name in any script. For several years in the early 1850s, Zadik-Leyb served as a yardman to a petty noble, who found him to be a good worker, but ultimately let him go. Zadik-Leyb wandered to the city of Kovno, where he worked as a day laborer, and ultimately applied for baptism in the Orthodox Church, which he entered as Lev Ivanovich Shakhovich.[30]

A similar fate awaited a Jew from a different part of the empire twenty years later: Zekharia Shtein was from Friedrichstadt in Kurland, which he left in 1863 to wander for several years through the Pale, without documents, working intermittently as a tailor. Finally, in the town of Belsk, the authorities caught up with him, arrested him for traveling about without permission and informed the Jewish community of Friedrichstadt of his whereabouts. His *landslayt* were happy to hear about him: they wanted to enlist him as a recruit to fill their conscription quota, despite his being twenty-seven years old. Faced with this prospect, Zekharia decided to convert, which he did in 1870.[31]

Another resident of the town of Belsk had a very different reason for seeking conversion. Eighteen-year-old Malka Lin could not write her story down, since she was illiterate, but the drama of her life was captured by the monk to whom she told it. Malka was the daughter of Mendel, a Jew registered in the community of Bialystok who kept a tavern near Belsk. In 1871, Malka met and fell in love with a soldier in the local regiment, Filip Erokhinin. He promised to marry her after she converted, and they began to live together. When she realized she was pregnant, Malka decided that Belsk was too dangerous a place for her, and she sought the protection of her boyfriend's commanding officer. At the army camp, she gave birth to a son. Soon thereafter, she was removed to the women's monastery in Grodno, where she began to study the dogmas of the Orthodox faith, but became deathly ill, struck by the cholera epidemic then raging in the area. Erokhinin stayed by her side and promised to marry her after her conversion, which took place later that year.[32]

Finally, quite a different set of circumstances surrounded Rivka Yofe's decision to embrace the Christian faith in 1903: she was an unmarried woman from Dvinsk who was working as a servant girl in Kovno. She came to the local Orthodox church and asked to be converted, but never appeared at catechism lessons, despite being sent for by the priest. He soon found out that Rivka was not simply skipping class: she had discovered that the neighborhood Catholic priest required fewer lessons and had a bigger fund to reward his converts. The Orthodox priest was not surprised—he had all along suspected that Rivka was seeking temporal, not eternal, deliverance.[33]

In sum, from these stories and statistics it seems possible to conclude that the fifth and largest category of the Jews who converted to Russian Orthodoxy in Lithuania from 1819 to 1911 were the destitute and the desperate, a segment of the massive flotsam of Russian Jewry that failed to find secure moorings in that rocky society: young people just at the point at which normal adult life begins, who could find no partner, no profession, no stable place in society. They were not yeshivah students or poets or adherents of the *haskalah*, but they were nonetheless affected by currents that transformed their society as a whole—the breakdown of rabbinical authority and the traditional educational system; the tendency toward Russification; a wide-scale pauperization that reduced some part of Russian Jewry to a life that resembled that of the peasantry. Perhaps the crisis was more marked for Jewish women, who had fewer alternatives available to them than did the men: the roads out of the Pale of Settlement— education, artisanship, commercial success, emigration—were far more accessible to males than females. Conversion to Christianity for these women, and their male counterparts, at least provided temporary succor and some meager financial rewards.

In the end, it seems plausible to hypothesize that this typology of apostates—those forced to convert, those seeking educational or professional advancement, the haute bourgeoisie, the criminals, the believers, and the poor and destitute—is appropriate not only to the small sample of Jews whose records are extant, but to the tens of thousands of Russian Jews who took this radical step out of Jewish life in the nineteenth century. If additonal, and more complete, data on

Jewish converts to Christianity can be located, the categories and generalizations here proposed will undoubtedly require restatement or amplification. But it seems fair to conclude that out of the files of the Lithuanian Consistory here analyzed, Jewish apostasy in tsarist Russia emerges as but one grave symptom of the deep-seated social, political, and cultural malaise that gripped Russian Jewry even in its most optimistic hours.

NOTES

1. I. Cherikover, "Obrashchenie v khristianstvo" [Conversion to Christianity], *Evreiskaia entsiklopediia*, vol. 11, cols. 884–95. This informative but all too brief encyclopedia entry is the only reliable scholarly account of Russian-Jewish apostasy. On the period before the Polish Partitions, see the recent article by Jacob Goldberg, "Die getauften Juden in Polen-Litauen im 16.–18. Jahrhundert," *Jahrbücher für Geschichte Osteuropas* 30 (1982): 54–99.

2. Shmuel Leib Tsitron, *Meshumodim: tipn un siluetn fun noentn over*, 4 vols. (Warsaw: Ahisefer, n.d.); Shaul Ginzburg, *Meshumodim in tsarishn rusland* (New York: CYCO-Bicher Farlag, 1946).

3. For details on the original publication of Ginzburg's sketches, see Yitshak Rivkind, "Shaul Ginzburg bibliografie" [Shaul Ginzburg's Bibliography], in Shaul Ginzburg, *Historishe verk* (New York: S. M. Ginsburg Testimonial Committee, 1937), 3: 377–416.

4. Cherikover, "Obrashchenie," col. 894, corroborated from archival sources by Shaul Ginzburg in his unpublished materials in the Shaul Ginzburg Materials, Rivkind Archive, Manuscript Division, Jewish National and University Library, Jerusalem, Collection 4' 1281A, file 6, no. 6. These numbers correspond exactly to those included in the official report of the Procurator of the Holy Synod for 1825–55, "Otchet Ober-Prokurator Sviateishago Synoda, 1825–1855," *Sbornik Imp. russkago istoricheskago obshchestva* 98 (1890): 457–60. Although it stands to reason that the synod would have known how many Jews were converted by its priests, it cannot be assumed that its recordkeepers were precise—especially since the other Russian ministry involved in conversions, the Ministry of the Interior, regularly published figures on Jewish conversion which were at odds with the synod's statistics. On this problem, see my *Tsar Nicholas I and the Jews: The Transformation of Jewish Society in Russia, 1825–1855* (Philadelphia: Jewish Publication Society, 1983), p. 213n.

5. J. F. A. de le Roi, *Judentaufen im 19. Jahrhundert* (Leipzig, 1899), pp. 31, 40–45; and N. Samter, *Judentaufen im 19. Jahrhundert* (Berlin, 1906), p. 91. The statistics on Jewish conversions to Roman Catholicism, and especially to Protestantism, seem low, though there is no way to estimate the actual numbers.

6. This chronology is based on Cherikover, "Obrashchenie," cols. 893–95. On Alexander I's Society, see Simon Dubnow, *History of the Jews in Russia and Poland*, 3 vols. (Philadelphia: Jewish Publication Society, 1916), 1: 396–401.

7. These records are located in the Archives of the YIVO Institute for Jewish Research in New York, as the Archive of the Lithuanian Consistory in Vilna (below abbreviated to LC). My analysis of the pre-1855 materials and a preliminary typology of Jewish apostasy in Russia were published in *Tsar Nicholas I and the Jews*, pp. 141–43.

8. *Svod zakonov rossiiskoi imperii* [The Code of Laws of the Russian Empire], 1896 redaction, vol. 11, "Regulations on the Spiritual Affairs of Foreign Faiths," articles 4– 7.

9. Ibid., supplementary regulations, 1–5.

10. See the correspondence on the readmission of the Society to Poland during the reign of Alexander II preserved in the papers of the Church Mission to the Jews, formerly the London Society for the Promotion of Christianity among the Jews, housed in the Bodleian Library, file d.51. See, too, Iulii Gessen, "Angliiskie mission-ery v Rossii" [English Missionaries in Russia], *Evreiskaia Entsiklopediia*, vol.1, cols. 491–94.

11. *Polnoe sobranie zakonov rossisskoi imperii* [Complete Collection of Laws of the Russian Empire], Second Collection: 1825–55, 25: 23,905. The "purity of blood" laws were rescinded in Portugal in 1773 and in Spain in 1860.

12. See *Tsar Nicholas I and the Jews*, pp. 13–34, and Shaul Ginzburg, "Yidishe kantonistn" [Jewish Cantonists], in his *Historishe verk*, pp. 3–135.

13. See Ginzburg, "Yidishe kantonistn," pp. 131–35, and for a more extensive but less rigorous treatment, Avrohom Levin, *Kantonistn* [Cantonists] (Warsaw, 1934). A thoroughgoing study of the post-1855 *nikolaevskii soldat* either in fact or in fiction has not yet been written.

14. Samuel A. Portnoy, editor and translator, *The Memoirs of Vladimir Medem: The Life and Soul of a Legendary Jewish Socialist* (New York: Ktav, 1979), p. 6. See also pp.4– 17.

15. LC box IV, file 113.

16. On Chwolson see, among others, Ginzburg, *Meshumodim*, pp. 119–56; Tsitron, *Meshumodim*, 2: 3–38; and the anonymous entry in *Evreiskaia entsiklopediia*, vol. 15, cols 584–87.

17 See Ginzburg, *Meshumodim*, pp. 65–79; Tsitron, *Meshumodim*, 1: 1–31; and the entry by Iulii Gessen and M. G.Morgulis in *Evreiskaia entsiklopediia*, vol. 4, cols. 917–22.

18. LC box IV, file 115.

19. LC box III, file 64.

20. LC box IV, file 127.

21. LC box III, file 68.

22. On the Polish case, see the studies cited by Jacob Goldberg, "Die getauften Juden," referred to in note 1 above.

23. LC box V, file 131.

24. LC box II, file 39.

25. LC box III, file 52.

26. LC box III, file 56.

27. LC box III, file 83.

28. See Cherikover, "Obraschenie," cols. 897–98.

29. LC box VII, file 188.

30. LC box VII, file 179.

31. LC box I, file 11.

32. LC box II, file 27.

33. LC box VII, file 183.

8

Heresy, Apostasy, and the Transformation of Joseph Rabinovich

STEVEN J. ZIPPERSTEIN

THE wave of pogroms that erupted in the provinces of southern Russia in the spring of 1881 and spread until the summer of 1882 was accompanied by widespread ideological reassessment and institutional realignment in the Russian Jewish community. Riots broke out in more than two hundred cities and townlets. Appearing as they did in the wake of the assassination of Alexander II, whose reign (1855–81) had held out the promise of thoroughgoing reform and even emancipation, they undermined the progressivist assumptions shared by many Jewish intellectuals about Russia's ultimately liberal direction. New, often bold alternatives—including the advocacy of a Jewish return to Palestine—gained currency and respectability. It was during this turbulent period that both Lev Pinsker and Moses Leib Lilienblum produced their influential nationalist manifestos. In the wake of the pogroms hundreds of russified Jewish youths in Kharkov, Ekaterinoslav, and other south Russian cities refocused their populist-inspired visions of the future and its tasks to include their Jewish

I would like to thank Evyatar Friesel, Sara Kochav, Eli Lederhandler, Ada Rapoport-Albert, and John Walsh for their helpful comments and suggestions. Several of the Hebrew-language newspaper articles cited in this study came to my attention by way of references in the file on Joseph Rabinovich in the Kressel Archives of the Oxford Centre for Postgraduate Hebrew Studies. The archives of the Church Ministry for the Jews, housed in the Bodleian Library, Oxford, were most helpful. I am appreciative to the Church Ministry (formerly the London Society for Promoting Christianity amongst the Jews) for permitting me to quote from this material.

brethren, and now worked toward the establishment of Jewish agrarian societies in North America or Palestine rather than peasant utopias in Russia.[1]

The belief that the pogroms were prompted and even planned by St. Petersburg officials (and perhaps approved of by Tsar Alexander III)—a belief that historians have conclusively shown to be unfounded but which was widespread at the time—reinforced the need felt by Jewish intellectuals for new ideological programs and communal priorities. Older, now tarnished, strategies had been based on the assumption that Russia was moving inexorably in the direction of the West: its economy would be modernized, its political structure liberalized, its minorities emancipated. The government's alleged support for the urban and rural rioters of southern Russia, its well-publicized assertion that the pogroms resulted from Jewish exploitation of gentiles, and its announcement of a series of new and restrictive Jewish regulations in their wake, convinced many Jews that Russia's social and political development would not follow the liberalizing course charted by the West. The year 1881, suggests Jonathan Frankel in his magisterial work *Prophecy and Politics*, constitutes the birth of "post-liberal" Jewish ideology.[2]

Most of the secondary literature devoted to this period concentrates on the emergence of Zionism, ultimately the most successful movement generated by the traumatic events of the 1880s. Insufficient attention is paid to the sheer turmoil experienced by much of Russian Jewry in these years, the rapidity with which many Jews of the time embraced and discarded new ideologies, and, perhaps most importantly, the widespread despair that persuaded tens of thousands of Jews to abandon Russia for the United States or, alternatively, left many others immobilized and hopeless.

Among the various options then open to Russian Jews was conversion to Christianity, though few voluntarily chose this course. At times, especially during the reign of Nicholas I (1825–55), the regime was keen to encourage Jews to do so; Russian and Polish Jewry also exerted considerable fascination on western missionaries who spent large sums here (especially in Poland where the imperial regime permitted them to work with few restrictions) hoping to win over this pious, populous, and economically vulnerable community. Modest gains were reported by missionaries working in nineteenth-century Warsaw, but successes elsewhere in the empire were rare.[3]

Yet the pogroms did contribute to an increase in the number of

Jewish converts, a rise not considerable in terms of sheer numbers but one that particularly affected the most russified, literate, and urbanized segment of the Jewish community. The average number of annual Jewish converts in Russia to Russian Orthodoxy in the 1870s was 460; by the mid-1880s the number had risen to 700. Many were young men fearful of new quotas on Jews in Russian schools and other restrictions, and disaffected with Jewish customs that they felt were atavistic and inferior. Among them were a number of writers for the St. Petersburg Jewish weekly *Razsvet*, who had publicly supported a Jewish nationalist solution and been prominent advocates of communal solidarity until their conversions in the wake of the pogroms of the 1880s.[4]

In this period of intense ideological ferment movements also appeared that promoted, at one and the same time, a belief in Jesus and the need for continued Jewish self-assertion. These constituted a widely discussed phenomenon in the late 1870s and early 1880s. The Jewish leaders of these movements Jacob Priluker, Jacob Gordin (later a popular Yiddish dramatist), and Joseph Rabinovich—did not make substantial inroads, and though their movements generated a great deal of heat (the Jewish press in Russia followed them with keen interest), they left little mark on the community as a whole. Yet Joseph Rabinovich in particular is worthy of examination, for his ideology was in many respects a product of the turmoil that engulfed Russian Jewry in the wake of the pogroms. It was, he stated explicitly, born out of despair and a pained acknowledgment that past options were discredited and must be abandoned for fresh and unprecedented schemes. Rabinovich embraced a firm belief in continued Jewish survival that owed much in terms of its conceptual underpinnings to Jewish nationalist thinkers like Perez Smolenskin. Rabinovich's announcement that Jesus was the messiah excluded him from continued involvement in Jewish communal life, but this socially cloistered provincial *maskil* (he was born in a small Bessarabian town and lived most of his adult life in Kishinev) continued to see himself and his followers as living apart from gentiles in a special society circumscribed by Jewish customs and informed by a pervasive sense of Jewish superiority.

An examination of Rabinovich, who was a respected Jewish communal figure before his spiritual turnabout in the early 1880s, sheds light on the fervid cultural life of Russian Jewry in the wake of the pogroms. His transformation illuminates the often tenuous line between the realist and the fanatic, the visionary and the charlatan, distinctions that are particularly elusive during periods of intense ideological crisis and widespread communal despair. His ideology emerged out of an unstable, fractious climate, at a time when otherwise fantastic schemes were suddenly thrust into the center of the Jewish communal agenda, when previously marginal figures suddenly assumed center stage, and when the certainties of the past seemed to many thoroughly discredited and outdated.

The son of a wealthy *ḥasid*, Rabinovich was born in Bessarabia, either in Orge'ev or Rezina. His education was standard for his milieu and was enhanced by periodic visits to the court of the Belzer *rebbe* in East Galicia. On one visit, when Rabinovich was still a boy, he was betrothed to the daughter of another Belzer devotee. Several years later, after he was married, his father lost most of his wealth in a fire. The young *ḥasid* was eventually won over to the *haskalah* (the Jewish enlightenment movement), according to one account, by a Lithuanian Jewish primary school teacher who persuaded him after one nightlong conversation.[5]

Rabinovich learned Russian and acquired certification as a notary. He was keenly interested in communal affairs and assisted in the opening of a *talmud torah* (a school for indigent and orphaned children) in Orge'ev, where he served as the Russian-language tutor. He eventually moved to the much larger city of Kishinev with his wife, three daughters, and a son and here worked as a notary and established a wide network of contacts with other *maskilim*, including Alexander Zederbaum, who later invited Rabinovich to serve as agent for *Ha-Melits* and *Dos Yidishe Folksblatt* in the southern provinces of the Pale of Settlement.

Rabinovich published a number of articles in the maskilic press of the 1870s—in *Ha-Melits, Kol Mevasser, Ha-Tsefirah,* and *Ha-Boker Or.*[6] The bibliographer Chaim David Lippe described him in 1881 as "the esteemed and wise man who has published articles of value, all of which reflect honorably on him."[7]

When viewed within the context of Lippe's typically hyperbolic descriptions of Rabinovich's contemporaries, his characterization of Rabinovich was but mildly complimentary—respectful rather than enthusiastic. Indeed Rabinovich was a rather typical *maskil*, one of two hundred or so occasional contributors to the Hebrew press of the period and a man distinguished, if at all, by his ambitious and passionate, even obsessive, desire to lift himself above his peers. His first major article, published in two parts in *Ha-Boker Or* in 1879, gave vent to these desires. It also offered a revealing glimpse at the religious heterodoxy apparent just below the surface in this otherwise unremarkable man.

Rabinovich wrote the article, entitled "Masters and Rabbis," a year earlier, when he heard that a rabbinical commission would be convened by the Russian government. The news of this prospective meeting—which would bring together rabbis and communal leaders from all parts of Russia for the first time in seventeen years—was understood by many Jews to signal that Emperor Alexander II wished to use the opportunity to emancipate Russian Jewry.[8] This seemed likely, since he had already freed the serfs (in 1861), large numbers of Jews were now in attendance in Russian schools, and Jewish soldiers had just fought bravely the year before in the Balkan war as conscripts of the Russian army. The commission, predicted even the normally skeptical and laconic Moses Leib Lilienblum, was likely a "gateway to hope."[9] As things turned out, only issues of minor importance were discussed at the meetings. But Rabinovich too, writing before the commission met, was carried away with enthusiasm by news of it and he began his essay with unqualified praise for the tsar and the coming deliberations: "Now all Russian Jews lift their eyes to the rabbinical commission with great longing and fully expect that Israel's deliverance will result from it. . . ."[10]

The article evaluated the role played by rabbis in Jewish society. Drawing on the ideas of the influential Jewish nationalist Perez Smolenskin, editor of *Ha-Shahar*, Rabinovich accepted Smolenskin's contention that Judaism was a product of "nationalist sentiment" rather than vice versa, but whereas Smolenskin attributed Jewish national cohesion to the Hebrew language, Rabinovich viewed the rabbi as the linchpin of Jewish unity. The rabbi's role, he argued, was unparalleled in any other community. It required that he serve as a substitute for a cultic center, a government, and an army. Almost singlehandedly the rabbi maintained Jewry's national integrity. The rabbinic legal system protected Jews so that "the forces of the world do not undermine" their spirit.[11]

The halakhic literature was produced by rabbis who, Rabinovich insisted repeatedly, were never elected in any formal sense by their communities but were chosen by acclamation. It answered Jewry's fundamental needs and was essential for Jewish religious and social well-being. In recent times, however, the stature of Jewry's leadership had declined precipitously; new, misguided rabbis had placed too much emphasis on talmudic sophistry and too little attention had been paid to Jewry's real needs. What occurred, argued Rabinovich, was a confusion of ends and means. Talmudic study, promoted in the past with larger, social goals in mind—namely, the strengthening of Jewry's national spirit—had come to assume a significance quite independent of overriding national concerns. This had resulted in widespread religious sterility and social paralysis. The rabbis, wrote Rabinovich, now spent their time "in the construction of a great monument whose upper reaches stretch to the heavens and . . . they paid no attention to the true spirit of the people and for them this spirit became only a way to ceaselessly promote the Torah. . . ."[12] The Talmud should ideally serve a provisional role in Jewish life and its primary function should be to bring Jewry intact "to the new age . . . both physically and spiritually."[13] Tragically, however, it had recently acquired a new importance and its devotees had come to see the entire world as but a vast talmudic study hall where they insisted upon resolving life's problems as if they were confronted by the opaque, hair-splitting disputations of the rabbis.[14]

The essay was of interest for two reasons. On one level, it could be read as a plea for communal recognition. Rabinovich wrote the article at a time when he still hoped to be elected to the position of crown rabbi of Kishinev (and perhaps also to a place on the commission), and his frustration with the vagaries of popular opinion and electoral politics was reflected in "Masters and Rabbis." This frustration was justified, for he never captured the coveted position and his anger on this score came to be related in his mind, as his later essays suggest, with anger over his people's apparent lack of momentum and direction. Born into a wealthy family, Rabinovich probably would have commanded a more important position in Jewish communal life had his family's wealth not been lost and he may have felt cheated out of a role that was, in his view, rightfully his.[15]

"Masters and Rabbis" was also revealing in another respect, for it shed light on Rabinovich's intense preoccupation with spiritual matters despite his rejection of the centrality of the Talmud. This preoccupation contrasted markedly with the typical late-nineteenth-century Russian maskilic attitude towards spiritual concerns: conformity with traditional practices and moderate orthodoxy were not uncommon for *maskilim* of Rabinovich's background. Some twenty years later, even the acerbic secularist Shai Hurwitz publicly assured traditionalist critics of his loyal adherence to religious standards when he came under attack in the Jewish press. Such conformity, however, was rarely the product of spiritual attachment: it generally resulted from a combination of factors that included caution, a commitment to a national solidarity, and even sentimentality. In truth the term *spirituality (ruḥaniut)*, used frequently by *maskilim* in this period, was infused by them with cultural, and not specifically with religious, connotations. They offered largely if not exclusively secular explanations for the unfolding of historical and contemporary events, even when examining Jewish religious life itself.[16]

In contrast, Rabinovich spoke with intensity and seriousness about spirituality, God, and religious redemption. "There will come a time," he wrote in the same essay, "when God will remember his creation, and Abraham, Isaac and Jacob, and He and He alone will bring an end to strife and redeem [the Jews] from their suffering."[17] Similar statements reappeared several times. Yet it was to the Pentateuch and the Prophets that he turned for religious inspiration, not merely out of a heightened appreciation of the aesthetic charms or the nationalist ethos expressed in these sacred works (which was rather typical of *maskilim*) but because he saw in them the prime sources for Judaism's religious truths.[18] Not surprisingly, he did not share the Russian Jewish intelligentsia's renewed appreciation in the 1870s of traditional Jewish folk customs, which they viewed as reflections of authentic national urges. His Judaism, in contrast to that of the highly acculturated editors of the St. Petersburg weekly *Razsvet*, who in a dramatic show of Jewish solidarity danced with *ḥasidim* on Purim in 1879,[19] took the spiritual dimension very seriously and posited an alternative to the dominant rabbinic or hasidic models. He was unable to look upon Jewish religious practices with the cheerful distance, the sense of nostalgic longing, and the bemusement of his more secular contemporaries.

It is unlikely that Rabinovich came to this idiosyncratic appreciation for a spirituality that deemphasized the Talmud through his hasidic background, for the Belzer *ḥasidim* placed a heavy stress on rabbinic study. Nor did his thinking show the influence of German or Hungarian Reform circles. His reliance on the Bible as a source of fundamental religious authority probably stemmed from other, rather more obscure quarters. One very plausible influence was Jehiel Zevi Hirschensohn-Lichtenstein, an erudite and mysterious figure who had been living secretly as an unbaptized Christian since 1855 and who arrived in Kishinev in 1878 and married Rabinovich's sister. Lichtenstein, who lived intermittently as a *ḥasid* in Belorussia and a missionary in Leipzig, published several books including an anti-Karaite tract and an anthology of rabbinic sayings about geography. He was a respected figure in maskilic as well as traditional Jewish circles. His *Sheva Ḥokhmot* [The Seven Wisdoms] was introduced by letters of praise from important scholars such as Mattityahu Strashun, Samuel Joseph Fuenn, and others, though the book appeared three years after Lichtenstein was first denounced as a missionary (by the rather mercurial and widely disliked Ephraim Deinard) in the newspaper *Ha-Maggid*.[20] Interestingly, Lichtenstein's understanding of Judeo-Christianity, as he explained it to a nonplussed Scottish evangelist in 1888, allowed for a Judaism which, as the missionary explained, would not be "dissolved and disappear in Christianity but [would] renew itself, gaining new life in the resurrection of Christ." He refused to be baptized because "he hoped to bring over his people with him to Christianity and . . . he would do this better by remaining an unbaptized Jew, than by another course."[21] According to one report, Lichtenstein gave Rabinovich a copy of the New Testament that he took with him on his tour of Palestine in 1882.[22] But when he wrote his article in *Ha-Boker Or*, Rabinovich still couched his criticism of rabbinic Judaism in maskilic terms. It was not, in any event, Rabinovich's first reading of the New Testament in the late 1870s (if indeed he did read it then) that led to his avowal of Jesus but the crisis facing Jewry in the immediate aftermath of the pogroms of the 1880s. The platform he would embrace was informed, in both its substance and in the terminology it employed, by an acute preoccupation with the pogroms. In this as well as in other respects it bears a close resemblance to other post-liberal Jewish ideologies of the period.

The pogroms propelled Rabinovich, once again as in 1879, into a state of intense communal involvement that was followed by profound disappointment. In general, the traditional Jewish expectation of the convergence of the catastrophic and the messianic helped reinforce a mood of acute anticipation among Russian Jews. The pogroms were followed by rumors, believed by many Jews, of the imminent opening of Palestine to Jewish settlement, of the creation of numerous Jewish societies abroad to transport eastern European Jews to the West, and of a well-placed and generous Englishman whose love for the Jews had moved him to acquire for them the Land of Israel. These reports, some partially true but all exaggerated, spread rapidly. Much expectation centered around what Jonathan Frankel has called the "Oliphant cult," which eagerly looked toward the Palestinophile activity of the English mystic and traveler Laurence Oliphant, who was, as Moses Leib Lilienblum half-seriously suggested at the time, the Jewish messiah.[23] Rumors now circulated that Oliphant—whose enthusiasm for Jewish colonization was in fact the product of a mixture of avarice, sympathy, mysticism, and an eagerness for intrigue—had pledged a million pounds of his own fortune toward the rebuilding of the Land and that several of his friends had also agreed to contribute. It was claimed that Jews would be resettled in Palestine free of charge.[24]

In truth, Oliphant had little money and earned his living from journalism. He did have some important contacts and had won support for his scheme to resettle Jewry in Palestine from the Prince of Wales. When he first embarked on his negotiations with the Turks in 1879 (his interest in Jews predated the pogroms), the governor general of Damascus, the grand vizier, and the minister of public works had all agreed that the plan seemed feasible. Even the sultan appeared sympathetic to it. When Anglo-Turkish relations soured over conflicts in Egypt in 1880, negotiations between Oliphant and the sultan were broken off. Oliphant returned to Constantinople in 1881—amidst widespread Jewish speculation that his reappearance signaled a decisive change in Jewish fortunes—hoping that the sultan's mood had changed. By late 1882, it was generally agreed by Jews that Oliphant's plans were chimerical, but before then his praises were sung in extravagant terms. As the Odessa Palestinophile society stated in a letter to Oliphant, "If Nebuchadnezzar took from Palestine that which Moses first gave them, and if Titus destroyed that which Cyrus bestowed, your accomplishments will stand forever and ever."[25]

Rabinovich too had placed much faith in Oliphant. He threw himself into Palestinophile activity in Kishinev and made his way to the center of a local group devoted to the resettlement of Jews. He preached about Palestine in local synagogues and when his group decided in early 1882 to investigate the prospect of purchasing land in Palestine, Rabinovich was sent as its emissary.[26]

He arrived in Constantinople on his way to the Holy Land and naturally hoped to confer with Oliphant. But he was rebuffed. Rabinovich then heard rumors of Oliphant's meager financial resources and his unfriendly relations with the sultan and his entourage. Such rumors were apparently widespread among the disgruntled

Palestinophile colony in the Turkish capital. In an article in *Ha-Melits* in May 1882 Rabinovich called Oliphant a "Bar Kozivah disguised as Bar Kochba," a liar or false messiah who "is not looked upon with favor by the princes of Turkey because of a book he wrote which criticized the Turks." In addition, "he has no money with which to help resettle the Land of Israel."[27]

Rabinovich's essay gave the impression that he himself was at the center of important negotiations and was privy to confidential information. He wrote that the Haham Bashi of Jaffa had given him assurances that the rabbi would attempt to obtain permission for Jewish settlement. Rabinovich noted that the settlement of individual Jews in Palestine, as distinct from large, organized groups, was still feasible. He described at length his discussion with an investor with international backing who hoped to build a Syrian railroad which would end just north of the Holy Land. Colonization by Jews of the land adjacent to the railway would be easy to obtain, Rabinovich speculated. Yet these prospects, he admitted, were modest when compared with the grand expectations associated with Oliphant, whose sweet visions of speedy redemption were vacuous and misleading.[28]

The two weeks Rabinovich spent in Jerusalem after sending the article to St. Petersburg only further dampened his hopes for a dramatic and rapid solution to the problems plaguing eastern European Jewry. He found the city desolate and impoverished. He left Palestine no longer convinced that it was worthwhile to purchase land there for Jewish settlement. Upon returning to Kishinev, he discovered that he had been savaged in the pages of *Ha-Melits* by many of the most prominent Jewish nationalists of the time—including Lilienblum, David Gordon, and Smolenskin—who accused him of spreading baseless allegations about Oliphant and of undermining the goodwill of gentiles and the resolve of Jews. Even his friend Zederbaum accused Rabinovich of maliciously destroying the good reputation that *Ha-Melits* had so carefully built up. Palestinophile activists in Minsk claimed that Rabinovich's letter made their fundraising activities particularly difficult; the Moscow *Ḥibbat Tsiyyon* group sent a telegram to the organization's central office in Odessa requesting clarification after members read the article.[29]

Some time between his arrival in Jerusalem and late 1883, when he made his first public statements about Jesus, Rabinovich concluded that Jesus was the messiah and that Jewry's suffering was the result of its rejection of him. Rabinovich later claimed that this revelation first occurred to him on Mt. Zion and that it was here that the meaning of and full importance of the prediction in the final chapter of Chronicles 2, verse 16—that Jewry would be "ridiculed by the messengers of God, they despised His words, they laughed at His prophets, until at last the wrath of God rose so high against His people that there was no further remedy"—were first clarified for him. It was the phrase "no further remedy" that Rabinovich found particularly revealing. In the wake of Oliphant's failure, the utopianism of the Palestinophile movement, his loss of faith in *haskalah*, and perhaps also his loss of communal standing following his denunciation of Oliphant, the biblical prediction lent some clarity to both his wretched personal affairs and his people's ever-worsening, apparently hopeless situation. A similar emphasis on the way in which utter despair, as engendered by the pogroms, led to a new and radically different understanding of Jewish destiny was evident in much of the work generated by Russian Jewish nationalists of the period; it was indeed this nexus of anguish and subsequent illumination that was the most salient theme in Lilienblum's autobiographical work on these years, *Derekh Teshuvah* [The Path to Repentance].[30]

In late 1883, Rabinovich announced in a series of meetings with Kishinev Jews and with representatives of German and English missionary societies that he was convinced that Jesus was the messiah.[31] He appeared at these meetings with his then mentor, a local Lutheran preacher, the Reverend R. Faltin, who took credit for Rabinovich's transformation. By Russian standards, Faltin was a very successful missionary, having converted some fifty Jews in the 1860s and 1870s.[32] Over the course of the next year, Rabinovich met other Protestant clergymen. He became particularly friendly with a young Hungarian-born Jewish apostate named Venetianer, who served a congregation in Rohrbach. Russian Orthodoxy, in contrast to Protestantism, did not attract Rabinovich and he viewed its clergymen as primitive in comparison with the cultivated Europeans who were now seeking him out. In December 1884, the Russian government granted him permission to open a synagogue which he called Bethlehem, probably for both christological and Palestinophile reasons. His followers he called New Israelites.[33]

Rabinovich's New Israelites were but one of several groups in Russia in the later 1870s and early 1880s that saw themselves as Jewish-Christians. All these groups surfaced in the provinces of New

Russia—the Biblical Brotherhood headed by Jacob Gordin in Elizavetgrad (started in 1879) and the New Israel led by a Jewish teacher
in a Russian government school for Jews, Jacob Priluker of Odessa
(started in 1880). What they had in common with the Kishinev-based
New Israelites was a commitment to a radical rapprochement between
Jews and Christians and a belief that such a transformation would lead
to changes in Jewry as a whole rather than changes merely in the lives
of individual Jews.

Leaders of the various groups were in close contact. Rabinovich
met Priluker when visiting Odessa before the Kishinev notary announced his espousal of Jesus. In 1884, the Biblical Brotherhood and
New Israel merged but Rabinovich's group remained independent.
Jews of similar background were attracted to the three groups: most
were skilled artisans and workers; a handful were students or russified
intellectuals. (Few European Jewish intellectuals who chose to convert
in Russia or elsewhere did so as part of an organized evangelical
movement.) That all the sects appeared in New Russia was probably a
reflection of the inability of traditional Jewish leaders to dominate
Jewish communal life in the region to the extent to which they were
able to elsewhere, in the more settled, less remote areas of the Pale. It
was also a product of the somewhat less pervasive barriers between
Jews and non-Jews in the cities of New Russia and the impact of
russification here, in a region where a second generation of Jews
literate in Russian had reached maturity by the 1880s.[34]

Yet Rabinovich's group, in its continued commitment to Jewish
solidarity and nationalism, its continued preoccupation with *haskalah*
and its failings, and its belief in Jewish specialness and even superiority, more closely resembled Jewish postliberal ideologies than it did
the other explicitly assimilationist and enthusiastically Christian
groups. Indeed the ideology formulated by Rabinovich—and which
he preached to as many as two hundred congregants at a time at his
Kishinev synagogue—was strikingly similar in several of its premises
to those of Jewish nationalists of the period.[35] They shared a criticism,
for instance, of *haskalah*. The *haskalah*, with its belief in the connection
between Jewish perfectibility and emancipation and its assumption
that Jews should transform their inner lives in order to gain gentile
acceptance, was a program that provided Jewry with guidelines for
action even if its understanding of salvation was predicated on the
decisions of gentiles rather than Jews. The pogroms undermined these
beliefs, especially since they occurred at a time of accelerated Jewish

acculturation and when the cultural gap between Jew and gentile seemed to be narrowing. In the wake of this ideological crisis, Palestinophilism provided an alternative course of action. It did not necessarily reject the possibility of emancipation outright (note the title of Pinsker's seminal work, *Autoemancipation*) but it suggested the need for a radical change in tactics and expectations.[36]

Rabinovich's own ideological-theological program should be seen in this light. He too had lost faith in the prospect that changes in Jewish behavior would alter the attitudes of gentiles. He also ceased to believe that Jews could rebuild Palestine either on their own, or, for that matter, with the help of well-meaning gentiles. At the same time he emphasized the need for Jews to regain power over their own destinies. This, he now concluded, could only be achieved once a wrong committed centuries earlier was redressed and Jews finally embraced Jesus. Their acceptance of him would not, he insisted, win the hearts of gentiles. Rabinovich did not stress such social or political benefits of conversion, at least not in his earlier writings about Jesus. Rather, their acceptance of Jesus would win the favor of God, and He, and only He, would put an end to Jewish suffering. Moreover, Rabinovich did not believe that the acceptance of Jesus by the Jews would in itself diminish the social distance that existed between Jew and gentile. Nor did he minimize gentile responsibility for the pogroms, but, he argued, the pogroms had discredited all other ideologies embraced by Jews and now it was time—as predicted in the Chronicles—to rediscover the true cause of Jewish suffering.[37]

Palestinophilism continued to figure prominently in his thought. An early slogan of his group affirmed that "the key to the Holy Land lies in the hand of our Brother Jesus."[38] To be sure, missionaries of Jewish origin typically highlighted allegedly christological statements in Judaic sources in order to authenticate their breakaway beliefs. This is not in fact what Rabinovich did. He turned to the Hebrew Bible for evidence but he did not ground a set of otherwise orthodox Christian assertions in the form of provocative glosses on Jewish texts. On the contrary, he did not seek to win Jews over to a particular, preexisting form of Christianity but promoted a new ideology that was based on an idiosyncratic interpretation of the nature of Judaism and Jesus and which continued to owe much to Jewish nationalism. He continued to express a commitment to Judaic concepts that ran contrary to Christian universalistic claims and that even negated Christianity's belief in its superiority over Judaism. In other words, it was Jesus that

Rabinovich embraced in 1883 and not specifically Christianity in any of its forms.

Not surprisingly, some of his would-be Christian allies grew restive when confronted with his views, and the eminent Protestant biblical scholar Franz Delitzsch, concerned about their doubts, wrote in 1885: "We are not blind to the veil which still shades the dawning light; the strong expressions of [the New Israelites'] national sentiments and their comments on the development of the Gentile Church may not meet with the general approval of Christians. . . . [Yet] we have full confidence that if they continue to love Jesus as their savior this love will lead them safely past all the rocks and quicksands."[39] Similarly a writer for the *Jewish Intelligence*, published by the London Society for the Promotion of Christianity amongst the Jews, attempted to minimize Rabinovich's heterodoxy, by explaining that "theologically, he appears thoroughly Orthodox; but as might be expected, he betrays his Jewish and Rabbinical training by occasional subtleties of interpretation, as e.g., when he finds the Trinity in the three names of the Deity—God, Jehova, and Lord."[40] Even vociferous Jewish critics acknowledged that his beliefs were atypical for a missionary. For instance, in January 1884, Zederbaum, who had initially refused to believe the news of Rabinovich's conversion, explained to his readers, quite incorrectly, that Rabinovich accepted Jesus as the messiah but not as the son of God.[41] London's *Jewish Chronicle* reacted to the efforts of Rabinovich with sarcasm and expressed amazement that a man could believe himself to be both a Jew and a Christian. A Russian correspondent for the *Jewish Chronicle* later admitted that he was pleased when he heard of Rabinovich's conversion in 1885. Finally, Rabinovich was showing his true colors.[42]

But was he really? The reasons for Rabinovich's conversion in a Congregationalist church in Leipzig in March 1885 are obscure. The panic he felt just before making the decision was, according to the Christians who accompanied him at the time, intense, but they interpreted his wildly changing moods as indicative of religious ecstasy. Promises of financial aid for his fledgling movement and the excitement of being courted by Delitzsch and by other Christian dignitaries probably influenced what was, by all accounts, a sudden and surprising decision. The refusal of the London Society in December 1884 to hire him as a missionary, despite Faltin's recommendation, may also have persuaded him to convert; Faltin was reminded by the society that their policy forbade them to employ an "unbaptized agent."[43]

After his conversion, to be sure, his references to the need to maintain a separate Jewish identity within the church eventually assumed the air of institutional inertia rather than ideological fervor.[44] But this was not originally the case.

The first eight of his "Twelve Articles of Faith," published in 1884, were all but identical to the confessions of a religious Jewish nationalist. They affirmed the unity of God, his noncorporeal nature, the eternally binding Ten Commandments, and the teachings of the Prophets. Of special interest were articles three and four:

> 3. I sincerely believe that the Creator, blessed be His name, has made by His Word a covenant with our Father Abraham, to be his God, and the God of his seed after him, and to give him all the land of Canaan for an everlasting possession, and that the sign of the covenant is circumcision in the flesh, a sign of an everlasting covenant.
>
> 4. I steadfastly believe that the Creator, blessed be His name, has, according to His promise, brought out the children of Israel from the bondage of Egypt with a mighty hand through Moses His chosen one, and commanded us to keep the Sabbath-day and the Feast of Unleavened Bread as an ordinance for ever.

Article nine stated that the Jews had been persecuted through the ages because of their rejection of Jesus.[45]

Rabinovich's insistence on the need for Jews to maintain what he called Jewish national forms in spite of pressure from his wary evangelical allies was one of the most pronounced features of his teachings. He continued to view Jewish ritual, much as he did in his 1879 article in *Ha-Boker Or*, as subordinate to the needs of Jewish nationalism. Certain practices should be retained, he argued, because they expressed national solidarity and commitment rather than for their religious significance per se.[46] He rejected the binding character of the Talmud, seeing it as a monument to a time "when Israel in blindness and hardness of heart groped in the darkness." Yet he affirmed that circumcision was essential for Jews, not because an uncircumcised Jew sinned against God but rather because he separated himself irrevocably from his people.[47] Rabinovich's most important departure, from the vantage point of his new Christian supporters, was his stress in his early (pre-1885) christological writings on the Oneness of God and his rejection of the Trinity.

He argued his position partly on tactical grounds—because he was convinced that Jews would be unprepared to believe in the Trinity—but he also showed why such belief was thoroughly unnecessary for the New Israelites. Rabinovich explained that while the vast majority of Jews had rejected Jesus' teachings during his lifetime, they nonetheless possessed, then as well as now, a set of tenets that made it easier for them to accept these truths. Jews were already committed to a belief in the unity of God, the sanctity of the Bible and the eventual coming of the messiah. For these reasons, the message preached by Jesus, originally aimed only at Jews, was a simple one, demanding only belief in him and his mission. Once Jews refused to accept him, his apostles were forced to direct their message to pagans, and for this reason the church found it necessary to formulate its teachings in a series of dogmatic and complex statements.[48]

Christianity therefore introduced practices and ideas that were alien to the simple and unadorned beauty of Jesus' original message. Pagan converts, wrote Rabinovich, had "been living in idolatry under degrading influences . . . [and] . . . they were so singleminded as to be ready to believe in anything." Hence Christian belief in the Holy Ghost and Resurrection. Jews today who embrace the teachings of Jesus, Rabinovich concluded, were not required to "accept all the specialities and distinctions which the Christian church, in the course of time, ordained for themselves."[49] Elaborate dogmas were necessary for pagans since "the word of Christ was then quite new, and they never heard anything about it before." Rabinovich stated quite clearly that he believed that the concept of the Trinity was also introduced in order to gradually win over Christian neophytes from polytheism. Jews had always accepted that God had three "faces" (*partsufim*) but that these were aspects of the same one God. Rabinovich did agree, after considerable pressure from the Christians who advised him when he formulated the Articles of Faith, that the term "unity" might be substituted for "one" as a translation of the Hebrew work *ehad* in the English version of the document's description of God. The term *ehad* (which is accurately translated as meaning one) remained in the Hebrew original and Rabinovich would compromise no further on this point.[50]

Moreover, he retained a belief in Jewish specialness, even superiority, and did not see this as provisional in character, marking off the Jews temporarily until their fall from grace could be rectified and their absorption into the church realized. Rather, the Jews would continue to function within their own national unit as long as national differences of any kind retained their relevance. Allusions to Jewish superiority even found their way into the prayers composed for his synagogue and he had his congregation affirm, for example, "Before

our eyes our possessions [in the Temple] have been plundered, removed and carried away. Our enemies laid upon us their yoke; we
carried it on our shoulders. Servants rule over us; there was none to
deliver us."[51] It is possible that Rabinovich was influenced in his
description of the evolution of Christian dogma by the well-known
explanation of Maimonides (in *The Guide to the Perplexed* 3: 26–32) of the
origins of the Mosaic sacrifices, a passage with which Rabinovich, as a
literate Jew, was probably familiar, though we have no way of knowing
for certain. Maimonides saw the sacrifices as having originated in
response to the Jews' unfortunate condition upon their release from
slavery in Egypt. He explained that abstractions could not then be
effectively communicated to Jews and that God's teachings had to be
concretized into forms, however base, that would be comprehensible.
Surely it is not surprising that Rabinovich, who embraced Jesus when
he was over forty years of age, would continue to be influenced by
such seminal Jewish texts.

We can now appreciate how different Rabinovich's beliefs were
from those of Priluker and Gordin. Gordin's Biblical Brotherhood was
above all devoted to rationalism and viewed all ritualism as irrelevant.
Inspired by the Stundists, an evangelical sect with strong roots in Kiev
and Elizavetgrad (and, interestingly, with a rather negative attitude
toward Jews), the Biblical Brotherhood was openly indifferent to
spiritual concerns per se and saw Jewry's chief dilemma in its need to
transform its unfortunate occupational structure by abandoning petty
commerce for agriculture. As a result, it taught that all particularistic
Jewish practices, including circumcision and endogamous marriage,
should be abandoned.[52] Priluker's group in Odessa took spiritual
concerns more seriously but advocated, with little compunction, that
Jews accept the beliefs and practices of Protestantism. In Priluker's
mind, his group served a provisional function: to bring Jewry into the
Christian fold; once this goal was achieved, it would disappear and
with it the need for Jewish separateness. Priluker renounced talmudic
law, embraced Sunday as the Sabbath, rejected Jewish dietary laws,
legitimized mixed marriage, and limited membership of his group to
those literate in Russian. He insisted (as did Jacob Gordin) that his
group be rewarded for its efforts by political emancipation before it
was granted to the rest of Russian Jewry.[53]

An integral feature of the platforms of both the Elizavetgrad and
Odessa groups was an insistence on the parochial character of contemporary Jewish life, this in contrast to Christianity. As Priluker wrote

in his novel *The New Israelite, or Rabbi Shalom on the Shores of the Black Sea* about an elderly rabbi who was won over to the Odessa-based sect: "He clearly realized his own deep ignorance of anything outside his own Synagogue. The speeches [of the New Israel] opened out before the eager eyes of the old Rabbi a new world, a new horizon of thought and ideals, that shattered the very ground he had been standing on all his life long."[54]

Rabinovich, on the other hand, embraced Jesus but nonetheless remained committed to a belief in the superiority of the Jews. There was no hint in his early pronouncements that he felt Jewish life to be insular or provincial. Nor did he advocate the eventual assimilation of Jewry into a larger, ethnically homogeneous society. Rabinovich took for granted a world in which nationalities lived separately; in this respect too he was a rather typical Russian *maskil*. He anticipated greater harmony among the nations but not amalgamation. Rabinovich reminded his followers that in the end of days the wolf would lie down with the lamb but, he stressed, "The wolf does not become a lamb but his nature will be purified from all evil. So also the words, 'One flock and one shepherd' do not mean that all members of the flock will be exactly alike but that the many peculiarities and special gifts of the many individual members will be sanctified."[55]

Rabinovich was not a particularly successful missionary. When his synagogue, Bethlehem, first opened its doors in December 1884, its Sabbath services attracted large crowds, so large in fact that Rabinovich claimed that he had hundreds of followers. Most of his congregants, though, were curiosity-seekers, Jews eager to witness the remarkable sight of a Jew preaching about Jesus in Yiddish;[56] missionary offices in Warsaw and elsewhere in eastern Europe were similarly deluged by Jews seeking the amusement of baiting missionaries, testing their knowledge of biblical texts, engaging them in witty, sometimes engrossing conversation. Indeed on a number of occasions so many Jews sought out this form of amusement that rabbinic authorities prohibited them from even walking in the vicinity of missionary libraries, information centers, and houses of worship. In rather remote Kishinev, where the power of the rabbinate was less decisive than in older, more established communities, this activity was more difficult to check.[57] For several months hundreds of Jews crowded weekly into Bethlehem. They were often boisterous, sometimes abusive. But Rabinovich's sermons were very long and dry—devoted, according to one disappointed gentile listener, to "long harangues about peculiar Jewish apparel, their ceremonies and habits"[58]—and eventually the crowds thinned down. Within a few years, Rabinovich's brother took to stopping Jews passing by the synagogue on the Sabbath, attempting to lure them into services.[59]

Government restrictions prohibited Rabinovich (along with all other non-Orthodox clergy in the empire, with the exception of Poland) from engaging in conversion and this also proved to be a hardship. Followers of Rabinovich interested in conversion were instructed to go to clergymen in Austria or Germany, most often it seems to Leipzig. According to the records of the London Society for the Promotion of Christianity amongst the Jews, Rabinovich was directly responsible for the conversion, by 1888, of no more than thirteen persons, among whom were his three daughters, his wife, and his brother. His insistence on the desirability of Jewish separateness was apparently lost on his daughters. When they were converted by Venetianer in 1885, they requested that he change their names to Christian ones. He dissuaded them from doing so.[60]

Rabinovich died in 1899, a largely forgotten and isolated figure who had fallen into a deep depression in the last years of his life. Since the time of his espousal of Jesus he led a restricted social life, cut off from most Jews and with close contact with few gentiles. He was closest, not surprisingly, to converts like himself; an intimate associate was Joseph Axelrod, Rabinovich's son-in-law, who worked as a missionary in Odessa.[61] By 1888, his erstwhile supporter, the Lutheran preacher Faltin, was waging a bitter campaign against him, relations between the two having been strained since Rabinovich's decision to convert in Leipzig rather than in Kishinev under Faltin's care. Rabinovich explained that his former mentor had only "theological" love for the Jews and not a "true and genuine love, springing from the depth of a man's heart within. . . ."[62] From the mid-1890s, even the London Society lost faith in Rabinovich and was hesitant to continue sending his movement an annual donation of £400. It is not clear whether or not it stopped payments but there was considerable support within the group to do so.[63] When the official history of the London Society, Rabinovich's major financial backer, was published in 1908, the author devoted no more than one paragraph to his life and work.[64]

Despite the fact that Rabinovich died a failure with few Jewish souls to his credit and having all but lost the goodwill of his Christian backers abroad, his biography remains of interest. To be sure, he was boastful, self-important, and something of a crank. But his spiritual transformation occurred at a moment in Jewish history when cranks (like Oliphant), marginal, powerless intellectuals (like Lilienblum, Mordecai Ben Hillel Ha-Cohen and many others), and political visionaries (like the members of Am Olam and Bilu) assumed unusual prominence. Their prominence was short-lived. Within the span of two or three years—once the poor economic conditions of Palestine became widely known, the Russian-Jewish agrarian societies in the United States failed, and the Russian government's new restrictions appeared less oppressive than previously feared—the older, conservative leadership regained its importance and the young men, so visible in the wake of the pogroms, were once again marginalized. A significant, if subtle, shift had indeed occurred in Jewish cultural and institutional life in Russia in these years that would contribute to the eventual consolidation of postliberal ideologies like Zionism and their supplanting of older ideological currents. In the immediate aftermath of this turbulent period, this was by no means clear.

Rabinovich should be viewed within this cultural context. He was shaken by the same events that caused many men and women with backgrounds similar to his to embrace Palestinophilism, Jewish socialism, and Am Olam. Had he not undergone a radical religious transformation, he would probably be remembered today as a Zionist who was the first outspoken critic of Oliphant and whose commitment to the rebuilding of Palestine was based on a peculiarly intense if idiosyncratic set of religious convictions. "A man who loves his people and is truthful to *haskalah* and religious precepts alike," as the editor of *Ha-Melits*, Alexander Zederbaum, once characterized him.[65]

His subsequent intellectual odyssey provides an interesting perspective on a period of intense ideological crisis that gave birth to Jewish nationalism. It is at some midway point between heresy and apostasy that Rabinovich must be placed, closer to the former and further (until 1885, at any rate) from the latter. He had violated a profound taboo and embraced a symbol of Jewish humiliation and oppression. Yet his attachment to Judaic textual sources was intense and, ironically, he drew his startling conclusions from his reading of them. He embraced Jesus for many of the same reasons that other Jews of the time would call for mass Jewish migration and for a radical reassessment of the optimistic prescriptions of the *haskalah*. Rabinovich's writings, moreover, were informed by an internal consistency that united his maskilic phase of the 1870s with his first christological statements of the 1880s.

Rabinovich did not merely remain attached to things Jewish after his discovery of Jesus; paradoxically, he arrived at his conclusions about the nature of Jewish salvation for peculiarly Jewish reasons and out of an overriding sense of commitment to his people and their destiny. Personal ambition, greed, and thwarted desires may very well have influenced him, but probably not much more than such factors influenced his more respectable contemporaries. To acknowledge that he occupies a place in Jewish cultural history, however minor, perhaps raises methodological questions as to the boundaries of Jewish historical research. To place Rabinovich outside these boundaries, however, is both unrealistic and unnecessarily vindictive.

NOTES

1. Jonathan Frankel, *Prophecy and Politics: Socialism, Nationalism and the Russian Jews, 1862–1917* (Cambridge: Cambridge University Press, 1981), pp. 49–132.

2. Ibid., pp. 1–4.

3. Michael Stanislawski, *Tsar Nicholas I and the Jews: The Transformation of Jewish Society in Russia, 1825–1855* (Philadelphia: Jewish Publication Society, 1983), pp. 141–54; Samuel Wilkinson, *In the Land of the North: The Evangelization of the Jews in Russia* (London: Marshall Brothers, 1905). For a description of missionary activity in Poland and Russia, see W. T. Gidney, *The History of the London Society for Promoting Christianity Amongst the Jews from 1809–1908* (London: London Society for Promoting Christianity Amongst the Jews, 1908), pp. 87–95.

4. For information on the number of Jewish conversions to Christianity in Russia see the entry "Obrashchenie v khristianstvo" [Conversion to Christianity] *Evreiskaia entsiklopediia*, esp. cols. 894–95. Also see two studies by Yehuda Slutsky: *Ha-itonut ha-yehudit russit ba-meah ha-tesha esreh* [The Russian-Jewish Press in the Nineteenth Century] (Jerusalem: Mosad Bialik, 1970), pp. 125–27, and *Ha-itonut ha-yehudit-russit ba-meah ha-esrim, 1900–1918* [The Russian-Jewish Press in the Twentieth Century, 1900–1918] (Tel Aviv: Tel Aviv University Press, 1978), pp. 363–65.

5. Biographies of Joseph Rabinovich may be found in Shaul Ginsburg, *Meshumodim in tsarishn rusland* [Jewish Apostates in Tsarist Russia] (New York: Cyco-Bicher Farlag, 1946) and Sh. L. Tsitron, *Meshumodim* [Apostates], 4 vols. (Warsaw: Central, 1923). Tsitron's work was translated into Hebrew and entitled *Mei-aḥorei ha-pargod* [Behind the Curtains], 2 vols. (Vilna: Z. Mats, 1923–25), and for reasons of

---

availability I shall quote from the Hebrew translation. Very useful is the entry under "Rabinovich, Yosef" in Zalman Rejzen, *Leksikon fun der yidisher literatur, prese, un filologie* [Lexicon of Yiddish Literature, Press and Philology], 2d ed., vol. 4. The fire that impoverished the Rabinovich family was described in the *Jewish Herald*, 1 May 1887. (This monthly periodical, which carefully followed Rabinovich's career, was published by the British Society for the Propagation of the Gospel amongst the Jews.) Tsitron, *Mei-aḥorei ha-pargod*, 1: 116–18, told of Rabinovich's conversion to *haskalah*. A Kishinev correspondent writing for *Ha-Melits*, 11 January 1885, after the appearance of Rabinovich's New Israelites, suggested that his hasidic background may have prevented him from fully committing himself to *haskalah*. He was always, the writer speculated, a man of two different characters (*ba'al shetei partsufim*).

6. Not included in Rejzen's list of Rabinovich's writings were articles published in *Ha-Tsefirah*, 2 June 1876, and *Ha-Melits*, 3 August 1882.

7. Ch[aim] D. Lippe, *Bibliographisches Lexicon der gesamten Jüdischen Literatur der Gegenwart* (Vienna: D. Lowy, 1879–81), p. 643.

8. "Ravvinskaia komissia" [Rabbinical Commission], *Evreiskaia entsiklopediia*, cols. 233–38; Mordekhai Ben Hillel Ha-Cohen, *Olami* [My World], 5 vols. (Jerusalem: Defus ha-poalim, 1927–29), 1: 107–11.

9. Quoted in Ha-Cohen, *Olami*, 1: 109.

10. *Ha-Boker Or* 4 (1879): 1071.

11. Ibid. Smolenskin is not mentioned by name in the article, probably because it appeared in a journal edited by his rival, Abraham Baer Gottlober.

12. Ibid., p. 1132.

13. Ibid., p.1072.

14. Ibid., p.1131.

15. Ginsburg, *Meshumodim*, p. 81; *Ha-Melits*, 11 January 1885.

16. Stanley Nash, *In Search of Hebraism: Shai Hurwitz and His Polemics in the Hebrew Press* (Leiden: E. J. Brill, 1980), p. 213.

17. *Ha-Boker Or* 4 (1879): 1071.

18. Ibid, pp. 1071, 1131–32.

19. S. L. (Israel) Zinberg, *Istoriia evreiskoi pechati v Rossii* [History of the Jewish Press in Russia] (Petrograd: I. Fleitman, 1915), pp. 238–46; Ha-Cohen, *Olami*, 1: 142–51.

20. See Tsitron's surprisingly sympathetic appraisal of Lichtenstein in volume 2 of *Mei-aḥorei ha-pargod*. On Lichtenstein also see the press clippings in the archives of the Church Ministry for the Jews (subsequently referred to as CMJ) d. 50/ 10–11.

21. *Jewish Herald*, 1 July 1888.

22. CMJ 55/ 10:21.

23. Frankel, *Prophecy and Politics*, pp. 81–82.

24. On Oliphant's Palestinophile activities see Philip Henderson, *The Life of Laurence Oliphant* (London: Robert Hale, 1956), pp. 203–12, and Anne Taylor, *Laurence Oliphant, 1829–1888* (Oxford: Oxford University Press, 1982), pp. 190–212.

25. Quoted by Sh. L. Tsitron, *Toledot ḥibbat tsiyyon* [History of the Love of Zion Movement] (Odessa: Moriah, 1914), 1:118.

26. See the entry on Rabinovich in Rejzen, *Leksikon*, vol. 4. The Odessa pogrom of 1871 persuaded Rabinovich, according to the *Jewish Herald*, 1 May 1887, that the better educated Jews were, the more likely would be their persecution—a notion that contradicted the *haskalah*'s progressivist beliefs but which was shared by several Russian Jewish intellectuals in Odessa and elsewhere in the aftermath of the pogrom. See Steven J. Zipperstein, *The Jews of Odessa: A Cultural History, 1794–1881* (Stanford: Stanford University Press, 1985), pp. 114–28.

27. *Ha-Melits*, 30 May 1882. The article was reprinted in Shulamit Laskov, ed., *Ketavim le-toledot ḥibbat tsiyyon ve-yishuv erets yisrael* [Documents on the History of the Love of Zion Movement and the Settlement of the Land of Israel] (Tel Aviv: Tel Aviv University and Kibbutz Ha-Me'uḥad, 1982), 1: 268–72.

28. Ibid.

29. Ibid., pp. 298–99, 315, 318–21, 322–25, 431. Also see *Ha-Melits*, 13 June 1882; 20 June 1882; and 27 June 1882.

30. On *Derekh Teshuvah* see Alan Mintz, "Guenzburg, Lilienblum and the Shape of Haskalah Autobiography," *Association for Jewish Studies Review* 4 (1979): 71–110. For Rabinovich's account of his transformation see the *Christian*, 3 March 1887. Interestingly, this account was contradicted elsewhere by Rabinovich himself. In a letter Rabinovich wrote to Zederbaum several months after his return to Kishinev from Palestine—and published in *Ha-Melits*, 3 August 1882, more than two years before Rabinovich announced his new beliefs—he stated that it was crucial that the pages of *Ha-Melits* be reopened to him so that he might act upon a pledge he made at the foot of Mt. Zion. He had promised to wage war against pernicious (and unnamed) writers who had misused their standing with the Jewish people. Rabinovich warned Zederbaum that if he closed his newspaper to him a plot, involving a coalition of nihilists and missionaries who had banded together to do harm to the Jewish people, which he had discovered during his stay in Jerusalem, would go unexposed. The megalomania was typical of Rabinovich. What was striking about the letter was his coupling of nihilists and missionaries months after his supposed discovery of Jesus and his contention that these groups intended to harm Jews. Quite possibly, Rabinovich had come by now to feel both a strong attraction and (not surprisingly, given his background) also an intense aversion, to missionaries, feelings that were wreaking havoc—hence perhaps the allusion to nihilists—with his inner life.

31. CMJ d. 50/ 3.

32. W. T. Gidney, *The Jews and Their Evangelization* (London, 1899), p. 101. Also see CMJ 55/ 10:22.

33. The opening of Bethlehem was described in Tsitron, *Mei-aḥorei ha-pargod*, 1: 127.

34. On these sects see V[enyamin O.] Portugalov, *Znametel'nyia dvizheniia v evreistve* [A Remarkable Movement among the Jews] (St. Petersburg: privately printed, 1884). Information on the followers of the groups may be found in *Ha-Tsefirah*, 27 February 1884 and 10 April 1884, and in the *Jewish Herald*, 1 November 1887. For a discussion of Jewish life in the southern cities of imperial Russia, see Steven J. Zipperstein, "Jewish Enlightenment in Odessa: Cultural Characteristics, 1794–1871," *Jewish Social Studies* 44 (1982): 19–36.

35. A handwritten Hebrew-language version of Rabinovich's "Twelve Articles of Faith" may be found in CMJ d. 50/ 1–11. An English translation was published in the *Jewish Herald*, 1 October 1884. Also see the article "The Sons of the New Covenant on Expositions of the Articles of Faith," in the *Jewish Herald*, 1 November 1884 and 1 December 1884. The Articles were formulated at a meeting held in Kishinev on 14 March 1884. A copy of the protocol from the meeting, signed by Rabinovich along with several local followers and the representatives of missionary societies from abroad, is to be found in CMJ d. 50/ 3.

36. Frankel, *Prophecy and Politics*, pp. 81–90. On the social underpinnings of *haskalah* ideology, see Zipperstein, *The Jews of Odessa*, pp. 9–20.

37. *Jewish Herald*, 1 November 1884.

38. Ibid., 1 October 1884.

39. Ibid., 1 January 1885.

40. *Jewish Intelligence*, August 1885.

41. *Ha-Melits*, 20 January 1884.

42. *Jewish Chronicle*, 23 January and 22 May 1885.

43. On Rabinovich's conversion, see CMJ FC 3835/ 13, and the *Jewish Herald*, 1 May 1887. Faltin's letter and the reply of the Society were summarized in the CMJ Minute Book, 1884, item 961.

44. See Rabinovich's harsh assessment of Judaism in the *Jewish Herald*, 1 January 1890. Also see his *Yeshu ha-notsri melekh ha-yehudim* [Jesus the Christian, King of the Jews] (New York: Hope of Israel, n.d.) and *What Is an Israelite of the New Covenant? A Dialogue between Two Jews* (London: London Council of the Rabinowitch Fund, n.d.). Both pamphlets were written by Rabinovich either in the late 1880s or early 1890s. In the latter work Rabinovich eschews Palestinophilism and contrasts the "carnal" Jew with the Christian (pp. 11–12).

45. *Jewish Herald*, 1 October 1884.

46. Ibid. Also see the *Jewish Herald*, 1 January 1885.

47. Ibid., 1 December 1884.

48. *Jewish Intelligence*, October 1884; the *Jewish Herald*, 1 November 1884.

49. *Jewish Herald*, 1 November 1884.

50. Ibid., 1 December 1884.

51. CMJ Miscellaneous Papers, 55/10.

52. For a detailed description of the Biblical Brotherhood see *Jewish Encyclopedia*, s.v. "Bibleitzy (Bibleiskoe Bratstvo)." Many items were listed in the *Sistematicheskii ukazatel' literatury o evreyakh . . . (1708–1889)* [Systematic guide to the literature on the Hebrews in the Russian language . . . 1708–1889] (St. Petersburg: Mefizei Haskalah, 1892).

53. The beliefs of New Israel were enumerated in *Jewish Intelligence*, January 1884. A biographical sketch of Priluker by Helen Franks may be found in a collection of his essays, *Russian Flashlights* (London: Chapman and Hall, 1911). Priluker eventually moved to England where he worked as a journalist and publisher. He died in 1935. Also see Priluker's autobiography, *Under the Russian and British Flags: A Study of a True Experience* (London: Spriggs Publishing Agency, 1912).

54. Yakov M. Priluker, *The New Israelite, or Rabbi Shalom on the Shores of the Black Sea* (London: Simpkin, Marshall, and Co., 1903), p. 109.

55. Quoted in the *Jewish Herald*, 1 May 1884.

56. Rabinovich gave the impression in his first public statements that some 200 Jews were within the orbit of his group. See, for instance, the *Jewish Herald*, 1 February 1885, where he stated that "about 200 of my people are inclined toward Christianity." Such claims were improbable and were scored by several Christians critical of his work. An Odessa pharmacist, Alexander Lampert, wrote in a letter to the press that was brought to the attention of the London Society (see CMJ d. 50/ 10) in response to a similar report in *Le Réveil D'Israel*, February 1889: "Alas, the real facts do not come up at all to the overdrawn picture and in fact the real truth is in entire disagreement with his statements." Zederbaum suggested that many Jews attended services at Bethlehem out of sheer curiosity; see *Ha-Melits*, 28 January 1884. Elimelekh Veksler, an Odessa-based correspondent for Warsaw's weekly Hebrew newspaper *Ha-Tsefirah*, wrote that Rabinovich had attracted little support in Kishinev but had captured the interest of some Jews in the smaller towns of Bessarabia; Veksler's reports appeared on 20 January and 27 February 1884.

57. W. T. Gidney, *At Home and Abroad: A Description of Missions to Jews in Great Britain and on the Continent* (London: Operative Jewish Convert's Institution, 1900), p. 115.

58. CMJ d. 50/ 17.

59. Tsitron, *Mei-aḥorei ha-pargod*, 1:127. Rabinovich would eventually suggest (in the *Jewish Herald*, 1 December 1887), "The importance of the movement in South Russia must be established not by its numerical strength but by its intrinsic character."

60. CMJ d. 22/ 2.

61. Wilkinson, *In the Land of the North*, p. 79; Ginsburg, *Meshumodim*, pp. 88–89.

62. *Jewish Herald*, 1 July 1888.

63. CMJ d. 50/ 16.

64. Gidney, *The History of the Church Society*, p. 542.

65. *Ha-Melits*, 20 January 1887.

9

The Impact of Nineteenth-Century Christian Missions on American Jews

JONATHAN D. SARNA

Most historical discussions of Christian efforts to convert American Jews concentrate on the goals set by the missionaries themselves. After evaluating the efforts expended, the money spent, and the relatively small number of souls converted by the missionary organizations, they conclude—unsurprisingly, given the weight of the evidence—that "these attempts have failed." "If the historical importance of such associations is measured by their success in promoting a cause," Professor Lorman Ratner thus writes, "then [the American Society for Meliorating the Condition of the Jews] should be left in obscurity, for it accomplished very little."[1]

This negative appraisal of missionary accomplishments, while accurate in some respects, leaves much unsaid. Indeed, the evidence seems to me to suggest that missionaries, albeit unknowingly and unwittingly, actually contributed in important ways to the development and strengthening of the American Jewish community. American Jews might have been happier had missionaries not posed their challenge, but they would also have been substantially worse off.

To explore this surprising paradox, this paper, after briefly reviewing the history of nineteenth-century Christian missions to the

I am grateful to Professors Benny Kraut and Jacob R. Marcus and to Rabbi Lance S. Sussman for their comments on earlier drafts of this paper, and to the Memorial Foundation for Jewish Culture and the American Council of Learned Societies for their generous support of some of the research upon which this paper is based.

Jews in the United States, will focus on two critically important areas of missionary impact on American Jewish life. It will argue that missionaries ultimately strengthened the Jewish community by forcing Jews to confront first, the uncertainties of American religious pluralism, and second, serious community problems that they had hitherto neglected.

1

The history of Christian efforts to convert American Jews may be summarized briefly.[2] In the colonial and early national periods such efforts were private and often casual religious solicitations undertaken either by ministers or laymen, usually with the intent of converting someone with whom they were already socially acquainted. The eagerness of Ezra Stiles to convert his friend Aaron Lopez of Newport, and efforts by people in Warrenton, North Carolina, to convert Jacob Mordecai typify situations that numerous Jews faced at one time or another.[3] In many cases, asking a Jewish friend to convert was not a fanatical or even an unfriendly act, nor did Jews view it as such. The suggestion, indeed, was often a backhanded compliment, a way of inviting popular but not yet completely acceptable members of the community to upgrade their civic status by becoming "good Christians," and joining a church like everyone else.

The first organized American societies dedicated to Jewish evangelization were formed in New York (the American Society for Evangelizing the Jews) and Boston (the Female Society of Boston and the Vicinity for Promoting Christianity among the Jews) in 1816, during what is known in America as the Second Great Awakening. Societies for the promotion of innumerable benevolent causes were formed during this period, among them the American Bible Society (1815), the American Colonization Society (1817), and the American Tract Society (1825), and many of the same reform-minded evangelicals were involved in each group.[4]

Spurred on by Joseph S. C. F. Frey,[5] a founder of the London Society for Promoting Christianity among the Jews, author of a best-selling missionary autobiography, and himself a convert, recently removed to New York; and also spurred by "intelligence from Germany announcing the desire of a number of Christian Jews to emigrate to the United States for the purpose of forming a Christian-Jewish settlement,"[6] the American Society for Evangelizing the Jews reorganized in 1820 and applied for a state charter. It received one, in April of that year, and emerged both with a new name, the American Society for Meliorating the Condition of the Jews (ASMCJ), and with a new objective:

> to invite and receive from any part of the world such Jews as do already profess the Christian religion or are desirous to receive Christian instruction, to form them into a settlement and to furnish them with the ordinances of the Gospel and with such employment in the settlement as shall be assigned to them.[7]

Numerous notables connected themselves with the ASMCJ during this period. Elias Boudinot, former president of the Continental Congress, served as its president. John Quincy Adams, William Phillips, Stephen Van Rensselaer, Jeremiah Day, Ashbel Green, Philip Milledoler (the last three, respectively, presidents of Yale, Princeton, and Rutgers), and former New York governor DeWitt Clinton, all served at various times as honorary vice-presidents. Peter Jay, son of the diplomat John Jay, served as treasurer. By the mid-1820s, the ASMCJ enjoyed prestige, publicity, and liberal support from several hundred auxiliary societies scattered in different states of the union.[8]

Nothing came of the ASMCJ's effort to colonize Jews. In 1826, following a spate of bad publicity and a shift in public attitudes back toward more secular concerns, the society collapsed amid factional and legal squabbling.[9] It continued to languish, although periodically showing renewed spurts of vigor, particularly in the 1840s, but it never regained its former eminence. Henceforward, the ASMCJ and missions to American Jews generally attracted fewer supporters, more detractors (Jewish and non-Jewish), and far less money. Premillennial hopes that Jewish converts would spur the onset of the "end of days" waned, confidence in colonization schemes faded away, and missionizing assumed the form, known as direct missionizing, that remains familiar. Societies—the ASMCJ and denominational societies like those of the Baptists and Presbyterians—hired individuals, many of them Jewish apostates, and sent them into Jewish neighborhoods, where they formed a visible presence (sometimes in storefronts), and could confront "potential converts" on a one-to-one basis. Over the years, this missionary presence grew stronger or weaker depending both on the religious temper of the times and on the perceived potential for success. In 1900, according to A. E. Thompson, the Jewish missionary enterprise in America consisted of some seventy-five missionaries, representing twenty-nine different societies, in thirteen United States cities.[10]

2

From early on, American Jews viewed Christian missionary activities directed against them both as a serious threat to their own immediate well-being, and, more broadly, as another in a long series of Christian efforts to undermine Jewish civilization. Jews knew that they had to respond to such challenges, and respond they did—vigorously. American Jewish responses to missionaries[11] began in 1816, with *Tobit's Letter to Levi*, or, since that seems to have been penned by a gentile, in 1820, with *Israel Vindicated* (written by one who called himself "An Israelite," even if he wasn't),[12] and continued to appear right through the century, with the antimissionary fulminations of Rabbi Isaac Mayer Wise being particularly noteworthy. The literature is enormous, considering the small size of the American Jewish population at the time, and it covers a wide spectrum from theological arguments, to historical arguments, to ad hominem arguments. It borrows liberally from European polemics, particularly those of Isaac Troki and Isaac Orobio de Castro, as well as from deistic tracts. Yet at the same time, it includes arguments and emphases peculiarly appropriate to American Jews' own situation—for example, arguments based on the Jewish contribution to American independence. It thus displays elements both of continuity and of change. It reflects, in this sense, the American Jewish experience as a whole.

While American Jewish antimissionary literature portrays an ostensibly unified community responding as one to a common threat, in fact the missionary challenge set off a highly significant—and hitherto overlooked—tactical debate within that community over how best to formulate a response appropriate to America's distinctive religious situation. In Europe, after all, Jews had always been forced to respond to missionaries from a position of weakness, particularly in the post-emancipation period when Jews depended on Christians for toleration, and feared to offend them. Even in England, Jewish opponents of the London Society for Promoting Christianity amongst the Jews had to remember that they were a minority fighting an established church at a time when Jews had yet to win full legal equality.[13] In the United States, by contrast, "free exercise of religion" was guaranteed by the Constitution, if not always by the states, and there was no established church at all. Legally, at least, Jews had won equality, not mere toleration.[14] They were one minority religious group among many others.

Some American Jews, conscious of the freedom America afforded them, wanted to respond to missionaries more forcefully than was possible in other countries. Rather than just defending Judaism respectfully by disputing Christian interpretations of Scripture and casting aspersions on individual missionaries, these Jews, whom we might term extremists, sought openly to revile Christianity, putting it, rather than Judaism, on the defensive. At the same time, other Jews, particularly those who regularly interacted with the Christian majority, opposed these tactics. Not wishing to alienate all Christians because of the missionary tactics of some, they advocated moderate, nonthreatening responses, the kind that could be effective without being offensive. The debate is difficult to reconstruct, and positions were naturally more varied than this idealized model suggests. Broadly speaking, however, we can say that extremists viewed Jewish-Christian relations in triumphalistic terms as a battle between two religions in which one—the more correct one—would emerge victorious. Moderates, by contrast, viewed the relationship in pluralistic terms, and therefore searched for a middle ground on which Jews and Christians could continue to coexist. The missionary threat brought these two conflicting outlooks into the open, with the result that each side produced polemics suitable to the particular end that it sought to advance.

Two examples illustrate this point. The first involves Mordecai Manuel Noah, the leading Jew in early America, and Solomon Jackson, the leading Jewish antimissionary. Noah worked as a New York journalist and politician, and spent the majority of his time in the company of non-Jews. It therefore comes as no surprise that his reaction to missionaries fell into what I have labeled the moderate camp. For several years, in his newspaper, he ignored American missions to the Jews completely. When he did break his silence, in 1818, he did so with words carefully chosen to ensure that no Christian would take offense:

> We have seen some remarks . . . concerning the pious labours of Mr. Frey in converting the Jews in this country, and the success attending his efforts. We have not noticed this person since his arrival in this country, as we are very indifferent on the subject of his labours to make an honest living by making proselytes: but this we

know, that the Society in London where there are 20,000 Jews who employed him, bade him farewell without regret, and in this country he has not made a single convert. We have no objections to his success, if sincerity and piety really govern his motives, but we have no idea of permitting the community to be deceived on this subject. We could say much more on the occasion, but religion should not occupy the columns of a newspaper.[15]

Noah later felt himself more free to express antimissionary views, and he did so effectively. But he never attacked Christianity as a religion. He limited himself to fulminations against missionaries' misappropriation of funds, lack of success, false piety, and immoral tactics.[16] He did not allow those whom he denominated "pious frauds" to sway him from his generally pluralistic religious stance, his image of Jews and Christians traveling side by side along roads so closely parallel as to be virtually indistinguishable:

There are two packets belonging to the New York and Boston line, one named *Jew* and the other *Gentile*. They carry equal freight, and sail with equal swiftness. They sail from the same port and arrive at the same destination. So it is with human *Jews* and *Gentiles* of the great world.[17]

Noah's pluralism was lost on Solomon Jackson,[18] a New York printer who displayed a more extremist and triumphalistic bent. Jackson, as a youth, had immigrated to America from England, settled in Pike County, Pennsylvania, and married a Christian woman, believing as he then did that "all religion was imposition—a mere trick of state."[19] But following his wife's death and numerous personal tribulations, Jackson became a *baal teshuvah*, a Jewish penitent, and thereafter he devoted much of his life to strengthening the Jewish faith. He published a translation of the prayer-book (1826) and the first American edition of the Passover Haggadah (1837), he supported Jewish education, and he led the Jewish Agricultural Society *Tseire ha-Tson*, which, among other things, barred from membership anyone married to a non-Jew and anyone "in the habit of violating the Sabbath."[20] In 1823, Jackson published what he is best remembered for: *The Jew*, the first Jewish periodical in America, "Being a Defence of Judaism against All Adversaries, and Particularly against the Insidious Attacks of *Israel's Advocate*."

In his periodical, Jackson expressed impatience with Jews of "trembling heart," who saw "danger" in his effort to defend Judaism. "Caution is now fear," he admonished these moderates, "and instead of being a virtue is in truth a weakness."[21] One of his contributors used Scripture to prove that "We are not to consider whether our answer

237

will offend or not; we are not to fear the consequence of doing our imperious duty. . . . It is the duty of every man of our persuasion, when attacked, to defend, as much as in his power, the religious tenets and peculiar doctrines of the unity of the Godhead."[22] To Jackson, moderation in defense of Judaism was a vice. He, therefore, attacked Christianity as "idolatry," and looked forward triumphantly to the day "that all the world will become of the Jewish persuasion, and be of their religion which is the only true religion."[23]

The dispute between Noah and Jackson was a basic one, argued time and again over the span of American Jewish history. The contrasting antimissionary styles of the two greatest American Jewish religious figures of the nineteenth century, rabbis Isaac Leeser and Isaac Mayer Wise, display the same moderate-extremist dichotomy. Leeser, especially in his early years, advocated a Mendelssohnian approach to missionaries: he sought to avoid religious controversy altogether if possible. In two books, *The Jews and the Mosaic Law* (1834) and *The Claims of the Jews to an Equality of Rights* (1841), and in one article, "The Jews and Their Religion" (1844), all three directed to gentile audiences, Leeser pleaded with missionaries ("we claim as children of one Father, as followers of his law, as supporters of a highly social system, to remain Jews, without the interference of our Christian neighbors and fellow-citizens; just as we act towards them"), and defended the good character of the Jewish people. He stressed the "common ground" that Jews and Christians shared, notwithstanding the many differences between the two religions. He forbore polemics and personal attacks, and at least when speaking to non-Jews made no triumphalistic claims. All he asked was that Jews "be left alone undisturbed." "We wish to live in peace," he assured his Christian readers, "doing to others as we wish to be done by."[24]

Isaac Mayer Wise, by contrast, went to any length to oppose missionaries. He considered it a "sacred duty" to expose missionaries' "rascality," and wasted no opportunity to catch them at their "lying."[25] Like Solomon Jackson, he sought "always to wage an offensive, rather than to fight a defensive war."[26] He opened the pages of his newspaper to a variety of anti-Christian critics, and trumpeted his view that Judaism would ultimately triumph: "the essence of Judaism is destined to become the universal religion . . . before this century will close, the essence of Judaism will be THE religion of the great majority of the intelligent men in this country."[27]

Disputes such as these between moderates and extremists, pluralists and triumphalists, Jews who sought coexistence with Christianity and those who foresaw nothing but an endless series of confrontations with it, did not originate in America. Similar debates, Jacob Katz has shown, raged much earlier in Jewish history as well.[28] The challenge which Christian missions to the Jews posed, however, did bring these debates into focus. By dramatizing the threat which Jews as members of a minority religion faced, missionaries forced Jews to confront, sooner and more directly than they might otherwise have done, their own religious situation in America, specifically their position vis-à-vis the Protestant majority. That Jews reached no consensus on the question of exclusiveness and tolerance is ultimately far less important than the fact that, thanks to the missionaries, the problem became a subject for spirited debate.

One aspect of the Jewish antimissionaries argument deserves special attention: the uniquely American debate over the meaning of the free exercise clause of the First Amendment to the Constitution. Jews, of course, had no monopoly on this debate. Americans have argued about what the constitutional guarantee of religious liberty means ever since that guarantee was proposed for ratification.[29] Still, the introduction of constitutional arguments into Jewish antimissionary polemics represents a new departure. It underlines again how missionaries forced Jews to confront their situation relative to America's other faiths.

Early on, many American Jews considered missionary activities directed against them to be an "invasion of the primary articles of our Constitution" or at least "contrary to the true spirit and meaning of the *constitution*."[30] Although the First Amendment only prohibited Congress from making any law "respecting an establishment of religion or prohibiting the free exercise thereof," Jews reasoned that it was generally improper, as Isaac Leeser put it, "for the many to combine to do the smallest minority the injury of depriving them of their conscientious conviction by systematic efforts."[31] Leeser may have been interpreting religious liberty in terms of the Northwest Ordinance of 1787's guarantee that "No person demeaning himself in a peaceable and orderly manner shall ever be molested on account of his mode of worship or religious sentiment."

By the 1840s, American Jews realized that no such broad interpretation of religious liberty had taken hold in the United States. With many continuing to argue, as Daniel Webster did, that Christianity formed part of the common law,[32] Jews fell back on an argument based on equality: "by the Constitution of the Union we are guaranteed, *pari passu* with our neighbors, the right to think, say and do."[33] Though they no longer believed that they could on constitutional grounds stop missionaries, Jews did insist that they had the same rights as missionaries. "I beg to address you as a God-fearing American citizen, recognized as such by the Constitution of the land," a Jew signing himself "M.S." wrote in an open letter to the *Churchman*.[34] Other Jews made the same point by asking, as Isaac Leeser once did, "how would missionary efforts by Jews be received among Christians?"[35] Having been taught by missionaries that religious liberty in America could imply free market competition between religious groups, Jews served notice that they were prepared to vie as equals. They proceeded to do so.

3

Missions directed at gentiles might at first glance have seemed like the most appropriate American Jewish response to Christian missions. How better to make the point that, in America, Jews could do whatever Christians could do? To evangelize Christians, however, Jews would have had to abandon both a longstanding diaspora tradition, one consistent with Jews' minority status, and also a powerful antimissionary polemic: the argument that Jews had no need to missionize since they did not deny to non-Jews the possibility of salvation. Even more important, sending missionaries out to the gentiles would not have solved the very real internal communal problems that left Jews prey to missionary blandishments in the first place. Missionaries, after all, directed their thrust at precisely those four areas where the Jewish community was weakest and most vulnerable. They concentrated on winning over ignorant Jews, isolated Jews, Jews confined to hospitals, and impoverished Jews. In so doing, they reminded Jewish leaders that apathy and neglect on their part could result in dire consequences. In a competitive environment, missionaries were free to exploit Jewish shortcomings to their own advantage.

It followed that "when we see today Christian missions springing up among our neglected Jews, we have no right to condemn them." So Minnie Louis, a prominent New York Jewish social worker, made clear in a paper read at the 1893 Jewish Women's Congress in Chicago. Before her audience could disagree, she explained that "it is we who deserve the condemnation for unfaithfulness to our duty."[36] Jews came to understand in the nineteenth century that missionary successes were symptoms of Jewish communal problems. By investigating where missionaries made inroads, Jews learned where they themselves had failed. They also learned that to defeat missionaries they often had to imitate them. They had to find ways to create Jewish functional alternatives to missionary activities, alternatives as fulfilling as whatever the missionaries offered, but designed at the same time to keep Jews firmly within the fold.

The resulting dynamic interaction between missionary challenges and Jewish responses operated in all four areas of Jewish vulnerability, but most particularly in education. In early America, the overall state of Jewish education was, notwithstanding certain exceptions, wretchedly poor. Few early American Jews knew Hebrew. Very few Jewish textbooks and no Jewish translation of the Bible existed for those who knew only English. And even given those books that were available, "Jewish schools functioned irregularly and inefficiently and Jewish education could not rise above the elementary level."[37] Missionaries frequently commented on this "deplorable ignorance" to prove how benighted Jews were, and they then exploited the ignorance by posing questions which the average Jew, to his embarrassment, could not answer.[38] Isaac Leeser's plea—"do not as honest men, interfere with young children or ignorant persons"—went unheeded.[39] In an open society, ignorant Jews could not be quarantined away from Christians. They had instead to be educated.

Realizing this situation, Jews slowly came to see education not just as a religious duty, but as a vital component of their whole countermissionary program. They proceeded to copy successful Christian educational patterns in order to use them for Jewish ends. The Jewish Sunday school, introduced by Rebecca Gratz and Isaac Leeser in 1838, is a good example. It was modeled on its Christian namesake, but with decidedly Jewish purposes in view. Isaac Leeser had determined that missionary successes proceeded from two causes: "either from ignorance of our religion, or because it is made the interest of converts." He expressed certainty that it was "not the interest of Christianity to bribe the interested to an outward profession which their soul does not feel." "As to the ignorant . . . ," he continued, "we have established Sunday-schools within the last two years, for the gratuitous instruction in religion in New York, Philadelphia and Charleston, and similar ones are proposed for Richmond and St.

241

Thomas. It is to be hoped that the good thus commenced will be ardently and earnestly followed up, until in all the world there shall not be a Jewish child ignorant *why* he is a Jew."[40] There were, of course, other motivations behind the Jewish Sunday school movement as well, but its antimissionary function cannot be too strongly stressed.

The Jewish Miscellany, a tract series, also introduced by Isaac Leeser, proceeded from the same strategy. According to its publishers, gentiles spared no effort "to diffuse false views . . . propagated through books, tracts, and publications of all kinds." Since this "mass of erroneous views" could result in "the loss to Israel of many precious souls who are now of our communion," it was time for Jewish "counter action." What better than to create a Jewish publication society, "to prepare suitable publications to be circulated among all classes of our people, from which they may obtain a knowledge of their faith and proper weapons to defend it against the assaults of proselyte-makers on the one side, and of infidels on the other . . ."

Propaganda of this sort, as the publishers realized, was "in fact the plan adopted by our opponents," but, of course, for different ends. "Shall we not profit by them," they wondered rhetorically. Their response, soon translated into terms of concrete action, was to learn everything possible from the missionaries and to use that knowledge to strengthen Judaism from the inside.[41]

Later on in the nineteenth century, this pattern repeated itself. Beginning in New York in 1864, and then in other cities too, missionaries set up free "mission schools" in Jewish immigrant areas, ostensibly to offer instruction in the Hebrew language, but in fact designed to Americanize Jewish children and in the process to convert them. Jews attacked these schools, verbally and even physically, but they had to admit that they themselves had done nothing about setting up a system of free Jewish education for those too poor to pay. The problem was soon solved: "the principal men of thirteen or fifteen synagogues assembled, and, after long consultation, passed resolutions to the effect that the Jews of New York should establish a sufficient number of free-schools where the children of all classes, who might wish to avail themselves of the means offered to them, should receive a Hebrew education."[42] The conversionist specter called forth the necessary funds, and shortly thereafter the first Jewish free schools, sometimes actually called "Jewish mission schools," came into being, temporarily driving the missionary schools from the field. Years later, the *Jewish Messenger* ironically observed that "if there had been no 'Jewish missions' in New York, we should have had no Hebrew Free Schools with nearly 3000 children as pupils. . . . The conversionists are our benefactors."[43] Missionaries had identified a need and showed how it could be met. Jews did the rest.

Isolated Jews in small towns and rural villages formed another area of Jewish vulnerability. They fell prey to formal and informal conversionist efforts on a continual basis. "Missionary tours" undertaken by rabbis and laymen, ongoing efforts to set up "circuit preachers" to serve outlying communities, and various mail order publications all sought to stem these threats, using techniques borrowed from the missionaries themselves. Isaac Leeser understood very early that many American Jews abandoned their faith "owing to their being entirely isolated from our people and in constant intercourse with ministers of Christianity . . . imbibing foreign manners from a constant intermixture with persons who are not Israelites."[44] He therefore urged American Jews to become "lay preachers":

> We wish Israel to take example from the activity and missionary zeal of all the sects which surround us . . . we call upon Israelites of every degree to become missionaries, not to carry the good tidings beyond the sea and into desert lands, but to the bosom of their own families, to their neighbors, to their friends.[45]

Leeser saw his own publications as missionary surrogates, designed to maintain contact with Jews "dispersed over so wide a space of country that we are precluded from waiting upon all individually to speak with them upon the concerns of their immortal souls."[46] Even the *Occident*, his monthly magazine, initially proceeded from this need. The ASMCJ had founded the *Jewish Chronicle*, a nationwide conversionist periodical. Leeser replied with a periodical of his own. His understanding of the relationship between the two periodicals says much about the relationship between missionaries and countermissionaries generally:

> two such little planets revolving around their peculiar axis; the former to malign the Jews and to report all their faults and apostacies, the latter to be in a measure their advocate, and to reprove without hesitation and reserve when errors and wrong are discovered.[47]

Missionaries challenged; Jews responded. In this case, as in many others, the Jewish response surpassed the challenge both in magnitude and significance. Without the missionary challenge, however, the appearance of Jewish periodicals in America would probably have been far longer delayed.

The third vulnerable sector of American Jewry to attract missionary attention in the nineteenth century consisted of Jews confined to hospitals. Most American hospitals during this period were maintained by religious denominations, and many nurses pursued their vocation from a sense of religious calling. In some cases, missionaries or nurses baptized dying Jews in perhaps well-meaning, but to Jews thoroughly reprehensible, efforts to save them. Reports of deathbed conversions abounded.[48] As a response, the first communitywide Jewish hospital in America, the Jewish Hospital of Cincinnati (1850), came into being. In seeking financial support for it, Isaac Leeser stressed its countermissionary appeal:

> every Jew must be anxious to have around him in the moments of suffering those who sympathize with him, not alone by pitying his pains and sorrows, but by sharing his religious sentiments, and his hopes of the future; and he must ardently desire not to have his hours of illness embittered by the appeals of those who prowl about sanitary establishments, and omit no opportunity to preach their unwelcome doctrines to all ears, in season and out of season; not to mention the dread which the conscientious invalid must feel of being tampered with in moments of unconsciousness, *as there are zealots who would not hesitate to baptize, as they call it, a Jew or heretic, or infidel, in extremis, so as to prepare his soul for heaven,* even if he be entirely unaware of the act or ceremony which is performed on him.[49]

There were, of course, other reasons for supporting Jewish hospitals that found expression. Abraham Sulzberger, in 1864, told Philadelphia Jews that it reflected the "greatest discredit" on them that their "friendless brothers" were forced "to seek in sickness and prospect of death the shelter of un-Jewish Hospitals; to eat forbidden food; to be dissected after death; and sometimes even to be buried with the stranger." He noted several cases where "Israelites of this city have died in Christian Hospitals without having the privilege of hearing the *Shemang Yisrael*—the watch-word of their faith and nation."[50] Some Jews considered it a source of embarrassment that non-Jews provided hospital care for the sick of all faiths while Jews did not provide it for any. By the end of the nineteenth century, discrimination against Jewish personnel in Christian hospitals had become yet another irritant with which the community had to contend. Still, the missionary problem—the specter of deathbed conversions—was the spur, if not the only cause, of efforts aimed at creating Jewish hospitals, open to

Jews and non-Jews alike, in Cincinnati, New York, Philadelphia, and Baltimore. If Christians could have hospitals where they displayed the benefits of their religion to Jews, Jews could counter with equally sumptuous hospitals, designed both as protection against conversionists, and as proof to Christians that Jews were every bit as generous and charitable as they were.[51]

The final major area in which missionaries made a substantial impact on nineteenth-century American Jewish life is the area of philanthropy. Jews had, of course, developed a comprehensive system of community aid going back to colonial days.[52] In response to missionary activities, however, they extended their efforts in new directions, to meet new problems.

In the 1820s, missionaries attempted to set up a colony in Ulster County, New York, for meliorating the condition (termed "grievous in the extreme") of persecuted European Jews: converts and potential converts who were then being victimized by riots and reactionary laws.[53] American Jews had considered the possibility of their country becoming a haven for European Jews before, but in the wake of the missionary thrust they offered several new and concrete proposals. *Israel Vindicated* (1820) suggested an interfaith relief effort:

> If these Nazarenes . . . are really desirous of doing a service to the poor of our nation, thousands of whom at this moment feel real distress in Europe . . . let them lay aside, in the outset at least, all attempts to interfere with our religious principles; let them consider our needy brethren only in the light of men suffering under the pressure of a common calamity, and, as such, entitled to their compassion; let them unite their efforts with the more wealthy of our nation, in endeavouring to procure an allotment of land for them in this widely extended country; and having succeeded in obtaining this, let them, as with one heart and with one voice, invite them to take possession of it, by holding out suitable inducements, and proffering them pecuniary aid.[54]

Mordecai Noah put forward a more comprehensive plan for setting up "an asylum for the oppressed," his well-known Ararat plan.[55] In 1826, Jacob Solis, then living in Mt. Pleasant, New York, suggested yet another plan for "establishing a JEWISH ASYLUM in this Country, to improve the future condition of the Jews." He noted that missionaries "had expended thousands of thousands of dollars to no purpose, because the great object was lost sight of." With "but little more than one year's interest of the amount expended by that [missionary] Society," he promised to do the job better by creating what he called "The American Jewish Asylum," designed "to admit all those

Jewish youth of both sexes, flying from oppressive governments here for refuge."[56] Since, as it turned out, Jews did not fly to America in the 1820s, Solis's plan, like all those that preceded it, Jewish and non-Jewish, came to naught. But that should not obscure the process, now familiar, whereby missionaries challenged Jews, and Jews then imitated missionaries in order to subvert them. The pattern recurred throughout the subsequent history of American Jewish philanthropy.

By the 1840s, Jewish immigrants began to flow to America's shores in larger numbers. In New York, owing to depressed economic conditions, many of them lived amidst squalor in the poorest sections of town—areas where wealthier Jews never traveled. Missionaries, however, did discover these forgotten people, and in October 1842 they appointed a special missionary, James Forrester, "to labor steadily and daily among the Jews, by visiting from house to house." The scenes Forrester described finding in New York revealed a problem far greater than American Jews had realized:

> The number of Jews now in this city has been ascertained to be nearly ten thousand. A large portion of them consists of emigrants from Europe, mostly from Germany, and many very recently. These are generally poor—some extremely so—and many touching recitals are contained in Mr. Forrester's journal, of scenes of suffering which he was compelled to witness, and sometimes had the gratification to relieve. . . . Sick and destitute females have been found in lonely garrets, without fire, in the coldest season, struggling to subsist themselves and their shivering infants upon a few crusts. Families, on the verge of being driven by their landlords from their scarcely habitable lodgings into the streets, have implored the missionary for aid in their time of need. The Board are gratified to add, that, in several of these cases, they have been enabled to afford relief; and that the small sums bestowed by their agent out of the moderate fund placed at his disposal, have been received with the most heartfelt expressions of gratitude.[57]

How New York Jews responded to these reports cannot be known for certain, but a strong indication of their alarm may be seen in an emergency twelve-page report of the Committee of the Society for the Education of Poor Children and Relief of Indigent Persons of the Jewish Persuasion, commissioned on 8 January 1843 and published just twenty-two days later under the names of three of New York's leading Jews: Benjamin Nathan, Henry Hendricks, and Solomon I. Joseph. Without mentioning missionary Forrester by name, the report confirmed much of what he had alleged. It went on to urge reforms in the whole system of Jewish poor relief in New York City.[58]

Writing from Philadelphia soon afterward, Isaac Leeser, likewise concerned about the missionary threat, urged New York Jewish leaders "to be up and adoing, to counteract any evil the [missionary] society or its agents may attempt."[59] That, apparently, is just what New York Jews did, for by 1845 Forrester was complaining about violence perpetrated against him, and his missionary activities seem to have abated. At the same time, Jewish charities, particularly the Hebrew Benevolent Society, expanded their efforts, and Jews generally became more conscious of the new responsibilities that immigration had thrust upon them.[60]

In the ensuing years, Jews periodically grew lax in their charities, and when they did, reports of some missionary success usually led them to redoubled efforts. In 1859, for example, the *Jewish Messenger* reported that a Jewish child, placed in a non-Jewish orphanage for lack of a Jewish home, had been converted there to Christianity. The resulting outcry brought about two long-discussed but hitherto postponed developments: the merger of the Hebrew Benevolent Society with the German Hebrew Benevolent Society, and the founding of the Hebrew Orphan Asylum.[61] Jewish hospitals and Jewish free schools, as we have already seen, came about in similar fashion, occasioned by well-publicized reports of what missionaries had done.[62]

All of these developments might, of course, have taken place even in the absence of the missionary challenge, just as a result of Jews' ongoing and abiding concern for the fate of their brethren in need. But the fact remains that throughout the nineteenth century, missionary challenges did stimulate both the direction and timing of Jewish social reforms. "Our sleeping fellow-Israelites," Isaac Leeser once lamented, "are aroused to action only when they see a sign of some danger."[63] Since in Jewish eyes no greater danger existed than missionaries, they played a considerable if unintentional part in galvanizing Jews into action, teaching them about the problems that existed in their midst, and showing them how those problems might be resolved.

On the face of it, this looks like just another example of Jews marching to the cadence of Christian drummers.[64] In fact, however, a more complex post-emancipation process was at work. Jews in America formed a beleaguered minority competing against a powerful majority in a more or less free religious marketplace.[65] Missionaries sold the religious wares of the majority, and in good businesslike fashion they tailored their marketing program to those areas where the minority's hold seemed weakest. Thoroughly alarmed, Jews rushed in with products of their own, modeled on those of the competition but promising more, designed to shore up their areas of weakness so as to retain, so to speak, their market share. Soon, the majority returned to the offensive, perceiving some new way to exploit Jewish weakness, and the cycle began once more. Round and round it continues, down to the present day.

So frankly adversarial a model, applying to religion the principles of free market capitalism, seems dismal indeed, particularly since it offers no hope for relief. Yet, as we have seen, missionary competition has actually led to the strengthening of the American Jewish community on a myriad of fronts. Competitive challenges, even if they weakened Judaism at first, have ultimately led to a stronger and more viable Judaism than existed before.[66] Missionaries have served as a kind of Jewish early warning system, pointing up problems that would have grown far worse if left untended. Where Jews might have been lulled into complacency, allowing evils to fester, missionary provocations compelled them to deal with problems vigorously and at once. Losses, real or feared, prompted necessary and effective counteractive measures.

Seen in a broader perspective, this American Jewish encounter with missionaries reveals how, quite generally, religious competition has worked to the advantage of Jews[67] serving as a critical factor in the survival and strengthening of American Jewry. Competitive challenges have, of course, always weakened Judaism at first, and have inevitably led the faint of heart to question whether Judaism can maintain itself. But in the long run, these challenges have had a salutary effect. By stimulating new efforts and programs, they have contributed to making the American Jewish community stronger, more viable, and far more socially conscious.

NOTES

1. David Max Eichhorn, *Evangelizing the American Jew* (Middle Village, N.Y.: Jonathan David Publishers, 1978), p. 193; Lorman Ratner, "Conversion of the Jews and Pre–Civil War Reform," *American Quarterly* 13 (1961): 43.

2. For further details, see, in addition to works cited above, Max Eisen, "Christian Missions to the Jews in North America and Great Britain," *Jewish Social Studies* 10 (1948): 31–66; Marshall Sklare, "The Conversion of the Jews," *Commentary* 56 (1973): 44–53; Lee M. Friedman, "The American Society for Meliorating the

Condition of the Jews and Joseph S. C. F. Frey," in Lee M. Friedman, *Early American Jews* (Cambridge: Harvard University Press, 1934), pp. 96–112; Robert M. Healey, "From Conversion to Dialogue: Protestant American Mission to the Jews in the Nineteenth and Twentieth Centuries," *Journal of Ecumenical Studies* 18 (1981): 375–87; and Louis Meyer, "Hebrew-Christian Brotherhood Unions and Alliances of the Past and Present," *Minutes of the First Hebrew-Christian Conference of the United States* (Pittsburg, 1903), pp. 16–31.

3. Arthur A. Chiel, "Ezra Stiles and the Jews: A Study in Ambivalence," in *A Bicentennial Festschrift for Jacob Rader Marcus*, ed. Bertram W. Korn (Waltham, Mass.: American Jewish Historical Society, 1976), pp. 63–76; Myron Berman, *Richmond's Jewry, 1769–1976* (Charlottesville: University Press of Virginia, 1970), pp. 110–24. For the situation in later periods, see Louis Schmier, ed., *Reflections of Southern Jewry* (Macon, Ga.: Mercer University Press, 1982), p. 32; Eli N. Evans, *The Provincials* (New York: Atheneum, 1973), pp. 120–39; and Kenneth Scott Latourette, *A History of the Expansion of Christianity*, vol. 4, *The Great Century*, A.D. *1800*–A.D. *1914, Europe and the United States of America* (New York: Harper, 1941), p. 293: "chance contacts seem to have been the chief sources of conversion."

4. Donald G. Mathews, "The Second Great Awakening as an Organizing Process, 1780–1830," *American Quarterly* 21 (1969): 23–43; Clifford S. Griffin, *Their Brothers' Keepers: Moral Stewardship in the United States, 1800–1865* (New Brunswick, N.J.: Rutgers University Press, 1960); Charles L. Chaney, *The Birth of Missions in America* (South Pasadena, Calif.: William Carey Library, 1976), and Ronald G. Walters, *American Reformers 1815–1860* (New York: Hill & Wang, 1978), offer useful introductions to various aspects of this period, and cite other sources.

5. George L. Berlin, "Joseph S. C. F. Frey, the Jews, and Early Nineteenth Century Millenarianism," *Journal of the Early Republic* 1 (1981): 27–49.

6. Philip Milledoler, quoted in *Occident* 1 (1844): 43.

7. Quoted in Ratner, "Conversion of the Jews," p. 45.

8. American Society for Meliorating the Condition of the Jews, *Constitution of the American Society for Ameliorating the Condition of the Jews; with an Address from the Hon. Elias Boudinot . . .* (New York, 1820); Joseph S. C. F. Frey, *Judah and Israel* (New York: D. Franshaw, 1840), pp. 81–93; Joseph L. Blau and Salo W. Baron, eds. *The Jews of the United States, 1790–1840: A Documentary History*, 3 vols. (New York: Columbia University Press, 1963), 3: 714–73; Jonathan D. Sarna, *Jacksonian Jew: The Two Worlds of Mordecai Noah* (New York: Holmes & Meier, 1981), pp. 56–57; Marion L. Bell, *Crusade in the City: Revivalism in Nineteenth Century Philadelphia*, (Lewisburg, Pa.: Bucknell University Press, 1977), pp. 137–59.

9. On the decline of the ASMCJ in the 1820s, see the secondary literature cited in note 2; *Israel's Advocate* 2 (1824): 67–68; 3 (1825): 6, 151; 4 (1826): 65–67, 86; and especially the final volume, 5 (1827) now found in microfilm, American Periodical Series #401; as well as *Religious Intelligencer* 10 (1825): 486; 12 (1828): 485. Ratner, "Conversion of the Jews," pp. 49–50, claims that the ASMCJ renewed its efforts in 1836. No evidence substantiates this claim; for contrary evidence, see Frey, *Judah and Israel*, p. 100; and *Jewish Chronicle* 10 (1854): 252.

10. A. E. Thompson, *A Century of Jewish Missions* (Chicago: Fleming H. Revell Company, 1902), pp. 277–78.

11. Jonathan D. Sarna, "The American Jewish Response to Nineteenth-Century Christian Missions," *Journal of American History* 68 (1981): 35–51.

12. Jonathan D. Sarna, "The Freethinker, the Jews, and the Missionaries: George Houston and the Mystery of *Israel Vindicated*," *AJS Review* 5 (1980): 101–14.

13. Harvey W. Meirovich, "Ashkenazic Reactions to the Conversionists, 1800–1850," *Transactions of the Jewish Historical Society of England* 26 (1979): 8–15; Todd M. Endelman, *The Jews of Georgian England, 1714–1830* (Philadelphia: Jewish Publication Society, 1979), pp. 71–76, 285–86; Bill Williams, *The Making of Manchester Jewry, 1740–1875* (New York: Holmes & Meier, 1976), pp. 45–48, 148–50; Sarna, "American Jewish Response," p. 46, n. 41.

14. George Houston, *Israel Vindicated* (New York: Abraham Collins, 1820), pp. 100–101, and Isaac Leeser, *The Claims of the Jews to an Equality of Rights* (Philadelphia: C. Sherman & Co., 1841), p. 51, both make this point; cf. Sarna, "The Freethinker, the Jews, and the Missionaries," p. 104.

15. Quoted in the *Federal Republican and Baltimore Telegraph*, 12 September 1818, in the collection of the American Jewish Historical Society, Waltham, Mass.

16. Sarna, *Jacksonian Jew*, pp. 56–57, 132, 179 n. 68.

17. Ibid, p. 131.

18. George L. Berlin, "Solomon Jackson's *The Jew:* An Early American Jewish Response to the Missionaries," *American Jewish History* 71 (1981): 10–28, and Abraham J. Karp, *Beginnings: Early American Judaica* (Philadelphia: Jewish Publication Society, 1975), pp. 37–40, contain the best short biographies of Jackson and cite earlier literature.

19. *The Jew* 1–2 (1823–25): 480.

20. *Address and Articles of the Association Tseire ha-Tson* (New York, 1837), p. 6.

21. *The Jew* 1–2 (1823–25): vi, vii.

22. *The Jew* 1–2 (1823–25): 53.

23. *The Jew* 1–2 (1823–25): 77, 158, and cf. 153, 306. See also Jackson's attack on Noah and others deemed too friendly with Christians, in his "Address to Joseph Dreyfous . . . 1829," reprinted in Solomon Solis-Cohen, "A Unique Jewish Document of a Century Ago," *Jewish Exponent*, 25 October 1929, p. 8.

24. Quotations are, in order, from Leeser, *Claims of the Jews*, pp. 11–12; I. Leeser, "The Jews and Their Religion," in I. Daniel Rupp, *An Original History of the Religious Denominations at Present Existing in the United States* (Philadelphia: J. Y. Humphreys, 1844), pp. 357, 362; and *Claims of the Jews*, p. 87. See also Sarna, "American Jewish Response," pp. 41–42; and the advertisement in *Occident* 18 (29 March 1860), supplement, p. 1, where Leeser praises Benjamin Dias Fernandes, *A Series of Letters on the*

Evidences of Christianity (Philadelphia: Bloch, 1853) for being "so gentlemanly in its tone."

25. Quoted in Sarna, "American Jewish Response," p. 47.

26. Isaac M. Wise, "The World of My Books," trans. Albert H. Friedlander, in *Critical Studies in American Jewish History*, ed. Jacob R. Marcus (Cincinnati: American Jewish Archives, 1971), 1: 174.

27. James G. Heller, *Isaac M. Wise: His Life, Work, and Thought* (New York: Union of American Hebrew Congregations, 1965), pp. 537–38; cf. Benny Kraut, "Judaism Triumphant: Isaac Mayer Wise on Unitarianism and Liberal Christianity," *AJS Review* 7–8 (1982–83): 179–230.

28. Jacob Katz, *Exclusiveness and Tolerance* (New York: Schocken Books, 1961).

29. Anson Phelps Stokes and Leo Pfeffer, *Church and State in the United States* (New York: Harper & Row, 1964); Paul G. Kauper, *Religion and the Constitution* (Baton Rouge: Louisiana State University Press, 1964), esp. pp. 45–53; Philip Kurland, *Church and State: The Supreme Court and the First Amendment* (Chicago: University of Chicago Press, 1975).

30. "Of the House of Israel," in *New York Evening Post*, 15 March 1829, p. 2; Houston, *Israel Vindicated*, p. v; and see generally Morton Borden, *Jews, Turks and Infidels* (Chapel Hill: University of North Carolina Press, 1984).

31. *Occident* 3 (1845): 42.

32. Stokes and Pfeffer, *Church and State in the United States*, p. 106.

33. [Prospectus for] *The Asmonean* (1849) in Lyons Collection, item 91b, American Jewish Historical Society, Waltham, Mass.; cf. "Honestus," *A Critical Review of the Claims Presented by Christianity for Inducing Apostacy in Israel* (New York, 1852), p. 21.

34. Reprinted in *New York Tribune*, 30 March 1855.

35. *Occident* 3 (1845): 42; see Sarna, "American Jewish Response," pp. 45–46.

36. Minnie Louis, "Mission-Work Among the Unenlightened Jews," *Papers of the Jewish Women's Congress* (Philadelphia, 1894), pp. 185–86.

37. Seymour Fromer, "In the Colonial Period," in *A History of Jewish Education in America*, ed. Judah Pilch (New York: National Curriculum Research Institute of the American Association for Jewish Education, 1969), p. 23; Hyman B. Grinstein, *The Rise of the Jewish Community of New York, 1654–1860* (Philadelphia: Jewish Publication Society, 1945), pp. 225–59; Jacob R. Marcus, *The Colonial American Jew, 1942–1776* (Detroit: Wayne State University Press, 1970), 2: 1056–68.

38. *Jewish Chronicle* 2 (1846): 275; cf. *The Jew* 1–2 (1823–25): 228–29; Leeser, *Claims of the Jews*, p. 15.

39. Leeser, *Claims of the Jews*, p. 15.

40. Ibid., p. 86. Cf. Naomi W. Cohen, *Encounter With Emancipation: The German Jews in the United States, 1830–1914* (Philadelphia: Jewish Publication Society, 1984), pp. 71–187. In 1876, the Rebecca Gratz Sewing School was founded for the same reason: "Jewish children . . . attended mission schools of another religious denomination." See Solomon Solis-Cohen, "The Hebrew Sunday School Society." *Judaism and Science* (Philadelphia, 1940), p. 10.

41. *Address of the Jewish Publication Committee to the Israelites of America* (Philadelphia, 1845), reprinted as the introduction to *Caleb Asher* (1845), the first number of *The Jewish Miscellany* to be published.

42. *Israelite Indeed* 8 (1864): 10.

43. *Jewish Messenger*, 18 May 1888, p. 4; see Isaac S. Moses, "Missionary Efforts in Judaism," *CCAR Yearbook* 5 (1895): 87, "Copy the methods employed by Christianity." Alexander M. Dushkin, *Jewish Education in New York City* (New York: Bureau of Jewish Education, 1918), pp. 53–59; Hyman B. Grinstein, "In the Course of the Nineteenth Century," in Pilch, *History of Jewish Education in America*, p. 37; Myron Berman, *The Attitude of American Jewry Towards East European Jewish Immigration, 1881–1914* (New York: Arno Press, 1980), pp. 313–14; Ida Cohen Selavan, "The Founding of Columbian Council," *American Jewish Archives* 30 (1978): 32–33; and for a related example, David Philipson, *My Life as an American Jew* (Cincinnati: J. G. Kidd & Son, 1941), p. 133.

44. Leeser, *Claims of the Jews*, p. 84.

45. *Occident* 2 (1844): 63.

46. *Address of the Jewish Publication Committee*, p. 2.

47. *New York Tribune*, 2 July 1848; Sarna, "American Jewish Response," p. 49.

48. Moshe Davis, *The Emergence of Conservative Judaism* (Philadelphia: Jewish Publication Society, 1963), p. 69; Allan Tarshish, "The Rise of American Judaism" (D.H.L. thesis, Hebrew Union College, 1938), pp. 274–76, 324–25.

49. *Occident* 8 (1850): 260; cf. 6 (1849): 537. Maxwell Whiteman, "The Legacy of Isaac Leeser," in *Jewish Life in Philadelphia, 1830–1940*, ed. Murray Friedman (Philadelphia: Institute for the Study of Human Issues, 1983), pp. 37–38.

50. Henry S. Morais, *The Jews of Philadelphia* (Philadelphia: Levytype Co., 1894), p. 117.

51. Morris U. Schappes, ed., *A Documentary History of the Jews in the United States 1654–1875* (New York: Schocken Books, 1971), p. 220; Alfred J. Kutzik, "The Social Basis of American Jewish Philanthropy," (Ph.D. diss., Brandeis University, 1967), pp. 309–10; see also Tina Levitan, *Islands of Compassion* (New York: Twayne Publishers, 1964).

52. Standard surveys include Marcus, *Colonial American Jew*, 2: 1032–55; Grinstein, *Rise of the Jewish Community of New York*, pp. 131–62; David and Tamar de Sola Pool, *An Old Faith in the New World* (New York: Columbia University Press, 1955), pp. 341–78; and Kutzik, "Social Basis of American Jewish Philanthropy," pp. 114–43.

53. Blau and Baron, *The Jews of the United States*, 3: 714–58 (quote is from p. 736); S. Joshua Kohn, "Mordecai Manuel Noah's Ararat Project and the Missionaries," *American Jewish Historical Quarterly* 55 (1965): 162–98; Sarna, *Jacksonian Jew*, pp. 61–62.

54. Houston, *Israel Vindicated*, p. 10.

55. Sarna, *Jacksonian Jew*, pp. 61–75; see pp. 221–22 for earlier literature.

56. Solis's plan "For Improving the Condition of Jewish Youth of Both Sexes" is reprinted in *The Jewish Experience in America*, ed. Abraham J. Karp, 5 vols. (Waltham, Mass.: American Jewish Historical Society, 1969), 2: 184–86. Edwin Wolf, "Unrecorded American Judaica Printed Before 1851," *Essays in American Jewish History* (Cincinnati, 1958), p. 205, no. 61, misdates this item. For contemporary discussions of the Solis plan, see *New York American*, 27 June 1826, p. 2; 23 August 1826, p. 2; 16 September 1826, p. 2; and *Connecticut Observer*, 5 June 1826, p. 3.

57. *Twentieth Report of the American Society for Meliorating the Condition of the Jews* (New York, 1843), p. 11; cf. Jackson, "Address to Joseph Dreyfous" (cited above, n. 23). The process whereby missionaries "discovered" poverty in New York is described in Carroll Smith Rosenberg, *Religion and the Rise of the American City* (Ithaca: Cornell University Press, 1971); for a broader perspective, see Edward K. Spann, *The New Metropolis: New York City, 1840–1857* (New York: Columbia University Press, 1981), pp. 67–91.

58. The report is reprinted in Schappes, *Documentary History*, pp. 217–22.

59. *Occident* 1 (1843): 47; *Caleb Asher* (n. 41 above), a fictional tract, underlined the relationship between poverty and conversionism.

60. *Jewish Chronicle* 1 (1845): 177, 270, 274–75; Sarna, *Jacksonian Jew*, pp. 128–29.

61. Grinstein, *Rise of the Jewish Community of New York*, p. 160.

62. Jewish prison chaplains also came about in this fashion. See Adolph M. Radin, *Report of Visiting Chaplain to the Jewish Ministers' Association of New York* (New York, 1893), p. 17: "Your honorable Board has done an important and laudable step in . . . having established this missionary chaplainship. We imitate the good example of our Christian brethren as far as compassion and sympathies for prisoners is concerned." For Emma Lazarus's effort to use the missionary specter to rouse Jews to action, see her letter to the *American Hebrew* (9 May 1883), reprinted in *The Letters of Emma Lazarus*, ed. Morris V. Schappes (New York, 1949), p. 58.

63. *Occident* 3(1845): 42.

64. For a different perspective on gentile influences, see Michael A. Meyer, "Christian Influence on Early German Reform Judaism," in *Studies in Jewish Bibliography, History and Literature in Honor of I. Edward Kiev*, ed. Charles Berlin (New York: Ktav Publishing House, 1971), pp. 289–303.

65. On competition in American religion, see Sidney E. Mead, *The Lively Experiment* (New York: Harper & Row, 1976), pp. 129–33; and Peter L. Berger, *The Sacred Canopy* (Garden City, N.Y.: Doubleday, 1967), pp. 142, 171. For a marketing perspective on missionary activities, see Arnold S. Stiebel, "The Marketing of Jesus:

JONATHAN D. SARNA

An Analysis of Propaganda Techniques Utilized by Christian Missionaries in Their Attempt to Proselytize the American Jew" (ordination thesis, Hebrew Union College–Jewish Institute of Religion, 1982).

66. As early as 1816, *Tobit's Letters to Levy* (New York, 1816), p. 26, warned that missions would backfire and unify Jews. Protestants, too, had to learn the value of religious competition; see Winthrop Hudson's discussion of "Lyman Beecher's Great Discovery," in his *The Great Tradition of the American Churches* (New York, 1963), pp. 63–79.

67. For an earlier perspective, see Asher Ginzberg, *Selected Essays by Ahad Ha'am*, trans. Leon Simon (Philadelphia, 1912), pp. 107–24.

254

10

Jewish Communal Divisiveness in Response to Christian Influences on the Lower East Side, 1900–1910

JEFFREY S. GUROCK

IN 1905 there were no fewer than seven Christian missions on the Lower East Side devoted explicitly to luring Jewish children, and to a lesser degree Jewish adults, from their ancestral faith. They were the People's Home Church, which proudly pronounced that "evangelism must be first in our experience," three settlements founded by the New York City Mission and Tract Society, and the independent Church Settlement House, the Grace Church Settlement, and the Jewish Bible Mission. In addition the Federation of Churches and Christian Organizations of New York City sponsored eight daily summer vacation Bible schools in the predominantly Jewish downtown vicinity which enrolled more than 2,000 Jewish children in 1905. These Bible schools never openly proclaimed the conversion of the Jews to be an institutional goal. Indeed, the parent Christian Federation took great pains to explain that while "their inspiration is Christian, their management is human and their mission is not a proselytizing one." However, the summer schools frequently met in City Mission centers like God's Providence House and the People's Home Church while their study-guides and curricula placed great emphasis on christological explanations of the Hebrew Bible and textual explication of the New Testament. Furthermore, the Mission Society saw its Bible school work as an important addition to its year-round program, which produced, in its estimation, "good results."

Christian teachings were also propagated to Jewish residents of the Lower East Side at Mott Street's Gospel Settlement and

Chrystodora of 7th Street. These institutions, like the vacation Bible schools, did not openly admit to conversionist aims but advertised Christian religious services and Bible classes as a regular part of their social program. Finally, Christian influence was fostered downtown by the Jacob A. Riis and College Settlements, which held periodic—primarily Christmas and Easter-time—observances organized by founders committed to doing good Christian works among the ghetto poor.[1]

While it is impossible to determine how many Jews these organizations converted, it is clear that literally thousands of Jewish children attended these settlements and church centers and that in the minds of many downtowners the potential for missionary triumphs constituted a major communal problem. Newly arrived Americans, coming from an eastern European world where the Cross meant only conversion, if not deprivations and pogroms, drew upon their own unhappy experiences in fearing these American institutions. They were little attuned to the subtle distinctions between Christian charity and Christianizing goals. Some of those who had been in America somewhat longer—and it is their organized reaction to this problem that we shall detail presently—recognized the symbolic significance of the presence of missionaries and their fellow travelers in the ghetto. It said to them, as it had said to opponents of conversionists in their communities for almost a century, that Judaism and Jewish status were under attack. They believed that Christian instruction in their schools and settlements cast the Jewish faith as degenerate, unenlightened, and decidedly un-American. And they noted what Christian efforts in their community's midst said about their equality and minority status in this country. To be proselytized implied that Jews and Judaism were somehow subordinate to other groups and confessions in this legally nonsectarian country.[2]

These popular fears and concerns were heightened when press reports appeared about Christian institutions either forcing or tricking Jewish children into participating in Christian services as a first step toward their ultimate conversion. Such was the case when the *New York World*, in July 1905, described the alleged physical ill-treatment of Jewish girls at a summer camp in Milford Haven, Connecticut, conducted by God's Providence House. Soon thereafter the *Yiddishes Tageblatt* and the *Hebrew Standard*, which represented the views of immigrant Jewry, and the *American Hebrew*, which reflected the outlook of the more Americanized uptown Jews, all reported the story of youngsters who reportedly refused to participate in morning Christian prayers and were "placed in a garret and fed . . . on bread and water." Although subsequent investigations questioned whether the punishments were meted out because the campers balked against Christianity being imposed on them or were, rather, a result of the campers' "flagrant insubordination which had nothing to do with prayer," the incident provided Jewish editorialists and other observers with the opportunity to reiterate their long-standing grievance about Christians using the lure of fresh-air camps to expose Jewish children to Christian services and teachings without the knowledge and approval of their parents. Jewish journalists and some of their readers used the occasion to call for a comprehensive organizational response to what they would later term "masked institutions." The *American Hebrew*, for example, called for "American 'self-defense' work . . . to make impossible one-half of the missionary institutions" that it asserted touched "fully one tenth of the homes of the East Side." In a similar vein, the *Hebrew Standard* sought to "arouse the Jewish community to its sense of duty." Albert Lucas, the most celebrated opponent of missionary work of his day, asked: "How much longer is the Jewish community going to stand idly by? When will something be done to offset the missionizing influences in our Jewish homes?" Private citizen Walter H. V. Epstein had no answer. But in a letter to the editor of the *American Hebrew*, he cried out: "Young men and women of the Eastside . . . what are you going to do about it? Will you allow your little brothers and sisters to attend schools where the service of a God, not recognized by the Israelites, is forced upon them?"[3]

These calls for Jewish communal activities—together with the ongoing anger and upset about Christian missionizing recharged by the Milford Haven incident—led to the creation of a loose confederation of organizations on the Lower East Side headed by the Jewish Endeavor Society and the teachers of the Albert Lucas Classes. The Endeavor Society, which was organized in 1901 by the early students and first graduates of the Jewish Theological Seminary, sought to provide the children of eastern European immigrants who were well on the road to Americanization with Jewish educational and cultural programs and with "dignified services" designed, in their own words, "to recall indifferent Jewry to their ancestral faith." For the Endeavor Society, Christian missionary successes were proof that Old-World styles of prayer and learning, as embodied in the *landsmanshaft* synagogue and *ḥeder*, could not be successfully transplanted in American soil. As an alternative to Christian after-school programs, they initiated in 1902 *talmud torah* classes with a modern curriculum that included Bible, history, religion, spelling and grammar, and so forth. Similar training was available at the Albert Lucas Classes explicitly constituted as an institutional bulwark against Christian missions. Working first out of Pike and then Rivington and ultimately Chrystie Streets' large synagogues, teachers recruited by their zealous antimissionary leader offered Jewish religious instruction in "English exclusively" on an equal basis to boys and girls, earning for the schools—in the words of one friend—"a reputation for thoroughly practical instruction in Judaism."[4]

These independent activities were strongly supported by the recently founded Union of Orthodox Jewish Congregations of America. This organization, which was established in 1898 by leaders of many of America's earliest Sephardic and central European congregations—the most traditional Jews in this country prior to the arrival of the eastern European Jews—worked for "the protection of Orthodox Judaism [in this case immigrant Jews] whenever occasions arise in civic and social matters." Antimissionary work clearly fell within that purview. The union's zeal to meet the missionary challenge was further strengthened by the personal interest displayed by its foremost spokesman in this campaign. The union's first secretary, Rabbi Bernard Drachman, then professor of codes at the Jewish Theological Seminary, was the prime mover behind the student-run Jewish Endeavor Society. He had opposed missionaries a decade earlier and told his students to do the same. Orthodox Union president Henry Pereira Mendes had likewise long championed, and in the 1890s personally initiated, anticonversionist campaigns. And Albert Lucas was since 1900 the energetic secretary of the Orthodox Union. The Orthodox Union leadership provided their younger colleagues working in the field with encouragement and financial support. The young Endeavor Society members, to their minds, were continuing a holy tradition of which they themselves had been proudly part. This coalition against the missionary foe was solidified further by the support Harry Fischel, Leon Kamaiky, Otto Rosalsky, and William Fischman gave to the cause. They were spokesmen for an emerging Americanized Orthodox leadership of eastern European heritage from within the ghetto itself.[5]

Fischel, a builder and real estate developer, Kamaiky, a newspaper publisher, Rosalsky, a lawyer, and Fischman, a prosperous merchant, were each representative of a new elite within the immigrant community. Born in the Old World, they had come, as youths, to these shores in the early 1880s and had by the turn of the century succeeded in both establishing themselves economically and becoming attuned to the ways of the land. They offered themselves as financial patrons and/or social guides to their fellow immigrants and their children in adjusting to America. Like the younger Jewish Endeavor members, they saw conversionist inroads as glaring evidence that American Jews were increasingly uncomfortable with the religious styles and trappings of the past. They willingly supported communal programs to solve the socio-religious dilemmas that seemingly encouraged missionary successes.[6]

In 1906 this coalition of groups concerned with Christianizing influence on the Lower East Side responded to the challenge through the Jewish Centres Association. The Association's tactics included the publication in the Yiddish and Anglo-Jewish press of the names and addresses of alleged missionary centers, the infiltration of Christian groups to ascertain their true ends, the instigation of public demonstrations in the streets against Christian Homes, demanding the return of Jewish children, and most dramatically, the planned creation on Henry Street of the first of what they hoped would be numerous Jewish Centres. These enlarged versions of the Albert Lucas and Jewish Endeavor Society classes would, they hoped, beat the conversionists at their own game through, as one contemporary described it, "a school for school, picnic for picnic warfare."[7]

These concerted antimissionary efforts failed, however, to gain either mass local backing or even unquestioned community support. Ghetto-based rabbis, for example, like those associated with the Agudat Ha-Rabbanim (Union of Orthodox Rabbis of the United States and Canada), were explicitly critical of their work. And although the Association did succeed in garnering enough backing to establish one Jewish Centre on Henry Street, it closed after two years due to lack of funds. Lucas, the Endeavor Society, and their supporters observed to their dismay that while most—if not all—Jews worried about their children falling into the hands of proselytizers, when it came to actually fighting the missions, the coalition, in fact, stood alone.[8] Indeed, they found that their antimissionary work, which at first glance seemed to be a cause around which all Jews could rally, was often scorned and censured, when not ignored, by other groups.

Uptown German Jewish leaders denigrated "[Jewish Centre] religious enthusiasts" as having "done more harm in the world than all the rest of the workers for the betterment of mankind can overcome." And downtown rabbinic leaders simply stayed away.[9] Why was this so?

To be sure, uptown leaders shared the antimissionary coalition's concern about conversionists setting up shop in the ghetto. There is, for example, evidence that Jacob H. Schiff, who did not back Jewish Centre era battles, quietly bankrolled Adolph Benjamin—Albert Lucas's acknowledged teacher—during the former's battle against the apostate missionary Herman Warszawiak before the turn of the century.[10] Schiff and many of his German friends refused, though, to fund Jewish Centre activities because they perceived that Lucas and his supporters were intent on doing more than just driving the missionaries out of the Lower East Side. In their eyes, Lucas and his group opposed almost all outside efforts to Americanize the Jew. They were seen as prepared to denounce with equal intensity as personae non gratae Christian settlement house workers and Christian public school teachers as well as the so-called "subtle conversionists." And the Germans recognized that their names too appeared on the list of those who were unwelcome in the ghetto.

Uptowners, moreover, accurately understood that the Jewish Centre people represented a new type of immigrant opposition to their acculturation efforts. These activists were not newcomers unversed in American ways. The term "greenhorn" certainly could not be hung upon their Orthodox Union mentors. The Jewish Centres Association's work was, in fact, informed by the belief that the process of immigrant acculturation to the English language and American cultural values was both inevitable and a positive good. Where the Association differed from the uptowners—and the source of tension between the two groups—was the Association's belief that other persons advocating Americanization did not have the best interests of the Jews and Judaism at heart. Only they, Association stalwarts publicly asserted, understood how to reconcile Judaism and Americanization, only they were committed to making the immigrant proud of his heritage and at home in America.

The Association thus sought to deny Christian groups any role in the Americanization of Jewish immigrants. Avowed missionaries, subtle conversionists, devout Christian social workers who spoke only of their desire to do Christ's work among the poor, school officials who organized Christmas pageants, and Christian schoolmarms who taught that Jewish traditions were barriers to becoming good Americans—all were seen as equally threatening to Jewish continuity. Though the Association recognized that only avowed conversionists and their subtle missionizing colleagues were explicitly dedicated to formal missionary activity, it viewed all of these Christian workers as united in their depiction of Judaism as a degenerate system unworthy of perpetuation in America.[11]

However, to the Association's way of thinking, Christians were not the only Americanizers who sought to undermine the Jewishness of their clients. Members and supporters of the Jewish Centres Association publicly questioned the intentions of Jewish settlement house patrons, some of whom were the very uptowners whose support they were seeking for their communal work. They asserted that German-run institutions, particularly the Educational Alliance, purposely undermined Jewish identification and attachments because settlement house workers believed they blocked rapid and complete adaptation to American life. Such were the sentiments of A. H. Fromenson, an editor of the *Yiddishes Tageblatt* and a charter member of the Jewish Centres Association, who defined the term "Jewish institution" in such a way as to exclude the Educational Alliance. A "Jewish institution," he wrote, "is one which stands for Jewish ethics and Jewish ideals and engraves its Jewishness over its door posts." The Educational Alliance, which is "ashamed of the name 'Hebrew Institute' graven over its portals . . . and which stands for something 'broader' than Judaism—an invertebrate, anemic, condescending, patronizing sentimentalism . . . has lost for all the regenerative work on the East Side the full means of its usefulness." Some critics even suggested that Jewish settlements were nothing more than "in reality a less pernicious method of Christian missionizing."[12]

Jewish Centre affiliates saw themselves as the only Americanizers working in the ghetto with an appropriate institutional solution to the dilemma of how to make the immigrants more attuned to the ways of this country without destroying their ties with their ancestral past. Thus, they scoffed when the Educational Alliance attempted to "cope with the irreligiousness of so many of our young people" through its People's Synagogue. The Jewish Centres Association denounced the synagogue's English-language service, with its Reform Jewish liturgical bent, as straying too far from the historical and residual sociological underpinnings of Judaism to be effective. They, in effect, told their potential German benefactors that although their financial support was certainly appreciated, they had little respect for their approach to meeting Americanization problems.[13]

Beyond whatever personal offense the patrons of the Educational Alliance felt, they remained convinced that these parochial zealots were unworthy of support because they misread the intentions of their fellow Americanizers. As the older uptown elite saw it, a broad spectrum of organizations and individuals, Jewish and Christian, with good motives and intentions, were successfully helping Jewish immigrants adapt to their new surroundings. Only the few groups with explicitly nefarious goals had to be kept from interacting with ghetto youngsters.[14]

These German Jews included themselves among those "attempting," as Louis Marshall, a long-time patron of the Educational Alliance, put it, "to inculcate ideas of self-respecting citizenship in conjunction with the true Jewish spirit." And if their religious activities did not conform to their critics' narrow definition of Judaism, Jewish settlement supporters were quick to assert that the Jewish East Side itself was "by no means of one opinion on religious matters," nor, significantly, was the settlement constituency ever entirely Jewish. "There are quite a goodly number of Christians living in our midst," one observer remarked, "whose rights and privileges deserve our due respect." Their downtown critics, Marshall suggested, wanted to see the settlements Americanize only Jews and teach—when they spoke of religion—one parochial form of that faith, which would create "a ghetto in fact as it is today in name." They, on the other hand, were facilitating mass eastern European acculturation without denigrating Judaism's basic universal moral and ethical teachings. The Educational Alliance, its friends averred, "deserve[d] credit for pursuing a policy which not altogether free from sectarianism cannot be open to charges of religious bigotry and small-mindedness."[15]

Educational Alliance backers believed, moreover, that their policy of teaching religion's universal message, devoid of "bigotry and small-mindedness," also characterized the intent and labors of many of their Christian counterparts. Indeed, some felt that immigrant Jews could learn American ways not only from Christians but from the universal teachings of Christianity as well. Such was the attitude of Rabbi Stephen S. Wise, who rallied to the defense of the muckraking settlement house leader Jacob A. Riis when the latter was accused in 1908 by the Jewish Centres Association of subtle missionizing in his "nonsectarian" settlement house. For Wise, Christmas observances, which greatly angered Jewish Centre men, were not a problem. Yuletide commemorations that celebrated not so much the birth of Christianity's messiah but rather the American principles of brotherhood, peace, and goodwill were no more inappropriately sectarian than the moral religious instruction offered at the Educational Alliance.[16] At the time Wise had come to Riis's defense, he had been supported by a number of Jewish settlement house workers who saw the attack as part of a broader battle over how "Jewish" their labors should be. They were under siege from Association quarters over their nonsectarian educational policies, which allegedly said nothing positive to immigrant clients about their ancestral heritage. And while they slavishly followed an approach that the Jewish masses did not want or need, Riis, said the association, used the same "non-sectarian" calling as a missionizing subterfuge. Rabbi Judah L. Magnes reacted in an almost identical fashion to Wise in response to Jewish Centre protests against Christmas activities in the public schools. Magnes saw such pageants as highlighting the universal teachings of "peace on earth, good will to men . . . a thought in which we as Jews can join."[17]

However, in the case of overt conversionist activity and the perpetuation of blue laws that recognized Christianity as the established faith of the American people, uptown Jews took a less tolerant stance. Indeed, uptowners, led by Marshall and some Reform rabbis, fought valiantly, if unsuccessfully, over the course of a generation to see Sunday laws changed.[18] The same Louis Marshall who was unmoved by Christmas celebrations in the schools was angered when New York State School Regents penalized Jewish students by scheduling promotion examinations on Sabbath and holidays, thus forcing pupils to decide between Jewish observance and educational advancement. And the same Jacob Schiff who made contributions to Jacob A. Riis's good works actively opposed overt conversionists having their way in the ghetto.[19] For them, when missionaries seemed to have their way and Jews were punished for observing their faith, vocal responses were clearly necessary.

However, even when uptown and downtown Jews perceived matters in the same light, the former failed to react affirmatively to calls for cooperative efforts. One contemporary source suggested that this reluctance stemmed from the "rich Jewish community's . . . unmistakeable tendency to stay clear of movements that have their origins or are in the hands of downtown Jews." But even beyond the issue of power sharing, another fundamental difference of opinion divided Jewish groups. The Germans frequently expressed the opinion that the tactics employed by the ghetto-based activists undermined Jewish status in America.[20]

Overt, noisy anti-Christian work was viewed in many uptown quarters as "rousing anti-Jewish feeling . . . [as likely] to bring about a *Juden Hetze* here" in the United States.[21] In attempting to drive Christian schools from the ghetto, Jews showed themselves ungrateful to those sincere Christians offering them assistance in becoming good Americans. And in persecuting the avowed missionaries, Jewish activists were seen as denying Christians their basic constitutional rights. Such was the stance taken by the *New York Sun* toward the Milford Haven furor. An editorial titled "Does This Not Look Very Much Like Bigotry?" castigated Lucas and his fellows for describing Christians doing good work in the ghetto as promoters of "anti-Jewish sentiments": Who, except the bigot, they argued, would object to "Christians stepping in" and working until "there will be no more suffering to relieve." Placing the missionaries within and their "bigoted" opponents without the spirit of the American Constitution, they continued, "In this country of religious freedom shall anybody be debarred from inculcating the precepts of religion and from practicing its charity?"[22]

Uptowners wanted to avoid acrimonious debate over the Jewish Centres Association's implicit critique of Christianity. Antagonism from gentile newspapers, in their view, would not enhance Christian support for their own campaigns against the blue laws. Nor did they want to debate publicly the implications of the *Sun*'s closing salvo, which further legitimized Christian missions to Jews: "Jews, no less than Christians, must accept the truth of the saying of Jesus. 'Let your light so shine before men that they may see your good works and glorify our Father in Heaven.'"[23]

For one Jewish critic of the Association's tactics, the more efficacious method of dealing with offensive Christian works was "quiet, dignified house-to-house work . . . to end the ignorance on the part of the parents and self-indulgence on the part of the children." Public "welfare is dangerous and ridiculous."[24]

Lucas and his confederates would have nothing of the uptowners' understanding of Americanization nor of their defensive, self-effacing posture toward criticizing the dissemination of Christian views. In their view, the nonsectarianism of settlement houses substantially undermined Jewish consciousness, while the unwillingness of German Jews to recognize the perniciousness of Christian "non-sectarianism" contributed to missionary successes. In addition, they were appalled by their coreligionists' careful maneuvering in this area of Jewish-Christian relations. For them, it was silent testimony to a lack of will or courage on the Jews' part. Thus there was little more that could be said and little basis for cooperation. German Jews considered the instances of Christian missionary successes a limited problem that had to be dealt with judiciously. The Association saw widespread conversionist activity and anticipated even greater success in the wake of an unbridled Americanization gone wild, a communal malady for which they held German Jews partly responsible. And convinced as they were that if missionaries were not stopped American Jewry's future would be endangered, Association leaders were not about to trim their ideological or tactical sails to garner German approbation and support. They would stand against the Christian missions even without the uptowners' financial backing.[25]

The Jewish Centres Association coalition also found, much to their dismay, that active spiritual and logistical support for their crusade was also not forthcoming from the immigrant Orthodox religious leadership. To be sure, members of organizations like the Agudat Ha-Rabbanim shared the Association's concern over lost children, and they certainly had no respect for the concept of nonsectarianism in Jewish life. Nor did they care how their views were received in the gentile world. They were ultimately less concerned about American law respecting the immigrants than about new Americans observing Jewish law. And so, immigrant synagogues and rabbis stood apart from the anticonversionist campaigns, thereby causing Lucas to lament more than once "the blind obstinacy of the 'majority' rulers of the synagogues, who wrap themselves in the 'Yehus' of their own piety and blind themselves with the 'Yods' of their own phylacteries."[26]

The unwillingness of immigrant rabbis to support the Jewish Centres stemmed, ironically, from their perception that groups like the Endeavor Society and the Lucas Class leaders, rather than constituting a major part of the solution to conversionism, were in reality a significant part of the problem. Rabbis and their lay supporters would not open their synagogues for Jewish school activities designed to counter missionary activities and later would not fall in behind the Henry Street Centre because, to their minds, the Christian downtown, the German Reform philanthropists, and the Centre activists were all guilty of spreading, each to a varying degree, the anti-Jewish ideology of Americanization.

The immigrant rabbis saw the missionaries as the most nefarious of these groups because they used Americanization ideas and techniques to Christianize the immigrants. But all the so-called "Jewish" organizations were also dangerous: they sought to destroy the ancestral teachings and observances of Judaism in their zeal to assimilate the immigrants. The uptowners offered a foreign conception of the faith that they promoted as legitimately Jewish, and the Association, which fostered the study of Judaism in English, modified the sociology of synagogue life, and offered religious education on an equal basis to girls and boys, as well as deviating from traditional procedures and attitudes in other ways that also undermined the links with Jewish tradition. Indeed, in their rejection of the new methods of Jewish education that emerged in part from the antimissionary campaigns, immigrant synagogue leaders implicitly suggested that these modernist departures paved the way for missionary successes by acknowledging and accommodating the doubts in young minds about the resilience of transplanted ways in America. For them, as with all other Jewish groups that reacted to Christian influences downtown, missionary response—or nonresponse—was part of a broader ideological understanding of Americanization. As they saw it, Americanization had to be resisted whether it emanated from Christian, German, or even from association "Orthodox" sources.[27]

Consequently, the Agudat Ha-Rabbanim failed to develop in the first decade of the twentieth century any specific program to counteract downtown Christian influences. Antimissionary work was not among the many communal problems noted by the Agudat Ha-Rabbanim, for example, at its founding. Nor did that issue come before its early conventions. They touched on the conversionist issue only inferentially, when they considered means of transplanting older European forms of Jewish education to American soil. But then, even if they had been disposed to fight conversionists with weapons similar to those of the association activists, these still unacculturated Jews were manifestly ill-equipped by language and training to do so.[28]

Thus the battle against Christianity's influence on the Lower East Side, which at first glance seemed to be a cause around which Jews of all stripes could unite, was in the end as divisive as any other in communal politics. Only that segment of New York Jewry that accepted the inevitability of acculturation and yet was ambivalent about the promises and pitfalls of the process possessed both the energy and cultural capabilities to oppose what they defined as the conversionist threat. They, who were clearly suspicious of all Americanizers other than themselves and who were relatively unconcerned about how their public protests were received outside their own community, found the portals of the uptown charity establishments closed to them. The doors of downtown synagogues were also barred to them because they were seen by others as Americanization advocates foreign to their own immigrant community.

NOTES

The following abbreviations are used:

> *AH = American Hebrew*
> *AJH = American Jewish History*
> *AJYB = American Jewish Year Book*
> *HS = Hebrew Standard*
> *JCR = Jewish Communal Register*
> *PAAJR = Proceedings of the American Academy for Jewish Research*
> *YT = Yiddishes Tageblatt*

1. Robert A. Woods and Albert J. Kennedy, eds., *Handbook of Settlements* (New York: Charities Publication Committee, 1911), pp. 235–43; M. Katherine Jones, comp., *Bibliography of College, Social and University Settlements* (New York, 1896), pp. 22, 28; College Settlements Association, *Second Annual Report of the College Settlements Association for the Year 1891* (New York, 1892), pp. 13–14; Federation of Churches and Christian Organizations in New York City, *Eleventh Annual Report of the Federation of Churches and Church Organizations in New York City* (New York, 1906), pp. 2, 19, 44, 45, 57; New York City Mission and Tract Society, *Annual Report for the Year 1905* (New York, 1906), pp. 10, 12, 22, 25.

2. New York City Mission and Tract Society, *Annual Report . . . 1905*, pp. 12, 25. One statistical indication of the popularity of Christian-run settlements among Jewish youngsters is the *Eleventh Annual Report of the Colleges Settlements Association, October 1, 1899–October 1, 1900* (New York, 1900), p. 41, which notes that approximately 1,000 children were enrolled in their kindergarten, domestic work classes, clubs, and summer excursions during that year. If these figures are at all reliable and are projected for other similar groups, their impact on Jewish youth was considerable. One should also note, however, with reference to the numbers actually converting that the De Witt Memorial Church's proud declaration that some 31 Jews had seen the light in 1905, if accurate, reflected a not particularly cost-effective operation based

JEFFREY S. GUROCK

on an expenditure of $7,500 of the City Mission's yearly budget of $33,000. See for background on the history of American Jewish responses to Christianity in their midst prior to 1905, Jonathan D. Sarna, "The American Jewish Response to Nineteenth Century Christian Missions," *Journal of American History* 68 (1981): 35–51, and his article in this volume.

3. *New York World*, 3 July 1905, p. 12; *YT*, 12 July 1905, p. 8; *AH*, 14 July 1905, p. 181; *HS*, 21 July 1905, p. 8; *YT*, 21 July 1905, p. 8; *AH*, 21 July 1905, p. 207; *AH*, 28 July 1905, pp. 234, 236.

This 1905 event was by no means the first example of published reports of Christian influence on Jewish children complete with the assertion that Jewish parents had no knowledge of the Christianizing influence. Nor was it the first time calls were heard for a comprehensive Jewish response. If anything, this present "horror story," as one contemporary called it, simply recalled the almost decade-long festering issue and thus constituted the culmination of calls for activity. Prior protests involved the Pro-Cathedral (1901), the City Mission's notorious proselytizer Herman Warszawiak (1902), the Gospel Settlement (1903), and the same God's Providence House (1903). And the Lower East Side was also bestirred by the downtown campaign against Jacob A. Riis of 1903 for his alleged secret proselytizing at his Henry Street Settlement. This 1905 event is most striking, as we will see presently, by its impact upon the New York press and its leading to a semipermanent Jewish institutional response. See on the pre-1905 legacy of missionary conflict which involved many of the actors in the 1905 drama, *AH*, 6 Dec. 1901, p. 143, 21 Feb. 1902, p. 432; 25 April, 1902, p. 696; *HS*, 14 Aug. 1903; *AH*, 22 May 1902, p. 23. See my "Jacob A. Riis: Christian Friend or Missionary Foe: Two Jewish Views," *AJH* 71 (1981): 29–47, for the sources describing that controversy.

4. *AH*, 18 Jan. 1901, p. 284; *AH*, 8 Feb. 1901, p. 375; *AH*, 4 May 1901, p. 596; *AH*, 13 June 1902, p. 105; *YT*, 2 Nov. 1903, p. 8; *HS*, 13 March 1903, p. 4; *AH*, 22 March 1903, p. 631; *AJYB* (5666): p. 85. For a short history of the Jewish Endeavor Society, see my "Jewish Endeavor Society," in *American Jewish Voluntary Organizations*, ed. Michael Dobkowski (Westport, Conn.: Greenwood Press, 1985).

5. See *AH*, 4 Dec. 1904, p. 231, for a discussion of the early purposes of the Orthodox Union and for a listing of the members of the organization's early board of directors. See my "Why Albert Lucas Did Not Join the New York Kehillah," *PAAJR* 51 (1984): 55–56, for an analysis of the Jewish ethnic composition of the Union in its formative years. See Drachman's autobiography, *The Unfailing Light* (New York: Rabbinical Council of America, 1948), pp. 225–26, for his account of his relationship with the Endeavor Society. See Eugene Markovitz, "Henry P. Mendes: Builder of Traditional Judaism in America," (D. H. L. diss., Yeshiva University, 1961), pp. 53–54, for a discussion of that leader's early antimissionary work.

6. Basic biographical information on these and other new elite members was derived from "Biographical Sketches of Jews Prominent in the Professions etc. in the United States," *AJYB* (1904–5): 52–213; "Biographical Sketches of Jewish Communal Workers in the United States," *AJYB* (1905–6): 32–118, and *JCR*, passim. For more on Fischel and the other new elite eastern Europeans, see Herbert S. Goldstein, ed., *Forty Years of Struggle for a Principle: The Biography of Harry Fischel* (New York: Bloch

Publishing Co., 1928), pp. 38–39 and passim. See also Arthur A. Goren, *New York Jews and the Quest for Community* (New York: Columbia University Press, 1970), pp. 32, 38, 65, 127, 201, 274.

7. *AH*, 28 July 1905, p. 235; 5 Aug. 1905, p. 266; *HS*, 15 Dec. 1905, p. 9; *YT*, 11 Jan. 1905, p. 8; *AH*, 30 March 1906, p. 578; *HS*, 30 March 1906, p. 4.

8. The history of the rise and rapid fall of the Jewish Centre must be followed through newspaper accounts appearing primarily in the Anglo-Jewish press. Unfortunately neither Lucas nor the coalition left records of their activities. See on that institutional experiment, *AH*, 17 Feb. 1905, p. 399; 5 Aug. 1905, p. 266; 20 April 1906, p. 671; *HS*, 30 March 1906, p. 8; 21 Sept. 1906, p. 4; 11 May 1906, p. 20; 31 Aug. 1906, p. 8; 28 Sept. 1906, p. 3; 11 May 1906, p. 20; 17 May 1906, p. 8; 21 June 1907, p. 28; 30 June 1907, p. 11; 19 July 1907, pp. 8–9.

9. *HS*, 8 July 1904, p. 10.

10. See David Max Eichhorn, *Evangelizing the American Jew* (New York: Jonathan David Publishers, 1978), p. 179, for the suggestion that Schiff bankrolled Benjamin. See *AH*, p. 432, for a glimpse at the Benjamin-Warszawiak battles.

11. See Leonard Bloom, "A Successful Jewish Boycott of the New York City Public Schools," *AJH* 70 (1980): 180–88, for one published secondary account of the role members of this coalition—particularly Lucas's followers—played in a protest against school sectarianism. See also the author's "Jacob A. Riis," which discusses the issue of how one differentiates among forms of Christian influence in the ghetto. See below for further discussion of conflicting Jewish attitudes toward Christianity's multifarious influences downtown.

12. *HS*, 27 May 1904, pp. 50–51; *YT*, 30 Dec. 1903, p. 8. For other, similar criticisms of the Educational Alliance emanating from groups associated with the Jewish Centres, see *HS*, 24 Jan. 1902, p. 6; *AH*, 26 Aug. 1904, pp. 377–78; 23 Sept. 1904, p. 491.

13. *AH*, 24 Jan. 1902, p. 6; 29 Feb. 1904, p. 278. Clearly the Jewish Endeavor Society was not alone in the early years of this century in promoting American-style services attractive to those becoming uncomfortable with *landsmanshaft*-style Orthodoxy. Great public debates ensued as to what synagogue functions had to remain unchanged and what ceremonials could be abridged or discarded. Fromenson spoke out strongly for the legitimacy of the Jewish Endeavor Society's changing the trappings of synagogue life and against both the old-line Orthodox, who opposed all changes, and Reform elements behind the Emanuel-Brotherhood and People's Synagogue, which wanted to go further than the JES in making changes. Fromenson, Lucas, S. P. Frank and other Orthodox Union leaders—later to be Jewish Centre Leaders—also participated in the great debates held in 1904 on the possible unification of all these youth synagogue efforts. See on this issue and on these groups: *AH*, 4 Sept. 1903, p. 503; 4 Dec. 1903, p. 81; 11 Dec. 1903, p. 153; 29 Jan. 1904, p. 346; 5 Feb. 1904, pp. 378, 389, 391; 14 March 1904, p. 443; 8 April 1904, p. 663.

14. See Morton Rosenstock, *Louis Marshall: Defender of Jewish Rights* (Detroit: Wayne State University Press, 1965), p. 268, and Charles Reznikoff, ed., *Louis*

JEFFREY S. GUROCK

Marshall: Champion of Liberty (Philadelphia: Jewish Publication Society, 1957), pp. xxv, xxxviii–xxxix, 936–54, 967–71, for discussions of his anti–blue law work. See Gurock, "Jacob A. Riis," p. 31, n. 5, for the Lucas-Marshall letter of 1903. Marshall probably also had strong words to say about Lucas's definition of the Reform Judaism which Marshall practiced: "Christless Christianity . . . useless for anyone who desired permanently to improve the conditions of Judaism." See *HS*, 6 June 1903, pp. 1, 3, for Lucas's attack against Reform Judaism.

15. *HS*, 31 Jan. 1902, p. 8; *AH*, 3 June 1904, p. 76; 10 June 1904, p. 103; 9 Sept. 1904, p. 431. See also *AH*, 29 Jan. 1904, p. 349, for a discussion of uptown's understanding of the ghetto dwellers' religious needs.

16. *Outlook*, 9 May 1908, pp. 69–71. *New York Times*, 21 Dec. 1908, p. 2. Stephen S. Wise to Newell Dwight Hillis, 12 June 1914, Jacob A. Riis Papers, New York Public Library, all quoted and analyzed in Gurock, "Jacob A. Riis," pp. 35–36, 42–43.

17. David Blaustein, director of the Educational Alliance, Henry Moskowitz, a Jewish leader of the Ethical Culture Society downtown, and Charles Bernheimer, assistant head worker of the University Settlement, were among the vocal defenders of Riis. See Gurock, "Jacob A. Riis," p. 34; *HS*, 28 Dec. 1906, p. 8. See also on Magnes's point of view, *HS*, 15 Dec. 1905, p. 5; *AH*, 11 Jan. 1907, p. 256, all quoted in Gurock, "Jacob A. Riis," p. 44.

18. Uptown lay and religious leaders were in the forefront of the movement which led to the introduction, first in 1907, of the Straus/Levy Sabbath Observance Bill which, interestingly, repeatedly failed to win passage through the 1910s. See on the early attempts at this bill's passage, *HS*, 24 April 1908, p. 6. See *AH*, 7 Dec. 1906, p. 114, for an account of the criticism of avowed missionary work by Dr. Joseph Silverman of Temple Emanuel and Dr. Samuel Schulman of Temple Beth El. Significantly, neither responded to the *Hebrew Standard* editorial of the next week urging support for the Jewish Centres in reaction to the same Christian statements which exercised these Reform leaders. See *HS*, 14 Dec. 1906, p. 8. See also Silverman's statement "United States Not a Christian Nation," reported in *HS*, 2 March 1906, p. 4.

19. For evidence of Schiff's backing of Riis's activities, see Jacob A. Riis to Julian Heath, 18 Dec. 1902, Jacob A. Riis Papers, New York Public Library, which discusses Schiff's contribution to a Riis building campaign. See also an undated Jacob H. Schiff to Riis letter, found in the Schiff Papers, American Jewish Archives, Cincinnati, which notes Schiff's contribution to a 1906 campaign. Significantly, Schiff did not express himself publicly on the Riis question in 1908.

20. *AH*, 22 May 1903, p. 23.

21. *HS*, 8 Jan. 1909, pp. 1–3.

22. *New York Sun*, 2 Aug. 1905, quoted in *HS*, 11 Aug. 1905, pp. 6–7.

23. Ibid.

24. *AH*, 28 July 1905, p. 235. See also on anti-activist criticisms, *HS*, 8 July 1904, p. 10.

25. *YT*, 30 Dec. 1903, p. 8; *HS*, 11 Aug. 1905, p. 8; *AH*, 29 Dec. 1905, p. 210.

26. *AH*, 21 Aug. 1903, pp. 439–40.

27. For discussions of the ideological reservations transplanted eastern European religious leaders and their downtown lay supporters had toward the JES, Albert Lucas Classes and all other types of American Judaizing influences see *YT*, 25 March 1903, p. 8; 20 Nov. 1903, p. 8; *AH*, 16 Jan. 1903, p. 298; 4 Sept. 1904, p. 503; 5 June 1903, p. 81; 2 Oct. 1903, p. 634; 13 May 1904, p. 794. There are also some sources that suggest that downtown ghetto Orthodox groups saw American Jewry as in consort with Christian conversionists. See on this view *HS*, 8 Jan. 1909, pp. 1–3; and Goren, *New York Jews*, p. 284. Lucas's critique of the immigrant religious leadership was that they took a too narrow view of immigrant problems. They were seen as intent only on insulating themselves from contemporary problems, not involving themselves in reaching large numbers of disaffected Jews.

28. The nonintersection of antimissionary concerns and conceptions of Jewish education in America is seen in the declarations of the Agudat Ha-Rabbanim recorded in its *Sefer ha-yovel shel agudat ha-rabbanim ha-ortodoktsim de-artsot ha-brit ve-kanada*, (New York: Arias Press, 1928), pp. 25–26. See also on early Agudat Ha-Rabbanim conventions which discussed Jewish continuity and religious education with no reference to the missionary problem, *AJYB* (1903–4): 160; (1904–5): 782; and *AH*, 8 July 1904, pp. 204–5.

11

A Unitarian Rabbi? The Case of Solomon H. Sonneschein

BENNY KRAUT

In the wake of continued ill will between himself and members of his synagogue board, Rabbi Solomon Hirsch Sonneschein (1839–1908) resigned his pulpit at Reform Shaare Emeth Congregation in St. Louis on 1 April 1886. Approximately one week later he secretly ventured to Boston, the "American Mecca of Unitarianism," to confer with some of the preeminent intellectual and institutional leaders of the Unitarian movement to determine whether and under what circumstances he might be given a Unitarian pulpit and become a member of the American Unitarian Association (A.U.A.). Sonneschein's discussions with Revs. Minot J. Savage, Edward Everett Hale, and Grindall Reynolds, secretary of the A.U.A., did not lead to any new religious affiliation on his part—he remained in the Reform rabbinate and did not join the Unitarian ranks. But when this episode became public knowledge one month later, in late May 1886, it provoked an enormous furor in American Jewish life. Sonneschein's action scandalized American Jews. Much of the Jewish press, as well as rabbis and laymen across the country, vilified him as a renegade and denounced him as unfit to hold rabbinic office. The strident tone of the abuse was reminiscent of the initial press and rabbinic reactions to another individual deemed a traitor to Judaism, Felix Adler, founder of the New York Society for Ethical Culture; not a few of Sonneschein's critics drew explicit parallels between the two men and their religious departures.[1]

How can one explain the near adherence of a rabbi to the Unitarian movement? Other well-known Reform defectors, such as Felix Adler and Charles Fleischer, who left Boston's Temple Israel to found the Boston Sunday Commons in 1912, established universal, nonsectarian religious organizations. Solomon Schindler, Fleischer's predecessor at Temple Israel, left the congregation in 1893 and, for a time, Judaism also, to pursue Edward Bellamy's socialist vision of American nationalism.[2] But why did Sonneschein seek out the Unitarians?

Certainly multiple explanations need to be considered. The rabbi's personal circumstances at the time were not good. A very impetuous and erratic man, trapped in a terribly unhappy marriage, Sonneschein feuded bitterly and frequently in the 1880s with important members of his congregation. Indeed it was friction with his congregation that gave the mercurial Sonneschein the occasion to take this step, which he himself later admitted was "hasty." But Sonneschein's overture specifically to the Unitarians illuminates a larger historical process that transcends his own individual idiosyncrasies and negative personal experiences. This episode highlights an emerging religious, intellectual, and, to a lesser degree, social rapprochement between leading Unitarians and Reform Jews in the last third of the nineteenth century, a rapprochement fraught with considerable ambivalence for Reformers, for it caused them to reconsider the rationale for the continued existence of American Reform Judaism.[3] Sonneschein himself was profoundly involved in this rapprochement and in the intellectual assessment of its implications for the continuation of Judaism. His near defection and the uproar it engendered only underscored the problematic relationship between the two liberal faiths, which continued into the twentieth century.[4] Moreover, in retrospect, Sonneschein's near entry into the Unitarian fold is quite suggestive about the nature of modern Jewish apostasy; the contemptuous Jewish denunciations of his action and the varied sources from which they came, reveal much about the true limits of American Reform Judaism which were demarcated as much by ethnic-communal concerns as by religious-theological ones.

Born in 1839 in Turoz St. Martin, Hungary, Solomon Sonneschein grew up in an orthodox Jewish home under the tutelage of his father Moses, chief rabbi of the town. Following his bar mitzvah he was sent to study at advanced *yeshivot* in Austria and, in 1860, received his *semikhah* from Abraham Placzek, chief rabbi of Moravia. He taught at a Jewish school in Hamburg for two years, but he found his traditional Jewish education stultifying and his rabbinic diploma, by itself, professionally restrictive. He sought wider intellectual horizons, and in 1864 received his doctorate at the University of Jena. Like so many future Reform leaders, under the impact of modern ideas, he broke with the traditional religion of his parents and considered himself an advocate of Reform Judaism, arguing that Judaism must be harmonized with progress and reason. From 1864–1868 he held rabbinic positions in Warasdin, Croatia, and in Prague, but in each case he found the synagogue uncongenial to his more liberal religious views. Offered a pulpit by New York's Shaare Hashamayim Congregation in 1868, he accepted with alacrity only to find shortly after his arrival that it too was unprepared for radical religious reform. His great oratorical skills, however, made him a desirable rabbinical candidate; hence, when the unanimous call came in 1869 from the Shaare Emeth board in St. Louis, he moved to the Midwest and remained as rabbi of this temple until 1886.[5]

Sonneschein was a highly temperamental individual. He could be charming, affable, and engaging, but also impolitic and volatile. If he sometimes exuded the elegance of a gentleman of good breeding, his uncontrollable temper frequently startled friends and foes alike.[6] Indeed, an angry tone suffuses his writings, letters, and actions. His espousal of classical Reform ideology, for example, included excessive, intemperate polemics against the Talmud and Orthodoxy, the notion of Jewish nationality, and even against moderate Reform. Haughty, imperious, and self-righteous, Sonneschein possessed an exaggerated sense of self-worth which nonetheless masked a pervasive feeling of insecurity, hurt pride, and frustration over never quite winning the national recognition that he felt he deserved, which other Reform leaders like Kaufmann Kohler, Emil Hirsch, Bernhard Felsenthal, and Isaac Mayer Wise had gained. And this rankled deeply.

His hopeless, horrendous marriage in 1862 to Rosa Fassel, daughter of the eminent Hungarian rabbi Hirsch Baer Fassel, was a source of great despair. A disaster from the start, the marriage found the two partners bickering constantly. Rosa often taunted Solomon that his sermons did not compare to the great ones of her father; for his part, Solomon drank excessively and was known to get drunk on a number of occasions. While the 1870s saw them putting up a front of domestic tranquillity, intimate friends knew that the reality was otherwise. Both found a release from their marital frustrations in extramarital affairs.[7]

Sonneschein sublimated his miserable family life by thrusting himself energetically into his rabbinic and public career, which by most standards was quite successful: he built Shaare Emeth into the largest Reform temple in the Midwest; he edited and wrote at various times for two English newspapers and three German journals, and he was twice elected a vice-president of the National Conference of Charities and Corrections.[8] A poetic and eloquent, if sensationalist, preacher,[9] Sonneschein, religiously and theologically, was an ardent exponent in the pulpit and in his writings of radical Reform, best crystallized by the Pittsburgh Platform of November 1885, which he himself helped draw up. This eight-point rabbinic affirmation, which avowed ethical monotheism as the core of Judaism and its dissemination as the central mission of the Jews and rejected Jewish nationalism, ritualism, and any and all ideas not consonant with reason and progress, expressed succinctly his religious views.[10] His closest friend within the Reform movement was Isaac Mayer Wise, with whose views he generally, although not always, agreed.[11] Sonneschein, like Wise, acknowledged the centrality of the Decalogue and upheld the inviolability and sanctity of the Saturday Sabbath;[12] but he was far more willing than Wise to drop ritual practices and customs; he favored applying biblical criticism to the *tanach* [Hebrew Scriptures], which Wise did not; and, in opposition to Wise, he looked favorably upon Felix Adler and his Ethical Culture movement, at least in the early 1880s.[13] Sonneschein remained one of Wise's most ardent supporters in the latter's many projects, including the Hebrew Union College,[14] the *American Israelite* and its German supplement, *Die Deborah*,[15] which Sonneschein edited exclusively between 1874 and 1879. He privately and publicly defended Wise from his numerous detractors on many occasions, a faithfulness Wise repaid when Sonneschein himself periodically came under attack.[16]

Sonneschein's Unitarian affair came on the heels of a rapidly disintegrating relationship with his Shaare Emeth board in the 1880s. For over a decade, his tenure had been a fairly satisfactory one in the temple: he introduced ritual innovations, adopted the Einhorn prayer book, and streamlined the services.[17] He attracted new members and helped raise the esteem of St. Louis Jews in the eyes of their Christian neighbors. While his temper involved him in minor personality skirmishes and while a few members opposed their rabbi because of the reforms he instituted, during the 1870s no serious public eruptions occurred, or none that are recorded.[18]

But by the 1880s, the relationship between rabbi and congregation had soured. Sonneschein's unstable personality, alleged personal excesses, radical religious orientation, and fundamental difference with the board over the scope of his rabbinic prerogatives saw him embroiled, almost continuously, in one confrontation after another.

Indeed, the strains that arose between the rabbi and his board illuminate one of the more vital themes in late-nineteenth-century American Jewish history, although in an exaggerated way: the evolving friction between the laity and their ostensible employees, the rabbis, who increasingly vied for authority over the congregation.[19] The contours of this competition were shaped by personality conflicts among the principals, as well as by disagreements over religious ideology, ritual change, and the scope of rabbinic prerogatives. In Sonneschein's troubles with Shaare Emeth, all four factors came into play. The board took strong exception to his drinking and frequenting of saloons, and was quite perturbed by persistent rumors of his marital infidelities. At a Friday night lecture on 17 December 1883, Sonneschein outraged many congregants with his musing that, in the future, American Jews and non-Jews would celebrate Hanukkah, the twenty-fifth day of the Hebrew month of Kislev and Christmas, the twenty-fifth day of December, together as one festive, national holiday. Their anger was undoubtedly deepened by the negative publicity their rabbi and temple received because of the speech at the hands of a jeering Jewish press in cities across the country.[20]

Sonneschein's perceived trespasses continued. In the early months of 1885, Sonneschein offended many congregants by mocking the alleged religious inconsistencies in the temple's Sabbath School curriculum.[21] In the summer of 1885, some temple members protested his having conducted Sunday services at the Independent German Protestant School, whose pastor was on vacation, and in October, Sonneschein was rebuked by the board for having invited a Christian minister to preach from the temple pulpit. The board, moreover, censured Sonneschein for holding Friday night debates in December 1885–January 1886 to defend the Pittsburgh Platform because he used the temple for purposes "other than the conduct of the usual religious services."[22] In all these instances, an unrepentant Sonneschein reiterated his resistance to lay interference with his rabbinic freedoms and upheld his right to follow the dictates of reason and progress against what he took to be congregational fanaticism and wickedness.

Matters came to a head in March 1886 when Sonneschein's impulsiveness and insensitivity to the sentiments evoked by ritual gravely insulted a bereaved family. Called to preside at the funeral of a twenty-year-old Sephardi girl, he not only arrived late and inebriated, but when he entered the hall of her parents' house and saw the mirror covered, as was customary in houses of mourning, he threw off the covering in a raging fury and fulminated in German against what he saw as a ludicrous superstition. Then, when he ended the service with the benediction "May the God of Truth and Justice in His mercy never visit this house," one indignant congregant moved to fight the rabbi in the living room of the bereaved. The congregational president, no admirer of Sonneschein, interceded to protect him and to prevent a riot.[23]

A few weeks later, on 28 March, a new board was elected which Sonneschein regarded as so antagonistic to him that in matters of disagreement with it he realized his supporters could not win in any vote. Hence, when on 1 April 1886 his request of the new board for an advance on his salary was denied, breaking precedent, he promptly resigned as Shaare Emeth rabbi, stipulating that in accordance with his contract, his resignation would take effect six months later, on 1 October 1886. The board accepted his resignation unanimously at a special meeting on 5 April, pending the approval of the full congregation at a meeting which it scheduled for 18 April.[24]

The St. Louis press speculated freely about the motives of the rabbi's resignation. Charitable interpretations, generally found in the secular press like the *Missouri Republican* and *Post Dispatch*, attributed it to ideological differences between a radical rabbi and a conservative congregation. Less charitable views, generally emanating from the Jewish press like the *St. Louis Jewish Free Press*, saw Sonneschein's action as a bluff to exact better financial terms from a new board.[25] Not everyone was surprised, therefore, when Solomon Sonneschein appeared at the open congregational meeting on 18 April seeking to have his resignation rescinded, defending his reputation against his critics and begrudgingly apologizing for "the sudden tempest" which swept over him and caused him to resign in haste. All to no avail—the congregation voted 82 to 64 to uphold the board's acceptance of the rabbi's resignation, which was to go into effect on 1 October, and it proceeded to advertise the anticipated vacancy.[26]

Sonneschein's supporters, however, did not give up the fight. In early May, they presented their rabbi with a petition requesting that he reapply for his own position. They reasoned correctly that few rabbis would dare apply if they knew Sonneschein still sought the job. Whether Sonneschein orchestrated this brilliant stroke is not clear, but on 23 May he formally applied for the vacant position.[27] Virtually no one in St. Louis knew, however, that Sonneschein in the meantime had traveled to Boston to explore the possibility of joining the Unitarians, nor that it was his having been rebuffed, however gently, by the Unitarian leadership that probably prompted his seeking reinstatement as rabbi of Shaare Emeth at the meeting of 18 April.

The publication of this information set off a veritable tremor in the St. Louis and American Jewish community at large. M. C. Reefer, a moderate Reform Jew who managed and edited the *Jewish Free Press*, released the story.[28] Reefer had been a former newspaper collaborator with Sonneschein but now was one of the rabbi's most serious critics; having received an anonymous tip from Boston which he then corroborated with that city's Rabbi Solomon Schindler and Rev. Minot Savage, he published all the known details of the episode and pursued it relentlessly.[29]

What actually happened in Boston? Sonneschein arrived during the second week of April, not giving any of the city's rabbis advance notice nor even attending Sabbath services. Rather, he preached at Rev. Edward Everett Hale's Unitarian Church on Sunday and conferred with Hale, Savage, and Grindall Reynolds about possibly serving a Unitarian pulpit because "the Jewish pulpit had become too narrow for him" and because of his opposition to his congregational board. When Hale raised the issue of baptism, Sonneschein, ever true to his antiritualism—he was a strong opponent of *brit milah* (circumcision)—rejected the possibility. The Unitarians sensed that the rabbi was "prospecting," informed him that no pulpit was available at present, and tried to persuade him to go on a missioning tour "among the German element" in the West. (Whether Jewish German or general German is unclear.) Not having been encouraged in a way that he might have hoped for, Sonneschein departed and never formally applied to join the Unitarian denomination.

Reefer lost no time in labeling Sonneschein more Unitarian than Jewish, and he recalled for his readers two Sonneschein incidents in the past weeks that had confounded St. Louis Jewry, but which now, in retrospect, seemed to make a good deal of sense and testified to his non-Jewish, if not universalist or even Christian, leanings. On 19 April, the first night of Passover and one day after Shaare Emeth voted to accept the rabbi's resignation, Sonneschein violated a longstanding personal opposition to intermarriage by officiating in his office at a marriage between a Jewish woman and a Presbyterian man.[30] Then on the seventh day of Passover, he had delivered a terribly incoherent, rambling discourse whose message, in light of the Boston trip, Reefer and others suddenly understood as if a veil had been lifted from their eyes.[31] Entitled "What Judaism Must Do to Be Saved," the salient point of the speech, ostensibly, was the need for Judaism to emancipate itself from its dead formalism and thereby help save the world and itself. But not only did it contain high praise for Christian virtues, it also was suffused with christological allusions in which Sonneschein—speaking in the first person singular, sometimes referring to himself and other times metaphorically personifying Judaism—cast himself as a new messianic savior. Some of the more obvious thoughts evoking christological sentiments appear at the beginning of the speech:

> I will not die because I shall live. I shall not die because I will live. I must not die because I ought to live. That is the lesson of creation, which has been inculcated upon that plan for *the last eighteen hundred and eighty-five years*. (Emphasis added)

Note the date of the last phrase, a virtually explicit reference to Jesus which suggests that he—Jesus—taught mankind how to attain everlasting life. Sonneschein continued:

> What I say of myself I have a right to say of Judaism. Judaism cannot die because it lives. It is not the lesson of the so-called resurrection of the Savior that teaches the world today, the lesson of a new life, but it is the grace of a loving Christ, of Jesus who teaches this lesson.

Here, Sonneschein appears to have underscored the nondogmatic source of the lesson of how to live; not the *dogma* of having to believe in resurrection teaches it, but the acceptance of a loving Christ. If this interpretation has merit, then the juxtaposition of the message of a loving Christ to the notion of a living Judaism is as oblique as it is suggestive: Does Judaism live by virtue of the message of eternal life of a human Christ? The next section is equally telling on this point:

> Judaism in order to be saved must be ready and not only able and enthusiastic, but willing to sacrifice everything for the sake of humanity. That is the Savior who dies on the cross?[32] Judaism dies and has been dying for the last eighteen hundred years. Dying and dying and dying and dying and crying out, My God, why hast thou forsaken me?

It is extremely revealing that Sonneschein described Judaism as dying for the last eighteen hundred years. That is precisely what Christians, including liberal Unitarians, argued: with the coming of Jesus, Judaism was supplanted, or in more crass terms, was dead. It is no less revealing that Sonneschein depicted a dying Judaism muttering the precise phrase attributed to a dying Jesus on the cross. Sonneschein then concluded his speech by returning to the supposed main theme— that in order to be saved, Judaism must have the courage to save the world—but not before climaxing with a joyous messianic flourish:

> Throw every vestige of the past away; every reminiscence of the middle age. Down with everlasting superstition, away with every vestige of ignorance and fanaticism and superstition. Life, human life, have life, spring life, lengthening of the days, shortening of the nights, come. I am ready to save you and can. I shall be saved again.

This sermon is one of the most extraordinary, if elusive, ever given by an American rabbi. Certainly to Reefer and many others, against the background of his trip, this proved that Sonneschein was an apostate to Unitarianism trying to reconcile Reform Judaism and Christian theology.[33] Perhaps. An equally tenable interpretation is that this sermon reflected a temporary aberration, not indicative of Sonneschein's real religious convictions. The sermon bespeaks the psychological distress of an individual twice rejected—by both his congregation and the Unitarians—who at worst ventured into a domain of "theological irregularity," or who lapsed momentarily into messianic delusions: he, the rejected man, had the formula to save Judaism and the world. Jesus may have appeared as an appropriate messianic model because, as "Jew-Christian," Jesus linked the two worlds between which Sonneschein was oscillating.

Regardless of one's interpretation, Sonneschein in June and July of 1886 became a favorite topic all over Jewish America. The Shaare Emeth board, caught in the maelstrom, tried at first to contain the story,[34] but when that proved futile, it established a committee chaired by Samuel N. Lederer, a prominent St. Louis attorney not affiliated with the congregation, to investigate the circumstances of Sonneschein's Boston trip. Lederer was charged to visit Boston and interview the individuals involved in the episode and to obtain in writing affidavits that would elucidate what had actually occurred during Sonneschein's trip to Boston. He did so, and his summary report to the committee confirmed what Reefer had already been publishing in the *Jewish Free Press*. With this evidence in hand, at a meeting on 20 June, the board called a special meeting for 23 June to give Sonneschein an opportunity to explain and vindicate his actions and to respond to the charge of apostasy that had arisen in so many quarters.

Sonneschein steadfastly repudiated all charges of apostasy; he re-affirmed loyalty to the Jewish cause and launched a bitter attack against his critics. He asserted that, given his disputes with the congregation, his trip to Boston merely attempted to ascertain

> how far I, as a *Hebrew theologian* could conscientiously go to be accepted by the A.U.A. as a public lecturer for the advancement of the sacred cause which both the advanced American Jew and the advanced American Christian have in common without losing the integrity and identity of my Hebrew affiliations of birth and conviction.[35]

In a subsequent meeting of the congregation on 30 June, Sonneschein defended his trip by proclaiming that he felt he could "preach and teach the doctrines of an unsectarian and at the same time strictly Jewish divine humanity to all the people, Hebrew and Gentile alike," wherever he found an audience. And if Reform Judaism was "nothing else but an empty shell," he, for one, need not polish it "for luxury's sake" but could move on to another area where he might be a true religious builder. Sonneschein, in all his defenses, reaffirmed that he was not a *zaken mamre*, a theological apostate, that all he would have done had he joined the Unitarians would have been to preach pure Judaism to a wider audience, and that even as a member of the American Unitarian Association, he could have remained the "same spiritually thoroughbred Jew I ever was and ever will remain." To cite his words in a letter he had written to Kaufmann Kohler categorically repudiating his being a renegade, *"Sonneschein shmadt sich nicht."*

The issue simmered over the summer. The temple had voted not to fire him at its 30 June meeting, since his resignation of 1 October was still in effect anyway and there was no reason to disgrace the rabbi or the congregation any further.[36] But on 12 September, over two hundred congregants met again to deliberate on Sonneschein's application to be rehired, which was still pending. During the course of the meeting, a committee representing both Sonneschein supporters and detractors privately negotiated a compromise that was then presented to the full congregation. The compromise proposed that Sonneschein be rehired for a term of not more than one year at his present salary of $5,000 per year. The terms and hidden assumptions of this proposal were neither brought up nor clarified for those assembled, for the mere announcement in the hall elicited a spontaneous outpouring of approval and thunderous applause. It was as if the grueling, internecine tension of months and the pent-up longing for congregational tranquillity exploded at the news of the impressive breakthrough.[37]

The real significance of the compromise, however, became apparent only a rew days later. On 24 September, a circular was issued inviting friends to a meeting in order to discuss the possibility of establishing a new congregation. Resolutions reached at the meeting asserted that owing to irreconcilable differences within Shaare Emeth that precluded congregational harmony, a new congregation, Temple Israel, was necessary. The breakaway congregation met for the high holidays that fall, with a policy of open seating and with Solomon Sonneschein as its rabbi. On 8 October, the *Jewish Free Press* reported that Temple Israel's membership stood at 147, of whose number 27 were individuals who had withdrawn from Shaare Emeth. The paper, however, estimated that another 75 would yet leave Shaare Emeth for Temple Israel, leaving the mother congregation with about 225 to 230 members.

In a letter to his former student David Philipson on 26 September, Isaac M. Wise, who was in constant contact with Sonneschein during the spring and summer of 1886, probably offered the true interpretation of the 12 September compromise at Shaare Emeth as a face-saving gesture, although Sonneschein's friends later denied the claim whenever it surfaced in public.

> Dr. Sonneschein has been honorably defeated. He was elected for one year with a salary of $5000 with the understanding that he will resign, and a new congregation is in process of formation; perhaps it is accomplished by this time to retain Dr. Sonneschein.[38]

Wise's evaluation of the whole affair, that of a loyal friend, represented the most charitable estimation of Sonneschein as a victim of vigilantes. "This is the first time on record," he wrote Philipson, "that an American Rabbi was tried by a congregation for heresy by new methods of the inquisition. It seems to me an ugly spot on the history of American Judaism." Indeed, to spare Sonneschein any further pain or embarrassment, Wise canceled the July meeting of the Union of American Hebrew Congregations (UAHC) scheduled in Cincinnati. The ostensible excuse was the death of Rev. James K. Gutheim of New Orleans, but the transparency of this pretext was obvious to all. Even before the St. Louis congregation had fully grappled with the Unitarian imbroglio, let alone resolved it, Wise had already canvassed the opinions of his rabbinic colleagues as to the desirability of Sonneschein's participation in the forthcoming conference. Kohler, for one, responded on 11 June that "Sonneschein should not participate" in the wake of his approach to the Unitarians.[39] Rather than have the Sonneschein issue rock the UAHC and possibly polarize its members, rather than have to confront the UAHC with the need to take an official stand on the topic, and rather than hurt his good friend, Wise sagaciously canceled the conference.

What were the real reasons for Sonneschein's approach to the Unitarians? Was he a self-seeking opportunist and spiteful Jewish renegade seeking to avenge himself against his congregation, as Henry Gersoni and many others speculated? Or was he but an unstable sensationalist dreaming of the national stir his action would cause? Or was Sonneschein's own self-perception accurate—was he indeed the high-minded idealist seeking a broader and more appreciative audience for his message of prophetic Judaism, for which his own flock was as yet unprepared? Apostasy or pure Judaism taught in a new social framework—how ought the historian to judge?

The truth is that Sonneschein needed a new job, and had the Unitarians been more forthcoming he might well have taken a Unitarian pulpit. He was extremely bitter and emotionally overwrought at the time. Given his disposition, one can also imagine that he would have relished the sensation his defection would have caused; one can picture him on the way to Boston blissfully imagining the storm that would erupt following his entry into Unitarianism. Certainly, he would have been immensely gratified at being accepted by the nation's social, cultural, and intellectual elite. And yet, while these personal considerations undoubtedly figured in Sonneschein's decision, his near defection should not be construed merely as an act of vindictiveness or opportunism. Rather, his rejection of the charge of theological apostasy and his avowed desire to teach pure Judaism in a wider social context ought to be accepted as sincere convictions. For in a sense, Sonneschein's trip to Boston culminated more than a decade of forging personal ties with leading Unitarian figures with whom he felt a growing spiritual kinship. Moreover, during these years, his study of Unitarianism led him to conclude that precious little, conceptually or religiously, distinguished the ethical monotheism of Reform Judaism from the "religion of humanity" and "free religion" preached by Unitarian colleagues. His application specifically to the Unitarians, therefore, was not a quirky aberration, but the outcome of his sustained social and intellectual interaction with Unitarians and Unitarianism.

During the 1870s, Sonneschein learned to admire the Unitarians.

Invited to lecture on Reform Judaism to the radical Free Religious Association (F.R.A.) in 1874, Sonneschein was exposed first-hand to the urbane, Yankee culture of this largely Unitarian, Boston-based organization. He was so deeply impressed by his hosts that his talk, in comparison to those delivered to the F.R.A. by other Reform rabbis such as Isaac M. Wise, Max Lilienthal, and Raphael Lasker, was by far the most sycophantic in tone.[40] Sonneschein kept up his contacts with the Unitarian movement by subscribing to the Unitarian press, such as the *Christian Register* of the Eastern Unitarians and *Unity* of the Western Unitarians; he could not help but keep abreast of the problematic search for a Unitarian consensus during the 1870s and 1880s. He corresponded with some of the most illustrious figures in the Unitarian world: Boston's James Freeman Clarke[41] and Minot Savage,[42] Chicago's Robert Collyer[43] and Jenkin Lloyd Jones,[44] St. Paul's William Channing Gannett,[45] and London's Moncure Conway,[46] as well as many others. He published some of their essays in his *Jewish Tribune*, heaping lavish praise upon them both in the paper and in his letters to them. Indeed, Sonneschein seems to have sought intellectual recognition from the Unitarians almost as much as from the Jews. He tried, usually without success, to publish his own sermons and essays in Unitarian papers. He also failed to persuade the liberal publisher of most Unitarian material, George H. Ellis, to bring out a projected book of his, an enterprise for which he sought Minot Savage, also apparently in vain, as a sponsor.[47] Needless to say, when his sermons did elicit praise from Unitarians Sonneschein was delighted.

Closer to home, Sonneschein established a very amiable relationship with the most prominent Unitarian in St. Louis, William G. Eliot, pastor of the Unitarian Church of the Messiah and grandfather of T. S. Eliot. The Eliots were transplanted Bostonians who in the midnineteenth century were the acknowledged bearers of culture and intellectual life in "a nominally Catholic city which seemed devoted to gambling, drunkenness, dueling, and the pursuit of wealth."[48] A graduate of the Harvard Divinity School, Eliot remained strongly rooted in his Yankee background; he represented the best sentiment of liberal religion in St. Louis and founded the nonsectarian Washington University, which he served at different times as president and chancellor. It was Eliot who gave Sonneschein a personal letter of introduction to the Boston Unitarians in anticipation of his April visit, thereby suggesting that the Unitarian Eliot, rather than any Jewish colleague or friend, was perhaps the only person in St. Louis outside the family who knew in advance of Sonneschein's trip. Eliot, who Sonneschein termed "my highly honored and venerable friend," may well have served as the model American religious liberal for him, the socially and intellectually "significant other."

Sonneschein spoke as guest minister at Unitarian churches in St. Louis and in other cities in the 1870s and 1880s and even led Sunday Unitarian services on two occasions in the summer of 1885 when the regular clergy were on vacation. He greatly enjoyed these opportunities; in fact, three years after his first sermon in Collyer's Unitarian Church in Chicago in 1874, he wrote the minister asking if he could do it again.[49] Sonneschein allowed the Second Baptist Church of Rev. W. W. Boyd to meet temporarily at Shaare Emeth in the spring of 1879 when the church building burned down, for which he was publicly lauded and given a twelve-piece silver tea set. Later, Boyd rose to defend Sonneschein in the pages of the *Jewish Free Press* in the midst of the Unitarian scandal.[50] The rabbi, moreover, was quite effective in attracting Unitarians to his own services and lectures, a fact that pleased many congregants in the 1870s, since it confirmed their status in the eyes of the Christian community.[51] But opponents of Sonneschein in the 1880s criticized him for attracting too many Unitarians and insufficient numbers of Jews, particularly during the debates on the Pittsburgh Platform in late December 1885 and early January 1886.[52] Sonneschein clearly regarded the approval of Unitarians as very important. In a letter to Rabbi Max Landsberg of Rochester, who was at work on a new prayerbook, *Ritual for Jewish Worship* (1885), for which he received the stylistic help of his Unitarian colleague, Rev. Newton M. Mann, Sonneschein remarked that American Jews needed a Jewish *American* prayerbook that would, among other things, "attract the liberal Christian so well and so forcibly, that he will come to us to catch the real and complete spirit of modern devotion in public worship."[53]

Sonneschein's personal contacts with Unitarians were representative of a broader interchange taking place among Unitarians and Reformers in many cities and towns across the country. While mostly restricted to the clergy and the educated laity, this rapprochement was nevertheless seen and felt by the general public. The last third of the nineteenth century witnessed the innovation of pulpit exchanges between liberal Jewish and Christian ministers, exchanges of newspaper subscriptions between editors of Jewish and Unitarian papers, and the participation of liberal Jews and Christians in the radical religious societies emerging from within one another's religious tradition. A number of Jews joined the Free Religious Association, while a much more substantial number of Christians joined Ethical Culture. Jews participated in various Congresses of Liberal Societies and, together with the Unitarians and others, joined forces to promote the complete separation of church and state in America.

A variety of intellectual and socio-religious forces fostered this rapprochement between Reform Judaism and Unitarianism in the last decades of the nineteenth century. Each represented the major liberal institutional expression of its respective faith. Both were by-products of Enlightenment ideology in nineteenth-century garb, and both sought to articulate their tenets in full consonance with reason, progress, and modern scholarship in science, Bible criticism, and comparative religion. Reform rabbis and Unitarian ministers affirmed with equal vigor their commitment to religious universalism and preached with equal fervor the imminent arrival of the "Religion of Humanity," characterized by the "Fatherhood of God and the Brotherhood of Man."[54]

Reformers and Unitarians were also drawn together because they were perceived as dissenters from commonly accepted religious consensuses, such as movements of religious revivalism. Between them "was the bond of the disaffected";[55] they began as outsiders from their respective religious traditions. Indeed, Reformers and Unitarians shared another compelling characteristic: each group grappled with problems of self-definition, not only of defining its movement's central beliefs but of determining its position within the parameters of its faith.[56] Both liberal movements were attacked by religious figures to their right, who charged them with propagating inauthentic forms of Judaism and Christianity. Reformers confronted the polemics of conservative and orthodox Jews who argued that Reform's dismissal of such beliefs as the personal messiah, resurrection, and Jewish nationalism, and of ritual practices such as circumcision and the transfer of the Saturday Sabbath to Sunday disqualified them as Jews. Similarly, Unitarians' rejection of all Christian dogmas and their humanization of Jesus provoked denunciation of them as apostates by conservative Protestant groups; Unitarians were deemed renegades and simply read out of the Christian religious fellowship.

Consequently, both the Reform and the Unitarian movements grappled with the same religious dilemma, prototypical of religious liberals: how to reconcile religious liberalism with religious tradition

286

and how to redefine that tradition so that it could accommodate theological innovation. Both Reform Judaism and Unitarianism underwent considerable internal strains in the process, as individual adherents within the respective faiths proposed their own solutions to the issue. Certainly, liberals like Sonneschein and William G. Eliot felt compelled to legitimate themselves in the eyes of their co-religionists. Against this background therefore, it is not surprising that the liberal Eliot, a minister at one of only two Unitarian congregations out of 148 churches in St. Louis,[57] would find common ground for intellectual, religious, and cultural discourse with his Reform counterpart, as did Schindler with Savage in Boston, Isaac M. Wise with Thomas Vickers in Cincinnati, Max Landsberg with Newton Mann in Rochester, Rebecca Gratz with William H. Furness in Philadelphia and, in the twentieth century, Stephen S. Wise and John Haynes Holmes in New York, to cite but a few examples.

Interestingly, although emerging from very different social settings and religious frameworks—American Unitarians were natives, American Jewish Reformers were generally central European immigrants or children of these immigrants; Unitarianism was evolving from within Christianity, Reform Judaism from within Judaism—the religious liberals in both camps, heavily influenced by similar forces of modernity and conceptions of religious evolution, seemed to be converging at basically identical religious self-definitions and eschatological goals. In fact, one finds innumerable expressions of that perception in the public mind. To some observers, Reform Judaism and Unitarianism seemed to be identical faiths, and hence their fusion in the not too distant future could be anticipated. Some Jews and Christians indeed called for the merger of the two religious movements because on the surface they appeared to be indistinguishable.[58]

Understandably, the blurring of distinctions between Unitarianism and Reform Judaism and the expectation of their imminent merger deeply troubled some Reform rabbis, for these tendencies implied that Reform Judaism was redundant and irrelevant and continued Jewish existence in America meaningless. These rabbis confronted the challenge directly. Already in the 1870s, but especially in the 1880s and 1890s, and to some extent into the twentieth century, they published sermons and essays that sought to define the relationship between Reform Judaism and Unitarianism and affirm the need for Jewish religious continuity. Some of them have suggestive titles, such as "Why I am a Jew," in which the spectre of Unitarianism lurks in the background; others, with such titles as "Judaism and Unitarianism," are far more obvious. Rabbis such as Kaufmann Kohler, Emil Hirsch, Solomon Schindler, Bernhard Felsenthal, Isaac M. Wise, Gustav Gottheil, Adolph Moses, Maurice Harris, David Philipson, Stephen Wise, Hyman Enclow and others took great pains to delineate what they felt to be the surface similarities yet fundamental distinctions between the two faiths. In the process, they articulated and refined a synthetic American Jewish identity which melded the affirmations of religious universalism, liberalism, and Americanism with Jewish separateness and chosenness. In large measure, therefore, Unitarianism and the Jewish interaction with Unitarians stimulated Jewish introspection to seek an intellectual and religious justification for continued Jewish existence. And this serves to highlight the deeply ambivalent relationship and dialectical struggle typifying the Reform Jewish encounter with Unitarians. On the one hand, Reformers wanted to align themselves and their religion with Unitarianism and cultivate a true coalition of liberal religionists seeking the same ends and working for common religious, social, and political goals. On the other hand, the more Reformers fraternized with Unitarians, resulting in their religion being equated in the public eye with Unitarianism, the more they were driven to articulate the necessity of Jewish separateness and to justify it. In effect, to borrow a metaphor from Genesis, for Reform Judaism, Unitarianism was the tempting, succulent apple (or fig, according to the *Midrash*) which when bitten into gave one greater insight into the world and into oneself, but which, in consequence of that knowledge, ineluctably carried with it the need for new strategies for survival and self-defense.

Solomon Sonneschein, having "bitten into the apple" of Unitarianism years before the 1886 incident, was quite cognizant of the necessity of distinguishing between the two seemingly identical liberal faiths for his congregation. In January–February 1881, he delivered a series of seven lectures entitled "Reform Judaism and the Unitarian Church."[59] Sonneschein easily and successfully limned the conceptual similarities between the two religions, but he had greater difficulty in portraying their differences. The fundamental differences outlined, therefore, were more residual than conceptual, more a matter of group historic memories, pragmatic ritual differentiations, and the preference for the "Christian" or the "Jewish" name rather than emanating from substantive, intellectual disagreements. Reform Judaism and Unitarianism were running parallel histories, he wrote, fighting for tolerance, freedom, and the religion of humanity. Their religious tendencies were the same but varied "only in the shading," with the "affinity of the two movements . . . clearly marked." Wherein did they differ? Unitarianism still preserved the form of Christianity by insisting on being called Christian, but it accepted the borrowed but true ideas of Jewish monotheism. Reform Judaism thought its ideas correct, but discarded the unnecessary forms, the rituals. Hence, although the unification idea was a good one and "has swelled the heart of many a pious and noble man in the two wings of the progressive denominations of the day," it was not yet feasible because the masses were not yet ripe for it. Moreover, he asked, who would be recognized as the founding father of the merged faiths—Moses or Jesus? Which day of rest would prevail—Saturday or Sunday? Also, Sonneschein added, Jews unfortunately were still regarded as a race, and Christian race prejudice still existed against Jews, even among Unitarians; if the faiths merged, who would secure the rights of persecuted Jews across the globe? Finally, he pointed out, neither (liberal) Christians nor (liberal) Jews viewed each other's history very favorably; the "aggressive" stances they had adopted toward each other's religious past had first to be overcome. Religious unity was therefore still a dream, Sonneschein concluded, a dream not yet able to be realized. In the interim, it was better that Reform Jews and Unitarians fulfill their inner missions first—the former, by disseminating the teachings of progress and reason to orthodox Jews and the latter by making these same truths available to Baptists, Presbyterians, and Lutherans. This attempt to differentiate Reform from Unitarianism helped Sonneschein wrestle with the general dilemma of reconciling his personal commitments both to religious universalism and to Jewish self-preservation.

As some voices within Unitarianism became increasingly radical, particularly within the Western Unitarian Conference, which was defining Unitarianism in the broadest possible terms of human spirituality and religious commitment,[60] the pressures on a Jewish radical like Sonneschein to continue to justify his Jewish separatism mounted. In an extraordinarily telling letter of 25 April 1883, to Moncure D. Conway in London, Sonneschein explained why he, a universalist liberal, unhampered by rituals or "race," remained a Jew:

> I now believe more firmly than ever before that Judaism, once entirely freed from its racial and fossilized encumbrances of the past is destined to infuse a new life into the dry bones of superannuated theology. It will take some time yet, of course, but

> it is bound to come. . . . Let Reformed Judaism first find its own home task, and then let the world at large see whether it may or may not claim the title of the "true Religion of Humanity."

Sonneschein here sounded the clarion call of Jewish religious triumphalism, much as Isaac M. Wise did, a trait symptomatic, paradoxically, of the universalism of liberal religious thinkers.[61] Unitarians and Reformers may have envisioned the advent of an enlightened, eschatological religion of humanity that would embrace all mankind, but with only a few exceptions, notably Felix Adler and Francis Ellingwood Abbot, they all projected this religion to be the universalization of their own faith, whether a universalized liberal Christianity or a universalized Reform Judaism. Therefore, the preservation of Judaism—the religion of the future—was urgent, and the mission of Reform Judaism until the arrival of the messianic era was to educate Jews to the universalism within Judaism. This idea of inner mission to fellow Jews constituted a nuanced variation of the standard expression of the mission theory of classical Reform Judaism, which projected Jews as a religious model for the world at large.

But Sonneschein added one further, crucial reason for having stayed within Jewry:

> It is by no means necessary that all those who anticipate such glorious results *must* abandon forthwith the different isolated standpoints which they shall have to occupy for the sake of those who surround them, and that leaving all time honored and sacred associations behind them, they *must* spontaneously join the steadily increasing caravan of religious pathfinders *who could not stay* where they found no satisfaction whatsoever. Nay!

Sonneschein regarded himself as a universalist fully prepared *now* for the realization of the religion of humanity; hence he was a potential advocate of a universal religious fellowship, such as that of Felix Adler. But he, the rational, intellectually advanced thinker, "who [could] anticipate such glorious results," would not leave his fellowship because he would not leave behind "those that surround him," the unprepared masses. His triumphalism, which defined Judaism as the religion of humanity, together with his conception of Reform's mission to elevate unenlightened Jewry, helped sustain his continuing identification as a Jew.

Three years later, in defending himself before Shaare Emeth on 23 June 1886, Sonneschein elaborated on this same earnest and profound conviction of the role of the Reform Jewish leader that had found expression in his letter to Conway. The goal of the rabbi in the modern era, he declared, was

> to aid Judaism in entering fully upon the platform of pure civilization and to assist at the same time modern civilization to understand and to accept the tenets of the prophetic promises of old. . . . A Jewish rabbi of our age means a teacher of religion who is going to bear Judaism into the fields of classic thought—that is prophetic Judaism.[62]

On this occasion, however, he proclaimed that if one's own congregation did not want to hear the message of prophetic Judaism and allow itself to be elevated, then the sensitive rabbi had no other choice than to seek a wider audience for his sacred message.

Sonneschein's intellectual grappling with Unitarianism and its implications for Jewish survival can be seen in bold detail shortly after the promulgation of the Pittsburgh Platform. To many Jews—orthodox, conservative, and moderate reform—this declaration effectively demolished the differences between Reform Judaism and its liberal Christian counterpart. In the face of hostile denunciations of the Platform emanating from Jews who represented a wide spectrum of Jewish beliefs and feelings, the religious challenges to radicals like Sonneschein became acute; finding the opportunity to defuse the criticism, to explain precisely what the Platform had intended, and to legitimate its brand of Judaism became of paramount importance. Consequently, in December 1885–January 1886, Sonneschein inaugurated a series of Friday night debates on the Pittsburgh proclamation in order to give himself a platform both to explain and defend it.[63] Not only was he confronted by some congregants about the declaration's apparently inconsistent retention of Jewish chosenness in the face of its affirmation of universalism—Sonneschein's retort: God is "wedded" to Israel and God is not a polygamist[64]—but he subsequently received a letter from a participant in the debates, Lewis Godlove, former treasurer of the *Jewish Tribune* and member of Shaare Emeth, which posed this trenchant question:

> If the mission of Judaism is to bring about the common Brotherhood of Man, if the doctrines of Judaism are the three named: Unity of God, Immortality of the soul and the binding force of the Mosaic moral code, why not take a heroic step and become Unitarians? We could then become part of the majority (represented by Christianity) instead of remaining a powerless minority daily growing weaker.[65]

In reply, Sonneschein disputed Godlove's concluding premise, emphatically rejected union with the Unitarians, and defended Jewish separation. Arguing that Christianity represented only 20 percent of all the inhabitants of the globe and that "there are twice as many Israelites in the United States as there are Unitarians," he saw no point in joining "the minority of the minority." (During the Unitarian fiasco he defended his action by referring then to the *larger* field of action he anticipated had he joined them.) Moreover, he retorted, while Christianity is on the wane in strength and influence, the "pure Hebrew idea [of ethical monotheism] stripped of all its ritualistic blindness is marching ahead splendidly." He reiterated that the time was not yet ripe for union because the "messianic hopes of mankind are not fulfilled yet. . . . Jesus was one of the *Great* and sainted saviors of the race but he is not *The* Savior. In that belief I live and I shall die a true Jew!" Sonneschein expressed his admiration for the Unitarian church's independent and courageous search for truth and for its humanity and indomitable intellectual energy, but while he considered himself the truest friend of Unitarianism, willingly extending to them his hand of fellowship at any time "to worship with them 'our Father who is in Heaven,'" he nevertheless must proclaim *"But I remain a Jew."*

Whether Sonneschein's response satisfied Godlove is not known, but less than two months later, the radical reformer wrote a remarkably revealing letter to the renowned Unitarian scholar and minister, James Freeman Clarke, which suggests a vacillating man not nearly so firm in his advocacy of continued Jewish survival.

> Many a time for the past few months I intended to ask you the plain question, whether you would honor or rather favor me with your enlightened and guiding words, should I address you in matters of Advanced Judaism *versus* Advanced Christianity as we both understand and pursue it, each of course his own denominational ideal [sic]. I am and the longer I observe things and persons and currents of events, *I am so the more intensely the believer in a possibility of blending both Rational Christianity and purified Judaism into one sunbeam of Eternal Truth.*[66]

For years, Sonneschein had preached that this ideal of achieving the universal rational religion of humanity, which he identified as Judaism, was to occur only in the future, imminent perhaps, but the future nonetheless. In this letter, two months before the Unitarian episode, Sonneschein seems to have intimated that he was prepared to explore with Clarke the possibility of quickening the *eschaton*, that is, of "blending Rational Christianity and purified Judaism." If the wish to discuss "blending" was offered seriously, there is no question that Sonneschein's conception of this "blending" would have consisted of two disparate social groups and religious communities, the Reform and the Unitarian, fusing under the banner of pure religion, that is, prophetic Judaism.

A concatenation of personal and institutional frustrations propelled Sonneschein toward the Unitarians, but it is clear that his Unitarian adventure two months later was not merely the outcome of unreflective action and impetuous behavior. Sonneschein had been profoundly involved in the Unitarian-Reform interchange and had intellectually struggled to work out a rationale for continued Jewish existence and identity. A devotee of the religion of humanity who felt liberated from all ritual forms and ethnic sentiment, Sonneschein lived on the margins of Jewish identity and on the brink of achieved universalism; his outlook was rooted in a triumphalist ideology that defined his understanding of prophetic Judaism as the universal religion of the future. A hyper-emotional man whose instability was aggravated by congregational circumstances, he was willing to approach the Unitarians after having been rejected by his own community. He considered seriously, for however short a period of time, the dissemination of his Judaism in a larger social framework, although vigorously denying the charge of apostasy against him. He had no intention of preaching anything other than triumphant, prophetic Judaism.

If it is true, as has been argued, that Sonneschein honestly believed his overture to the Unitarians was not an act of apostasy whereas his outspoken critics were utterly convinced that it was, how can one explain these antithetical perceptions? Moreover, what larger lessons about the phenomenon of apostasy might be gleaned from this unusual episode? Clearly, to those Jews who characterized Unitarianism as a Christian denomination—admittedly liberal, but Christian nonetheless—Sonneschein's mere attempt to join that movement was an unconscionable act of treason. It should be emphasized that their perception of Unitarianism as Christian was not unjustified. Most Unitarians did indeed conceive of themselves as Christians and sought to retain the name "Christian" for their denomination; they were nurtured on the sermons of a historic Christian past and they still looked to Jesus, albeit for the most part in an idealized, human form, for spiritual inspiration. In the 1870s and 1880s, the American Unitarian Association and the National Conference of Unitarian Churches attempted to define principles affirming their Christian roots, on the one hand, without placing a credal test on any person wishing to join, on the other. But the overwhelming majority of Unitarians upheld their Christian identity.[67] To American Jews, however, especially to the rabbis who differentiated between Unitarianism and Judaism by underscoring the religious significance of the Jewish historical past and its contemporary relevance and who dismissed the religious value even of a nondogmatic, humanized Jesus, the concept of a "Unitarian Rabbi" was contradictory and inherently untenable.[68]

In denying his apostasy was Sonneschein thus guilty of misreading the Unitarians by thinking that they would welcome him to preach prophetic Judaism as the religion of humanity? Given his distraught emotional state at the time, this conclusion is certainly possible. Or, perhaps, due to his anger and possible desire for revenge, he simply did not care whether Unitarians considered themselves Christian or not—he would teach his message of prophetic Judaism in any case. But it is also equally plausible that Sonneschein did not misjudge the Unitarians. As a regular reader of the Unitarian press, he was aware of the difficulties of Unitarians in trying to formulate a statement of religious identity and of the wide spectrum of religious orientations within the movement. He could easily have discovered spiritual kinsmen within Unitarian ranks. While the Unitarians included evangelical types on the right such as Rufus Ellis, they also included free religionists on the left, such as Octavius B. Frothingham and William J. Potter. Moreover, the radical Western Unitarian Conference, centered in Chicago and dubbed by the *American Hebrew* "agnostic Unitarian,"[69] was formally non-Christian in self-identification. Its proclamation of 11 May 1886 conditioning "its fellowship on no dogmatic tests" and welcoming "all who wished to join it to help establish truth, righteousness and love in the world"[70] left room for non-Christians like Sonneschein to join. Admittedly, Sonneschein traveled east, to the center of "historical Unitarianism," and not north to Chicago, because Boston was indeed the "Mecca" of the denomination and because William Eliot, a former Bostonian, gave him letters of introduction to the movement's most important divines. But Sonneschein undoubtedly could have hoped and even expected to find Unitarians who would agree with the basic contours of his religion of humanity. Certainly Minot Savage preached a universal religion that appeared identical to his own understanding of Reform Judaism.[71] In rationalizing his journey to Boston, Sonneschein may well have convinced himself that given the lack of conceptual differences between the two liberal faiths in religious principles and in eschatological vision, sentimental memories of past religious associations need not prevent his preaching prophetic Judaism among the Unitarians. He may consciously and deliberately have reasoned that it was not apostasy to teach Judaism in a non-Jewish socio-religious context.

While it may not be wise to construct a historical model based on such a singular character as Solomon Sonneschein, whose alleged apostasy was very short-lived in any event, this Unitarian affair nevertheless suggests a modern paradigm of apostasy that merits at least cursory examination. By his willingness, however temporary, to leave the rabbinate and preach his conception of Judaism within the Unitarian fellowship, Sonneschein was guilty not of *theological* apostasy (judged in reference to his own definition of Judaism) but of *social* apostasy, of leaving the community of Israel. For the modern period, as distinct from medieval times, this kind of distinction may prove useful in understanding the phenomenon of Jews leaving the socio-religious fabric of Jewish life.

In the premodern age, theological and social apostasy were virtually inseparable. Jewish apostasy carried with it the abandonment of the norms of Jewish religious thought and, simultaneously, the social framework of the Jewish community. For the modern age, however, the meaning of apostasy has to be adjusted. The nature of Jewish historical experience in the modern period has dissolved the intimate connection between Jewish thought and social affiliation. Jews can be theological apostates, alienated from Judaism completely, and yet remain within the Jewish consensus by choice and even with the begrudging assent of Jewish religious critics. Examples of the phenomenon abound and would include secular Zionists, Yiddishists, or indeed anyone whose Jewish attachments are strictly ethnic or national in nature. In the Sonneschein case, however, we encounter the reverse (and far less representative) dynamic: social or group defection without theological apostasy. In fact, Sonneschein considered committing social apostasy *for the sake of* propagating sound Jewish theology (as he understood it) in another socio-religious context. To him, the notion of a Unitarian Rabbi was conceptually feasible, while negative Jewish social consequences seemed irrelevant. Sonneschein, as a model, therefore, is to be distinguished from religious universalists such as Felix Adler and Charles Fleischer who, like apostates of old, understood themselves to transcend both Judaism and the Jewish group.

It is, moreover, equally instructive to underline the precise lines separating Sonneschein from other Reform thinkers. One might argue that what separated them were religious ideas, that other Reformers perceived him to be willing to affirm Christian beliefs. In reality, however, it was the social or communal aspect of his near defection, rather than his religious ideas, that distinguished him from other Reform radicals like Kaufmann Kohler and Emil Hirsch. Theologically and religiously, the latter two were every bit as radical as Sonneschein, and, if Sonneschein was a theological apostate, so were they. From the point of view of religious ideas, the traditionalists and moderate reformers who accused all three of having left Judaism were right to lump them together. Some even suggested that Sonneschein was merely being used as a scapegoat for the whole radical group. Indeed, if one compares Sonneschein and Hirsch theologically, Sonneschein's devout theistic faith, his belief in all-encompassing spiritual force—he frequently included the notations of "P.G." (please God) or the Hebrew abbreviation for *"im yirtseh ha-shem"* (if God wills) in his letters—was far more traditional than Hirsch's more humanistic or immanentist orientation, which bordered on agnosticism. As Solomon Schindler said of a Hirsch speech in 1883, its "confession is a nice conglomerate of fine sentiments expressed in beautiful words but it is not the confession of Judaism."[72] Sonneschein himself attacked Hirsch when the latter declared that "the God worshipped by true Judaism is not in the Heavens, but in a living active principle in man." "Judaism believes in a *living* God," Sonneschein retorted, "but not in a mere principle."[73] Eight years later, Sonneschein again reacted angrily to what he perceived to be Hirsch's "agnostic flirtations."[74] Over the years, Hirsch's views changed little. As he wrote Felix Adler in 1918, "Sometime[s] I regret that I did not take the step which you have."[75] From a theological standpoint, therefore, neither Hirsch nor Kohler had the right to criticize Sonneschein, his aberrant christological Passover sermon excepted. Ultimately, then, what really separated Sonneschein from his fellow Reform colleagues was less his radical religion than his willingness to leave the Jewish community.

Ironically, for all their vaunted liberalism and universalism, despite their avowed antinational feelings and their preference for designating Jews a "religious community," even radical reformers felt the powerful emotional pull of Jewish group solidarity. They were enormously loyal to the Jewish group qua group, and while Felsenthal alone among the radicals became an outspoken advocate of Zionism, by the turn of the century even Hirsch and Kohler employed terms like "Jewish people," "Jewish race," and "Jewish nation" in acknowledging the Jewish collective.[76] This ethnic commitment of even classical Reform Jews, despite their often public protestations to the contrary, is a theme not yet adequately explored or explained. Indeed it seems almost contradictory to the standard dichotomous stereotype of an anti-ethnic or antinational classical Reform Judaism. Viewed *sub specie aeternitatis* or from the vantage of later history, it seems that what ultimately separated Reformers from the Jewish consensus—the limits of Reform Judaism, if you will—was not this idea or that idea by itself, or this supposedly deviant practice or that, but their conscious departure from, or their perceived socio-religious betrayal of, the Jewish group. Immediately prior to his Boston trip, Solomon Sonneschein, feeling terribly betrayed by his "group" or "religious community," saw neither social nor religious constraints to dissuade him from stepping outside its bounds.

The furor over Sonneschein died down rapidly. If he had been labeled an apostate or enfant terrible for a few months in 1886, he was nonetheless quickly reintegrated into Jewish life and welcomed back into the Reform Jewish fold; indeed, he had never actually left it. Not only did he minister to the newly established Temple Israel, but later he held three other pulpits: a small congregation in San Francisco, from which he broke because of its "semi-orthodoxy"; Shaare Hashomayim of New York, the congregation in America that had originally called him from Europe; and Temple B'nai Yeshurun in Des Moines, Iowa, which invited him in 1899 to serve as its rabbi when he lost his job at Shaare Hashomayim due to its merger with Congregation Ahavat Chesed. A few years following his divorce from Rosa, Sonneschein married the daughter of a personal friend and fellow Reform rabbi, Judah Wechsler, and he seemed to enjoy a measure of domestic tranquillity, and even happiness, which he had previously never enjoyed. His own religious radicalism in the last decade of his life was also tempered, in style if not in content, as he entered a phase which he himself called "constructive radicalism."[77] By invitation, he attended the first meeting of the board of the Jewish Publication Society in 1888[78] and was elected a member of the executive committee of the Central Conference of American Rabbis in 1890, occasionally lecturing at its annual meetings and serving on or chairing some of its committees.[79] Sonneschein reconciled himself with his old antagonists, M. C. Reefer and Moritz Spitz, and apparently admitted that in his headstrong radicalism and flirtation with the Unitarians he had erred.[80]

In the last years of his life, Solomon Sonneschein's declining health and degenerating eyesight, which finally left him blind, caused him great anguish. He ceased his wanderings of the prior fifteen years and retired to St. Louis in 1905. He died on 3 October 1908 from an intracerebral hemorrhage, with the *Shema Yisrael*, the traditional and ultimate expression of Jewish faith, on his lips. His Unitarian overture, for all the excitement it had caused in 1886, had no long-term repercussions in the history of American Judaism, save for the creation of a new St. Louis temple. It remains but a fascinating curiosity, although revealing much about the patterns of American Jewish religious history. We will never know for sure what would have happened had the Unitarians actually taken in Solomon Sonneschein. As it turned out, however, the figure of a Unitarian rabbi remained but a hypothetical construct in American Jewish life.

NOTES

1. See, for example, the views of correspondent M. L. G. to the *Hebrew Standard*, cited in the St. Louis *Jewish Free Press*, 30 July 1886. Examples of the extreme nature of the charges against him are seen in his being characterized as *aḥer* both by Kaufmann Kohler in the *Jewish Free Press*, 16 July 1886, and by Rabbi Moritz Spitz, *Jewish Free Press*, 3 Sept. 1886. On Felix Adler, see Benny Kraut, *From Reform Judaism to Ethical Culture: The Religious Evolution of Felix Adler* (Cincinnati: Hebrew Union College Press, 1979), esp. pp. 135–68.

2. On Solomon Schindler, see Arthur Mann, *Yankee Reformer in an Urban Age* (Cambridge: Harvard University Press, Belknap Press, 1954), pp. 52–72; on Charles Fleischer, see Arthur Mann, "Charles Fleischer's Religion of Democracy," *Commentary* 17 (1954): 557–65. Most of both essays were incorporated into Arthur Mann, *Growth and Achievement: Temple Israel* (Cambridge, Mass.: Temple Adath Israel, 1954), pp. 45–83.

3. This theme is developed more fully in Benny Kraut, "The Ambivalent Relations between American Reform Judaism and Unitarianism in the Last Third of the Nineteenth Century," *Journal of Ecumenical Studies* 23 (1986); it is also discussed in Benny Kraut, "Judaism Triumphant: Isaac Mayer Wise on Unitarianism and Liberal Christianity," *AJS Review* 7–8 (1982–83): 179–81.

4. See the sermon initially given in 1920 by Hyman Enelow, "Need Jews Become Unitarians?" in *Selected Works of Hyman Enelow* (Kingsport, Tenn., 1935), 3:

103–10; cf. Milton Ellis, "Judaism and Unitarianism" (rabbinic thesis, Hebrew Union College, 1921); Abraham J. Feldman, *Judaism and Unitarianism* (Cincinnati: Tract Commission of the Union of American Hebrew Congregations and the Central Conference of American Rabbis, 1930); Solomon B. Freehof's responsum on the issue "Jews Joining the Unitarian Church," in his *Recent Reform Responsa* (Cincinnati; Hebrew Union College Press, 1963), pp. 56–58; see too the 1977 publicity brochure of the Unitarian Universalist Association disseminated from its national Boston headquarters by Linda Weltner, "Do I Have to Stop Being Jewish to be Unitarian Universalist?"

5. The best sources of biographical information on Sonneschein are the obituaries written by friends and colleagues. See the *Jewish Voice*, 6 Oct. 1908, for an obituary by Rabbi Moritz Spitz; *American Israelite*, 5 Oct. 1908, for one by Rabbi Max Heller; *Jewish Voice*, Oct. 1908, for a small essay on Sonneschein by Rabbi Rudolph Farber. Other information on Sonneschein can be found in the obituary column of the *St. Louis Post-Dispatch*, 4 Oct. 1908, and in Isaac Markens, *The Hebrews in America* (New York, 1888), pp. 301–2. The most probing and comprehensive secondary source is the series of reminiscences about Sonneschein by his friend Rabbi Leopold Wintner, which appeared in successive weeks in the *Jewish Voice* from 29 Jan. 1909 through 26 Feb. 1909, and which was published as a separate pamphlet, *S. H. Sonneschein* (New York, 1909). Good as introductions to Sonneschein, these secondary works clearly must give way to the fairly extensive primary sources on Sonneschein from which one can glean the full measure of the man: a set of four volumes of Sonneschein's personal correspondence spanning the 1870s to the late 1890s (Letterbooks), his published writings, the newspapers which he edited or coedited, notably the *Jewish Tribune*, and the many references to Sonneschein in the Jewish and secular press. Archival material is found in the Solomon H. Sonneschein Papers, American Jewish Archives (AJA), Cincinnati, Ohio.

6. For an example, see Sonneschein's vituperative letter to Moses Fraley, one of his staunchest supporters, on 21 November 1890, in the Sonneschein Papers, letterbook 4, box 968. Also, refer to his caustic comments about Moritz Spitz in the *Jewish Tribune*, 28 Dec. 1883, and in a letter to Leo Wise, 9 Mar. 1891, letterbook 4. See too his reference to Kaufmann Kohler as a "born fool" in his letter to David Philipson, 14 July 1891, letterbook 4.

7. See the revealing remarks of Sonneschein's grandson, David Loth, transcribed by Jack Nusan Porter, "Rosa Sonnenschein [sic] and the *American Jewess* Revisited: New Historical Information on an Early American Zionist and Jewish Feminist," *American Jewish Archives* 32 (1980): 128–31. This Porter article supplements and emends his previous article on Rosa, Solomon Sonneschein's wife, "Rosa Sonnenschein and the *American Jewess:* The First Independent English Language Jewish Women's Journal in the United States," *American Jewish History* 68 (1978): 57–63. Porter's own comments on Rosa, particularly with respect to her relationship to Solomon, should not be resorted to uncritically since he did not utilize all available sources on the subject and tended to lionize her. One vital source Porter did not use was the diary of Augustus Binswanger, box 2304, AJA, which adds much personal and firsthand knowledge to David Loth's comments. A confidant of Rosa, Binswanger in his diary illuminates much about the Sonneschein family and its failing rela-

tionships. His entry of 14–15 Nov. notes his being informed by Rosa of her husband's infidelities and affairs with the household staff. Rosa's utter contempt for Solomon, at a time when Binswanger was still her husband's friend, shines through clearly. See too the entries 29 June–July 1873. The marital difficulties of the two Sonnescheins were common knowledge, certainly by the 1880s, and Wintner's obituary also pointedly discusses them. As for Rosa, she was quite a tease with men and there exists an unbroken and persistent oral tradition of her own extramarital dalliances. Given her marital circumstances, and her flirtatious and in some ways outrageous personality, there is no good reason to doubt this tradition. Sonneschein himself ruminated about the terrible marriage and its impact on him. See letterbook 4, 16 Dec. 1892 and 30 Sept. 1892, and his letter to a Mr. and Mrs. J. Wolfort of St. Louis, 21 Feb. 1893, in which he called his wife a "false and fickle woman."

8. At various times, Sonneschein either coedited or edited the *American Israelite*, *Die Deborah*, the *Jewish Tribune*, *Sulamith* (a German supplement to the *Jewish Tribune*), and a literary magazine, *Die Wahrheit*. His commitment to the duty of *tsedakah* was both firm and on the public record. See his essay "Hebrew Charities during the Middle Ages," in the *Tenth Annual Conference of Charities and Corrections, Louisville, Sept. 24–30, 1883* (Madison, 1884).

9. Sonneschein's polished and dramatic oratorical style often elicited criticisms of his being too theatrical, a "Talmage Jew" in the words of Emil Hirsch and Liebman Adler. The Brooklyn preacher T. Dewitt Talmage was renowned for his theatrical pulpit exhortations. See the *Jewish Advance*, 1 Apr. 1881; also, *Jewish Advance*, 18 Mar. 1881, in which correspondent Yoez derides Sonneschein as a sensationalist. See, too, the *Jewish Times*, 2 Oct. 1874.

10. On the Pittsburgh Platform, consult Walter Jacob, ed. *The Changing World of Reform Judaism: The Pittsburgh Platform in Retrospect*. (Pittsburgh: Rodef Shalom Congregation, 1985); see too W. Gunther Plaut, *The Growth of Reform Judaism* (New York: World Union for Progressive Judaism, 1965), pp. 31–36, and the *Proceedings of the Pittsburgh Rabbinical Conference, Nov. 16, 17, 18, 1885* (Cincinnati: Central Conference of American Rabbis, 1923), pp. 18, 22–23, 27, 31, 35, 41, in which Sonneschein's role is illustrated. Sonneschein's radical reform beliefs surface in so many letters and in his *Jewish Tribune* that a few select references to his views will suffice. See his letter to the Shaare Emeth Congregation School Board, 5 Feb. 1885, letterbook 2, box X-132; letter to Moncure Conway, 25 Apr. 1883, letterbook 2; letter to Isaac M. Wise, 8 Nov. 1885, letterbook 3; letter to Rev. William Blackstone, 16 Sept. 1891, letterbook 4. See too the *Year Book of the Central Conference of American Rabbis* 12 (1902): 147, 13 (1903): 147–48, and 2 (1892): 198, in which Sonneschein declared that the Pittsburgh principles were the "unquestionable authoritative guide for my rabbinic actions and activities." See too his *Trial Issue of the New Ritual for Temple Israel*, and his letter to Bernhard Felsenthal, 16 Aug. 1888, soliciting comments on it, in Bernhard Felsenthal Papers, box 2158, file "Letters to and from Felsenthal, 1869–1907," AJA.

11. The Sonneschein letterbooks contain scores of letters to Wise, many of which clearly describe Sonneschein's attachment to him. Cf., e.g., his letters to Wise, 21 Dec. 1882, 11 Apr. 1883, and 20 June 1884, letterbook 2. See too his letter to Isaac M. Wise, 19 Apr. 1886, letterbook 3.

12. See his letter to Victor Rottman, 15 Oct. 1885, letterbook 3, and *Jewish Tribune*, 20 Feb. 1880, 6 Oct. 1882, 6 July 1882. Sonneschein insisted that his later Sunday lectures at Temple Israel from the fall of 1886 to 1891 were just that: lectures, and not a Sabbath prayer service. See the Constitution of Temple Israel which allowed for Sunday lectures, but which declared that they would interfere neither with the integrity nor the sanctity of the historical Sabbath, letterbook 3, Oct. 1886. Sonneschein consistently opposed transferring the main Sabbath services from Saturday to Sunday. In the 1870s, he opposed Kohler on this issue (cf. *Jewish Times*, 17 Apr. 1874, and *American Israelite*, 1 May 1874), while in the 1880s he reaffirmed his opposition to the transfer of the Jewish Sabbath to Sunday. See the *Proceedings of the Pittsburgh Rabbinical Conference*, p. 41; see Sonneschein's Sunday lectures, "Our New Institution: Sunday Lectures, Their Scope and Aim," 31 Oct. 1886, pp. 11–14, and "The Sunday Sabbath," 15 Nov. 1887, esp. pp. 18–19. On the general subject of the Sunday Sabbath, see Kerry Orlitzky, "The Sunday-Sabbath Controversy in Judaism," (rabbinic thesis, Hebrew Union College, 1981).

13. Historically, a contemporary's reaction to Adler actually constituted a religious barometer as to where one stood on the religious spectrum of American Judaism, and hence Sonneschein's numerous sympathetic comments on Adler through the mid-1880s testify to his radical religious orientation. Whereas Wise and most Reformers regarded Adler as a treacherous apostate, Sonneschein, like Rabbi Bernhard Felsenthal of Chicago, for a time understood ethical culture to be a vindication of Reform Judaism and a legitimate religious model for what he hoped Reform as a whole would yet become. For Wise's views on Adler, see Kraut, "Judaism Triumphant," pp. 212–16; for Felsenthal and other reactions to Adler, see Kraut, *From Reform Judaism*, pp. 150–65. Sonneschein's early attitudes to Adler can be traced through the *Jewish Tribune*, 28 May 1880, 4 June 1880, 1 Oct. 1880. In the beginning of 1883, Sonneschein held a seven-part series on Ethical Culture which he published in the *Jewish Tribune* between 10 Jan. 1883 and 9 Mar. 1883. In the 4 May 1883 issue, Sonneschein actually implied that Adler was returning to Judaism, but on 1 June 1883 he published an open letter to Adler, to which he never received a reply, asking the Ethical Culture founder whether or not he stood outside of Judaism. This letter was occasioned by the opening of the St. Louis Ethical Culture Society in which some of his own congregants were involved. Indeed, because of the society's presence in St. Louis, Sonneschein periodically received queries as to the difference between Ethical Culture and Reform Judaism, and he felt compelled to respond. See his Sunday lecture, "The Attitude of Judaism towards the Ethical Culture Society," 27 Feb. 1887. Ultimately what separated Sonneschein from Adler, given the antiritualistic streak in both, were their differing views on the meaning and ongoing relevance of ethical monotheism defined as the essence of Judaism. On this point, refer to Sonneschein's critique of Ethical Culture's concept of conscience, which the rabbi felt had no meaning without God, in his Sunday lecture "The Attitude of Judaism towards the Ethical Culture Society," 27 Feb. 1887, p. 22. Sonneschein in this address rendered the same judgment on Ethical Culture that Wise had rendered on Christianity: Whatever was true in it was not new to Judaism; whatever was new, was not true.

14. See the letter of Sonneschein to Wise, 21 Dec. 1882, letterbook 2. See, too, David Philipson, *My Life as American Jew* (Cincinnati: J. G. Kidd and Son, 1941), pp. 10, 12.

BENNY KRAUT

15. *Die Deborah*, 29 May 1874 and 1 Jan. 1875.

16. Refer to his letter to Bernhard Felsenthal, 4 Jan. 1884, letterbook 2. "You do injustice to Wise. It would be the time now that we, *who are all of the same opinion*, should come to an understanding. Call it a 'Conference.' What is in a name: Shall I play go-between between you and Wise? Not as an *actor*, but as your *friend?*" See too *Jewish Tribune*, 22 Jan. 1893. Henry Gersoni attacked Sonneschein for defending Wise, *Jewish Tribune*, 17 Dec. 1880, and Moritz Ellinger, another foe of Wise, earlier mocked Sonneschein and his literary journal *Die Wahrheit* in his *Jewish Times*, 17 Mar. 1871. See Kraut, "Judaism Triumphant," pp. 219–22, for a discussion of Wise's reactions to Sonneschein's Unitarian affair. Wise also defended Sonneschein during his December 1883 Christmas-Hanukkah controversy, *American Israelite*, 28 Dec. 1883. See letter of Sonneschein to Wise, 30 Dec. 1883, letterbook 2, thanking the Cincinnatian for his public support. See text below and n. 20. See M. A. Rosenblatt's glowing tribute to Sonneschein's achievements for the Temple and for Jewish-Christian relations in the *Jewish Free Press*, 7 May 1886. See too president Barney Hysinger's report at the annual meeting of Shaare Emeth in *Proceedings of the Fourteenth Meeting of the Members of the Congregation of Shaare Emeth for the year 1882–1883, March 26th, 1883* (St. Louis, 1883) p. 7. See the Binswanger diaries, 7 June 1870 and 16 Sept. 1871.

17. See Sonneschein's statement to his congregation as reported in the *Missouri Republican*, 20 June 1886.

18. *Jewish Free Press*, 23 Apr. 1886 and 2 July 1886; Binswanger diary, 8 Jan. 1871. Sonneschein did, however, alienate one man during the 1870s who later became a primary opponent. Augustus Binswanger, a future member of Shaare Emeth's board, who ultimately rose to the position of president of the Union of American Hebrew Congregations, began as Solomon's friend. Nevertheless, he became a social intimate of Rosa, who not only steered him to the woman he eventually married but also confided in him about her husband's sexual indiscretions. During the turmoil of the 1880s, Binswanger became a leading and vociferous critic of Sonneschein, almost entirely owing to personal reasons. Religiously, he was as radical as Sonneschein.

19. On the rabbis as "hired help," cf. Naomi Cohen, "Sermons and the Contemporary World: Two American Jewish Sources," in *Contemporary Jewry: Studies in Honor of Moshe Davis*, ed. Geoffrey Wigoder (Jerusalem: The Institute of Contemporary Jewry, 1984), pp. 25–26. The clash between laymen and rabbis spilled over into noncongregational frameworks as well, such as in the reconstituted Jewish Publication Society in 1888. See Jonathan D. Sarna's forthcoming history of the Jewish Publication Society, especially chapter 2.

20. One can trace the Christmas-Hanukkah furor in the pages of Sonneschein's *Jewish Tribune*, which published not only local but national reactions in its issues of 28 Dec. 1883, 4 Jan. 1884, and 11 Jan. 1884. Sonneschein was convinced that his enemies on the Shaare Emeth board, along with Rabbi Moritz Spitz, moderate Reform rabbi of St. Louis's Congregation Beth El, his friend and local coeditor of the *Jewish Tribune*, stirred up an unwarranted commotion. See his letters to Isaac M. Wise, 30 Dec. 1883, and to De Sola Mendes in the *American Hebrew*, 14 Jan. 1884, both in letterbook 2. See Sonneschein's later defense of his Christmas-Hanukkah remarks, especially in light of

the fact that he was unwilling to consider transferring his Jewish Sabbath to Sunday, in his lecture "The Sunday Sabbath," 15 Nov. 1887, pp. 13–14. On the challenges of Christmas to American Jews, consult Ken White, "American Jewish Responses to Christmas" (rabbinic thesis, Hebrew Union College, 1982). The resignation of Moritz Spitz as coeditor in mid-December of 1883 was interpreted by most people as a sign of his disgust with Sonneschein, but the latter insisted that Spitz had left for other reasons which, if they were made public, would terribly embarrass Spitz. Cf. the *Jewish Tribune*, 4 Jan. 1884, and Sonneschein's letter to Felsenthal, 4 Jan. 1884. Sonneschein's relationship with Spitz was tempestuous to say the least. It was Sonneschein, Spitz's friend while they were still in Europe, who recommended to Spitz that he apply for the St. Louis Beth El pulpit and leave his congregation in Milwaukee, which he did. On Saturday afternoons, after services, they went drinking in St. Louis restaurants. They collaborated on the *Jewish Tribune*, but ultimately Spitz's moderate reforming tendencies, coupled with Sonneschein's own radical ones, caused a severe rupture in relations that frequently gave rise to name calling and heated recriminations. In 1892, Sonneschein and Spitz were finally reconciled, and it was Spitz who was at Sonneschein's deathbed, reciting *Shema Yisrael* with him, who raised money in the St. Louis community for a suitable monument for his friend, and who published obituaries, including his own, praising Sonneschein in the *Jewish Voice*. See a biographical memoir of Moritz Spitz, written by his daughter Alma Spitz. I am extremely grateful to Rabbi Jeffrey Stiffman and to Mrs. Diana J. Kline, chairman of Congregation Shaare Emeth Archives, for having sent me copies of this and other important materials. Aspects of the confrontation between Spitz and Sonneschein, in addition to those manifested in the pages of the *Jewish Tribune*, can be seen in the *Jewish Free Press* (successor to the *Tribune*), 25 Dec. 1885, 3 Sept. and 10 Sept. 1886, and in the *American Hebrew*, 19 Mar. 1886. See too Sonneschein's letter to Leo Wise, 9 Mar. 1891, referring to Spitz's "treachery," and Sonneschein's poignant letter to Spitz, 28 Dec. 1892, suggesting they come together as brothers once again.

21. Sonneschein letter to the synagogue school board, 5 Feb. 1885, letterbook 2. See too *Jewish Free Press*, 6 Mar. 1885.

22. Cf. Sonneschein letter to president Barney Hysinger and the board, 16 Dec. 1885, letterbook 3. See too, *Jewish Free Press*, 26 June 1885, 3 July 1885, 23 Oct. 1885, 6 Nov. 1885, 11 Nov. 1885, 18 Dec. 1885, 25 Dec. 1885, and 1 Jan. 1886.

23. See *Jewish Free Press*, 5 Mar. 1886 and 12 Mar. 1886, and *American Hebrew*, 19 Mar. 1886.

24. Letter of Sonneschein to Barney Hysinger, 1 Apr. 1886, letterbook 3. See *Jewish Free Press*, 2 Apr. 1886, 9 Apr. 1886, 16 Apr. 1886, and 2 July 1886, which reconstructed the whole sequence of events.

25. *Jewish Free Press*, 23 Apr. 1886, 30 Apr. 1886, 7 May 1886, 14 May 1886; *American Hebrew*, 9 Apr. 1886 and 14 May 1886; and *St. Louis Post-Dispatch*, 2 Apr. 1886.

26. *Jewish Free Press*, 23 Apr. 1886, reported fully on the 18 April meeting and printed Sonneschein's remarks verbatim.

BENNY KRAUT

27. Letter to the president and board of trustees and members of the congregation, 23 May 1886, letterbook 3. See too *Jewish Free Press*, 21 May 1886. Also *Jewish Free Press*, 10 Sept. 1886, which indeed commented that very few applications for the job had been received.

28. See the *Jewish Tribune*, 21 Feb. 1881, 6 Oct. 1882, and 17 Aug. 1883.

29. Solomon Schindler wrote a comprehensive letter to Reefer, in which he reconstructs his understanding of the unfolding events, which was published in its entirety in the *Jewish Free Press*, 18 June 1886. See too the *Jewish Free Press*, 28 May 1886.

30. See *Jewish Free Press*, 23 Apr. 1886, 7 May 1886, and 28 May 1886. Sonneschein had been an ardent critic of intermarriage in the 1870s, but in the 1880s he gradually adopted a position which retroactively assented to a civil mixed marriage. He seemed pulled by the contrary needs of maintaining the Jewish group on the one hand and recognizing broad, liberal, humanitarian sentiments on the other. See his pilpulistic but fascinating responsum to a questioner in August 1883 as to whether or not an uncircumcised boy who attends synagogue, who was born to an unconverted gentile woman married to a Jewish male, may be considered a Jew and have a bar mitzvah, *Jewish Tribune*, 12 Aug. 1883, republished in the *Jewish Voice*, 1 Jan. 1909. In his responsum, Sonneschein expressly asserted: "I can under certain conditions, declare myself *B'dayved* in favor of a mixed marriage, though *le'chatchila* I must always, and without any exception, veto and expose it." See too his letter to Jacob Levy, 9 Mar. 1882, letterbook 2, in which Sonneschein claimed it would be suicidal to open the floodgates to intermarriage, but that a truly liberal humanitarian person would advise young people passionately in love to go to a civil court.

31. *Jewish Free Press*, 28 May 1886.

32. This sentence is all the more difficult in light of the question mark with which the sentence ends. Was this punctuation mark a printer's error? Or did he really end the thought with a question mark, and if so, why? Was it because he himself was undecided on the issue, or was it intended to tantalize his audience?

33. For an intriguing analysis of Sonneschein's actions reflecting a spiteful apostate, see the article by Henry Gersoni, Reefer's coeditor of the *Jewish Free Press*, then residing in New York, in *Jewish Free Press*, 18 June 1886.

34. *Jewish Free Press*, 18 June 1886; see too Sonneschein's 30 June 1886 statement. Two influential board members, Nicholas Scharff and Jacob Furth, both antagonists of the rabbi, visited him on 27 May and offered a compromise: they would suppress the Unitarian affair and all testimony pertaining to it on condition that Sonneschein withdraw his candidacy for the vacant rabbinical position. The rabbi scorned the offer.

35. *Jewish Free Press*, 2 July 1886.

36. Dismissing a rabbi was still a grave step. To ensure that their position was fully understood, the eight board members opposing the rabbi issued a circular on 24 June, with the pertinent affidavits attached, to all members of the congregation. They

also sent a separate circular to some of the more important rabbis in the United States, from religious radicals like Emil Hirsch and Kaufmann Kohler to conservatives like Benjamin Szold and Alexander Kohut, soliciting their response to the question whether or not, given the evidence, Sonneschein was fit to occupy a pulpit. This circular, as well as much other Sonneschein-related material also published in the *Jewish Free Press*, can be found in the Benjamin Szold Papers, box 1897, file 1886, in the AJA. According to the *Jewish Free Press*, 11 July 1886, among the rabbis polled were: Kaufmann Kohler, Emil Hirsch, Gustav Gottheil, Alexander Kohut, Benjamin Szold, Max Landsberg, Isaac M. Wise, L. Maier, Isaac L. Leucht, James K. Gutheim, H. P. Mendes, M. Jastrow, M. Samfield, S. Hirsch, Joseph Krauskopf, Jacob Voorsanger, I. Hahn, Isaac Moses, Adolph Moses, and M. Spitz. Some of the extant responses can be found in the *American Hebrew*, 2 July 1886; I. Szold letter to Jacob Furth, 28 June 1886 in the Szold Papers, AJA. On Wise's reactions see *American Israelite*, 2 July 1886 and 8 July 1886; see too the *American Hebrew*'s reactions to Wise's defense of Sonneschein, 23 July 1886. The *Jewish Free Press*, 2 July 1886, contains a complete description of the proceedings of the meeting of 20 June.

37. *Jewish Free Press*, 17 Sept. 1886, and *American Israelite*, 17 Sept. 1886. See too the *Missouri Republican*, 10 Sept. 1886, 11 Sept. 1886.

38. Letter of Isaac M. Wise to David Philipson, 26 Sept. 1886, box 2333, American Jewish Archives. See too the *Missouri Republican*, 26 Sept. 1886 and 27 Sept. 1886.

39. Letter of Kaufmann Kohler to Isaac M. Wise, 11 June 1886, Kohler Correspondence file, folder 1886, AJA.

40. See the address of Sonneschein to the F.R.A. published in the *Proceedings at the Seventh Annual Meeting of the Free Religious Association, May 28, 29, 1874*. (Boston, 1875), pp. 76–81. On Jews and the F.R.A., consult Benny Kraut, "Francis E. Abbot: Perceptions of a Nineteenth Century Religious Radical on Jews and Judaism," in *Studies in the American Jewish Experience*, ed. Jacob R. Marcus and Abraham J. Peck (Cincinnati: American Jewish Archives, 1981), pp. 90–113, and Kraut, "Judaism Triumphant," pp. 194–202. See too Sonneschein's letters to William J. Potter, 10 Apr. 1874 and 8 May 1874, letterbook 1, box X-132.

41. Letters to James Freeman Clarke, 19 Feb. 1886 and 12 Jan. 1887, letterbook 3.

42. Letters to Savage, 30 May 1882, letterbook 2, and 7 Jan. 1887, letterbook 3. See his poem dedicated to Savage, 31 Dec. 1882, letterbook 2.

43. Letter to Robert Collyer, 4 May 1877, letterbook 1.

44. Letters to Jenkin Lloyd Jones, 16 Nov and 30 Nov. 1886 and 17 Jan. 1887, letterbook 3.

45. Letters to William Channing Gannett, 24 May 1881, letterbook 1, and 23 May 1885, 29 Jan. 1886, letterbook 2.

46. Letter to Moncure Conway, 25 Apr. 1883, letterbook 2.

47. Cf. letter to Minot Savage, 30 May 1882, letterbook 2, and his letter to Samuel J. Barrows, editor of the *Christian Register,* 28 Apr. 1886, letterbook 2.

48. See Sonneschein's letter to Eliot, 20 Apr. 1884, letterbook 2. Citation is from Paul C. Nagel, *Missouri: A Bicentennial History* (New York, Norton, 1977), p. 25. On Eliot, see James Noel Primm, *Lion of the Valley: St. Louis, Missouri* (Boulder: Pruett Publishing Company, 1981), pp. 187, 265, 522; Ernest Kirschten, *Catfish and Crystal* (New York: Doubleday and Company, 1970), pp. 335–46.

49. *Jewish Free Press,* 30 June 1886; *Jewish Tribune,* 13 Apr. 1883; *Jewish Free Press,* 6 Nov 1885.

50. Cf. *Die Deborah,* 4 July 1879, 22 Aug. 1879; *Jewish Tribune,* 17 Oct. 1879, 7 May 1880, and 24 Sept. 1880; *Jewish Free Press,* 25 June 1886.

51. *Jewish Tribune,* 16 Jan. 1880.

52. See the critical comments by board member Nicholas Scharff on Sonneschein's excessive appeal to the Unitarians, *Jewish Free Press,* 18 June 1886.

53. Letter to Max Landsberg, 9 Feb. 1885, letterbook 2.

54. Cf. Kraut, "Judaism Triumphant," pp. 179–81.

55. Marion Bell, *Crusade in the City: Revivalism in Nineteenth Century Philadelphia* (Lewisburg: Bucknell University Press, 1977), p. 142. See too pp. 131–39.

56. For an excellent analysis of this theme within the Unitarian movement, consult Conrad Wright's chapter "Saluting the Arriving Movement," in *A Stream of Light,* ed. Conrad Wright (Boston: Unitarian Universalist Association, 1975), pp. 62–94.

57. Robert Allen Campbell, ed., *Campbell's Gazetteer of Missouri,* 2d ed. (St. Louis: R. A. Campbell, 1875), p. 555.

58. See Benny Kraut, "Reform Judaism and the Unitarian Challenge," in *The American Jewish Experience,* ed. Jonathan D. Sarna (New York: Holmes and Meier, 1986), pp. 89–96. Also cf. Naomi W. Cohen, "Sermons and the Contemporary World," p. 38. One fine example of the confusion in the public mind about differences between Unitarianism and Reform Judaism can be seen in the following comment of the *Missouri Republican,* 11 July 1886, on Sonneschein's Unitarian episode:

> Our surprise is not with the Unitarianism of Rabbi Sonneschein, but rather that his congregation should be able to distinguish between Judaism and Unitarianism. It has long seemed to us that the distinctions between Unitarianism and Judaism are so slight, that but for the circumcision only the most acute minds could discuss the essential differences.

59. Originally appearing weekly in the *Jewish Tribune,* starting with 27 Jan. 1881, the lectures were reprinted in serial form by Spitz in his *Jewish Voice,* 13 Nov.–11 Dec. 1908.

60. Wright, *A Stream of Light,* p. 87.

61. Kraut, "Judaism Triumphant," pp. 225–26. Sonneschein published similar

calls in his *Jewish Tribune*, 6 Apr. 1883 and 12 Sept. 1883. On 2 Oct. 1885, Sonneschein replied to a letter from Mrs. Henry Eliot in which he affirmed that contrary to (liberal) Christian suspicions that Judaism is dead, "the Glories of Israel are not past and the freedom of the Jewish faith is *not* gone. The hour is not very far, when that which the most liberal Christians call dead and count among the eternally lost, will appear among the living as their most lively and redeeming helpmeet in history." Letterbook 3. Shortly thereafter he wrote to Victor Rottman, 15 Oct. 1886, that "the time is soon upon us when the Christian will subscribe to and recognize the three principal tenets of Judaism: the Eternal God, the Decalogue as the only religious law, and the Saturday Sabbath as the only authentic Sabbath." Letterbook 3. See, too, Rabbi Bernhard Felsenthal's belief that Jews and Unitarians will unite on Jewish terms, *Jewish Advance*, 19 Dec. 1879.

62. *Jewish Free Press*, 2 July 1886.

63. The *Jewish Free Press* reported in detail on the debates and on the opposition which both the venue and the rabbi's ideas aroused. See the issues of 11 Dec. 1885, 18 Dec. 1885, 25 Dec. 1885, 1 Jan. 1886, 8 Jan. 1886, 15 Jan. 1886, 29 Jan. 1886, 16 Feb. 1886.

64. *Jewish Free Press*, 15 Jan. 1886.

65. This passage is contained in the letter of Sonneschein to Lewis Godlove, 29 Dec. 1885, letterbook 3. Godlove's letter which prompted this reply is not extant. Additional background on this exchange between Godlove and the rabbi can be found in the *Jewish Free Press*, 25 Dec. 1885, which reported on the public disagreement between the two men at the second Friday night debate.

66. Letter to James Freeman Clarke, 19 Feb. 1886, letterbook 3.

67. See Wright, *A Stream of Light*, pp. 62–94; Kraut, "Judaism Triumphant," pp. 202–30; Kraut, "Frances E. Abbot," pp. 92ff.

68. Kraut, "Reform Judaism and the Unitarian Challenge"; Naomi W. Cohen, "The Challenges of Darwinism and Biblical Criticism to American Judaism," *Modern Judaism* 4 (1984): 145–46; Cohen, "Sermons in the Contemporary World," p. 38.

69. *American Hebrew*, 23 July 1886.

70. Wright, *A Stream of Light*, p. 87.

71. Cf. for example, the speech by Savage, cited in Kraut, "Judaism Triumphant," pp. 210–12, which demonstrates how close Savage's views on religion were to those of reformers like Sonneschein and Wise.

72. *Boston Hebrew Observer*, 5 June 1883.

73. *Jewish Tribune*, 28 Sept. 1883.

74. Letter to Leo Wise, 9 Mar. 1891, letterbook 4. Any number of examples demonstrate Sonneschein's unflinching belief in an eternal Supreme Being. Cf. his *Confirmant's Manual: Temple Israel* (St. Louis, 1882), p. 2; his "The Jewish Creed," in *The Great Awakening on Temperance*, ed. J. B. McCullough (St. Louis: Anchor Publish-

ing, 1878), pp. 225–41; his lecture, "Our New Institution: Sunday-Lectures, Their Scope and Aim," 31 Oct. 1886, pp. 13–14.

75. Kraut, *From Reform Judaism*, p. 225. Hirsch, indeed, throughout his life wrestled with the theological issue of the nature of God. Cf. Bernard Martin, "The Social Philosophy of Emil G. Hirsch," *American Jewish Archives* 6 (1954) and his "The Religious Philosophy of Emil G. Hirsch," *American Jewish Archives* 4 (1952).

76. Cohen, "Challenges of Darwinism and Biblical Criticism," pp. 129–30; Kraut, "Reform Judaism and the Unitarian Challenge," pp. 95–96. See too David Strassler, "The Changing Definitions of the 'Jewish People' Concept in the Religious-Social Thought of American Reform Judaism during the Period of the Mass Immigration from East Europe, 1880–1914" (Ph.D. diss., Hebrew University, 1980).

77. Cf. his address at the laying of the cornerstone of Beth El, 4 Aug. 1887, his letter to Joseph Krauskopf, 29 Apr. 1887, letterbook 3, and his letter to Moritz Spitz, 28 Dec. 1982, letterbook 4.

78. My thanks to Professor Jonathan D. Sarna for having alerted me to this fact.

79. See *Year Book of the Central Conference of American Rabbis* 1 (1891): 22, 32.

80. See Rudolph Farber's obituary, 18 Oct. 1908. See too Sonneschein's letter to Henry Berkowitz, 2 Jan. 1889, letterbook 4, in which he commented on his admiration for Reefer who, at that time, functioned as business manager of the Kansas City Jewish newspaper. See too his letter to Moritz Spitz, 28 Dec. 1892, letterbook 4.

12

Intermarriage in the American West: A Historical Perspective

WILLIAM TOLL

A specter is haunting Jewry, the threat of its disintegration through intermarriage. Marshall Sklare, perhaps the most respected sociologist of American Jewry, has written, "Intermarriage is the quintessential dilemma for the American Jew. It calls into question the very basis on which American Jewish life has proceeded—that Jewish survival is possible in an open society." And Calvin Goldscheider has recently added, "No other issue symbolizes more clearly the conflict between universalism and particularism, between the American melting pot and pluralism, between assimilation and ethnic continuity. . . ."[1] The rate of intermarriage between born Jews and others has risen to its highest point in modern times in the United States since 1965, and nowhere higher than in the cities of the American West. Whether this extraordinary development should be considered a unique social phenomenon or the further extension of a postemancipation sense of Jewish identity will be considered later in this paper. Clearly the accelerating rate of intermarriage in America has accompanied other innovations in family life, like divorce and a low birth rate, which Jews under age forty share with most of their gentile counterparts. What may seem a personal disappointment, or even a social peril, to one generation may provide the basis for a new sense of communal identity for its children.

To set the social and personal meaning of intermarriage into a broader context we should first review its development in western Europe and in a new society like the United States since the midnineteenth century. Efforts to explain Jewish intermarriage in central Europe through the Nazi era have usually emphasized the atmosphere of pervasive antisemitism. Jewish young people, given the choice between Jewish and Christian identity, chose the latter in order to avoid stigma and to be able to pursue economic opportunity.[2] In Germany from the 1890s through the 1920s, a period coinciding with the concentration of Jews in the largest cities for three generations and their increased attendance at universities, intermarriage rates did accelerate. From 1901 to 1905, for every one hundred marriages between two Jews in Germany, there were eighteen intermarriages. Calculated differently, 18 Jews out of every 218 (8.5 percent) married non-Jews. By the 1920s, the proportion of intermarriages had tripled, so that for every one hundred marriages between two Jews, there were fifty-four intermarriages.[3] Again calculated individually, 21 percent of the Jews chose a non-Jewish mate.

In France from the 1870s through the 1930s, legal restraints against Jewish access to the civil service, the army, and the universities had been abolished, though social antisemitism persisted. In this ambiguous milieu intermarriage became a minor social drama, and scholars disagree on its incidence. Michael R. Marrus, in his impressive study of French Jewry in the era surrounding the Dreyfus Affair, claims that it was infrequent, while David Weinberg, in his history of Paris Jewry during the 1930s, argues that intermarriage among native French Jewry had been very high since the midnineteenth century.[4] Needless to say, the data are very sketchy.

A new study of Viennese Jewry by Marsha Rozenblit has uncovered curious trends and apparent mixed motives for intermarriage. Austrian law technically forbade intermarriage, so that one of the prospective partners had to choose the religion of the other. Between 1870 and 1910, the number of Jews converting to Christianity for intermarriage increased, but seems to have been only half the rate of that in Berlin. In addition, however, almost half as many Christians converted to Judaism in order to marry,[5] thus revealing more complex social patterns than hitherto imagined. While the individual reasons for intermarriage are not revealed, the social backgrounds of the two groups were sufficiently known to reveal different mobility routes within the Jewish community. The majority of Jews converting to Christianity were men, often civil servants or professionals from middle-class families already residing beyond areas of heavy Jewish residential concentration. Their intermarriage represented a further rise in status for their families from the stigma of Jewish origins. The great majority of Christians converting to Judaism, however, were working-class women who were not deterred by a rise in antisemitism in Vienna. Indeed, they may well have perceived their marriage as an elevation in class status as well as a source of personal stability. Rozenblit suggests most plausibly that individual decisions for intermarriage may simply have reflected the increased incidence of accidental contacts as the Jewish population grew to almost 200,000, or 10 percent of the city's population.[6] But the increased willingness of Jews to seek partners beyond the traditional ethnic community also reflected the greater range of interethnic contacts which occurred because of mobility beyond the ghetto. The pressures of Catholic culture and Austrian law deflected personal choice into patterns of conversion.

In Italy, where Jews have been a tiny minority in modern history, the majority have been members of urban elites in Rome, Milan, Turin, and elsewhere. Among this segment intermarriage has been very common for generations. Current estimates for Milan indicate that half the young Jews intermarry, though the figure is much lower for the much larger Jewish community in Rome.[7] H. Stuart Hughes, in a recent study of Italian Jewish novelists, argues that intermarriage with a Jew constitutes for many Italians an instance of upward social mobility. Mussolini himself, though opposed to his daughter's desire to marry the son of a Jewish army colonel, urged intermarriage as a means of bringing cultural unity to the Italian people.[8] Today, the intermarriage of a Jew does not lead to his separation from the organized Jewish communities.

Explanations of intermarriage in new societies like the United States talked not so much about social status, but about ecological constraints on choice. The very small size of some isolated communities or the proportionally large number of non-Jewish potential spouses in smaller cities were pointed to as understandable temptations.[9] By the mid-1950s students supplemented these corollaries to Frederick Jackson Turner's "Frontier Thesis" by turning to psychological explanations. They emphasized the rebellious character of many persons choosing non-Jewish spouses.[10] The presumption seemed to be that well adjusted persons would recognize the claims of ethnicity on mate selection. The most popular of the psychological explanations had actually been imported from Germany by the émigré psychologist Kurt Lewin. For him, intermarriage represented a form of "self-hatred" that grew from the Jew's stigmatized minority status.[11] However, actual data on Jewish intermarriage in the United States before 1950 are very rare and motives have simply not been investigated.

Nevertheless, when American scholars discussed the small group of the intermarried, they invariably deemed such a choice a personal and social disaster. The majority of the intermarried Jews, they argued, either left the community, created families that would be isolated from it, or would see their marriages end in divorce. Although divorce rates at that time were much higher among the intermarried than among Jews married to one another, the causes were simply a matter of speculation.[12] A small survey of Hillel rabbis in the early 1960s showed that the great majority felt intermarriage must lead to divorce.[13] But as scholars have since learned with the rise of divorce in every segment of American society, the relatively high rate of marital dissolution among the intermarried often has little to do with the differing religious origins of the partners.

Since the majority of persons writing on intermarriage since World War II have been either rabbis or counselors, they have stressed their own professional or personal concerns. The counselors felt a primary obligation to assist young people to find happiness, the rabbis to strengthen the Jewish community; yet neither group could feel exempt from the competing obligation incumbent upon the other. In the mid-1970s Gerald Bubis, director of the School of Jewish Communal Service at the Hebrew Union College in Los Angeles, explained the rabbi's dilemma in the following terms: "The rabbi works toward an accommodation between group expectations and individual demands. He is caught in the clash and conflict which sometimes results, and always must be guided by what's good for Jews and Judaism."[14] Many well-known rabbis have simply resigned themselves to intermarriage as the price Judaism must pay for the protections of a liberal democracy,[15] while some commentators have suggested that perhaps more Jewish education, classes on conversion, or even procedures for arranging contacts between young Jewish men and women, might stimulate a marriage market to stem the tide.[16]

Studies of intermarriage in the American West, however, document such extraordinary changes in the incidence and rate of intermarriage that they require that one think more imaginatively about both motives and consequences. While the data are often sketchy and based on samples which vary in size and reliability, trends everywhere since the late nineteenth century have been higher than in most other locales. Yet communities have been vibrant and civically active. In the

West, despite occasional antisemitism, Jews have not been stigmatized nor have they feared for their civic status. Instead, the marriage between liberal democracy and Jewish settlement has produced a new kind of Jewish identity, of which intermarriage is one characteristic. As Steven Cohen has argued, as Jews have integrated at various contact points into American society, traditional Judaism has been reduced in scope and intensity and major innovations have been made in Jewish practice.[17] Social patterns like intermarriage that horrified one generation become normal to the next without threatening the survival of the community. Almost twenty-five years ago, Judith Kramer and Seymour Leventman noted that in societies like the United States that encourage religious and ethnic diversity and also promote economic growth, the social and cultural synthesis produced by one generation provides merely a point of departure for the next.[18] For one generation, intermarriage may represent the ultimate intrusion of secularism into Jewish family relations. But for the children it usually culminates a series of breaks with the intensive ethnic network begun by the parents. Furthermore, it occurs in a culture that values rather than denigrates Judaism, and this has been nowhere more true than in the West. As I will demonstrate, in the West intermarriage does not require that either partner relinquish social status or civic pride, and as a personal decision, neither partner need feel stigmatized.

Statistical data on intermarriage in the American West are very sketchy, though there is some reason to believe that until World War I it may not have greatly exceeded national trends. A new study of Jews in the West in the nineteenth and early twentieth centuries cites the exotic cases of pack mule traders who married American Indian squaws, and explains these unions as examples of frontier isolation. More importantly, a rate of almost 25 percent is given for Jewish intermarriage in Los Angeles around 1876.[19] If this figure refers to individuals rather than to marriages, it is extremely high. The group to which it would apply would be Jewish pioneer merchants, who would already have relatively high status in their cities, and the motives for intermarriage would largely be a matter of proximity and personal choice. My own work in Portland uncovered only one prominent nineteenth-century Jewish man who married a gentile. Although he was excluded from the synagogue, he participated in civic affairs and was especially active in arranging programs for the Council of Jewish Women. A former mayor of Portland retained membership in the synagogue, but flirted with Unitarianism. He was described by a local gentile judge as "a Jew by race, but he might be called a rationalist. . . . He does not pretend to be a Jew in belief."[20] His sons were educated at Lawrenceville School in New Jersey and drifted away from Portland and the Jewish community.[21]

Documenting intermarriage on a larger scale is more difficult because neither the manuscript census nor marriage licenses record religion, either at birth or at the time of marriage. Marriage records at synagogues, however, may record some instances of intermarriage. Of the 269 marriages recorded at Temple Beth Israel in Portland between November 1884 and August 1912, about 11 percent (most after 1900) may have involved a non-Jew. Only one person was recorded as a convert and thus not technically intermarried. Twenty-eight others, primarily women, had English surnames like Holt, Hamilton, Laurence, Dean, Taylor, Hollister, and McFarlane that could not be traced to local Jewish families. Several of the marriages were civil ceremonies conducted in places like Boise and Lewiston, Idaho; Spokane, Washington; or Baker, Oregon.[22] In each case, though, one of the partners had family ties to Beth Israel and wanted the marriage recorded. Because the bulk of the probable non-Jews in these marriages were women, and because many of the Jewish men resided in remote towns, these unions seemed to follow one regular pattern of Jewish male intermarriage for frontier regions.

Nevertheless, the dominant theme in late nineteenth- and early twentieth-century family formation in the Pacific Northwest, as in San Francisco, was a localized marriage market, with sons and daughters of German or Polish Jewish families marrying one another. Jews were among the pioneer merchants on the Pacific slope, and the more successful were accepted into the fraternal and civic institutions of the developing elite. But they expected to have social institutions of their own. Intermarriage for most would not enhance their already high social status, nor necessarily increase their wealth. Their names already appeared in elite directories, their synagogues stood adjacent to those of elite Protestant churches, and their rabbis shared pulpits with liberal ministers.[23] The Jewish elite in the West was maintained through an elaborate institutional network, for women as well as for men, created largely by the second generation between the mid-1880s and 1910. It rested ultimately on an interlocking mercantile supply network with its hub in San Francisco. Just as the pioneer merchants before the 1870s had returned to German villages very often for brides, so the young men of the 1890s and 1900s turned to the regional supply center to marry. The letters of the merchant and philanthropist Ben Selling to his cousins and friends in remote towns throughout the Pacific Northwest are filled with gossip about impending engagements and marriages, and they were virtually all within the local elite.[24] After 1900, an increasing proportion of marriages was between residents of Portland and San Francisco, thus suggesting that deliberate efforts were being made to extend the Jewish marriage market to a wider region.[25] Perhaps the completion of the railroad between Portland and San Francisco in the early 1890s and the improved economic conditions after 1900 spurred these contacts. But between 1903 and 1910, the Levi, Ackerman, Sonnenberg, and Harris men of San Francisco came to Portland to marry Hirsch, Friendly, Blumenthal, and Lippitt women.

The demographic decline of German Jewish families which occurred after 1900 was not an outcome of wide-scale intermarriage, despite the undocumented figure for Los Angeles. Instead, men and women decided either to limit family size or not to marry at all. Second-generation Jewish women of German descent married at a higher age and had far fewer children than had their immigrant mothers. And many of their sisters, brothers, and cousins never married. In Portland, a pattern emerged similar to that in midnineteenth-century Germany, in which fully 17 percent of the second generation women and 13 percent of the men remained spinsters and bachelors. Often unmarried sisters and brothers shared the parental house or apartments in fashionable hotels. When a few elderly nieces of such unmarried persons were interviewed, they indicated that their maiden aunts had never considered intermarriage. One suggested that perhaps her aunts had never found men to match their father in determination and achievement. Several elderly bachelors from remote towns claimed they never had the time to marry. Instead, they found in bachelorhood or spinsterhood in companionship with their siblings a comfortable form of existence.[26]

The years from 1910 through 1945 saw western Jewish communities dominated demographically by immigrants of eastern European background, and then by their children. Subsequent data collected for cities like Los Angeles and San Francisco indicate that their older Jewish residents had very low rates of intermarriage, which did not differ from rates elsewhere in the country.[27] Beginning with the post–World War II period, the local Jewish Welfare Federations began to gather data to assess social needs so that their resources might be more efficiently allocated. Initially, intermarriage was not even considered worth examining. Where data were gathered, it was not correlated with the social background of the intermarried Jews or of their gentile partners. A 1947 statistical study in Portland, for example, was interested in the migration of Jews around the city, and in the age profile of Jews in different neighborhoods, because the second generation had moved so rapidly away from the immigrant district, with its settlement house, Jewish old age home, B'nai B'rith community center, and synagogues. The major concern was where to relocate resources, and no inquiry was made about intermarriage.[28] A 1951 survey of the Jewish population of Oakland included a question on intermarriage in the interview schedule, but no data were presented on the subject in the final report.[29]

Studies of Los Angeles in 1953 and of Long Beach in 1962 by Fred Massarik finally began to gather systematic data on the subject and to infer a few relationships between intermarriage and changes in local Jewish communities. The Los Angeles study, for example, indicated, first, that the local Jewish community with a population of over 315,000 was now the second largest in the country, and that it was rapidly growing. In a sample of some 600 households intermarriage was tested against what was called "religious identification," which meant the observance or nonobservance of a set of religious rituals. Among the 400 households that considered themselves "observant," only 1 percent were intermarried, but among the approximately 200 households which considered themselves "unobservant" almost 12 percent had intermarried, a proportion well above the national average at the time.[30] Having defined Jewishness as a religious affiliation marked by degrees of piety, Massarik was not surprised to find that the least pious were the most likely to defect.

A further breakdown according to geographic district, however, suggested an acceleration of intermarriage rates according to generation and income. In the oldest immigrant districts like Boyle Heights and City Terrace, intermarriage was virtually unknown. In other areas of early Jewish settlement like Beverly-Fairfax and Wilshire, rates were well under the national average. In the newer and wealthier districts like Beverly Hills and in the new suburb of Glendale, however, rates reached from 10.4 percent to almost 15 percent.[31] The study, however, did not directly correlate either generation, occupation, or income to intermarriage, though data suggested that the wealthier element in

Beverly Hills and the young upwardly mobile couples settling in the San Fernando Valley were over twice as likely to intermarry as second-generation middle-class people in older Jewish districts.

The Long Beach study of 4,450 households (about 14,500 persons) did not break the population into districts, but instead indicated an overall intermarriage rate of 9 percent, about the same as in nearby Los Angeles suburbs like Mar Vista and South Los Angeles, but substantially lower than for the San Fernando Valley. Again, intermarriage as a subject was not discussed in detail, but a clue to the social background was provided by forms of Jewish identification and income. The largest proportion of local Jews identified themselves as Conservative, and the next largest as Reform, while fewer than 5 percent of the household heads considered themselves Orthodox. And at a time when $10,000 a year was considered a solid middle-class income, 61.6 percent of Long Beach Jewish households fell below that figure. Only 9.5 percent earned more than $20,000. These characteristics suggest a predominantly second- and third-generation community whose denominational breakdown and rate of intermarriage were not very different from the suburban neighborhoods of Providence, Rhode Island, studied by Goldstein and Goldscheider at the same time.[32]

With a Massarik study of San Francisco, its peninsular suburbs, and Marin County in 1959, a very different picture began to emerge. Both intermarriage rates and those American-born Jews failing to identify with any denomination seemed so high that over the next decade Jewish spokesmen throughout the country commented ominously on these findings as a portent of the future. In San Francisco, which had a Jewish population of 46,000 and where over 13 percent of the population still considered itself Orthodox, 17.2 percent of the households were intermarried. In the more affluent peninsula communities, like Menlo Park and Palo Alto, where the Jewish population now reached 15,000, only 3 percent of whom considered themselves Orthodox, intermarriage characterized 20 percent of the couples. And in Marin County, with a small population of about 2,700 Jews and where only 1 percent considered themselves Orthodox, 43 percent did not identify with any Jewish denomination and fully 37 percent of the households were intermarried.[33] Regrettably, the author did not correlate intermarriage with social or economic variables nor did he directly measure its incidence in different neighborhoods, despite the fact that in 1959 San Francisco had an extraordinary proportion of older Jews compared with twenty years previously and with surveys of other western cities. Nevertheless, it seemed clear that Orthodoxy and very low rates of intermarriage could be associated with the downtown neighborhoods where so many older and smaller households lived. In the newer districts like the Western Addition and Park Merced where children were far more prominent, the intermarriage rate must have been substantially higher, perhaps approaching levels akin to those in Marin County. Though Massarik did not guess at the causes of intermarriage, general surveys in the 1960s attributed the higher rate to San Francisco's special status as a national center for persons in professional and managerial employment, an occupational stratum which was growing rapidly and which was identified as the one which had broken away from the Jewish community in the greatest number of ways.[34]

A follow-up study of Oakland, Berkeley, and the East Bay completed in 1968 demonstrated that while rates of intermarriage were gradually increasing, they were conjoined with two conflicting patterns: secularization and conversion to Judaism. Secularization had been measured in prior studies through issues like changing patterns of religious observance, nonaffiliation with synagogues, and membership in non-Jewish organizations. But this was the first study of a western city in which conversion to Judaism emerged as a significant new trend. In Oakland, where the population had grown very little since 1951, the proportion of married people and especially widows was higher than elsewhere in the East Bay, while the proportion of single people, including children, was substantially lower. Likewise, the intermarriage rate was about 10 percent, about the same as Long Beach and what it had been in Beverly Hills almost a generation before. In Berkeley, however, not only had the Jewish population tripled since 1951, but its proportion of single persons, including children, was more in line with that of the other expanding Jewish communities in the East Bay. Its intermarriage rate of 16 percent was about the same as San Francisco's. An additional question, however, discovered that many of the born Jews, as well as persons born into another religion but currently heading households containing Jews, now considered themselves to have no religious affiliation.[35] Obviously, the results reflected a student population, many of whom were influenced by radical political ideologies. But it also included many young married professionals. Were their opinions a fringe or a portent?

Apparently running counter to this trend, however, was the finding that almost 6 percent of heads of households had not been born Jewish but had converted. (Whether any nonheads of households had converted was not recorded.) Any implications (or reasons) for this finding were not discussed. Interestingly, Goldstein and Goldscheider had also encountered conversion in their study of the much older Jewish community of Providence, Rhode Island, in 1963. Perhaps because it had previously been so rare, they found that the rate of conversion was increasing much more rapidly than even the rising intermarriage rate. Without examining how converts or their spouses defined or felt about being Jewish, the authors moved to a social or cultural conclusion. With substantial gratification they observed that Judaism had achieved an elevated status as a religion in America and they found also that most children of mixed marriages were being raised as Jews.[36] Their findings were then corroborated by the National Jewish Population Study in 1972, which found that 27 percent of intermarrying gentile women had converted, and that most children of intermarrying Jewish women were being raised as Jews.[37]

The most recent studies, those of Phoenix and of Denver, move us into a different social world entirely. By comparison, two studies of Boston in 1965 and 1975 showed gradual and predictable increases in the level of education, especially graduate school, decreases in ritual observance, shifts from independent businessmen to salaried employment, and substantial increases in intermarriage.[38] In particular, salaried professionals, who had had a minuscule intermarriage rate of 1 percent in 1965, had increased to 8 percent in 1975, while salaried workers had increased from 3 percent to 20 percent. But Boston was an old and large Jewish community, segmented into many social clusters, from Orthodox immigrants to transient professionals attracted to the many local universities. Phoenix and Denver by contrast were largely new communities for Jews. The surveys revealed that while Denver-Boulder had over 42,000 Jews and the Phoenix area over 43,000 full-time Jewish residents, over 50 percent in Denver and over 60 percent in Phoenix had arrived no more than ten years prior to the respective surveys.[39] In size and social composition both the Denver and Phoenix communities offer important points of comparison with the San Francisco–area Jewry studied by Massarik almost twenty-five years before. All three were virtually identical in size and were diffused over the territory of the urban area, though each had some significant clustering. None had an intensively Jewish neighborhood, though Denver had had a famous area of second settlement for the immigrant generation before World War I.

All three had large contingents of children, with Phoenix (26 percent) slightly higher than San Francisco, and Denver (21 percent) slightly lower. In addition, the aged, persons over sixty-five, were about 5 percent lower than for San Francisco, even though Phoenix is a national retirement center.[40] But where rates of intermarriage seemed exceptionally high in San Francisco when almost 20 percent of the households were intermarried, the rates in contemporary Phoenix and Denver, especially for persons under age forty, are dramatically higher still. In conjunction with other changes in family size and composition, they indicate how an inner revolution has affected Jewish communities in the American West.

Where the study of San Francisco simply noted as anomalous that intermarriage was exceptionally high, the Denver study from the beginning treated intermarriage as an aspect of new family types. It separated the population into the intermarried, those "living together," the divorced, the single parents, and "multiple households." It contains a special section entitled, "Marriage, Re-marriage, and Intermarriage." Within the family section of the Phoenix study, intermarriage was the only special topic, in addition to the general outline of varying family structure. Intermarriage loomed large because in Phoenix 24 percent and in Denver 30 percent of all marriages are between born Jews and non-Jews. But this already high figure includes all couples, including the large contingent of retired people, among whom in Phoenix 85 percent of the men and 95 percent of the women are or were married to another Jewish person. Likewise in Denver, for persons fifty years of age and older, 85 percent of the couples include two born Jews. Among the younger cohorts the intermarriage picture is starkly different. For persons in their thirties in both cities, about half the marriages include a born Jew and a born gentile. For persons in their twenties in both cities, the intermarriage rate for individuals rose to 43 percent. This is 10 percent higher than the National Jewish Population Survey reported in 1972. To refine the impact of intermarriage on the religious character of the household, both studies then identified gentile partners who had converted to Judaism. For those in their thirties, 17 percent in Phoenix and 13.4 percent in Denver had married a convert to Judaism. For those in their twenties the figures were much lower, but many gentiles, women especially, convert to Judaism at a later stage in the life cycle.[41] For both cities the intermarriage rates among the young are higher than for Weimar Germany, which in the past had been taken as the measure for Jewish communities in the throes of disintegration.

How are we to interpret the rising tide of intermarriage? First, it seems clear that trends in the West do not differ in direction from trends elsewhere. The San Francisco survey of 1959 yielded intermarriage rates which did not differ markedly from those for Washington, D.C., in 1956. Sociologists like C. Bezalel Sherman and Albert Gordon pointed to the similar white collar occupational structure of the two cities, which because of their high proportion of salaried professionals attracted persons who in smaller numbers were everywhere prone to break from the ethnic community's social conventions.[42] A thorough study of Melbourne, Australia, Jewry in the mid-1960s demonstrated that college education more than any other variable fostered dramatically more liberal attitudes on all aspects of gentile-Jewish interaction. A college education virtually reversed the proportion of persons who had gentile friends, who disparaged Jewish parochial schools, who joined non-Jewish organizations, and who did not oppose intermarriage.[43]

Second, the surveys of Denver and Phoenix indicate that among larger Jewish communities in the American West a similar process of secularization has produced young people especially who perceive Jewishness very differently than was true twenty years ago. In a paper comparing Jewish with Japanese marriage patterns in the American West, Paul Spickard has catalogued those sociological variables that predisposed one generation, compared with its immediate predecessors, to widen the boundaries for selecting suitable mates. Because both Japanese and Jewish immigrants valued education, each succeeding generation increased its attendance at college, and in a society that progressively accepted minorities, it found more things in common with young people beyond their respective groups and less with provincials within them. Third-generation Jews, for example, were hardly aware of the ancestral tensions between Lithuanian and Ukrainian Jews.[44] Indeed, in West Coast cities like Los Angeles and Portland the immigrant *landsmanshaftn*, which institutionalized provincial European loyalties after resettlement in major eastern cities, seem never to have been created.[45] Instead, men and women founded benevolent societies to provide health and death benefits and to make interest-free loans to any Jew who wished to join. So from the beginning in the West provincial barriers within immigrant Jewry had been relegated to informal family traditions. Spickard also noted that Jews and Japanese had accepted the racial hierarchy of American culture. Although as late as 1970 each group was most likely to marry endogamously, when they did marry "out" they selected white Protestants, then Catholics, then "Orientals" (for the Japanese this most frequently meant Chinese), and least frequently blacks.[46]

Spickard's argument, however, slides over several points which provide a more complex meaning to the acceleration of Jewish intermarriage. First, he assumes that American Jews are above all an ethnic group. In fact, however, what permits continuity in Jewish life despite recurrent crises is the constant tension between Jewry as a vaguely defined cultural entity and Judaism as a religious ideology which gives a historically conscious people a sense of moral purpose.[47] Because Jews as a cultural entity have also defined themselves through a religious ideology, non-Jews can "convert." Both born Jews and converts can interdict a seemingly inevitable process of assimilation with emotionally satisfying innovative ritual forms. Indeed, early-twentieth-century rabbis in the West often gave much publicity to the capacity of Judaism to adjust to rational philosophies and to develop aesthetically pleasing ritual.

Persons raised in an intensely ethnic Jewish world and caught in an era of major social transition, however, are often not clear about how to interpret the ambiguity of the Jewish sense of self. For example, as sophisticated a sociologist as Marshall Sklare and as tolerant a rabbi and counselor as Albert Gordon opposed intermarriage vehemently, yet felt incapable of commenting on the increased incidence of conversion.[48] One suspects that their reticence sprang from their own ethnic sense of Jewishness, and Sklare in particular emphasized how parents felt that intermarriage, regardless of conversion, violated their ethnically bound sense of family. In a similar vein a new study of Jewish identity in France demonstrates that nonobservant Jewish shopkeepers in provincial towns could not conceive of a convert as an authentic Jew, while more sophisticated Parisian Orthodox Jews said they would welcome an observant convert as one of their own. Many of these Orthodox Jews had recently intensified their practices, and the author concluded that "the fact that some Jewish groups have perpetuated or rediscovered certain specific aspects of their cultural tradition suggests that intellectual consciousness is an essential ingredient of cultural perpetuation and *renewal*, and that different cultures lend themselves in different degrees to preservation and *reinterpretation* in the context of industrial society."[49] (Emphasis added.)

A second critical limitation of Spickard's analysis is his indifference to what specifically remains of Jewish identity for the intermarried. He recognizes the various poles around which the identities of third- and fourth-generation American Jews can turn, but he does not examine the effects of mobility on the subjective meaning of the Jewish component. Will Herberg and Marshall Sklare by the late 1950s had both noted how religion had replaced ethnicity as the basis for social identity in general in America.[50] However, for them religion itself had become a social, that is, still an ethnic, rather than a spiritual experience. Their assessment minimized the continuing tension between the religious and secular sense of self, yet Herberg was calling for a spiritual revitalization. More recently, Milton Plesur has perceptively noted that with the move of the third generation to the suburbs, Jewishness became a fragment of identity associated with specific religious acts. It no longer pervades social contacts and it is not a spontaneous expression of the self.[51]

What remains of Jewish religious expression is directly related to moments in the life cycle that tie generations together. Recent sociological studies demonstrate that Judaism remains identified with the home and synagogue and is most intensively expressed by middle-aged parents and their school-age children.[52] Most generally, conscious efforts to behave Jewishly are now approached primarily through synagogue activity rather than through spontaneous, exclusively Jewish social intercourse, the reverse of the case for the immigrant generation and their children. Yet because the second generation had grown indifferent to ritual observance in the home, many of their children did not regard Jewish identity as important when choosing a marriage partner with whom they would build their own families. However, the strong affective ties which have held Jewish families together have led most intermarried persons to want to provide their own children with a moral identity tied to their own psychological roots.[53] As one person, the graduate of an Orthodox yeshivah and now a thoroughly secularized psychological counselor, put it, he remains connected to his early training and he believes that his daughter should understand the compassion and social conscience that Judaism taught to him. In a view that he well recognizes as "irrational" and perhaps contradictory, he wants his daughter to understand the cultural roots of his own motivation, but not necessarily to join a Jewish community, which he associates with compulsive ritual.[54]

While a typology of motives for intermarriage can be constructed, as J. S. Slotkin did over forty years ago, the extraordinary increase in the phenomenon suggests that today most intermarried persons are not expressing antisocial or deviant behavior related to personality disorders. Indeed, Slotkin himself found that about half of his sample simply felt themselves indifferent to the view that a concern for Jewish destiny should limit their marital choice.[55] Interviews today suggest that intermarried persons reflect the same broad range of attitudes toward religion that one finds in the general population of the same age, but that most of them perceive the ethnic network as constrictive. What seems vital for intermarried third- and even fourth-generation Jews is not some sentimentalized "symbolic ethnicity," as Herbert Gans has argued.[56] Instead, the intermarried who remain serious about religion (at the appropriate stage in the life cycle) are searching for myths to transmit an ethical education across secularized generations. By 1971, Bernard Lazerwitz noted that Slotkin's emphasis on deviance had become archaic and that a large number of intermarried persons now retained relationships with the Jewish community. They were often aided by a spouse who had converted in order to join what he termed the "religio-ethnic" community. Indeed, Lazerwitz concluded, and both Arnold Schwartz and Steven Cohen agreed, that intermarriage as such did not threaten the Jewish community because it was only a symptom of a growing dissatisfaction with exclusively Jewish social affiliations that had marked the previous generation.[57] Cohen found that the younger the person in both the second and third generations, the higher the proportion failing to join Jewish organizations but maintaining membership in secular organizations, having many gentile friends, and intermarrying.[58] The Denver and Phoenix studies verify these findings.

Rather than attempt to create a new typology of the intermarried on the basis of a small sample of interviews, I instead wish to present a general hypothesis about the meaning of intermarriage to those concerned. The interviews with the intermarried (including a few with persons who spontaneously converted to Judaism though their spouses were not Jewish) dramatized primarily how Judaism and Jewishness are moving rapidly through an intergenerational crisis, accentuated by the open social structure of western cities. Persons raised in the period from the 1930s through the early 1950s, especially in major urban centers, found social cohesion in intensive neighborhoods, extended family contacts, and a Jewish business network. Today, however, young Jewish adults, especially in western cities, perceive family as a set of nuclear units and approach Jewishness through a set of institutions to which each person can owe allegiance as conscience and family needs dictate. Only at certain points in the life cycle does contact with tradition seem necessary. And if parents require a ceremony that satisfies their expectations, they seem to question the freedom of conscience which led children away from tradition in the first place. Among the interviewees this led some to a "nondenominational" wedding which neither partner felt to be morally satisfying.[59] In other cases a hurried conversion of the gentile partner under intellectually dishonest circumstances accentuated the intergenerational misunderstanding.[60] But when the married couple must face the moral education and historical positioning of their own children, a new understanding of Jewishness arises. At this point a new religious approach to Jewishness is worked out, sometimes in *ḥevrot*, often through learning with the children.

The high rates of intermarriage and the increased incidence of conversion indicate that young people of mixed parentage are a growing proportion of contemporary Jewry. Major segments of Jewry, perhaps especially in the West, can best be conceived of as persons held together by a sense of ethical need. Put another way, the identity of American Jews depends decreasingly on shared ancestry and "symbolic ethnicity" and depends increasingly on a shared belief that a religious tradition can bring spiritual buoyancy to segmented personalities.

NOTES

1. Marshall Sklare, *America's Jews* (New York: Random House, 1971), p. 193; Calvin Goldscheider and Alan S. Zuckerman, *The Transformation of the Jews* (Chicago: University of Chicago Press, 1984), p. 178.

2. Uriel Tal, *Christians and Jews in Germany: Religion, Politics and Ideology in the Second Reich, 1870–1914* (Ithaca: Cornell University Press, 1975), p. 291; Ismar Schorsch, *Jewish Reactions to German Anti-Semitism, 1870–1914* (New York: Columbia University Press, 1972), pp. 5, 14–15, 138, 143; Marjorie Lamberti, *Jewish Activism in*

Imperial Germany: The Struggle for Civil Equality (New Haven: Yale University Press, 1978), p. 179; Daniel I. Niewyk, *The Jews in Weimar Germany* (Baton Rouge: Louisiana State University Press, 1980), p. 96.

3. Niewyk, *Jews in Weimar Germany*, p. 98. Louis A. Berman, *Jews and Intermarriage: A Study in Personality and Culture* (New York: T. Yoseloff, 1968), p. 123, cites intermarriage data.

4. Michael R. Marrus, *The Politics of Assimilation: A Study of the French Jewish Community at the Time of the Dreyfus Affair* (New York: Oxford University Press, 1971), pp. 60–63; David H. Weinberg, *A Community on Trial: The Jews of Paris in the 1930s* (Chicago: University of Chicago Press, 1977), pp. 48–50.

5. Marsha L. Rozenblit, *The Jews of Vienna, 1868–1914: Assimilation and Identity* (Albany: State University of New York Press, 1984), pp. 129, 140.

6. Ibid., pp. 5, 138–42.

7. S. Della Pergola, *Jewish and Mixed Marriages in Milan, 1901–1968* (Jerusalem: Institute for Contemporary Jewry, Hebrew University, 1972), pp. 24, 37, 43, 47–48; Della Pergola, "A Note on Marriage Trends among Jews in Italy," *Jewish Journal of Sociology* 14 (1972): 198–200.

8. H. Stuart Hughes, *Prisoners of Hope: The Silver Age of Italian Jews* (Cambridge: Harvard University Press, 1983), p. 27; Meir Michaelis, *Mussolini and the Jews: German-Italian Relations and the Jewish Question* (London and Oxford: Clarendon Press, 1978), p. 33.

9. Berman, *Jews and Intermarriage*, pp. 86, 93; Peter I. Rose, *Mainstream and Margins: Jews, Blacks and Other Americans* (New Brunswick: Transaction Books, 1983), pp. 56–58; I. Harold Scharfman, *Jews on the Frontier* (Chicago: Henry Regnery, 1977), pp. 280–81.

10. The literature on intermarriage as adolescent rebellion is criticized in Berman, *Jews and Intermarriage*, pp. 112–13, 118–19.

11. Kurt Lewin, *Resolving Social Conflicts: Selected Papers on Group Dynamics* (New York: Harper, 1948), pp. 186–89; Albert I. Gordon, *Intermarriage: Interfaith, Interracial, Interethnic* (Boston: Beacon Press, 1964), p. 63, noted the decline of self-hatred in the 1960s because of an increased mood of interethnic tolerance. Whether Jewish self-hatred ever existed as a social phenomenon in the American West is unclear. I have found no evidence that it did.

12. Gordon, *Intermarriage*, p. 4.

13. Berman, *Jews and Intermarriage*, p. 178; Gordon, *Intermarriage*, p. 196.

14. Gerald D. Bubis, "Intermarriage, the Rabbi and the Jewish Communal Worker," in *Serving the Jewish Family*, ed. Bubis (New York: Ktav Publishing House, 1977), p. 72.

15. Comments of Rabbi Judah Cahn are quoted in Arnold Schwartz, "Intermarriage in the United States," *American Jewish Yearbook, 1970* (Philadelphia: Jewish

Publication Society, 1970), p. 101; Robert Gordis, *The Root and the Branch: Judaism and the Free Society* (Chicago: University of Chicago Press, 1962), p. 132, states opposition to intermarriage as a Jewish concern to preserve its traditions and to avoid "indifference to religion."

16. Stuart E. Rosenberg, *The Search for Jewish Identity in America* (New York: Doubleday Anchor Books, 1965), pp. 275–76; Erich Rosenthal, "Jewish Intermarriage in Indiana," *American Jewish Yearbook, 1967* (Philadelphia: Jewish Publication Society, 1967), pp. 263–64.

17. Steven M. Cohen, *American Modernity and Jewish Identity* (New York: Tavistock Publications, 1983), p. 37.

18. Judith Kramer and Seymour Leventman, *Children of the Gilded Ghetto: Conflict Resolutions of Three Generations of American Jews* (New Haven: Yale University Press, 1961), p. 4. Cohen, *American Modernity*, p. 21, comments on the emergence of "the generation" as a sociological concept.

19. The scholarly volumes are Albert Vorspan and Lloyd Gartner, *History of the Jews of Los Angeles* (San Marino: Henry E. Huntington Library, 1970); Allen D. Breck, Jr., *The Centennial History of the Jews of Colorado, 1859–1959* (Denver: Hirschfeld Press, 1960); William Toll, *The Making of an Ethnic Middle Class: Portland Jewry over Four Generations* (Albany: State University of New York Press, 1982); Harriet and Fred Rischlin, *Pioneer Jews: A New Life in the Far West* (Boston: Houghton Mifflin Co., 1984), p. 90.

20. "Judge Deady in Relation to B. Goldsmith," 3 December 1889, Bancroft Collection, Bancroft Library, University of California, Berkeley.

21. "Bernard Goldsmith," interview, 29 November 1889, Bancroft Collection.

22. Congregation Beth Israel, Portland, Oregon, marriage licenses, 1884–1912, American Jewish Archives, Cincinnati, Ohio.

23. Toll, *Ethnic Middle Class*, pp. 23–36; Peter R. Decker, "Jewish Merchants in San Francisco: Social Mobility on the Urban Frontier," in *The Jews of the West: The Metropolitan Years*, ed. Moses Rischin (Berkeley: Judah Magnes Library, 1979), pp. 21–22; Stephen M. Wise to Solomon Hirsch, 3 July 1900, Stephen Wise Papers, American Jewish Historical Society, Waltham, Mass.

24. Ben Selling Papers, Oregon Historical Society, Portland, Ore. See also Fred Rosenbaum, *Architects of Reform: Congregational and Community Leadership, Emanu-El of San Francisco, 1849–1980* (Berkeley: Judah Magnes Library, 1980), p. 35, which notes the intensive endogamy of the German Jewish elite.

25. Beth Israel marriage licenses show a slight increase in annual marriages and a decided increase in unions between Portland and San Francisco families after 1900. The data base is small, however, and it is difficult to conclude that intermarriage increased substantially after 1900.

26. Toll, *Ethnic Middle Class*, pp. 52–53. The historical populations of no other cities in the West have been studied with these questions in mind.

27. National data cited in Bernard Lazerwitz, "Intermarriage and Conversion: A Guide for Future Research," *Jewish Journal of Sociology* 13 (1971): 41.

28. "Papers Relating to the Portland, Oregon, Jewish Population Census, March, 1947," Judah Magnes Museum, Berkeley, California.

29. S. C. Kohs, "The Oakland, California, Population and Jewish Community Center Study" (1951), p. 112, Magnes Museum.

30. Fred Massarik, "A Report on the Jewish Population of Los Angeles" (January 1953), p. 49, Magnes Museum.

31. Ibid., p. 111.

32. Fred Massarik, "A Study of the Jewish Population of Long Beach, Lakewood, and Los Alamitos" (1962), p. 27 [table 20], Magnes Museum; Sidney Goldstein and Calvin Goldscheider, *Jewish Americans: Three Generations in a Jewish Community* (Englewood Cliffs, N.J.: Prentice Hall, 1968), pp. 51, 182.

33. Fred Massarik, "A Report on the Jewish Population of San Francisco, Marin County, and the Peninsula" (1959), p. 29 (table 13), p. 44 (table 24), Magnes Museum.

34. C. Bezalel Sherman, "Demographic and Social Aspects," in *The American Jew: A Reappraisal*, ed. Oscar Janowsky (Philadelphia: Jewish Publication Society, 1964), p. 40; Gordon, *Intermarriage*, pp. 204–6; Kramer and Leventman, *Gilded Ghetto*, pp. 14–15, 202–3.

35. Fred Massarik, "A Report on the Jewish Population of Alameda and Contra Costa Counties, California" (January 1970), p. 11 (table 2), p. 16 (table 7), p. 85 (tables 58 & 59), Magnes Museum.

36. Goldstein and Goldscheider, *Jewish Americans*, pp. 156–57.

37. Fred Massarik and Calvin Chenkin, "United States National Jewish Population Study: A First Report," *American Jewish Yearbook, 1973* (Philadelphia: Jewish Publication Society, 1973), pp. 292, 296.

38. Cohen, *American Modernity*, pp. 59–63.

39. Bruce A. Phillips and William S. Aron, "Phoenix Jewish Population Study, Part I, Demographic Overview" (September 1983), pp. 5, 24; Bruce A. Phillips and Eleanore P. Judd, *The Denver Jewish Population Study, 1981* (Denver: Allied Jewish Federation, 1982), pp. iii, 29–30 (table 15).

40. Phillips and Aron, "Phoenix Study," p. 8; Phillips and Judd, *Denver Jewish Population*, p. 3 (table 2).

41. Phillips and Aaron, "Phoenix Study," pp. 14–15; Phillips and Judd, *Denver Jewish Population*, pp. 44–46.

42. Sherman, "Demographic and Social Aspects," p. 40; Gordon, *Intermarriage*, pp. 204–6.

43. P. Y. Medding, *From Assimilation to Group Survival: A Political and Sociological*

Study of an Australian Jewish Community (Melbourne: Cheshire, 1968), pp. 110, 118, 123, 184.

44. Paul S. Spickard, "Intermarriage and Ethnic Identity: Jews and Japanese Americans in the Western United States," paper delivered at the American Historical Association Meeting, December 1983, San Francisco, pp. 5–7.

45. Vorspan and Gartner, *Jews of Los Angeles*, p. 114; Toll, *Ethnic Middle Class*, pp. 117–18.

46. Spickard, "Intermarriage and Ethnic Identity," p. 8.

47. The diversity of meanings for Jewishness developed by modern Jews was a major theme in the writings of Horace M. Kallen from 1915 through the 1960s. See, for example, essays like "Jewish Teaching and Learning in the American Scene," or "To Educate Jews in Our Time," in Kallen, *"Of Them Which Say They Are Jews," and Other Essays* (New York: Bloch Publishing Company, 1954). See also Martin Cohen, "Structuring American Jewish History," *American Jewish Historical Quarterly* 57 (1967): 140.

48. Sklare, *America's Jews*, pp. 201–6; Gordon, *Intermarriage*, p. 37; Sherman, "Demographic and Social Aspects." p. 40.

49. Dominique Schnapper, *Jewish Identities in France: An Analysis of Contemporary French Jewry* (Chicago: University of Chicago Press, 1983), pp. xxviii, 16, 124–25.

50. Will Herberg, *Protestant, Catholic, Jew: An Essay in American Religious Sociology* (New York: Doubleday Anchor Books, 1960), pp. 186–95; Sklare, *America's Jews*, p. 110.

51. Milton Plesur, *Jewish Life in Twentieth Century America: Challenge and Accommodation* (Chicago: Nelson-Hall, 1982), p. 158.

52. Ibid., p. 187; Cohen, *American Modernity*, pp. 55–63.

53. Massarik and Chenkin, "National Jewish Population Study," pp. 298–300, note a very high proportion of children of mixed marriages being raised as Jews.

54. M. S., male, born 21 January 1947, Brooklyn, N.Y. (interviewed, 20 September 1984).

55. J. S. Slotkin, "Jewish-Gentile Intermarriage in Chicago," *American Sociological Review* 7 (1942): 39 (table 1).

56. Herbert Gans, "Symbolic Ethnicity: The Future of the Ethnic Groups and Cultures in America," *Ethnic and Racial Studies* 2 (1979): 1–18.

57. Lazerwitz, "Intermarriage and Conversion," pp. 50, 60; Schwartz, "Intermarriage in the United States," p. 110; Cohen, *American Modernity*, pp. 122–24.

58. Cohen, *American Modernity*, pp. 59–63, 73–75.

59. R.T., female, born 3 January 1942, The Dalles, Ore. (interviewed, 23 August 1984); A.H.W., female, born 4 April 1945, New Haven, Conn. (interviewed, 2 August 1984).

60. M.W., female, born 24 March 1945, Grenoble, France (interviewed, 12 September 1984); M.W., male, born 25 October 1942, Atascadero, Calif. (interviewed, 14 August 1984); M. T., female, born 24 Februry 1947, Los Angeles, Calif. (interviewed, 17 September 1984).

Glossary of Hebrew and Yiddish Terms

aggadah, aggadot (plural): *the nonlegal contents of the Talmud and Midrash, including legends, tales, folklore, moral teachings, prayers, historical data, and theological speculation*

apikoris: *heretic, skeptic*

Ashkenaz: *medieval Hebrew term for Germany and northern France*

brit milah: *the covenant of circumcision; the circumcision ceremony*

cohen: *priest; a descendant of the priestly clan in ancient Israel*

halakhah: *Jewish law*

ḥalutsah: *widow whose brother-in-law refuses his levirate duty*

ḥasid, ḥasidim (plural): *adherents of the mystical revival movement Hasidism, originating in Poland in the second half of the eighteenth century*

haskalah: *the Jewish enlightenment, the movement for the modernization of Jewish life and thought in the eighteenth and nineteenth centuries*

ḥeder: *primitive, one-room Jewish elementary school*

ḥevrah, ḥevrot (plural): *society*

landslayt: *Jews from the same town or vicinity in eastern Europe*

landsmanshaft, landsmanshaftn (plural): *fraternal society of Jews from the same town or vicinity in eastern Europe*

mamzer: *a child born from an incestuous union or from an adulterous union between a married woman and a man other than her husband*

maddiaḥ: *seducer*

maskil, maskilim (plural): *adherents of the* haskalah

melamed: *teacher in a* ḥeder

GLOSSARY

meshummad: *apostate*

mohel: *ritual circumciser*

mumar: *apostate*

rebbe: *charismatic, rabbinic leader of a hasidic community*

semikhah: *rabbinical ordination*

tefillin: *phylacteries worn by Jewish males over age thirteen during weekday morning prayer*

talmud torah: *community-supported Jewish elementary school, usually for the children of the poor*

yeshivah, yeshivot (plural): *academy for the study of Talmud and other legal texts*

Select Bibliography

Abrahams, Beth-Zion Lask. "Stanislaus Hoga—Apostate and Penitent." *Transactions of the Jewish Historical Society of England* 15 (1946): 121–49.

Appel, John J. "Christian Science and the Jews." *Jewish Social Studies* 31 (1969): 100–121.

Cohen, Arthur A. "Three We Have Lost: The Problem of Conversion." *Conservative Judaism* 11 (Summer 1957): 7–19.

Davis, Moshe. "Mixed Marriage in Western Jewry: Historical Background to the Jewish Response." *Jewish Journal of Sociology* 10 (1968): 177–220.

Dunlop, John, ed. *Memories of Gospel Triumphs among the Jews during the Victorian Era.* London: S. W. Partridge & Co.; John Snow & Co., 1894.

Eichhorn, David Max. *Evangelizing the American Jew.* Middle Village, N.Y.: Jonathan David Publishers, 1978.

Endelman, Todd M. "Conversion as a Response to Antisemitism." In *Living with Antisemitism: Modern Jewish Responses.* Edited by Jehuda Reinharz. Hanover, N.H.: University Press of New England, 1987.

———. "Communal Solidarity and Family Loyalty among the Jewish Elite of Victorian London." *Victorian Studies* 28 (1985): 491–526.

———. "Disraeli's Jewishness Reconsidered." *Modern Judaism* 5 (1985): 109–23.

Feuer, Lewis S. "The Conversion of Karl Marx's Father." *Jewish Journal of Sociology* 14 (1972): 149–66.

Fishberg, Maurice. *The Jews: A Study in Race and Environment.* London: Walter Scott Publishing Co., 1911. Chap. 21.

Fixler, Michael. "Bernard Berenson of Butremanz." *Commentary* 36 (1963): 135–43.

Ginzburg, Shaul. *Meshumodim in tsarishn rusland* [Apostates in Tsarist Russia]. New York: CYCO-Bicher Farlag, 1946.

Goldberg, Jacob. "Die getauften Juden in Polen-Litauen im 16.–18. Jahrhundert." *Jahrbücher fur Geschichte Osteuropas* 30 (1982): 54–99.

———. *Ha-mumarim be-mamlekhet Polin-Lita* [Converts in the Kingdom of Poland-

BIBLIOGRAPHY

Lithuania] (Jerusalem: The Zalman Shazar Center for the Furtherance of the Study of Jewish History, 1985).

Hertz, Deborah. "Intermarriage in the Berlin Salons." *Central European History* 16 (1984): 303–46.

Isser, Natalie. "The Mallet Affair: Case Study of a Scandal." *Revue des Etudes Juives* 138 (1979): 291–305.

Isser, Natalie, and Lita Linzer Schwartz. "Sudden Conversion: The Case of Alphonse Ratisbonne." *Jewish Social Studies* 45 (1983): 17–30.

Kedar, Benjamin Zev. "Hemshekhiyyut ve-ḥiddush be-hamarah ha-yehudit be-ger-manyah shel ha-meah ha-shemonah-esreh" [Continuity and Change in Jewish Conversion to Christianity in 18th Century Germany]. In *Studies in the History of Jewish Society in the Middle Ages and in the Modern Period Presented to Jacob Katz*. Edited by Immanuel Etkes and Yosef Salmon. Jerusalem: Magnes Press, The Hebrew University, 1980.

Kish, Guido. *Judentaufen: Eine historisch-biographisch-psychologisch-soziologische Studie besonders für Berlin und Konigsberg*. Berlin: Colloquium Verlag, 1973.

Kraut, Benny. *From Reform Judaism to Ethical Culture: The Religious Evolution of Felix Adler*. Cincinnati: Hebrew Union College Press, 1979.

Mahler, Raphael. "Ha-mediniyyut kelafei ha-misyonarim be-polin ha-kongresait bi-tekufat 'ha-brit ha-kedushah'" [Policy toward Missionaries in Poland in the Era of the Holy Alliance]. In *Sefer Shiloh*, edited by Michael Handel. Tel Aviv: Department of Education and Culture, Municipality of Tel Aviv, 1960.

Martin, R. H. "United Conversionist Activities among the Jews in Great Britain, 1795–1815: Pan-Evangelicalism and the London Society for Promoting Christianity amongst the Jews." *Church History* 46 (1977): 437–52.

Meirovich, Harvey W. "Ashkenazic Reactions to the Conversionists, 1800–1850." *Transactions of the Jewish Historical Society of England* 26 (1979): 8–15.

Menes, Abram. "The Conversion Movement in Prussia during the First Half of the Nineteenth Century." *YIVO Annual* 6 (1951): 187–205.

Riff, Michael A. "Assimilation and Conversion in Bohemia—Secession from the Jewish Community in Prague, 1868–1917." *Leo Baeck Institute Year Book* 26 (1981): 73–88.

Rozenblit, Marsha L. *The Jews of Vienna, 1867–1914: Assimilation and Identity*. Albany: State University of New York Press, 1983. Chap. 6.

Ruppin, Arthur. *The Jews of Today*. Translated by Margery Bentwich. London: G. Bell and Sons, 1913. Chaps. 10–11.

Samter, Nathan. *Judentaufen im neunzehnten Jahrhundert*. Berlin: M. Poppelauer, 1906.

Sarna, Jonathan D. "The American Jewish Response to Nineteenth-Century Christian Missions." *Journal of American History* 68 (1981): 35–51.

Bibliography

Sherman, Michael D. "Christian Missions to the Jews in East London, 1870–1914." M.A. thesis, Yeshiva University, 1983.

Shohet, Azriel. *Im ḥilufei tekufot: reshit ha-haskalah be-yahadut germanyah* [Beginnings of the Haskalah among German Jewry]. Jerusalem: Mosad Bialik, 1960. Chap. 9.

Smith, David C. "The Berlin Mission to the Jews and its Ecclesiastical and Political Context, 1822–1848." *Neue Zeitschrift für Missionswissenschaft* 30 (1974): 182–90.

Sobel, B. Z. *Hebrew Christianity: The Thirteenth Tribe.* New York: John Wiley & Sons, 1974.

Szajkowski, Zosa. "Marriages, Mixed Marriages, and Conversions among French Jews during the Revolution of 1789." *Historia Judaica* 19 (1957): 33–44.

Theilhaber, Felix A. *Der Untergang der deutschen Juden: Eine volkswirtschaftliche Studie.* 2d ed. Berlin: Jüdischer Verlag, 1921. Chaps. 10–11.

Thompson, A. E. *A Century of Jewish Missions.* Chicago: Fleming H. Revell Co., 1902.

Torres, Tereska. *The Converts.* New York: Alfred A. Knopf, 1970.

Tsitron, Shmuel Leib. *Mei-aḥorei ha-pargod: mumarim, bogedim, mitkabshim* [From Behind the Screen: Converts, Traitors, Deniers]. 2 vols. Vilna: Zvi Matz, 1923–25.

Van Kaam, Adrian Leo. *A Light to the Gentiles: The Life Story of the Venerable Francis Libermann.* Pittsburgh: Duquesne University Press, 1959.

Notes on Contributors

BENJAMIN BRAUDE is Associate Professor of History at Boston College. He has also been Visiting Professor of History at Harvard University and Research Assistant in Near Eastern Studies at Princeton University. He coedited and contributed to *Christians and Jews in the Ottoman Empire: The Functioning of a Plural Society* and is currently completing *Bedouins, Priests and Spies: Palgrave and the Opening of Arabia*.

JEREMY COHEN holds the Samuel and Esther Melton Chair of Jewish History at Ohio State University. He is the author of *The Friars and the Jews: The Evolution of Medieval Anti-Judaism*, which won the National Jewish Book Award for scholarship in 1982.

DAVID ELLENSON is Associate Professor of Jewish Religious Thought at the Hebrew Union College-Jewish Institute of Religion, Los Angeles. He has published over thirty essays in a variety of journals, including *Modern Judaism*, *The Journal of the American Academy of Religion*, *Jewish Social Studies*, *American Jewish History*, and *Semeia*, and has completed a book-length study of Rabbi Esriel Hildesheimer and the creation of modern Jewish orthodoxy, which will soon appear.

TODD M. ENDELMAN has taught at Yeshiva University and Indiana University and is currently Professor of History at the University of Michigan. He is the author of *The Jews of Georgian England, 1714–1830: Tradition and Change in a Liberal Society*, which was awarded the National Jewish Book Award for history and the A. S. Diamond Memorial Prize of the Jewish Historical Society of England.

JEFFREY S. GUROCK is Associate Professor of American Jewish History in the Bernard Revel Graduate School of Yeshiva University. He is the author of *When Harlem Was Jewish* and *American Jewish History: A Bibliographical Guide*.

DEBORAH HERTZ is Assistant Professor of History at the State University of New York at Binghamton. She has published essays in *Central European History, New German Critique,* and several collections on the history of women in Germany; edited *Briefe an eine Freundin: Rahel Varnhagen an Rebecca Friedländer;* and just completed a book on the Jewish salons of eighteenth-century Berlin.

BENNY KRAUT is Associate Professor of Judaic Studies and Director of the Judaic Studies Program at the University of Cincinnati. He is the author of *From Reform Judaism to Ethical Culture: The Religious Evolution of Felix Adler* and numerous articles on the relationship between American Reform Judaism and liberal Protestantism.

WILLIAM O. MCCAGG, JR., teaches eastern European and Russian history at Michigan State University. He is the author of *Jewish Nobles and Geniuses in Modern Hungary* and *Stalin Embattled, 1943–1948.* He has just completed a book on the assimilation of Habsburg Jewry, 1670–1918.

JONATHAN D. SARNA is Associate Professor of American Jewish History at the Hebrew Union College-Jewish Institute of Religion in Cincinnati and Academic Director of its Center for the Study of the American Jewish Experience. His books include *Jacksonian Jew: The Two Worlds of Mordecai Noah, People Walk on Their Heads: Moses Weinberger's Jews and Judaism in New York,* and *The American Jewish Experience: A Reader.*

MICHAEL STANISLAWSKI is Assistant Professor of Jewish History on the Miller Endowment at Columbia University. He is the author of *Tsar Nicholas I and the Jews: The Transformation of Jewish Society in Russia, 1825–1855,* which won the National Jewish Book Award for history. He has recently completed a book about Yehudah Leib Gordon.

WILLIAM TOLL is the author of *The Resurgence of Race: Black Social Theory from Reconstruction to the Pan-African Conferences, The Making of an Ethnic Middle Class: Portland Jewry over Four Generations,* and over a dozen essays on black history and American Jewish social history.

STEVEN J. ZIPPERSTEIN has taught at Cornell University and the University of California, Los Angeles. He is currently Frank Green Fellow in Modern Jewish History at the Oxford Centre for Postgraduate Hebrew Studies and a Fellow of Wolfson College, Oxford. He is the author of *The Jews of Odessa: A Cultural History, 1794–1881.*

Index